FORTUNE AND ROMANCE:

Boiardo in America

MEDIEVAL & RENAISSANCE

TEXTS & STUDIES

VOLUME 183

FORTUNE AND ROMANCE

Boiardo in America

edited by

Jo Ann Cavallo & Charles Ross

MEDIEVAL & RENAISSANCE TEXTS & STUDIES
Tempe, Arizona
1998

The three plates that appear following page 60 are
reproduced by permission of the Folger Shakespeare Library.

The map of Georgia that appears on page 95 is reprinted from
David Braund's *Georgia in Antiquity* (Oxford University Press, 1994),
by permission of Oxford University Press.

Figures 8, 10 and 11 are reprinted courtesy of
Alinari/Art Resource, New York. Figure 9 is reprinted courtesy of
Scala, Art Resource, New York.

℗ Copyright 1998
The Italian Academy for Advanced Studies in America
at Columbia University

Library of Congress Cataloging-in-Publication Data

Fortune and romance : Boiardo in America / edited by Jo Ann Cavallo &
Charles S. Ross

    p. cm. — (Medieval & Renaissance texts & studies ; 183)
    Most of the essays in this volume stem from the American Boiardo
Quincentennial Conference, "Boiardo 1994 in America," held in Butler
Library, Columbia University, Oct. 7–9, 1994, sponsored by the Italian
Academy for Advanced Studies in America.
    Includes bibliographical references and index.
    ISBN 0-86698-225-6 (alk. paper)
    1. Boiardo, Matteo Maria, 1440 or 41–1494 — Criticism and interpreta-
tion — Congresses. I. Cavallo, Jo Ann. II. Ross, Charles Stanley.
III. American Boiardo Quincentennial Conference "Boairdo 1994 in
America" (1994 : Butler Library, Columbia University) IV. Italian Academy
for Advanced Studies in America. V. Series.
PQ4614.F67 1998
851'.2—dc21   98-11569
                                          CIP

This book is made to last.
It is set in Goudy, smyth-sewn,
and printed on acid-free paper
to library specifications.

Printed in the United States of America

CONTENTS

HUMANISM AND LITERACY

THE ARTS IN FERRARA

BOIARDO'S MINOR WORKS

PREFACE

MOST OF THE ESSAYS IN THIS VOLUME stem from the American Boiardo Quincentennial Conference "Boiardo 1994 in America," held in Butler Library on the Columbia University campus October 7–9, 1994. The conference was sponsored by the Italian Academy for Advanced Studies in America at Columbia University, with the collaboration of Purdue University's English Department, Italian Program, and School of Liberal Arts, the Department of Italian at Columbia University, and the Istituto di Studi Rinascimentali based in Ferrara, Italy. Ours was one of four major conferences on Boiardo held in 1994. The Italian Boiardo Quincentennial conference, entitled "Il Boiardo e il mondo estense nel quattrocento," was held in Scandiano, Modena, Reggio Emilia, and Ferrara on September 13–17. The other two conferences were held in St.-Etienne, France, on October 21–23, and London, England, on December 2–3.

The title of our conference, " Boiardo 1994 in America," deliberately echoed the title of the volume *Ariosto 1974 in America*, which grew out of an earlier conference on Ariosto, also held at Columbia University. Typical of the critical climate predominating until recently in Ariosto studies, the ten essays of that volume are without any reference to the poem that Ariosto's own masterpiece aimed to complete. Our goal, by contrast, has been to understand Boiardo by placing his writing in the context of medieval and Renaissance literature and culture. We therefore invited eminent scholars of classical, medieval, and Renaissance literature, art, music, and history to bring their expertise to the study of Boiardo. Our hope was to offer a plurality of voices that will engender debate and further research.

The volume opens with a section on fortune, exploring both the theme of Fortune in the *Orlando Innamorato* and beyond (Quint, Nohrnberg, Murrin) and the subsequent critical fortune of Boiardo's poem itself (Cavallo). The next section, on romance, examines different theoretical approaches to the *Orlando Innamorato*: psychology (Gundersheimer, Gragnolati) and gender studies (Ross). The section on humanism and literacy focuses on ethics (McMichaels), audience (Sorrentino, Sherberg), and philosophy (Egan). We then offer four essays on the arts in Ferrara: three on visual performances (Manca, Cranston, McIver), and one on music (Perkins). The volume concludes with two considerations of Boiardo's minor works: his major lyric sequence (Rodini), and his one play (Dersofi).

We would like to thank the Italian Academy for Advanced Studies in America at Columbia University for its continued support through the sponsorship of the present volume.

Jo Ann Cavallo
Charles Ross

ALLEN MANDELBAUM

Foreword

Un'altra fiata, se mi fia concesso,
Racontarovi il tutto per espresso.

Some other time, if God permits,
I'll tell you all there is to this.

WHAT BOIARDO DID NOT LIVE TO DO, the contributors to this volume have done: they have told it all. They have given us an exegetical *gozzoviglia*, a revel-wassail that is yet ever lucid. (My own sense of the Columbia symposium was only confirmed when I overheard one unbearded auditor mutter decisively on 9 October 1994: "He did not live to tell it all: that task was left to Butler Hall.")

As befits a revel, these contributors do not slight the energy, zest, and exuberance of Boiardo the romancer (even, at times, with garrulousness beyond his own). But above all—and deepest of all—they have dug into his 4,430 octaves with convincing force and numerous insights.

They have shed light on the ethical cruxes he confronts, on the resonances *for us* of his insistence on non-closure, his awareness of how elusive the "all" is; on his "romance" geography in relation to the commercial atlas of his own—and of earlier—times; on the pressures of chant and of transcribed text; and on the musical and pictorial contexts that bordered his discourse.

They have given us Boiardo not as "predecessor" but as brilliant contemporary of both his antecedents and his successors, a vital member of the fraternity that encompasses Ovidians, chansonists, and forgers of moral awareness in narrative form.

They have traced the syncretistic trail-task of molding the matter of

France and the matter of Britain and the resonances of Ovidian Latinity that compelled his audience and can compel us. I say Ovidian Latinity—but Vergil, too, is here, even the Ferraran's implicit awareness of the savage Juno's line so dear to Freud: "*Flectere si nequeo superos, Acheronte movebo*"—(or we might hear Juno as saying: "If I/can't bend the gods on high, then I'll move Hell"). And Boiardo does mobilize-analyze the underworld of desire.

Is Boiardo's non-closure a measure of the unattainability of a perfect state or a state of perfection? Certainly, the writers of this volume can lead us to see how interlacing is Boiardo's plot-web but, too, how intricate and probing is his moral vision.

Even the reversal—in this volume—of the chronological order of Boiardo's works, with Rodini concluding with a cadenza on Boiardo's earlier lyrics (in the wake of Di Tommaso's MRTS volume of perceptive facing-page translations), can incite us to see Boiardo the lyricist as one who may—finally—be aphasic, obsessed by his inability to encompass his beloved with his words. But, *at the same time*, we are free to find (early on in the *Amorum Libri*) another Latin layer in Boiardo, a fleeting but indelible reprise of the upbeat Lucretius of the invocation to Venus, making room for the *De rerum* as an index of Boiardo's love of *this* earth, an *un*-Petrarchan Boiardo.

* * *

Some say that Mark Twain said: "The difference between truth and fiction is that fiction has to make sense." I hope much that this present volume will spur the pedagogic itch of both the teachers and the taught. It would indeed be a "shame" (as Gundersheimer *might* say) if the "opportunity" were not seized (as Nohrnberg would *certainly* say) to find the rich, enduring sense of Boiardo's fiction.

INTRODUCTION

I

Boiardo's *Sfortuna*

THE WORLD WAS CHANGING RAPIDLY in the months before the poet
Matteo Maria Boiardo died on December 19, 1494. Leonardo da Vinci was
forty-two and working on the *Last Supper*. Michelangelo was nineteen
years old and living in Bologna as a protest against Medici hegemony in
Florence. Albrecht Dürer was twenty-three. Lorenzo de' Medici and Christopher Landino had passed away two years earlier. During 1494 Christopher Columbus lay near death on the island of Hispaniola, consumed by
the rigors of his second voyage and the problems of managing 1,500 colo-
nists. King Charles VIII of France penetrated Italy as far as Naples,
bringing new modes of warfare and foreign domination to the peninsula.
Angelo Poliziano, Boiardo's only poetic rival in the fifteenth century, and
Pico della Mirandola, Boiardo's philosophical cousin, both died that year.

A decade earlier Boiardo's masterpiece, the *Orlando Innamorato*, radically changed the face of chivalric literature. Whether or not Luigi Pulci's
Morgante prompted Boiardo's muse, Boiardo brought an educated, humanist intelligence to chivalric romance, creating a new form that displayed
classical erudition as well as an artist's grasp of the narrative structure of
Carolingian and Arthurian romance. Although the *Innamorato* was a
"poet's poem," with enormous impact on Ludovico Ariosto, Torquato
Tasso, and lesser-known authors, it was not a "critic's" poem. Due to a
number of variables, particularly language and style, it was pushed aside in
the debate on the heroic poem that dominated literary studies in the sec-

ond half of the sixteenth century. Ariosto was proclaimed the "champion" of the romance epic invented by Boiardo.[1]

The roots of Boiardo's *sfortuna* in later criticism are clearly laid out in the Valgrisi edition of the *Orlando Furioso* edited by Ieromino Ruscelli.[2] Ruscelli begins by stating that a knowledge of Boiardo is essential to understanding Ariosto's narrative: "It must first be noted that to fully comprehend from one end to another all of the stories . . . of the *Furioso*, one must have read the first three books of the *Innamoramento d'Orlando* composed by Count Matteo Maria Boiardo."[3] Yet, the editor then inserts an essay by Fausto da Longiano that praises Ariosto as a "diligent imitator" of the Greeks and Latins. Interested in creating a classical pedigree for Ariosto's text, Fausto lists several elements that have Homeric and Virgilian sources: he notes that just as the war against Troy could not begin without the help of Ulysses, Agramante's War cannot get started without the help of Brunello. He then proceeds to compare Ruggiero and Achilles. Among the other Ariostean characters and episodes for which Fausto finds classical precedent are Marfisa, Bradamante, Alcina, Orrilo, the horses Baiardo and Rabicano, the sword Balisardo (made by Falerina), the ring that makes one invisible, the twin fountains, and Malagigi's turning Draghinazzo into the image of Gradasso, which then jumps into a boat to deceive Rinaldo. He ends his list by saying, "If our Poet did not imitate Homer and Virgil in every little part, he nonetheless deserves praise because he varied his characters according to place and time."

What should be immediately striking to the reader is the fact that it was Boiardo rather than Ariosto who invented most of the events and characters cited in Fausto's list. Indeed, Fausto da Longiano had originally compared both Boiardo and Ariosto to their classical precedents.[4] Ruscelli kept all the material, but simply removed every mention of Boiardo's name in his attempt to canonize the *Furioso* as a classic. Unfortunately,

---

[1] Daniel Javitch has most recently studied Ariosto's prominent place in this debate. He shows how the literati were not as interested in understanding chivalric poetry as they were in finding a modern Italian "classic" that could rival Greek and (primarily) Latin epic. *Proclaiming a Classic: The Canonization of "Orlando Furioso"* (Princeton: Princeton Univ. Press, 1991). For Boiardo's place in this debate, see Giuseppe Sangirardi, *Boiardismo Ariostesco. Presenza e trattamento dell' "Orlando Innamorato" nel "Furioso"* (Lucca: Pacini Fazzi, 1993), 7–25.

[2] Ieronimo Ruscelli, "Le Annotationi, gli Avertimenti, & le Dichiarationi di Ieronimo Ruscelli," *Orlando Furioso* (Venice, 1573), 602.

[3] Ruscelli, "Le Annotationi," 602.

[4] Javitch mentions this peculiarity. *Proclaiming a Classic*, 41.

Fausto's original piece appeared in only a single edition, that of Pasini and Bindoni issued in 1542, while Ruscelli's modified insertion was reprinted regularly throughout the second half of the Cinquecento, thus contributing to the cultural eclipse of Boiardo's reputation.

Ruscelli's editorial excision of Boiardo's work may perhaps be explained in part by the *Innamorato*'s success outside Italy. The poem and its early continuations were quickly translated into Spanish. But when the Spanish version caught the attention of Italian *literati*, they thought that Boiardo had done no more than rewrite a Spanish original. Thus, ironically, the success of Boiardo's poem elsewhere worked against its critical standing within the peninsula.

Ruscelli does note that "Boiardo's book is very beautiful and worthy of all praise and held in high esteem throughout Italy" and that "Boiardo had obscured every other writer of romances in his time."[5] Yet, the very oblivion into which the *Innamorato* sent previous chivalric poems also indirectly contributed to its later critical *sfortuna* by making it virtually impossible for critics to gauge its break from the past.

The blind spots one can find in Ruscelli's essay were perpetuated in subsequent centuries. Even after the normative debate of the sixteenth century had evolved into descriptive critical analysis and the *Furioso* was no longer used to proclaim the validity of epic poetry in Italian, the precedent had already been set for regarding the *Orlando Furioso* as a break from a vast, amorphous body of chivalric material rather than a brilliant creative imitation of the innovations introduced by Boiardo.

Ruscelli's erasure of Boiardo's poem found an American equivalent in Thomas Bulfinch's *Mythology*, first published in the 1860s and still widely available in reprinted editions today. In his preface, Bulfinch names Dante and Ariosto as "the Italian poets" whose "literature of romance is a treasure-house of poetical material." The presence of Dante as a writer of romance and the omission of Boiardo may already be surprising. The real shock comes in the "Legends of Charlemagne" section, however, when Bulfinch summarizes (albeit not always reliably) vast amounts of narrative material from the *Innamorato*. Since he does not document his sources, a reader unfamiliar with Boiardo's work has no way of knowing that almost one-quarter of Bulfinch's recounting of the legends of Charlemagne is taken directly from the *Orlando Innamorato*. To make matters worse, modern editions provide an index that attributes to Ariosto elements that are

---

[5] Ruscelli, "Le Annotationi," 603.

typically Boiardan. For example, the index identifies "Balisarda" in this way: "In Ariosto's *Orlando Furioso*, a famous sword made in the garden of Orgagna by the sorceress Falerina." Needless to say, the garden of Orgagna and the sorceress Falerina are inventions of Boiardo that never even appear in Ariosto's poem.

A breakthrough was made near the end of the last century by the source-studies of Pio Rajna, who credited Boiardo with having revolutionized Italian narrative poetry: "Boiardo took from wherever he could. He transformed everything, and gave it his own imprint." In the same passage, Rajna also called attention to the sheer inventiveness of the *Innamorato*: "He took more from his own fantasy than any other Italian poet, except for Dante."[6] Nevertheless, Rajna's monumental source study of the *Orlando Furioso* lists the *Orlando Innamorato* as only one of many, mostly French, medieval sources. Perhaps assuming a full familiarity on the part of his readers with the work of Boiardo, Rajna did not bother to note to what extent the earlier material could have reached Ariosto through the *Innamorato*, nor did he generally distinguish Boiardo's poem from other texts.

The *Innamorato*'s *sfortuna* perhaps hit bottom during this century, when critics began to dismiss two things for which Boiardo had been generally credited: merging the Carolingian and Breton cycles, and creating a poem popular enough to warrant a continuation by Ariosto. Regarding the first issue, critics (beginning in 1927) pointed out incipient contamination between the two cycles in earlier Italian chivalric literature.[7] Regarding the second, Carlo Dionisotti (in 1970) said that pending further evidence, chivalric literature appeared to have fallen out of favor after Boiardo and was only revived by Ariosto.[8] Even though Dionisotti was the first to say that this hypothesis was provisional and that the research on the chivalric poem of the late fifteenth and early sixteenth centuries was "still almost entirely yet to do," his statement circulated "lazily," as Giuseppe Sangirardi says, among scholars for more than twenty years before anyone at-

---

[6] Pio Rajna, "*L'Orlando Innamorato*," *Studi su Matteo Maria Boiardo*, ed. N. Campanini (Bologna: Zanichelli, 1894).

[7] Fabio Cossutta, in *Gli ideali epici dell'Umanesimo e l'"Orlando Innamorato"* (Rome: Bulzoni, 1995), 34 n. 19, cites L. Cesati's "Contatti e interferenze tra il ciclo brettone e il carolingio prima del Boiardo," *Archivum Romanicum* 11:1 (1927): 108–17, as the first critical work to do so.

[8] Carlo Dionisotti, "Fortuna e sfortuna del Boiardo nel Cinquecento," *Il Boiardo e la critica contemporanea: atti del convegno di studi su Matteo Maria Boiardo* (Florence: Olschki, 1970), 224.

tempted to verify it.[9] It was repeated even among Boiardo critics who viewed it as an affirmation of Ariosto's courageous appraisal of his predecessor's poem. By seeing Ariosto's choice as a risk, it indirectly validated Boiardo's poem in Ariosto's estimation. At the same time, however, it denied the impact that his innovative poem had on the romance epic prior to Ariosto's continuation.

Although many lamented the lacuna pointed out by Dionisotti, it is only in the past ten years that scholars have begun to lay the groundwork for a history of the chivalric romance of the late fifteenth and early sixteenth centuries. By charting both Boiardo's radical break from what preceded him and his enormous influence on what followed, these new critical and historical studies finally permit us to begin correcting a critical blind spot that has persisted for over four centuries.[10]

The recovery of the *Innamorato* represents a significant addition to the canon of Italian poetry. But we also need to bring the criticism that has permitted that recovery into the classroom. The essays in this collection put us in touch with the best of the recent work on Boiardo. At the same time, we also need to keep in mind certain fundamentals of literary history in order to understand the very form of Boiardo's poem, a literary history that is increasingly neglected in the name of theory and popular culture. The purpose of the following section is to survey the literary background to Boiardo's poem, in order to suggest the richness of the *Orlando Innamorato* for comparative literature courses and to provide some suggestions for reducing the sheer strangeness of this poetic masterpiece. Boiardo's *Orlando Innamorato* allusively imitates earlier stories and themes. A brief look at a series of precursors will show how the poem synthesizes classical poetry, French romance, and humanist thought.

---

[9] Giuseppe Sangirardi, *Boiardismo Ariostesco. Presenza e trattamento dell'*Orlando Innamorato *nel* Furioso (Lucca: Pacini Fazzi, 1993), 291.

[10] For the most part, these studies come from a younger generation of Italian scholars. See, in particular, Marina Beer, *Romanzi di cavalleria: il* Furioso *e il romanzo italiano del primo cinquecento* (Rome: Bulzoni, 1987), especially the section "Il romanzo cavalleresco italiano del primo Cinquecento," 139–206; Marco Praloran, *"Maraviglioso artificio." Tecniche narrative e rappresentative nell'*Orlando Innamorato (Lucca: Pacini Fazzi, 1990); Sangirardi, *Boiardismo Ariostesco*, especially the section "1505–1516: la stagione del boiardismo," 27–37; Marco Villoresi, "Per lo studio delle relazioni fra il *Danese* e la *Reina Ancroia* e altri casi di intertestualità nel romanzo cavalleresco del Quattrocento," *Interpres* 14 (1994): 107–51, and "Il mercato delle meraviglie: strategie seriali, rititolazioni e riduzioni dei testi cavallereschi a stampa fra Quattro e Cinquecento," *Studi italiani* 14 (1995): 5–53"; and Alberto Casadei, "Riusi (e rifiuti) del modello dell'*Innamorato* tra il 1520 e il 1530," *Italianistica* 24.1 (1995): 87–100.

II
Teaching the *Innamorato*

The Iliad. In Homer's epic, written in the high style, Achilles sulks in his tent and refuses to fight for the Greek army at Troy. He is angry that Agamemnon has used his authority to deny Achilles a slave girl. Boiardo replays this theme in a more humorous key. Orlando secretly leaves Paris after Charlemagne, refusing to allow him to joust first for Angelica, instead institutes a lottery that relegates Orlando to the thirty-first position. As a result, Orlando is not present to defend the city against a series of invasions. Hector's killing of Achilles' friend Patroclus eventually brings the mainstay of the Greek army back into line. Similarly, Orlando returns to Paris and presumably to his senses—the poem is unfinished, but Angelica tends to disappear in the late portions—after he comes under the influence of a new friend, Brandimarte.

In his translation of *The Iliad*, Alexander Pope noted the delicate architecture of Homer's duels. In a similar way, much of the first book of the *Innamorato* is structured by a series of duels: Argalia (Angelica's brother) versus Astolfo (the English duke who wins Charlemagne's lottery), Argalia versus Feraguto, Feraguto versus Orlando. The series culminates when Orlando confronts Ranaldo at Albraca. Boiardo also imitates Homer's famous catalog of ships. He reviews the troops collected by King Gradasso at the Paris tournament, and he describes the armies led by King Sacripante from Circassia and King Agricane from Tartary at the battle of Albraca. What a later poet would call "fit work for a herald" expands in the second book of the poem as Boiardo lists first the armies and then the ships that sail from Africa when King Agramante invades France.

Homer's epic records the fall of Troy; Boiardo's poem chronicles the defense of Paris. Homer records the end of a civilization, while Boiardo celebrates ancient beginnings. The new hero Rugiero, destined to found the Este line, comes to the fore in the second book of the poem, and epic imitation therefore takes a dynastic turn in the third book as Rugiero explains to Bradamante that his family traces itself to Hector of Troy.

The Odyssey. Homer's second long poem records the story of Odysseus's belated return home to his faithful wife Penelope. Like the Greek wanderer, Orlando runs into strange, often magical adventures. He meets a giant with one eye on the road to the East, just as Odysseus faces the Cyclops. He is drugged by an enchantress named Dragontina, whose artwork recalls Homer's Circe. And just as Odysseus makes Circe swear to leave him alone, Orlando makes the fata Morgana take the same oath (2.13.29). Orlando's cousin Ranaldo imitates Odysseus too. He boards a ship without a pilot, aborting his duel with Gradasso, and slaughters the inhabitants of Castle Cruel, just as Homer's hero ruthlessly kills the Cicones during his initial homeward voyage.

The Odyssey is a masterpiece of narrative art because everything relates to the central theme of the *nostos*, or homecoming. Even seeming digressions contribute to the development of this central theme, as when Homer tells the story of Agamemnon, the leader of the Greek army, to contrast the fortune of Odysseus. Agamemnon returns home, and his jealous wife Clytemnestra murders him, while Penelope remains true despite the years Odysseus spent with the goddess Calypso in her cave. Boiardo constructs his narrative of several stories *interlaced* together. Often these stories seem wildly digressive, but each can be related, often in strange and unexpected ways, to the central theme of Orlando's truant passion for Angelica. Ranaldo, for example, drinks a love antidote and spends the first half of the story fleeing from Angelica. Then, about halfway through the poem, Ranaldo's disposition changes, causing him to pursue the woman he once fled. His relationship to Angelica contrasts to that of Orlando, just as Agamemnon's fate contrasts with that of Odysseus. Other characters and situations fit into a similar pattern of theme and variation, unexpected cause and effect. Boiardo rarely nods.

The Aeneid. A key filter for Homer's poems and the predominant classical influence on Boiardo, as for other writers of the Middle Ages and Renaissance, was Virgil's *Aeneid*. For Boiardo and poets who followed him, Virgil was the author who imitated Homer by combining romance and epic in a single work. The romance wanderings of the *Odyssey* account for the adventures of Aeneas in the first six books of the poem, as the hero follows his fortune from the fall of Troy to his sojourn in Carthage, where destiny prevents his finding happiness with Queen Dido. After funeral games for his father, Aeneas descends into the underworld, where he gains the knowledge needed to recognize the terminus of his travels. Early allegorists turned the *Aeneid* into a journey of the soul. They concentrated on the first six books, from the fall of Troy to Aeneas's journey through the underworld, which was generally the amount of material that could be covered in a school term. As a result, medieval readers interpreted Virgil as a magical and mystical figure. Dante most famously regarded the *Aeneid* and Virgil as guides through the errors in hell and purgatory to a renewed Christian dispensation. Boiardo knew the allegorical tradition but handled it with more complex irony. Thus, Orlando's worldwide pursuit of Angelica, the romance portion of the *Innamorato*, parodies the intertextual series at the heart of Western literature: the adventures and return home of Odysseus; Aeneas's driven quest to found Rome; and Dante's struggle to reach Beatrice and Heaven.

Although the allegorists concentrated on the first half of Virgil's epic, Boiardo and other Renaissance writers read all twelve books of the *Aeneid*. The wars Aeneas wages in the epic second half of the *Aeneid,* as he establishes in Italy the homeland that will give rise to Rome, imitate the military feats of the *Iliad*. The siege of Troy, rewritten by Virgil, is the model for the Christian defense of Paris in Boiardo's poem. But an epic action may also serve as a romance adventure. The fall of Troy is a story told by Aeneas during the romance half of Virgil's poem; Orlando's defense of Angelica at her castle of Albraca in the East is, similarly, a romance episode. The genres blur and overlap because of the long literary tradition that preceded the fifteenth century and because Virgil himself left a complex legacy. We can say that Boiardo does simultaneously what Virgil did by halves. He alternates love and war, romance and epic, intentionally to create contrast and variety.

In addition to alternating epic and romance elements in a single work, Boiardo maintains the generic feature that Renaissance theorists call the marvelous: flying demons, supernatural swords and horses, pilotless ships, books of magic, invulnerable heroes, enchanting ladies. The demons that the magician Malagise raises to distract Mandricardo and Gradasso are Christian equivalents to the pagan gods who enliven the epics of Homer and Virgil with their supernatural powers and all-too-human passions.

Ovid. "Let's be no Stoics nor no stocks, I pray, Or so devote to Aristotle's checks As Ovid be an outcast quite abjur'd," says Tranio to Lucentio as they enter Padua in Shakespeare's *Taming of the Shrew*. In other words, let us study not just virtue and philosophy, but love. For the Middle Ages and the Renaissance, the author of *The Metamorphoses, The Art of Love*, and *Amores* provided the literary model for the treatment of women. The idealization of heterosexual love, the rules of courtesy, the worship of the fairer sex, the *Romance of the Rose*: all these have been summed up in the phrase "Ovid misunderstood," although both the classical and medieval periods illustrate all too well the inverse relationship between the literary praise of women and their actual position in society.

Like other Renaissance humanists (poets like Spenser and Shakespeare) Boiardo rewrites Ovid's myths in his own way. Cupid's gold and lead arrows, which cause love and destroy it, become in Boiardo's poem the fountain of Merlin and the Stream of Love. When Angelica humorously pursues Ranaldo, she imitates Ovid's Apollo as he chases the nymph Daphne. Boiardo's gardens recall Ovid's description of the golden age, and the Naiades enter the *Innamorato* directly from the *Metamorphoses*. One could probably argue that Boiardo's flattery of Ercole d'Este at various points in the poem echoes Ovid's praise of Augustus, whom the poet commends in Book 1, for example, for taking pleasure in the firm devotion of his people.

Medieval romance. The main features of medieval French romance (courtly love, war, and the literary use of magic) reached Boiardo in two main forms, the matter of France and the matter of Britain. The Carolingian branch, called the *chansons de geste*, told stories about the defense of Christianity against Islam, which historically posed its greatest threat during the life of Charlemagne's grandfather King Pepin. Later romances represented these historical forces by means of so-called pagan armies; in Boiardo's work King Marsilio of Spain and King Agramante of Africa lead their Saracen forces to attack France.

King Gradasso's invasion of France, the first war in the poem, is actually an element of the second branch of French romance, the stories about King Arthur. Even though King Gradasso comes from the Far East, he imitates a character named Galehaut in the prose *Lancelot*, one of the important thirteenth-century stories about the court of King Arthur still familiar to us because Thomas Malory's fifteenth-century redaction, *Le Morte Darthur*, features the adventures of knights and ladies like Lancelot and Gawain, Guinevere and Morgan le Fay. In the prose *Lancelot*, Galehaut, like Gradasso, leads a large and threatening army, but turns out to be a man of honor who forestalls his campaign after observing the civility of the court he intended to conquer. He finds himself so impressed by Lancelot that he wishes only to be his friend. In similar fashion, Boiardo's King Gradasso stakes his entire campaign on a single joust. When he loses, he keeps his word and retires, like a gentleman.

Boiardo distinguished the two branches of French romance in the first two stanzas of Book 2, Canto 18, attributing love to King Arthur and war to Charlemagne's court:

> There was a time Great Britain was
> Illustrious in arms and love;
> Her name is celebrated still.
> The glory of King Arthur stems

> From when the good knights in his realm
> Displayed their worth in many battles
> And sought adventure with their ladies.
> Her fame has lasted to our day.
>
> Later, King Charles held court in France;
> His court was no equivalent,
> Though it was sturdy, confident,
> And had Ranaldo and the Count.
> Because it closed its gates to Love
> And only followed holy wars,
> It could not boast the worth, the fame
> The former showed, the first I named.

As we noted earlier, Boiardo is somewhat misleading since there are wars in Arthurian romance, and the matter of France, such as the *Entrée in Espagne*, includes stories in which Orlando chases princesses through the East. But students will find it easier to grasp literary history by recalling the distinction Boiardo corroborates: the subject of Carolingian romance (the *Chanson de Roland* tradition) is religious war, while love and magic are the main themes of Arthurian romance.

The Carolingian and Arthurian cycles are distinct not only in content but in form. Boiardo's fusion, therefore, could not but be reflected in the structure of his poem. The two features that characterize the *Innamorato* are *entrelacement* and the series of consecutive cantos. Marco Praloran has documented how Boiardo's "marvelous artifice" arises from his combination of the narrative techniques of the two cycles.[11] Whereas in the French romance, the end of a chapter coincides with the end of a narrative segment and new topics arise at the conclusion of an episode, Boiardo consistently carries over the episode from the end of one canto to the beginning of the next, and instead switches topics at a moment of high suspense.

As we have indicated, Boiardo's innovation regarding sources goes beyond his use of Carolingian and Arthurian texts. He incorporates Greek, Latin, and Italian material from genres as diverse as epic, tragedy, comedy, the novella, and the lyric. Marco Villoresi sums it up this way: "In effect, beyond the suturing of the elements of arms and love, the Arthurian and

---

[11] Marco Praloran, *"Maraviglioso artificio,"* 299.

the Carolingian cycles, the true innovation of Boiardo's romance consists in the decisive enlargement of the literary horizon opened up by the text. No longer limited to romances, the sources of the *Innamorato* lie in every direction, beyond the confines of the genre."[12] Boiardo's innovative use of classical and lyrical sources provides teachers with rich opportunities to introduce classical authors such as Propertius and Statius, as well as contemporaries writers like Niccolò da Correggio or Ludovico Sandeo.

Diverse materials and multiple storylines provide variety and contrast: the geometrical pairings of battles set up enchanting outdoor love scenes. The technique of interlace has been compared to that of the intricate scroll work surrounding medieval manuscript illustrations, but it is also not unlike the art of a banquet, where one course complements another. In fact, we have records of Boiardo's personal attendance at some of the enormous banquets in his day at the household of the pope in Rome or in Ferrara when the Holy Roman Emperor was guest.

The interlaced threads of the *Innamorato* tend to come together in allegorical centers such as the marvels of Circassia, Dragontina's Garden, Falerina's Garden, Morgana's realm of Fortune, and the Laughing Stream. Like the adventures that Odysseus relates, these enchanted domains seem to "mean" something. Multiple interpretations are possible, depending on the emphasis given to a particular theme or the situation of a particular character. Deciphering these meanings was part of the experience that Boiardo—who also composed riddles for a deck of Tarot cards—expected of his readers and listeners. As a result, the texture of the story raises perhaps the most fundamental theme of the poem, how does one know?

The Education Theme and Orlando's Early Adventures. Whereas Odysseus is naturally clever, a man of many wiles, in Boiardo's world of fifteenth-century Italian humanism, people often learned by reading. They turned to books for answers. Homer claims the inspiration of the muses, but Boiardo claims—he is lying, humorously—that he found his story in the writings of Turpin, who witnessed the events Boiardo tells. Boiardo's humor makes an important point, that a written source of knowledge presents problems because books can be wrong, or they can be hard to understand. Jane Austen's *Sense and Sensibility* offers the same epistemological dilemma: Marianne Dashwood is misled into being a "romantic" by reading eighteenth-century Gothic romances. Edward Ferrars recommends him-

---

[12] Marco Villoresi, "Per lo studio delle relazioni fra il *Danese* e la *Reina Ancroia*," 151 n. 58.

self to Elinor because he is well read and educated, but the alert reader is on notice that learning alone may produce sensibility, but not sense.

More important than reading itself is finding truth, and that lesson structures Orlando's earliest adventures. As the hero makes his way east, he is in quest of knowledge, since he is looking for Angelica. He encounters several major obstacles (a sphinx, the river of death, Dragontina's Garden) each composed of several elements. Orlando, like all romance heroes, is morally bewildered. But if we start with the assumption that romance represents the spiritual "truth" of epic, as Ann Astell argues in *Job, Boethius, and Epic Truth*,[13] then we can make sense of Orlando's adventures in Circassia. Early allegorists explained the adventures of Odysseus as a voyage of discovery, preparing the soul to return to its heavenly home. Boiardo parodies—in the sense that he creates a structure parallel to—the Platonic story of the soul gaining self-knowledge during its earthly existence.

We cannot at first glance read Orlando's early adventures and conclude that they are about gaining knowledge. But once we assume the general pattern, that his adventures form an allegory of education, the details of the episodes tend to conform to it. For example, Orlando first meets a man, a pilgrim or palmer, whose son has been kidnapped by a giant. The giant, it turns out, has been positioned by the King of Circassia to guard a sphinx. Orlando defeats the giant and rescues the boy. The palmer rewards him with a book that answers all questions. Orlando's curiosity then leads him to the sphinx, from which he learns that Angelica resides in her fortress of Albraca. The sphinx in turn asks him two questions. Unable to answer either, because he forgets to use his answer book, Orlando draws his sword. A battle ensues in which the count finally cuts his way free of the monster's folds. It is hard not to think of Red Crosse's first encounter with the dragon of Error in *The Faerie Queene*, where the knight must cut himself free after finding himself "wrapt in *Errours* endlesse traine" (*FQ* 1.1.18).

The episode fits the allegorical pattern of romance. As Orlando heads east searching for Angelica, his problem is one of knowledge: he needs to learn where she is. At its simplest, the encounter with the sphinx provides him with this information. But what about the other details? Their interpretation is elusive, but several answers suggest themselves, and creative students can come up with others. When Orlando forgets the book given him by the boy's father, he unnecessarily brutalizes the sphinx. Unable to

---

[13] Ann Astell, *Job, Boethius, and Epic Truth* (Cornell: Cornell Univ. Press, 1994).

answer her questions, he becomes angry and resorts to force, the typical re-action of the uneducated to learning, which they regard with fear.

Orlando's next adventure, at the Bridge of Death, reinforces the picture that his soul is at stake as he searches for Angelica. Here again there is opportunity for creative interpretation to account for Orlando's duel with the giant Zambardo, who catches the count in his net. Next, a Georgian friar lectures Orlando to be resolute unto death; the irony of the lecture will recur in a similar talk given by Duke Vincentio to Claudio in Shakespeare's *Measure for Measure*. Another telling moment comes during the subsequent adventure when Orlando releases the cyclops' prisoners by lifting a massive stone from the door to a cave. Plato compared the world to a cave where we see not truth, but only shadows. Perhaps that myth lies behind Orlando's release of the prisoners from the cave. The scene also occurs in stories about the quest for the holy grail, where it shades in with an image of Christian redemption: in the Bible, the removal of a large stone from a tomb offers proof that souls go to heaven.

Despite Orlando's prowess, and although it was typical of Renaissance thought to marvel at the coincidence between Plato and Christian doctrine, Orlando's journey only parodies the passage of the soul through this world. For after releasing the prisoners, Orlando again learns about Angelica, this time from a courier she herself has dispatched for assistance in her struggle against King Agricane. Certain of her location—the romance equivalent for the eternal heaven that renders memory of the world superfluous—Orlando enters Dragontina's Garden, where the enchantress slips him a drink that makes him forget everything, including Angelica. At this point the story returns to Ranaldo at Castle Cruel. While Orlando is morally bewildered by love but in a position to gain experience and knowledge that could save his soul, Ranaldo, who hates Angelica, winds up in a version of hell. Angelica eventually releases both Orlando and Ranaldo. Why that happens would be a suitable topic for a paper or in-class essay.

Several other large themes may help organize the four or five class days that can be profitably devoted to the abridged version of Boiardo's *Orlando Innamorato* in a sophomore, junior, or senior literature class on great narratives, romances, or Renaissance poetry.[14] Students may be assigned a character to keep track of and describe to the class. Or they may study in-

---

[14] An abridgment, including two new maps, has been published as Matteo Maria Boiardo, *Orlando Innamorato*, trans. Charles Ross (Oxford World's Classics, 1995).

dividual episodes, each of which has a particular theme: the problem of violence at Castle Cruel (1.8–9); Brandimarte and Fiordelisa as figures of true courtesy (1.9); the effects of friendship in the story of Tisbina, Iroldo, and Prasildo (1.12); the stories of unhappy marriages told by Leodilla (1.22) and Doristella (2.26); Origille and the problem of female identity (1.29); the politics of Falerina's Garden (2.4–5); the role of Fortune in Morgana's underworld (2.8–9). It is the purpose of the following essays to contribute to our understanding of these themes and episodes, to make the *Innamorato* available for critical study in the classroom, for professional scholars, and for the educated reader.

FORTUNE

DAVID QUINT

The Fortunes of Morgana:
From Boiardo to Marino

IT MAY SEEM A CONTRADICTION IN TERMS to single out a central or key episode in a poetic edifice as vast and capacious as the *Orlando innamorato*, whose organizing principle seems to be the deviation and dispersal of its storytelling from any main plot or narrative center. Nonetheless, the tradition of the Italian heroic poem that followed Boiardo's work chose one of its episodes and identified it, as a kind of emblem, with the *Innamorato* itself and with the generic structure of the chivalric *romanzo*. This is the episode of Orlando's journey to the subterranean realm of the Fata Morgana—Morgan the Fay of the Arthurian romances—and his liberation of her prisoners in the eighth and ninth cantos of Book 2. It is a double episode, for Orlando has to return in Canto 13 and liberate one more prisoner, Ziliante, the beloved favorite of Morgana. The ensuing tradition accorded a centrality to the episode of Morgana, repeatedly imitating and alluding to it: if this centrality seems paradoxical in light of the diffuse and multiform *Innamorato*, I will argue that it was not chosen arbitrarily. For the episode of Morgana offers an ideological motivation precisely for the centrifugal structure, the variety, and the open-endedness of Boiardo's poem.[1]

---

[1] An Italian version of this article appeared as "La fortuna di Morgana: dal Boiardo al Marino," in *Tipografie e romanzi in Val Padana fra Quattro e Cinquecento*, ed. Riccardo Bruscagli and Amedeo Quondam (Modena: Panini, 1992), 99–106. It incorporates material from other works of the author. For broader discussion of some points and more ample documentation, see David Quint, "The Figure of Atlante: Ariosto and Boiardo's Poem,"

Morgana, let us recall, is the allegorical personification of Fortune or, as she is alternatively called, of "Ventura." Boiardo provides her with a golden forelock and with the traditional iconography of *occasio* or *kairos*, the contingent moment that has to be grasped and exploited when it presents itself and that afterwards is sought in vain.[2] Morgana's prisoners, who include the other great Carolingian hero Ranaldo, Orlando's cousin, along with Dudone, Brandimarte, and seventy paladins and damsels, warn Orlando when he penetrates the labyrinth that surrounds the underground prison of the fay that he must seize the elusive Morgana by her forelock while it is still possible: when she turns her back on him to run away he will discover that she is bald. The warning comes too late and Orlando is obliged to give a long and painful chase after the fay. He finally succeeds in overcoming this formidable allegorical creature, and the text of the poem spells out the moral.

> Ogni cosa virtute vince al fine:
> Chi segue vince, pur che abbia virtute;
>
> Strength conquers all things in the end.
> He who persists, if he's strong, wins. (2.8.55)
>
> . . . ogni cosa vince l'omo forte;
>
> . . . strong men conquer everything. (2.8.63)

The episode is a pre-Machiavellian version of the struggle between virtue and fortune, already a commonplace in fifteenth-century letters.[3] Orlan-

---

Modern Language Notes 94 (1979): 77–91, and *Epic and Empire* (Princeton: Princeton Univ. Press, 1993).

I cite the following editions and translations: Matteo Maria Boiardo, *Orlando innamorato*, trans. Charles Stanley Ross, The Biblioteca Italiana (Berkeley and Los Angeles: Univ. of California Press, 1989); Ludovico Ariosto, *Orlando furioso*, ed. Lanfranco Caretti (Milan and Naples: Ricciardi, 1954); Ludovico Ariosto, *Cinque Canti / Five Cantos*, trans. Alexander Sheers and David Quint, The Biblioteca Italiana (Berkeley and Los Angeles: Univ. of California Press, 1996); Giovan Battista Marino, *L'Adone*, ed. Giovanni Pozzi (Milan: Mondadori, 1976). Except where I have just noted, the translations are my own.

[2] See Frederick Kiefer, "The Conflation of Fortuna and Occasio in Renaissance Thought and Iconography," *Journal of Medieval and Renaissance Studies* 9 (1979): 1–37; Rudolf Wittkower, "Chance, Time and Virtue," *Journal of the Warburg Institute* 1 (1937–38): 313–21.

[3] One can look, for example, at the prologue to Leon Battista Alberti's *Libri della famiglia* or at octaves 36–37 of the second book of the *Stanze* of Angelo Poliziano. The crisis of the humanist concept of Fortune is the subject of Mario Santoro, *Fortuna, ragione e prudenza nella civiltà letteraria del Cinquecento* (Naples: Liguori, 1971).

do's "virtue," clearly identified here with fortitude or strength, conquers the vicissitudes of Fortune. And just as chapter 25 of *The Prince* will divide the resistance to Fortune between the twin humanist virtues of fortitude and prudence, so the *Innamorato* depicts a *second* victory of Orlando over Morgana in Canto 13. This time, taught by experience, the prudent knight seizes the forelock of the fay right from the beginning and frees her prisoner Ziliante. Furthermore, he forces Morgana to swear by Demogorgon, the sovereign ruler of the fairies, that she will do him no further harm (2.13.26–29). In effect, Orlando, by his double virtue, has made himself immune to the blows of Fortune; this heroic virtue is just as powerful a shield to him as the enchantment that renders Orlando's body invulnerable (except for the soles of his feet).

Orlando has thus conquered time, or at least a certain humanist concept of time. The capricious and everchanging movement of Fortune distributes time in discrete moments of *occasio*, into so many opportunities that will not repeat themselves. The experience of this temporal multiplicity seems to condition the ideal of the universal man formulated by *quattrocento* humanist advocates of the active life: what we have come to know as the "Renaissance man." Time is perceived as a series of contingent and heterogeneous events, each the occasion for human exploitation. The adversary of Fortune adapts himself to every circumstance that may arise and thus becomes a chameleon-like opportunist. The versatile Renaissance man is the master of the situation, turning any contingency to his own advantage. The active life enjoins man to experience every moment to its fullest, and the seizing of the forelock of Fortune also contains the idea of *carpe diem*. So Boiardo's Mandricardo declares at the opening of Book 3.

> Tutto è perduto il tempo che ne avanza
> Se in amor non si spende o in cortesia,
> O nel mostrare in arme sua possanza;
>
> On my faith
> Spare time is time lost if its's not
> Given to love or courtesy
> Or demonstrating strength in arms. (3.1.52)

Mandricardo has already abandoned himself to Fortune, resolved to depend on his own prowess alone (3.1.12–14). The idea that this conflictual relationship with Fortune allows the human protagonist to exercise his virtue is accompanied in Boiardo's poem by a corresponding sense of the negative consequences of being the favorite of Fortune. Ziliante weeps when Orlando leaves him still a prisoner to Morgana after the knight's first journey into the realm of the fay. It turns out that Ziliante is the son of King Manodante, whose name might mean "giving hand" or "generosity," and who possesses more than half of the world's riches. Ziliante was thus favored by Fortune even before Morgana fell in love with him and made him her favorite, and he can be considered the prisoner of his own wealth. For Morgana, as the figure of Fortune, is also the "Treasure Fairy" ("la Fata del Tesoro"; 2.7.34; 22.12.24), the giver of all temporal and worldly goods. Her cavernous realm contains an enormous heap of golden furniture and objects that Ranaldo tries to rob without success: he has to renounce the fairy's gold if he wants to escape from her prison. The wiser Orlando had already renounced the riches of Morgana in the first book of the poem when he refused to hunt down and capture an enchanted deer which she had set in his path, a deer that sheds its golden antlers six times a day and promises infinite wealth to its possessor (1.25.4f.).[4]

If, as Fortuna, Morgana offers the paladin an opportunity to make his fortune, as Ventura, she is the dispenser of adventure, thus of all the multiform adventures that make the knights of the *Innamorato* zigzag up and down its boundless landscape. Adventure is a constitutive principle of romance narrative, the source of all of the apparently digressive episodes and proliferating subplots that acquire their own value and fascination. And in this sense, one could consider Morgana-Ventura as the chief creator, the first cause, of Boiardo's poem and of its narrative structure.

These adventures arise from chance and are purely episodic with regard to any single or central plot; each is a complete and autonomous point of time, the present moment that does not have a before or after. The *Innamorato* accumulates loosely connected and periferal episodes, whose organizing norm is variety itself, figured in the mixture of diverse flowers to which the narrator compares his poem (3.5.1).[5] Each episode offers in its turn a new and unique series of circumstances that Boiardo's protagonist

---

[4] See Charles S. Ross, "Angelica and the Fata Morgana: Boiardo's Allegory of Love," *Modern Language Notes* 96 (1981): 12–22.

[5] For adventure as a generating principle of romance, see the fundamental study of Riccardo Bruscagli, "*Ventura e inchiesta* fra Boiardo e Ariosto," in his *Stagioni della civiltà estense* (Pisa: Nistri-Lischi, 1983), 87–126. Boiardo's comparison of the *Innamorato* to a "mistura" of flowers is commented upon by A. Bartlett Giamatti in his introduction to the English translation by William Stewart Rose of the *Orlando furioso*, ed. Stewart A. Baker and A. Bartlett Giamatti (New York: Bobbs-Merrill, 1968), xxxi.

has to master, and they may thus all be read as differentiated versions of the victory of Orlando over Morgana, as so many encounters between human virtue and fortune. Boiardo thus unites to the episodic romance narrative a humanistic ideology that celebrates *life as adventure.* And because Orlando does not simply defeat Morgana, but extorts from her the oath that she will not harm him in the future, there seems to be no end to this series of episodes: the poem celebrates a human potential that is unlimited in its multiplicity and that is apparently without temporal limits as well. The *Innamorato* exists in a world where the laws of time and death have been virtually suspended, the world of the literary pastime. Its open-ended narrative appears infinitely expandable, not for nothing continued by so many other poets. Boiardo's romance itself did not end but remained incomplete at the 1494 death of its author, who did not enjoy an immunity to Fortune similar to the one his poem celebrates.

The Italian poets who succeeeded Boiardo as authors of heroic poetry would criticize the romance narrative form of the *Innamorato* and the ideology that informed it, and in doing so, they would repeatedly recall the episode of Morgana. In the *Orlando furioso* (1516) Ludovico Ariosto not only continued but gave an ending to the *Innamorato,* bringing to a conclusion the double epic plots of the foundation of the Este dynasty and of the world war between the forces of Charlemagne and King Agramante. The *Furioso* could thus consider the interminable romance adventures of the *Innamorato* as digressive obstacles to the completion of its own, newly teleological narrative.[6] Especially with regard to the culminating marriage of Ruggiero and Bradamante, the progenitors of the Este, these adventures resemble the strategies of deferral of the magician Atlante, who is determined to keep his pupil Ruggiero from his glorious destiny and from the premature death that is fated to accompany it. Ruggiero confronts the choice of Achilles, a choice that Atlante tries to make for him. The famous enchanted palace of desire that the magician builds to protect Ruggiero, but into which many other paladins becomes imprisoned (*OF* 12.7f.), can be read as a microcosm of the errors of romance, a miniature *Innamorato*; this structure must be destroyed at the center of the *Furioso* (22.23) before Ariosto's poem can introduce its own distinct narrative

---

[6] See Quint, "The Figure of Atlante"; Patricia Parker, *Inescapable Romance* (Princeton: Princeton Univ. Press, 1979), 31–37; Albert Russell Ascoli, *Ariosto's Bitter Harmony* (Princeton: Princeton Univ. Press, 1987), 362–65; Sergio Zatti, *Il "Furioso" fra epos e romanzo* (Lucca: Maria Pacini Fazzi, 1990), 9–37.

form, which bit by bit jettisons its multiple adventures and its numerous knights and ladies, killed off and buried along the way, in order to reach its epic conclusion. The labyrinthine palace of Atlante is, in fact, a critical rewriting of the labyrinth-prison of Morgana. For whereas Boiardo's Orlando had found an escape from the prison of Fortune by running down and capturing Morgana—and so symbolizing the capacity of human virtue to conquer time and give it significance—in the palace of Atlante the imprisoned Ruggiero and Orlando are both condemned to an endless chase after temporal objects revealed as illusory and ever unreachable phantoms of desire. This continuous error is Ariosto's dark and ironic judgment upon the romance adventures and open-ended narrative of his predecessor, doubly illusory because they confer humanistic value upon a frenetic, but futile life in the world of time *and* because their indefinite prolongation can suggest an escape or shelter from time and death. Boiardo's romance is thus categorized as a literature of evasion, a mere pastime.

Moreover, Ariosto depicts the titular episode of his poem, the madness of Orlando, as a symbolic undoing of Orlando's conquest of Morgana in the *Innamorato*. Tortured by the suspicion that his beloved Angelica has betrayed him with Medoro, he listens to the story of the two lovers recounted by the old shepherd who had been their host and who now shows Orlando the bracelet that the grateful Angelica had given him in recompense (23.120). This jewel, we have learned earlier, has its own history.

> Quel donò già Morgana a Ziliante,
> nel tempo che nel lago ascoso il tenne;
> ed esso, poich'al padre Monodante
> per opra e per virtù d'Orlando venne,
> lo diede a Orlando.

> Morgana had given it once to Ziliante, at the time when she kept him hidden under her lake, and he, after he had been restored to his father Manodante through Orlando's deeds and virtue, gave it to Orlando. (19.38)

And Orlando, in his turn, had bestowed the bracelet as a gift upon Angelica. The bracelet that belonged to Ziliante and that was a token of the favor of Fortune and the sign of the invincible virtue of Orlando, now reappears before the eyes of the knight, and this definitive, ocular proof of the infedelity of Angelica is the decisive trigger of his madness: it was "the axe that lifted his head from his neck with one blow" ("Questa conclusion fu la secure / Che 'l capo a un colpo gli levò dal collo"; 23.121.1-

2). Angelica thus assumes the features of an inconstant fortune, transferring her favor upon the lucky Medoro—"né persona fu mai sì *avventurosa*" (19.33.3). This recollection of the greatest act of prowess achieved by Boiardo's Orlando at the moment in Ariosto's poem where the paladin descends into madness constitutes a reversal of the humanist faith of the *Innamorato*, that faith in the human domination over fortune.

This reversal will become completely explicit in the first of the fragmentary *Cinque canti* (1519–20?), the sequel that Ariosto planned to the *Furioso*. At the council of the fairies summoned by Demogorgon in his temple high in the Himalayas, Morgana appears:

> squallida e negletta
> nel medesmo vestir ch'ella avea quando
> le diè la caccia, e poi la prese Orlando.

> dirty and neglected... in the same dress she had been wearing on the day when Orlando chased and later captured her. (CC 1.10.6–8).

In accordance with her oath to do Orlando no harm, Morgana keeps silent at the council, but her sister Alcina embraces her cause and makes it a pretext for a total war launched by the fays against Charlemagne's empire. It is Demogorgon himself, the father of time and creation, who declares:

> sia Orlando, sia Carlo sia il lignagggio
> di Francia, sia tutto l'Imperio spento;
> e non rimanga segno né vestigi
> né pur si sappia dir: "Qui fu Parigi."

> let Orlando, let Charles, let the lineage of France, let the entire Empire be wiped out; and let no sign or vestige remain, let no one even know enough to say: "Here once stood Paris." (1.30.5–8)

This impressive passage is Ariosto's last revision of the optimistic humanism of the *Innamorato*. If Boiardo's Orlando mastered Fortune and time in his conquest of Morgana, here, in the bitter and almost nihilistic world of the *Cinque canti*, Ariosto shows Morgana's revenge: the triumph of time and the reversion to chaos of all things human.

In Canto 11 of the *Italia liberata dai Goti* (1547) of Giangiorgio Trissino, Corsamonte, the poem's Achillean hero, leaves the camp of Belisarius in a sulk when the commander refuses to grant him the hand of the lovely Elpidia. He reaches Monte Circeo, the realm of the fairy Plutina, who, as her name suggests, is a treasure fairy like Morgana; her palace, too, overflows with golden objects (*ILDG* 11.901–10). And, like Morgana, Plutina is a transparent figure of Fortune: she has been blinded by God for having favored only "good, wise and just men" ("i buoni / E i savi, e i giusti"; 1043–44). Now she can only distribute her gifts randomly. Corsamonte is offered the "most high adventure" ("l'altissima ventura"; 785; 801) of curing Plutina of her blindness: he has to wait twenty-five days by her side and then slay a dragon. As a reward, Plutina promises to stay by Corsamonte's side for the rest of his life, pouring the bounty of Fortune upon him. A couple of cantos later (13.271f.), the magician Filodemo divines Corsamonte's whereabouts and sends two knights, Traiano and Ciro, to bring back the absent champion. Their embassy in Canto 14 is modelled on the embassy of the Greeks to the angered Achilles in Book 9 of the *Iliad*, and the negative answer they receive from Corsamonte (14.165f.) transforms his choice between epic battle and romance adventure into another choice of Achilles between a brief but glorious life and a long life under the protection of Fortune. Corsamonte will change his mind and return to battle and to his death in Canto 22. At the news that Elpidia has been captured and made a prisoner by the Goths, the hero rushes away from the realm of Plutina; refusing to wait four more days, he loses his chance to cure the fairy and receive the kind of immunity from Fortune that Morgana offered Orlando in the *Innamorato*.

Trissino's plot, where two knights, instructed by a magician, seek to bring an absent paladin back to the field of battle, is the evident model for the celebrated episode of Armida's enchanted island in Torquato Tasso's *Gerusalemme liberata* (1581): in Tasso's poem, the magus of Ascalon sends Carlo and Ubaldo to the distant island of the sorceress to search out the absent champion Rinaldo and return him to the Crusade outside Jerusalem. Perhaps less evident is the extent to which Armida, like Trissino's Plutina, is a figure of Fortune modelled on Morgana in the *Innamorato*. Armida's island lies among the *Fortunate* Isles; her palace has the form of a labyrinth (*GL* 16.1.8) with sculpted reliefs on its doors (16.2–7), and thus recalls Morgana's palace, which has sculpted on its doors a relief of the Cretan labyrinth itself (*OI* 2.8.14f.). And the famous embrace of Rinaldo and Armida while she looks at herself in her mirror (*GL* 16.20) echoes Boiardo's description of Morgana who embraces Ziliante: "She stared—his fair face was her mirror" ("Mirando come uno specchio il suo bel viso"; *OI* 2.13.22.2). Thus, the liberation of Rinaldo from the palace and island of Armida becomes a new version of the liberation of Ziliante from Morgana's realm, from a too favorable Fortune. It is also a version of the choice of Achilles, though of an earlier choice in the career of the Greek hero: as is well known, the scene of Rinaldo's coming to his senses, as he looks at himself in Ubaldo's diamond shield and sees his own softened and effeminate condition, is modelled on the episode in the *Achilleid* (1.852f.) of Statius, where the adolescent Achilles, up until then disguised in women's clothing on the island of Scyros, is brought back by Ulysses and Diomedes to fight in the Trojan War.[7]

But if the *Gerusalemme liberata* dresses up Armida in the guise of Fortune—the Fortune of romance adventure who draws the hero away from the historical world of epic—the poem at the same time presents Fortune as a separate character, the pilot of the marvellous ship that carries Carlo and Ubaldo to and from Armida's island. Bearing the forelock of occasion, a forelock that in an earlier version of the scene functioned as the sail of her ship, Fortune, too, imitates Boiardo's description of Morgana.[8] Tasso has earlier described Fortune as the servant of Divine Providence (*GL* 9.57) in a passage that recalls Dante's portrait of Fortune (*Inf.* 7.61–96): her actions are not at all random but bring to realization a preordained plot of human history. Here, she participates in the epic plot of the *Liberata*, ferrying Rinaldo back to the Crusader army. Tasso thus divides his imitations of Morgana in order to create two versions of Fortune, a romance Fortune and an epic Fortune. The epic Fortune is, of course, the real one: Armida only plays the role that belonged to Morgana in the *Innamorato*, the role of Fortune that holds the knight captive inside her realm of adventure and contingency. Tasso's poem does not allow her to hold on to that role for long.

Boiardo's episode of Morgana thus represents for Tasso—as it also did for Ariosto and Trissino—the genre of romance itself, a genre that was, however, only becoming theorized in Tasso's time and against which he himself polemicized in his *Discorsi*. This polemic was not only concerned with the formal multiplicity and endlessness of romance,[9] but also with

---

[7] See Beatrice Corrigan, "The Opposing Mirrors," *Italica* 33 (1956): 165–79.

[8] The marvel of Fortuna's forelock-sail is described in the discarded octave from Canto 15 (7) that is reprinted in the appendix of Luigi Bonfigli's edition of the *Gerusalemme liberata* (Bari: Laterza, 1930), 516: "La chioma ch'avvolgea si lunga e folta / ver' quella parte ch'è contraria al dorso / dispiega e spande a l'aura; e l'aura come / la vela suol, curvando empie le chiome."

[9] Tasso famously argues against romance that "de la moltitudine delle favole nasce

the ideology of human self-determination that Boiardo superimposed upon the romance adventure. If Ariosto criticized this ideology from the perspective of a disillusioned spectator of the Italian wars of the the first decades of the Cinquecento, Tasso's criticism of an earlier humanism is made in the name of an emerging counterreform orthodoxy.[10] On the island of Armida, Rinaldo is depicted *not* as Boiardo's Orlando, the conqueror of Fortune, but rather as Ziliante, her beloved prisoner. Moreover, this isolation of the hero—his attempt, as an adventurer, to create his own destiny independent of religious and political authority—transforms the errancy of romance into a moral and spiritual error.

In his *Adone* (1623), Giambattista Marino repeats Tasso's strategy, dividing and thus doubling his imitations of the episode of Morgana, but to a rather different effect. In the first canto of the poem, Adonis is hunting after a deer and minding his own business on the shores of Palestine when the allegorical figure of Fortune approaches him in her ship. She sings, inviting him to grasp her forelock: her song,

> Chi cerca in terra divenir beato
> goder tesori, e posseder imperi
> stenda la destra in questo crine aurato.

> Whoever searches to be happy on earth, to enjoy wealth and possess empires, let him extend his right hand to this golden lock of hair. (*Adone* 1.50)

is a clear citation of the song of Boiardo's Morgana when she meets up with Orlando:

> Qualunche cerca al mondo aver tesoro
> Over diletto, o segue onore e stato
> Ponga la mano a questa chioma d'oro
> Ch'io porto in fronte, e quel farò beato;

---

l'indeterminatezza, e può questo progresso andare in infinito, senza che lo sia da l'arte prefisso o circonscritto termine alcuno." See the *Discorso secondo dell'arte poetica* in Tasso, *Prose*, ed. Ettore Mazzali (Milan and Naples: Ricciardi, 1959), 374.

[10] For Ariosto and the crisis of the Italian wars, see Ascoli, *Ariosto's Bitter Harmony* and the fine chapter of Marina Beer in her *Romanzi di cavalleria* (Rome: Bulzoni, 1987), 109–38. Sergio Zatti has underscored Tasso's anti-humanist polemics in the *Liberata* in *L'uniforme cristiano e il multiforme pagano* (Milan: il Saggiatore, 1983).

> Whoever looks for wealth on earth
> Dominion, honor, or delight
> May seize this golden forelock I
> Wear on my brow: I'll give him bliss. (*OI* 2.8.58.1–4)

Adonis enters into the boat of Fortune and is carried to Cyprus and eventually to the garden of Venus. The action is a rewriting not only of the *Innamorato*, but also a rewriting and reversal of the *Liberata*: the ship of Fortune, secularized once again, sails to carry the hero not *from* a realm of romance back to the Holy Land, but from Palestine *to* a romance island of adventure and erotic delight.

Adonis would remain forever in the romance garden. But Mars, the god of martial epic, invades the realm of Venus in Canto 12, and the advent of his rival forces Adonis to flee, a scene described in verses (96f.) that recall the frightened Angelica at the beginning of the *Orlando furioso* when she flees from the battle between Charlemagne and Agramante (*OF* 1.33). Like Angelica, Adonis escapes into a nearby wood, a characteristic wood of romance error and adventure. There, he is immediately met by the enchanted deer of the fairy Falsirena (105f.). This beast, which jumps into the arms of Marino's passive hero and thus spares him even the effort of having to hunt after it, reproduces almost *in toto* Morgana's magic deer in the *Innamorato*, although it sheds its golden antlers only twice instead of six times a day. Falsirena, "the fairy of gold" ("la fata dell'oro"; 117), is herself closely modelled on Morgana, and Morgana's underground prison also reappears in the labyrinthine realm of Falsirena into which Adonis now descends: he sees where the riches of the fairy are generated beneath the earth and finally reaches her garden of pleasure. Falsirena falls in love with the handsome youth and he becomes another Ziliante, the prisoner of a demonic Fortune. When Falsirena offers herself to her unwilling lover,

> Intenerisci il tuo selvaggio ingegno
> prendi il crin che Fortuna or t'offre in dono.

> Soften your hard heart, take the forelock that Fortune now offers you as her gift. (12.249)

her words spell out her allegorical identity. The next two cantos, where Adonis escapes from the prison of Falsirena first transformed into a parrot, then in his own body, involve the hero in a whole series of romance adventures and hairbreadth close calls, especially in Canto 14 in which the fairy sends in pursuit of Adonis a band of robbers who come out of the

Ethiopica of Heliodorus. Mixing motifs of the chivalric romances, the *Innamorato* preeminent among them, with elements from the Greek novel, and thereby suggesting their generic affinities, Marino confirms the observations of late sixteenth-century literary theorists like Paolo Beni who grouped together these two historical forms of romance.[11] Presiding over these adventures, the Fortune-fairy Falsirena becomes identified with romance itself. And it is Falsirena who returns in Canto 18 to put in motion the plot that leads to the death of Adonis, a death that he has perhaps brought upon himself when he robbed the fatal arms of Meleager from Falsirena's treasury (18.40), unlike Boiardo's Ranaldo who was forced to renounce Morgana's gold. Thus, Falsirena is the instigator of the larger part of the plot—to the extent that there is a plot in Marino's static poem. She is a double of the Fortune who began the action of the poem, a Fortune that at its end transforms herself into Nemesis. She is also a double of that Venus who enthralls Adonis, fascinated as he is by the beauty of the goddess. When Falsirena attempts to seduce Adonis a second time, she disguises herself in the form of Venus, a counterfeit duplicate of the goddess of love (13.144f.). And Marino could have known a Renaissance mythographic tradition according to which Nemesis-Fortune was depicted in the guise of Venus.[12]

The effect of all these doublings is that—especially when it comes to the problem of the genre of the *Adone*—there is not much to choose from between Venus and Falsirena. What was in the earlier literary tradition a choice of Achilles between epic and romance collapses in Marino's poem where Adonis commutes between the garden of the goddess and the garden of the fairy, both idyllic realms of pleasure. There is no arena of heroic action for Adonis—his only act of prowess is to win a beauty pageant that has for its prize the throne of Cyprus—and the whole poem can be read as a deformation of epic into romance. The hero's choice is between two versions of romance—the stasis of his erotic idyll with Venus or the adventures sent his way by Falsirena—but these are illusory alternatives since Adonis remains passive in both cases, and it cannot be said

----

[11] Pado Beni, *In Aristotelis Poeticam commentarii* (Padua, 1613), 80–81. For the status of the *Ethiopica* in the literary theory of the late Renaissance, see Alban Forcione, *Cervantes, Aristotle, and the Persiles* (Princeton: Princeton Univ. Press, 1970), 49–87.

[12] See Lilio Gregorio Giraldi, *De deis gentium* (Basel, 1548), 640, 648 (Syntagma 16). For the tradition of Fortuna-Nemesis, see Erwin Panofsky, " 'Virgo e Victrix': A Note on Durer's Nemesis," in *Prints*, ed. Carl Zigrosser (New York: Holt, Rinehart and Winston, 1962), 13–38, 19 n. 28.

that he chooses one or the other. Thus, if Marino transforms the heroic poem along the romance lines of the *Innamorato*, giving control of the narrative action of the *Adone* to a version of Boiardo's Morgana, he nonetheless strips these romance structures of the humanistic values Boiardo had conferred on them. In Marino's cynical, Ovidian world, the figure of Fortune no longer represents *occasio*, the opportunity for the adventurous human protagonist to demonstrate his own virtue, but instead an all-powerful chance that reduces human agents to its playthings and eventually deprives them, through the metamorphosis that changes Adonis into a flower, of their very humanity.

The imitations of the episode of Morgana in the great tradition of Italian Renaissance narrative poetry thus constitutes a history of reception. They offer a quite coherent reading not only of the episode, but of the *Innamorato* itself for which the episode of the Fortune-fairy is an emblematic and miniaturized model. For the poet-successors to Boiardo, the *Innamorato* is defined as the romance of adventure; its narrative form, full of diverse and seemingly unconnected episodes, reflects the realm of Fortune, of contingent time. If, however, Boiardo valorized the adventure as the occasion and place for his paladins to exercise their heroic virtue, a humanistic virtue that overcomes the forces of Fortune, the later tradition will oppose the romance adventure to epic heroism, a heroism dependent not so much upon the virtue and self-determination of the individual as upon the historical plots and collective social-political goals in whose service that heroism is placed. The episodic structure of the romance narrative, the episode itself will be considered as evasions of an authentic human temporality and historicity represented by epic and by its teleological narrative; and the return to a poetic universe dominated, as is the *Innamorato*, by a figure of Fortune will take place in the *Adone*, the escapist poem *par excellence*.

This critique of the romance structures of the *Innamorato* is also a critique of the hopeful humanism of the late Quattrocento, a humanism that would become subject to new political and religious pressures in the following centuries. In the light of this poetic history of its reception, the humanistic values of the *Innamorato* become clearer and more manifest, and by the same token, the rupture of its last stanzas announcing the invasion of French troops in 1494 appears that much more decisive and bitter. The extent of this historical and cultural rupture can be measured in the century-long literary tradition that returned over and over again to reread and rewrite Boiardo's romance and its animating figure of Fortune.

JAMES NOHRNBERG

Orlando's Opportunity: Chance, Luck, Fortune, Occasion, Boats, and Blows in Boiardo's *Orlando Innamorato*

If a king were to give enormous booty to one who had done nothing in a war, and to those who had done the fighting barely just their salary, he could respond to the murmuring soldiers: am I injuring you by giving [to] the others freely and gratuitously? But really, how could one consider him just and gentle, if he crowned magnificently for his victory a general whom he had furnished with machines, troops, money and all supplies aplenty for war, while another, whom he had thrown into war without armaments, he ordered put to death on account of the war's unhappy ending? Before dying, could he not say with justice to the king: why do you punish me for what happened through your fault? If you had equipped me similarly, I would have won too.[1]

But I must tell you that there is no such thing as Fortune in the world. Nothing that happens here below, whether of good or evil, comes by chance, but by the special disposition of Providence, and that is why we have the proverb: "Every man is the maker of his own fortune." I, for my part, have been the maker of mine, but because I did not act with all the prudence necessary, my presump-

---

[1] Erasmus, *A Diatribe or Sermon Concerning Free Will*, VIII.54. Ernst F. Winter, trans., *Erasmus–Luther: Discourse on Free Will* (New York: Ungar, 1961), 82–83.

tions have brought me to my shame. I should have remembered
that my poor, feeble Rozinante could never withstand the strongly
built horse of the Knight of the White Moon.[2]

NEAR THE START OF HIS LIFE-STORY IN Book 3 of Boiardo's *Orlando Innamorato*, the future knight Mandricardo falls on a serpent at the bottom of
a cave and crushes it. A fortunate fall indeed: it is Mandricardo's exceptional *ventura* to have found this way of both cheating death (3.2.24) and
winning Hector's arms. These arms were Mandricardo's high *aventura*, his
Main Chance (3.2.37). When the same knight subsequently duels with
Gradasso, Gradasso falls under him, "by fortune or a tricky fall [*caso*]." A
lady thereafter consoles the frustrated contender with the observation,
"One can't forbid what fortune wants" (3.1.46, 48).[3] Fortune, it seems

---

[2] Don Quixote to Sancho Panza, in Cervantes, *Don Quixote* II.66. Walter Starkie,
trans., *Don Quixote* (New York: New American Library, 1967). Cf. Erasmus, *Adag.* II, iv,
30 (*Adagiorum Collectanea*, numbering of Paris edition of 1506/7), on "Sui mores fingunt
fortunam / Every man's character moulds his fortune": "Cornelius Nepos in his life of
Pomponius Atticus: 'And so he made the old proverb seem true, which says that every
man's character moulds his fortune.' And a little further on in the same work: 'We have
pointed out above that every man's character procures his fortune.' This is an aphorism
clearly derived from common experience; we generally see bad men come to a bad end,
as they deserve, and it is a common saying that a bad man comes to no good, and 'Evil
thrice over to the evil.' This is supported by a proverbial line of verse: 'To the good man
God gives a good reward.' Menander too, cited by Plutarch: 'Because the mind in us is
God.' And Hercalitus, whom he also cites: 'A man's character is his God' or 'his fortune.' Here belongs that phrase in Alcman, that 'Fortune is the sister of Good Principles,
Persuasion and Foresight,' as Plutarch records in his essay 'On the Fortune of the
Romans.' Plautus in the *Trinummus*: 'The wise man moulds his own fortune.' Livy in his
fourth decade, book 1, writes as follows about Marcius Porcius Cato: 'In this man such
was the force of personality and natural gifts that it seemed he would have made a great
name for himself, whatever the position in life to which he was born.' Pacatus in a *Panegyric*: 'Each man's own wisdom in his God.' Fulgentius in his essay on Virgil quotes from
the Telesiacus of Carneades 'All fortune dwells in the wise man's mind.' I take it that
the same point is made when Cicero quotes in the fifth of his *Paradoxes* from an unspeci-
fied poet (the text is defective, I think it should be corrected thus): 'Fortune herself, the
most powerful force, gives way to him, and, as a wise poet has said, is moulded for every
man by his own character.' For his point is that every man's character moulds his fortune." From *Adages: II.1.1. to II.vi.100*, trans. R.A.B. Mynors, *Collected Works of Erasmus*
(Toronto: Univ. of Toronto Press, 1991), 33: 205–6.

For Spanish sources for Don Quixote's doctrine, see Otis H. Green, *Spain and the
Western Tradition: The Castilian Mind in Literature from 'El Cid' to Calderón*, 4 vols. (Madison and Milwaukee: Univ. of Wisconsin Press, 1968), 2: 279–337, especially page 287,

obvious, wants Mandricardo to succeed.

Boiardo's long narration of fortuity and befallenness—or Fortune and Occasion—is always accompanied with these kinds of moralization, across a wide conspectus of the characters' reactions to their hap. Thus, the poem becomes an *anatomy* of Fortune: if only because the story itself so thoroughly replaces the deep causality of traditional epic with the deep accidentality of traditional romance. Romance tends to vitiate the authority of an epic source, even as it divinizes fortuitous causes: causes hidden *from*, rather than in, the will of Heaven—or the authority of tradition. Fortune may be defined by Aristotle "as *causa accidens* on human action, with the causes infinite and the fortune certain," but it is understood by the common man to be the kind of thing, positively, "which Alexander trusted and which contributed to his victories," or, negatively, as a "divine power, turning and reversing human affairs capriciously, offering nothing firm and safe." So Poggio wrote, in his *De Varietate Fortunae.*[4] The word fortuitous, Augustine notes in discussing the goddesses of Chance and Happiness, comes from *fortuna* (*Civ. Dei*, IV.18).

While the lady in Boiardo cannot contravene Gradasso's fortune, she *can* promise him an unmatched *strana ventura* the very next day: neither knight nor poet ever tires of this prospect, which depends equally on a

---

and the speeches in Joanot Martorell and Martí Joan de Galba, *Tirant Lo Blanc*, trans. David H. Rosenthall (New York: Schocken Books, 1984), 383: "No man should take umbrage at what Providence ordains and Fortune executes, for the human mind is not all-seeing, and brave knights are known by their forbearance"; and page 450: "You are like a farmer who instead of wheat reaps empty husks, as you should curse yourself rather than Fortune, which has no power over your free will. Do you know what made you err? Your own ignorance of reason's dictates. Fortune allots things like wealth, rank, and power, but the decision to love or hate, to behave well or badly, to seek or shun is in each man's power." Martorell's characters, however, readily refer to their fates, amorous and otherwise, as "monstrous," two-faced," "fickle," "adverse," "outrageous," or "unjust" fortune. A contemporary of the *Innamorato*, *Tirant Lo Blanc* (publ. 1490) is a source for the Ginevra-Ariodante episode in Ariosto's fifth canto (cf. Rosenthall, *Tirant Lo Blanc*, 427–29).

[3] Translations of Boiardo are generally taken from Charles Stanley Ross, *Orlando Innamorato* (Berkeley and Los Angeles: Univ. of California Press, 1989). Only occasionally have I hazarded a more literal rendering of my own.

[4] Cited in George Holmes, *The Florentine Enlightenment, 1400–50* (New York: Pegasus, 1969), 117–18. With the following citation of Augustine, cf. Isidore of Seville, *Etymologies*, VIII.xi.94: "*Fortuna* gets her name from *fortuitus*, because she is a goddess who makes sport of human affairs by reason of the fortuitousness and various nature of her action—which is why she is said to be blind: since she sometimes favors certain men without trying their merits, and visits both just and unjust."

medieval delight in a tale of "faery," and a "Renaissance penchant for embracing new worlds."[5] Late in Book 2, for example, Brandimart arrives at a palace portal beyond which a giant struggles with a dragon, and where he will soon have to kiss a serpent in a tomb. "The cavalier is quite happy to find here such a *strana aventura*" (2.25.26). At the palace where Mandricardo will acquire Hector's shield, the knight likewise hears the Siren song of *Strane aventure* (3.1.57). The term implies the novel and astonishing twists of fortune into which the characters are inevitably drawn, in a poem where accidents happen regularly, and haphazardness functions as a cause.

One way into our topic is through Boiardo's ostensible subject matter, which coincides with just those things that Fortune, as commonly understood, happens to dominate: war, love, the accident of birth, material outcomes (as in business ventures), and the long possession of anything beyond self-consciousness that we might want to call our own.

1.1. Fortunes of War

First, war. Astolfo's initial triumph over Grandonio is a *strana ventura*:

> Gano can't believe Astolfo could
> Have knocked [Grandonio] to the ground.
> Instead, he figures—he is sure—
> That some strange accident befell
> That giant. Some unheard-of thing
> Must be the cause of such a fall [*cascata*].

What could this intervening befallment, *qualche caso strano intervenuto* (1.3.10), be? "Is Fortune so insidious? / Did heaven license this buffoon / To make us look ridiculous?" ask the Magazans (1.3.17). Pitting themselves against Astolfo's sudden distinction, they also pit themselves against his Fortune. They are not merely engaged against Astolfo, but also in what Petrarch calls, at the outset of his *Remedies*, "the daily combat with Fortune" (I, Pref.),[6] in this case, the fortunes of war.

---

[5] The quoted words are taken from David Marsh, "Beyond the Pillars of Hercules: Voyage and Veracity in Exploration Narratives," in *Annali D'Italinistica*, vol. 10: *Images of America and Columbus in Italian Literature*, ed. Albert N. Mancini and Dino S. Cervigni (Chapel Hill: Univ. of North Carolina Press, 1992), 143.

[6] *Petrarch's Remedies for Fortune Fair and Foul*, 5 vols., trans. and comm. Conrad H. Rawski (Bloomington and Indianapolis: Indiana Univ. Press, 1991), 1: 4. All subsequent passages from Petrarch are taken from this source.

Fortune chooses one's generals in war, and she can choose carelessly (2.28.45). When the Guelfs prevailed in battle, however, the emblem under which they fought lacked neither *ventura* nor *virtû* (2.25.44). The effect of blows, however, is often merely a matter of chance: "Sword-strokes can't be predicted well" (2.11.41). When Feraguto arrives in the Forest of Arden to challenge Argalia for Angelica, he succeeds in knifing her champion in the groin. But he is not so happy with what has happened when Argalia proves mortal: "[T]he saddest thing to fall out has intravened: / as heaven and Fortune wished" (1.3.64). *Casa intravenuto*—this is the Magazans' language for Astolfo's success in the joust. It is the warrior Brontino's *mala ventura* that presents him to the violent Orlando on the field of battle (1.15.22), and gets him hacked up. Elsewhere the giant Ranchiero launches an amazing swing at Orlando: "It landed in a nearby tree / And split it till it reached its roots" (1.20.24). Bad luck for the tree, one might say. Rugiero swung fast at Olivier, but it was God's wish that his sword turn and strike flat (3.4.21): good fortune for Olivier.

Why *does* everyone hit so hard? The blows of Fortune are typically *outrageous* ones, just as a stroke of luck is usually an *amazing* one. The weapons in Boiardo are myriad, but the inflictions seem much the same. They are moralized only as fortunate or unfortunate, but the blows Orlando offers to a personification of Penitence in Morgana's underworld in Book 2, Canto 9, are also those he suffers. They might as well have been administered by Fortune's own disciplinary rod or cudgel. The proverbial *ictus fortunae* is found in Boethius (*De Cons. Phil.*, III, prosa 1); Fortune is armed with a *stick* or *hook*.[7] In Martianus, Fortune or Tyche ("luck") rewarded some, "but girlishly plucked the hairs of others, beating others on the head with a rod." She calls the shots, and she takes your chance—*away*.

1.2. Fortunes of Love

Boiardo's project of subjecting the peers of Charlemagne to the love experience of Arthur's knights implies that the fortunes of battle deserve equal billing with the fortunes of love. A heart-shaped French miniature, ca. 1460–67, printed by Conrad Rawski in his translation of Petrarch's *Remedies*, shows a lady in one panel; in the panel opposite, Cupid takes aim at her, over an icon of Fortune with her light and dark faces. In other

---

[7] *Virga* in Martianus Capella, *De Nuptiis*, I.88, in *De Nuptiis*, ed. James Willis (Leipzig: Teubner, 1983), 25. *Unco* in *De Cons. Phil.* II, prosa 8.

words, the lady is a person about to be subject to the fortunes of love. The unarmed and disarming girl that conquers Orlando is not only Angelica, we can argue, but also a Fortune. If Angelica smiles on him, he thinks, so does Fortune.[8]

In a long complaint about his pitiless misfortune, a bereft Brandimart speaks of his lost love:

> I do not want to live without her,
> For she's my only joy, my comfort,
> And if I live, I'll die a thousand
> Times! Ruthless Fortune, you were wrong
> To interfere in my affairs.
> Who will amuse you when I'm gone
> And my death ends your power? What
> Will you do then, cruel, faithless one? (1.21.44)

Yet, Petrarch submitted that, in his experience, "smiling Fortune is more to be feared and demonstrably more dangerous than frowning Fortune": he observed "those who had stood undefeated against all violence of adverse Fortune [were] overthrown by prosperous Fortune as if it were child's play, her flatteries overcoming the strength of a mind that threats could not subdue" (*Remedies*, I, Pref).[9] Angelica is later flattered to have Orlando for a lover, but only after she has inveigled him into a commitment to fight with Ranaldo in exchange for a kiss and a massage (1.25.47). The man made happy by smiling Fortune, we conclude, is much like a fool in love: committed to his own destruction.

Almost the first thing Orlando asks after spotting the tempting Angelica is "Where is my fortune guiding me?" (1.1.30). —Away from your wife, we might answer. Doesn't he see, Orlando asks himself, that sin is enticing him into disobedience to God? But the knight does not stay for an answer, and the wife is not mentioned even once again. Orlando is like Ovid's Medea, resolving to be called dear to the gods as she takes to the high seas with her lover: for it is Medea whom Orlando echoes when he says he sees what's best and picks what's worst (1.1.31).[10]

---

[8] Cf. 1.2.24 with 1.14.43, 1.16.37, 1.25.37, and 2.19.50, 53.

[9] Rawski, *Petrarch's Remedies*, 1: 6–7.

[10] "I see the better, I approve it too: / The worse I follow"; *Metam.* VII.20–21. *Ovid's Metamorphosis: Englished . . .*, ed. Karl K. Hulley and Stanley T. Vandersall (Lincoln: Univ. of Nebraska Press, 1970), 306.

Asleep with her blond hair on the grass, Angelica shortly thereafter presents the magician Malagise not only with an early emblem of opportunity, but also with the chance to defeat fortune. Charles Ross made the identification of Angelica with Occasio, via the Fay Morgana, more than twenty years ago. His reading is fundamental to the present essay's understanding of Boiardo. As the most complex of the poem's several enchantresses (Angelica being the first), Ross cites the triplex embodiment of Morgana:

> As the *Fata del Tesoro*, she owns a stag with golden antlers that attracts Brandimart, a treasure field that tempts Ranaldo, and a fickle heart that leads her to kidnap the son of the richest man in the world [Manodante]. As *Ventura* . . . by a small play on words Morgana represents the "adventure" that every romance knight constantly seeks, canto after canto. But most important, as Fortune she not only personifies the proverb "to seize time by the forelock," she also leads Orlando through her underworld (Book II, cantos viii–ix) on a chase that mirrors Orlando's endless pursuit of the beautiful Angelica, heroine of the poem.[11]

An early question raised by Ross's identification of Morgana as Orlando's object (Angelica) is this: why should Malagise be inspired to *kill* such an Opportunity, or Occasio figure, upon her first appearance in the poem? In fact, one notes that almost all of Boiardo's enchantresses are also the object of hostile heroic animus; the story requires that a majority of them be conquered or dispatched by one or another of the human protagonists. What fortune is being repelled?

Boiardo's conflicted choice between seizing an inviting opportunity and squelching a nascent evil apparently depends on a longstanding iconographic confusion between the traditional attributes of the classical Occasio and the medieval or Boethian Fortuna. This confusion must date at least from Old French translations of the word *occasio* as fortune or venture, in the famous distich of Cato on Opportunity's having hair in front and being bald behind. We can argue that the corresponding ethical ambiguity pervades the entire narrative of Boiardo's poem, especially in those places where the knights' heroics may be allegorized as answering the challenge that Fortune constitutes for Virtue.[12]

---

[11] Charles S. Ross, "Angelica and that Fata Morgana: Boiardo's Allegory of Love" *Modern Language Notes* 96 (1980): 13.

[12] I owe a great deal here—and throughout—to the work of David Burchmore,

2. The Love of Fortune: Subjective and Objective Genitive

Malagise has learned from a demon that the only reason Angelica is around is to lure Charlemagne's knights into defeat by her invincingly armed brother; the pair are the subversive secret agents of the pagan king Galafrone. Up close, however, Malagise hesitates (1.1.45), and he who hesitates is lost. Instead of killing the alluring girl, he seizes and starts kissing her. She embraces his unwelcome advances to his peril and in the end possess his magic book. Malagise thereupon becomes her captive.

The magic in the magician's book matters because divination, like astrology, offers an insight into one's *fortune*. But while magic has allowed Malagise to divine that Angelica is a lure, it has not enabled him to resist the sexual chance, or opportunity, presented by the apparent availability of her person. In the subsequent matches against Argalia (her brother) for Angelica's possession, other contenders also try their luck: "Since truly he'd be Fortune's son, / He'd wear the crown of happiness, / Whomever such a creature loved" (1.2.24). The mightiest aspirants are soon drawn to the forest of Arden in search of this "chance."

Ventura (1.2.29) is indeed the key word, and in the thematically climactic Morgana episode in Book 2, Canto 9, the terms Fortune and Venture are virtually interchangeable. "Few are found beneath the moon /

---

whose University of Virginia thesis on Chaucer and Spenser (and including Fortuna figures in these authors) I co-directed and examined. For the present essay, see especially his definitive article "The Medieval Sources of Spenser's Occasion Episode," in *Spenser Studies: A Renaissance Poetry Annual, II*, ed. Patrick Cullen and Thomas P. Roche, Jr., (Pittsburgh: Univ. of Pittsburgh Press, 1981), 93–120. Burchmore explains that despite her traditional forelock, Spenser's Occasion (in *Faerie Queene* II.iv–v) is not meant to signify that "opportunitie is a thing, that soone passeth, and is cleane lost, onlesse it be presently apprehended," because, on the contrary, "she appears when you least want to see her, and you cannot get rid of her when you try" (Burchmore, "The Medieval Sources," 94–95; the internal quote is from Thomas Cooper's *Thesaurus*). But this other side of the latter-day Occasio (as Occasion-for-Patience) does indeed seem to be represented by Boiardo's Angelica, if we choose to see her as Ranaldo's persistent *Misfortune*.

Burchmore, "The Medieval Sources," 98, cites "the substitution of Fortune or Aventure for Occasio in the Old French translations of Cato's *Distichs*" as the beginning of the transfer of the critical forelock from Occasio to Fortuna. (*Distiches Catonis*, "fronte capillata, post est Occasio calva"). Related statuary is found in Phaedrus X.viii, and Posidippus, *Greek Anthology*, XVI.275 (the latter is cited—as an addition to notices in Politian, *Miscellanea* c. 49—by Erasmus, *sub Adag.* I.vii.70, *Nosce tempus* [Gr. *gnothi kairon*, "know the right moment"], in *Adages: I.vi.1 to I.x.100* (1989), *Collected Works of Erasmus*, 32: 108–10). See also Rudolf Wittkower, "Patience and Chance: The Story of an Emblem for Ercole II of Ferrara," *Journal of the Warburg Institute*, vol. 1 (1937–38): 171, and, in the same volume, "Chance, Time, and Virtue," 313–21.

Able to handle Fortune's key," but "When one has Venture with him, he turns [it] to the exact right point through calculation" (2.9.25, 26). The great joust that ensues in Boiardo's second canto—a tournament that Charlemagne orders in the same stanza as the critical mention of *ventura*— has no particular motive in the story as told up to that point. But it is another chance for the many jousters to show whether or not they have "force or fortune" standing by them (1.2.30). Thus, the narrative alternates between those trying their luck or fortune at love and those trying it at arms. But if you're going to get lucky, you'd better be clever.

The poet-narrator ends his second canto with the promise of "more *strana ventura*" (1.2.68) than ever you heard or read. He then returns to those trying their fortune in love. The first of these, Ranaldo, comes upon the fountain that, through *sciagura* (bad luck), failed to save the *isventurato* (unfortunate) Tristan. The anti-romance motor of sexual distaste, or disillusion with love, we are told, cures not only thirst but also longing, and erases the impression of the idealized face of the beloved. How worthless "to follow a thing so vain," Ranaldo now thinks of his idol. Then he takes a nap beside another font, the cursed stream of infatuation—a natural product, the poet informs us. Angelica now arrives on the scene, and the audience is warned that it will hear something novel, corresponding to the *ventura* (1.3.39) that the poet tells us to behold in the sleeping knight. He seems to mean that he is giving us the rare chance to see, or hear described, a sexual aggression that is female. The narrator says that Angelica dismounts for a little drink; we assume that she took it, since he then reports that she felt her heart afire at the sight of Ranaldo asleep in the flowers.

"Bring me handfuls of lilies." Although Dante's good angel Beatrice thus announces herself in the sacred wood where Adam also met Eve (*Purg.* XXX.21), Angelica's emptying handfuls of petals on Ranaldo only sends him into flight. Ranaldo had the (good) luck to give up seeking his fortune in love, just before Angelica had the (bad) luck to fall in love with him. "Why couldn't [Ranaldo] have come to Merlin's Stone, / where I captured his sage cousin [Orlando]?" (1.5.18), Angelica is found whining a little later. And, indeed, "Guided by *fortuna* or his *ventura*" (2.20.44), Ranaldo, along with Orlando and Angelica, will eventually come this way again, where one drink releases Angelica from her fixation on Ranaldo, while another causes Ranaldo to think himself indeed *aventurato*, lucky, to come upon his chance once more (2.20.48). Having been chastened by Cupid for his earlier disdain, the reformed kill-courtesy then thanks God for the *ventura* and takes his drink (an evil one, *peggiore*, 2.25.26) from the fount of infatuation (2.15.61). But Angelica's love has again arrived too late, he's missed his chance—or his chance has arrived too late, and his love has missed hers. "I miss you," we say in English, with the double meaning narrativized here: no one wants to miss his chance for the right love, yet everyone suspects he already has.

The lot of the flowers, Angelica originally laments, is so very much more *aventurosa* than her own (1.3.48); she tossed the flowers on Ranaldo rather than jumping on him herself. But now she is left to fall asleep on the spot where Ranaldo lay, recomposing herself as the emblem of another opportunity. When Orlando arrives in the wood, cursing fell Fortune for his mischance in quest of Angelica, he suddenly comes upon the sleeping maid, while the nearby river speaks of love. He has the *tempo*, occasion, to seize her. "One who has the time, because he misses the time, will find himself with empty hands," and, the moralizing narrator sticks in, lose a great pleasure through hesitating. Orlando, however, misses the chance to "know his fortune's time," as Prasildo's go-between says to Tisbina on a different sexual occasion (1.12.14); that is, the chance to pluck the day, indulge the genius, seize the initiative, take time or fortune by the fore-lock, use advantage, and know the fit or due time[13]—for taking one's pleasure. "One who hesitates when asked to serve, / And *then* serves, forfeits his reward," Orlando lectures himself when he recalls the loving face of the one who has sent him to the battle with Agricane (1.19.8). Moreover, the knight misses his chance again: both in the bath of Book 1, Canto 25, and with the Leodilla of the preceding canto (1.24.15–19, 43–44). The advice offered by Leodilla, the lady whom Orlando and Brandimarte save from "fortune fell" (1.22.9), recommends an opportunistic hedonism:

> Let others seek renown throughout the world;
> The smart ones want their pleasure first,
> To live delightful, happy lives.
> May those who work for fame or things
> Ignore this—and the loss be theirs!" (1.22.27)

---

[13] Carpe diem quam minime credula postera ("Pluck today, believing in tomorrow as little as possible"): Horace, *Carm.*, I.ix.8. *Indulgere genio*: Persius, *Sat.*, V.151; cf. Servius *ad Georg.* i.302. *Utere sorte tua* ("use your fortune": the losing Turnus to the winning Aeneas, *Aen.*, XII.932). "Nosce tempus," *Adag.* I.vii.70, in *Adages: I.vi.1 to I.x.100* (1989), *Collected Works of Erasmus*, 32: 108–10. Erasmus explains the Persius tag, "indulge the genius," as proverbial "for doing as one pleases" (*Adag.* II.iv.74, *Adages: II.i.1 to II.vi.100* (1991), *Collected Works of Erasmus*, 33: 228.

"Is my face so *pauroso?*" (1.3.44), so appalling, Angelica asks, when Ranaldo first shuns her. Her misfortune looks rather like misfortune's *allegorical personification*: the foul face of impoverishment, which is fair Fortune's hidden aspect, the negative half of *Fortuna bifrons*. If Angelica were as desirable as she has presumed she is, then *she* would be the one being pursued. But she is being avoided, as if she were an evil, like the supposedly good fortune of a fair wife, as reprehended by Reason as "a most decorous but troublesome idol," in Petrarch's *Remedies for Fortune*. Reason describes such a mate as "a sweet poison, golden fetters, resplendent servitude" (*Remedies*, I.66).[14]

It is Feraguto's arrival that ends Orlando's original luck, *ventura*, in gazing on Angelica. But even as the lady disappears from the scene of the ensuing fight between the two rivals, the paladin is thoroughly hooked. The fight over this enslaving possession wakes up the damsel with the serene visage (1.3.78) and she herself quickly departs—*one can't say why* (so also in the similar case as 2.21.18, where it is Orlando and Ranaldo who are fighting over the lady). Suddenly the knight's fortune is not so good. Angelica is replaced in the narrative by a woman in black with bad news of the misfortunes of both Feraguto's father and his king. The newly arrived lady, Fiordespina, draws Feraguto off to fight for both; there's no better chance, she says, for him to acquire fame and glory than now offers (1.4.10).

Thus, the narrative is controlled by a ghostly paradigm of the two fortunes, the fair one being replaced by the foul one, the missed occasion for joy and roses being logically followed by the subsequently found occasion for dolor and thorns. The brothers Grifone and Aquilant, for a second example, meet two ladies, one in black, one in white. The one in black says that there is no defense against what the heavens have destined; the white one counters that "one can prolong one's time / And, if one's clever, sway one's fortune" (3.2.42–43). The brothers may be heading for death; it would indeed be good fortune if one could defer the time when the dark fortune will prevail over the light one.

The twofold aspect of Fortune—her two persons or faces, one light and fair, one dark and foul—is a commonplace of later medieval iconography as found, for example, in Book 8 of Alan de Lille's *Anticlaudianus*:

Her appearance with its twofold aspect misleads the viewer. The front of her head is covered with a rich growth of hair, the back

---

[14] Rawski, *Petrarch's Remedies*, 1: 194.

bemoans its baldness. One eye dances mischievously, the other overflows with tears; the latter is dull and heavy, the former sparkles. Part of her face is alive, aflame with natural colour; part is dying in the grip of pallor; as the charm of the countenance fades, the face grows dull and beauty melts away. One hand gives a gift, the other takes it away.[15]

The duality of *Fortuna bifrons* also appears in allegories of Fortune as a locus of architecture or landscape. Falerina's Garden and its various cogeners—that first are and then are not—seem like the "house" of Fortune as it is found in the text just quoted: "One part of the house glitters with silver, shines with gems, is alight with gold: the other part lies debased with worthless material. The former part prides itself on its lofty roof; the latter stands uncovered in a gaping cleft."[16] The behavior of Boiardo's gardens is similarly ambiguous and fickle. These gardens, moreover, do not change by themselves, but in relation to the heroes' fortunes when they visit them. Dragontina's Garden, for example, disappears when Angelica arrives there to recover Orlando's memory and his services (1.14.43–47). The garden disappears because she replaces both it and Dragontina, and thus she reoccupies the place of the adventurer's fortune. A house of fortune similar to the one in Alanus appears in *The Romance of the Rose* (6093–6174), and in the same context so do two founts of sweetness and bitterness (5978–6078). Boiardo's waters of infatuation and disinclination go back to the two waters of honey and gall in which Cupid dips his arrows on the Cyprian isle in Claudian's *De Nuptiis Honorii* (69–71), but the medieval analogue shows that they also represent the fondness and disdain of Lady Fortune.

At the time when Ranaldo is hoping to rescue his brother Ricciardetto from his disgrace by the fortunes of battle on behalf of the Spanish king, Angelica is employing her prisoner Malagise, in return for his freedom, to capture Ranaldo *for her*. Ranaldo refuses the chance the offer gives him to free the mage. He'd accept hard fortune and bad luck (*spaventosa*) on his friend's behalf, anything except going where Angelica is (1.5.29). In other words, he wants to free Ricciardetto without becoming Fortune's captive himself. Malagise, in revenge for Ranaldo's refusal to help him, works an enchantment that draws the cavalier off from battle and disgraces him by

---

[15] Alan of Lille, *Anticlaudianus or The Good and Perfect Man*, trans. James J. Sheridan (Toronto: Pontifical Institute of Mediaeval Studies, 1973), 90.

[16] Alan of Lille, *Anticlaudianus*, 189.

carrying him out to sea by boat, away from his duty and in search of an illusory enemy. Arriving at an island pleasure-palace contrived by Angelica, Ranaldo flees from this Lido-like temptation only to next end up in the monster-haunted Castle Cruel. Boiardo's inspiration in *Aeneid* X (after a divine-intervention motif from *Iliad* XXI) emphasizes the departure of a beleagured warrior, namely Turnus, from the fortunes of battle. But the *Innamorato* emphasizes the entry of a distracted chevalier, Ranaldo, upon the fortunes and misfortunes of, so to speak, the "fortunati."[17] Virgil's Turnus escapes from the necessity of epic to the uncanniness of romance; Boiardo's Ranaldo enters upon one uncanny romance after another.

At Castle Cruel, Boiardo's protagonist regains his claims to approbation as a warrior by a terrific show of valor in the loneliest of circumstances. Yet, his survival here depends, finally, on the intervention of Angelica. At the outset he complains that "ruinous fortune sends [him] disgraces one upon another" (1.8.24). Angelica may not *be* Ranaldo's fortune, but she is its instrument, or it is hers.

The *sea* may not be Ranaldo's fortune either, and yet things said about its power are also said about Fortune's, and it is Angelica who has put the knight on the sea. Here we recognize a confluence of traditional rhetoric about fortune in classical texts. Plato's *Laws* say that man's skill in handling the three forces of chance, occasion, and dependence of God is like that of a pilot in a storm. In Horace, Fortuna is "mistress of the sea," while in Sallust, "Fortune rules in all things." Thus, the sea becomes an image for the forces one must control in order to negotiate the totality of the world-space. In Boethius, "Life is . . . a sea of trouble stirred up by Fortuna, and with our light skiff we venture on its waves," as H. R. Patch summarizes the figurative tradition extending from *The Consolation of Philosophy*.[18] The marine motif may come from Cicero's *De Officiis*:

---

[17] "Fortunati" is suggested by the usage of Tasso at *Gerusalemne Liberata* XV.6, where the soldiers repatriating another Rinaldo for epic duty are conveyed to the Fortunate Isles by a pilot identified by her clothing's changeable colors and forelock as Fortuna: "O fortunate men (she says) come aboard this ship, on which I safely cross the ocean, to which all winds are favoring, all tempests tranquil, and every heavy load is light. My lord, unsparing of His favor, provides me now for you as minister and guide." *Jerusalem Delivered*, trans. Ralph Nash (Detroit: Wayne State Univ. Press, 1987). See James Nohrnberg, *The Analogy of "The Faerie Queene"* (Princeton: Princeton Univ. Press, 1976), 309–10, and for the comparison to the *Aeneid*, 9–10.

[18] Howard R. Patch, *The Goddess Fortuna in Medieval Literature* (Cambridge, MA: Harvard Univ. Press, 1927), 201. Plato, *Laws* IV, 709C (Loeb Classic Library edition, 1: 269–67), cited by Ficino in his Letter to Rucelli (perhaps, as Edgar Wind suggests, this

Who fails to comprehend the enormous, twofold power of Fortune for weal or woe? When we enjoy her favoring breeze, we are wafted over to the wished-for haven; when she blows against us, we are dashed to destruction. Fortune herself, then, does send those other less usual calamities, arising, first, from inanimate nature—hurricanes, storms, shipwrecks, catastrophes, conflagrations.[19]

---

is the source of the famous emblem of the Rucellai, the Fortune-figure running her own boat [Millard Meiss, ed., *De Artibus* (Zurich: Buehler Buchdruck, 1960), 1: 492]). Note *Laws* 790B: "One might be moved to say . . . that no law is ever made by a man, and that human history is all an affair of chance. Still, the same thing may be said with apparent plausibility of seafaring, navigation, medicine, or strategy . . ." (trans. A. E. Taylor). Patch's "a sea of trouble" is proverbial: so Erasmus, *Adag.* I.iii.28, "Mare malorum / A sea of troubles," in *Adages: I.i.1 to I.v.100* (1982), *Collected Works of Erasmus*, 31: 258. Cf. also Erasmus, *Adag.* I.1.91, "Servire scenea / To be a slave to your theatre": "To serve the time is indeed the part of the wise man, as Phocylides warns us: 'Remember, always wary, to serve the times; blow not against the wind.' However the metaphor here is taken from mariners, who once they have set out must be tossed at the will of winds and tides; it would be vain for them to strive to put a resistance" (*Adages: I.i.1 to I.v.100* (1982), *Collected Works of Erasmus*, 31: 130). Sallust (*Conspiracy of Catiline*, I) is quoted in Montaigne, *Essays*, II.xii, "Of Glory." The Horace tag is from *Carm.* I.xxxv.6. Cf. also Erasmus, *Adag.* I.iv.33, "Vela ventis permittere / To spread the sails to the winds," *Adages: I.i.1 to I.v.100* (1982), *Collected Works of Erasmus*, 31: 343–44. Anciently invented, the metaphors for the control of circumstance have never died; e.g., the following from A.J.P. Taylor, on the later policies of Bismarck:

> Once he had been ready to stake everything on fortune's wheel. Now he tried to stop it from spinning. . . . How strenuously he had warned against tying Prussia's trim, seaworthy frigate to Austria's worm-eaten galleon. . . . Prussia's frigate had become the great German man-of-war: Austria's galleon was more worm-eaten by twenty-five years. Yet Bismarck tied them together for the rest of their existence. . . . He allowed the Habsburg monarchy to survive. . . . No more events must be allowed to happen. The keeper of the Elbe dike had resumed his old employment.

Bismarck: The Man and Statesman (New York: Vintage Books, 1967), 190.

[19] *De Officiis* II.6, trans. Walter Miller, Loeb Classical Library (Cambridge, MA: Harvard Univ. Press, 1975), 187. A truly worthy philosopher, Cicero's argument elsewhere goes, will provide a remedy for the vexation and distress of life and the soul by means of the following kind of speech: "Why are you prostrated, or why do your mourn, or why do you tamely yield to fortune? She may possibly have pinched and pricked you, she cannot assuredly have undermined your strength. There is a mighty power in the virtues; rouse them, if maybe they slumber. At once you will have the foremost of all, I mean Fortitude, who will compel you to assume a spirit that will make you despise and count as nothing all that can fall to the lot of men." (*Tusculan Disputations*, III.xvii.36, trans. J. E. King, Loeb Classical Library [Cambridge, MA: Harvard Univ. Press, 1950], 268, 271). Boethius must have taken such a passage to heart when he wrote *De Cons. Phil.*, IV. prose vii, "You skirmish fiercely with any fortune, lest either affliction oppress you or prosperity corrupt you. Stay yourselves strongly in the mean! . . . For it is placed

The man born rich, or born to high estate, should only expect "a life of great worries," Petrarch's Reason argues similarly:

> Sailors, appropriately, call a great tempest Fortuna. A great fortune is a great tempest. And a great tempest requires both great know-how and strength. . . . Do you believe it is more fortunate to be born amidst the wide ocean than on a small river? . . . You have weighed anchor under an unlucky star. So see to it that after the stormy day the night finds you safely in port. . . . Those who fall from on high are gravely hurt, and it is seldom peaceful on the open sea. If you are at the bottom, you need not fear to fall, nor to be shipwrecked when on dry land. . . . Haven't you noticed that the affairs of man turn like a magic wheel—so that a calm ocean is whipped up by a howling storm, and clear morning is followed by a cloudy evening? Just as a plain path ends in craggy cliffs, so unexpected calamity follows the prideful insolence of prosperity, grim death beclouds the happiest course of life, and, often, the end is wholly unlike the beginning.[20]

The marine imagery is pervasive in the *Remedies*, and even leads Reason to suggest that would-be survivors on the high seas of life should be ready to cut themselves loose from the proverbial anchor of hope, which cannot help one far from shore (I.109).

"Human life and trips at sea / Are not assured stability. / One cannot trust in worldly things, / And no good wind endures for long," Boiardo's narrator says (2.27.40). In novellae based on Hellenic romances, misfortune separates families, and so does the sea. Boiardo's Elidonia, for example, abandoned the sail of her *navicella* to fortune (2.1.7). The self-propelled or drunken boats that carry off the various characters in Renaissance romance—as Don Quixote expects the "enchanted boat" will do in the "adventure" of chapter 29 in Cervantes' Part II—are all so many embodiments of the operations of Fortune as *Aventure*, with chance at the rudder, or in charge of the weather. The same *fortuna* that has toppled Carthage's lofty turrets must also be the one that raises

---

in your power to frame to yourselves what fortune you please." (*Tracts and De Consolatione Philosophiae*, trans. H. F. Stewart and E. K. Rand, Loeb Classical Library [Cambridge, MA: Harvard Univ. Press, 1973], 361). See also Erasmus as cited in note 2 above and notes 42–44 below.

[20] Rawski, *Petrarch's Remedies*, 1: 50–51.

the storm that forces Brandimart off course; *fortuna* drives him to a port in Africa where all Christians, unfortunately, are *persona non grata* (2.27.45, 46). Luciana, the *sventurata* (luckless one) chained by the sea for the Cyclopes, was originally taken from her father King Tibiano by fell fortune (3.3.35, 52). Tisbina, in yet another example of these tropes, complains that the plots of her *sventurato* (unfortunate) lover Iroldo have drowned her in the sea of misfortune (*mar di sventura*; 1.12.46).

It is also a *Fortuna prava*, depraved Fortune, that wills that Iroldo arrive at the domain of Orgagna ruled by Falerina (1.17.6). "A lady governed that domain," because its absent king was off trying to help another king win Angelica at Albraca; "The dame who holds the realm in hand / Knows all the mysteries of deceit and fraud" (1.17.7). The terms switch place: the lady governor of Orgagna and the goddess governing Iroldo's fate are equally *prava*. Falerina is in charge precisely because the king is not: while he tries his fortune in the war for love at Albraca, the power she exercises is the one ruling his kingdom. Angelica, Marfisa says, is "a meretrix . . . *prava*" (1.20.43).

The origin of the war at Albraca is Angelica's unrequited lover King Agricane, eventually a victim of bad fortune. The king's famous deathbed conversion is not really the result of the wise if tragicized governance of human affairs as exercised by Providence. Agricane has lost his horse Baiardo; "Don't let me [also] lose God," he demands (1.19.15). But he is found embracing Christianity only when he has lost worldly prizes—Baiardo or Angelica—while Orlando has fought only to win them, and *not* in defense of the faith (as he explicitly acknowledges; 1.18.48). There is an essential difference between Boiardo's scene and the comparable one in Tasso featuring the near-death of Tancredi. Rather than saving an immortal soul (or an endangered sanity, as in the *Furioso*), Agricane's conversion in effect recoups a lost fortune. (The eventual baptism of Manodante's reunited family can be cited to make the same point.) "All things that lie beneath the moon. / Great wealth and earthly kingdom—all / Have been assigned to Fortune's will . . . / But war is where she seems the most / Unstable, changing, hazardous. / Nothing else is as fraudulent," the narrator announces as he embarks upon the episode of the king's defeat. But Agricane has only hazarded his fortunes on a war he cannot win, in order to win a girl he cannot have. Since his quest has finally lost him all the contents of his royal power (1.16.1–2), it has cost him a fortune to lose a fortune. Fortune is like that; in modern parlance, Angelica's "opportunity cost" (originally a Scholastic notion) is prohibitively high.

Agricane's vast expenditure may enhance Angelica's value, and so contribute to her meaning, but it does not result in her possession. Much of Reason's argument in Petrarch's *Remedies* is that you cannot really ever truly retain the so-called goods of fortune; they're always as good as forfeit, like life itself.[21] Fortune will have her way with men, men will not have their way with Fortune. Only death overcomes her power: "Fortune has great power over one who comes into this world, but none over him who is dead. She overthrows the strongest of cities, routs knights in armor, destroys the mightiest kings—but the grave is an impregnable fortress: the worms rule there, not Fortune" (*Remedies*, I.14). So Iroldo, as he essays to commit suicide: "Fortune won't molest me more, / Because death overcomes her power: / Only thus is that proud one conquered" (1.12.58). Tisbina, "cursing Love and Fortune, which / Brought them to such a ruthless end" (1.12.60), drinks from the same doctrinal cup.

Orlando, of course, has high expectations of a much happier fortune. We can compare his relation to Angelica to the following passage from Petrarch's *Remedies*:

> REASON: . . . I submit that it is an indication of utter superficiality and mindlessness to embrace every hope that comes along and to consider it a sure thing. Knowledgeable and experienced people are very wary of doing this.
>
> HOPE: Meanwhile I hope for good things.
>
> REASON: You say "meanwhile," which, I think, means until your hopes have deceived you. But this is your habit: You hope compulsively and never abandon hope until it abandons you. Remarkably enough, many times when Hope has done just that, you are ready, and ready again, to embrace her when she returns. And as she approaches, you seem to forget her old wiles and restore her, who is armed with new plots, to the innermost recesses of your heart.
>
> HOPE: I shall not forsake my good hope to the very end.
>
> REASON: What if she forsakes you long before that? Will you call her back? Will you run after her? Or will you wait for her return? Go, do it, as long as nothing seems sweeter to you than to be deceived.[22]

When Angelica insists that it does not suit her position or nature to chase

---

[21] Cf. the homily in *Remedies*, II.9: "Harsh Fortune has robbed me of all I had."

[22] Rawski, *Petrarch's Remedies*, 1: 296.

after something when she's in flight or in motion, but rather to be herself
chased after (1.3.45), she inevitably implies that the venture for her stands
for the pursuit of happiness. But like the gold-horned stag of the Treasure
Fairy, "Nobody ever captures it" (1.22.58).[23]

The lady who tempts Orlando with the hunt after the stag speaks as
follows:

> You will accumulate such wealth
> When you have caught the magic stag,
> That you will always be content,
> If riches makes a happy man.
> Perhaps, too, you will gain the love
> Of that fay whom I've told you of:
> I mean Morgana, fair of face,
> Prettier than the sun at noon. (1.25.12)

Orlando listens with a smile, not only because he is too wise or noble to
venture after riches (1.25.16), but also because he does not think Morgana
can hold a candle to Angelica. He knows she waits, he thinks he hears
her call his name (1.25.22).

3. Fortune and Enterprise

Orlando is not entirely wrong. Whenever Angelica comes up in the poem,
so does the subject of her suitor's luck or fortunes. At one point Orlando's
fixation seems threatened by Ranaldo as his rival, and he complains that
human enjoyments are brief and always mingled with *sventura*: Fortune has
given Orlando only one day of joy (1.25.52–54), the one she's taken away.
In a later episode, Orlando takes on some ferocious man-eaters at great

---

[23] The hare-brained scheme proposed as Orlando's reward by Manodante is rejected,
one might think, because it is too good to be true. In Florence, on the other hand, the
scheme might have appeared as too true to be good: that is, merchant-banking might be
understood in Ferrara as a kind of unnatural magic, fiscal wealth always seeming nefarious
to proprietors of wealth that is land-based. For the stag makes gold at a great *rate*: the
(two) antlers moult six times a day, each divides into thirty points, and every horn
weighs a hundred pounds; 2 x 6 x 30 x 100 = 36,000 pounds. This sounds like a Platonic Great Year's worth of wealth: and that *per diem*. (Numerologists may want to add
that these numbers for proliferation dimly reflect those of the *Orlando Innamorato* itself,
or of Boiardo's *Amorum Libri*.) Much of Manodante's story belongs to an interpolated
tale, the place where the proverbial greed and miserliness of the merchant class also seem
to belong, in generic contrast with the generosity of the knightly class of cavaliers in the
romanzi proper.

risk to his life; but having saved the fair Angelica from them, he is contented with his *aventura* (2.19.50). Thereafter he tells King Norandino, "I lost everything at war / Except my arms and [Angelica], / Which Fortune kindly left to me" (2.19.59). Later still, Ranaldo despairs of possessing the maiden, but a messenger from the scene where Orlando seems to be winning says Ranaldo still has a chance to catch up; with such a fast horse, he "ought to try (*provar*) his *ventura*" (2.24.29).

By keeping Angelica on Orlando's case, the poet need not blame the hero's numerous inconveniences directly on Fortune herself. The blame is veiled in a way that cooperates with the hero's own obtuseness. But even if Orlando were to blame Angelica for his troubles by identifying her as Fortune, he might not have penetrated to the troubles' source. "Many who have come to grief through their own stupidity blame Fortune and complain of being tossed about by her stormy waves, when the fools have actually cast themselves into them," writes Alberti in his *On the Family*; the same author also concludes that "So long as we assert our dominion and power over everything we do not choose to abandon to the whims of external forces, no one can say that uncertain and fickle Fortune has the power to consume and destroy."[24] But often the quest for Angelica looks just like an abandonment of one's will and purposes to the whims of external forces. In that case, we must internalize the sources of the characters' disaster, rather than seeing their heroics as tests (*provi*; 1.1.1) of their readiness to dispute their fates.

Perhaps a given knight's private motives cannot be fully exposed in this poem until his fortune is personified or objectified as external to him. In the *Remedies*, Petrarch's Sorrow laments his exposure to a serious shipwreck, but Reason remedially replies that some prior collapse within the rational power is responsible for one's subjection to the waves of external affliction:

You relate the shipwreck at sea, but you say nothing about the shipwreck of the mind, as though there were any wreck more serious or more frequent than this. Here is the tempest of greedy desires and raptures, which, like the brawling winds, blow you through the surf of every coast and over every ocean, with the sails of desire and hope billowing, the rudder of the mind trailing, and

---

[24] *The Albertis of Florence: Leon Battista Alberti's Della famiglia*, trans. Guido A. Guarino (Lewisburg, PA: Bucknell Univ. Press, 1971), 28, 30.

the anchors of steadfastness dangling, lost on high. This is the shipwreck that has dragged you into this. Do away with desire, and you have, in large measure, done away with the voyage and, surely, the dangers of the voyage. Desire drives wretched men not only into ships, but into rocks and death. *Thus nearly all of those who of their own will go to sea and perish in the sea first perished in their mind and first drowned in the wave of greed before they died in the surges of the ocean.* Desire is rarely unaccompanied by heedless haste: what it wants, it wants forthwith; it hates delay and added expense, the companion of delay; it is the short road to destruction, and the foremost cause of frequent shipwreck.[25]

While the *aventura* appear to be external, they only externalize an antecedent disaster within the mind of the adventurer. The heroics in the fiction are tests (*provi*; 1.1.1) of the heroes' fortitude and will to self-determination, and/or proofs of their defiance of Fortune. At the same time, however, the more otherworldly trials are generated out of a self-ignorance that the knights exhibit when they opportunistically cast themselves into difficult spots in the first place. Consoling Astolfo for his apparent loss of Ranaldo at the bridge, the two damsels insist that "Virtue is / Never completely recognized / Till fortune is most malign!" (2.2.29). But neither is the knight's own motive fully exposed until his fortune is personified as a hostile force subtly cooperating with his prior self-destructive tendencies.

On the site where Agricane dies in Book 1, Brandimart in Book 2 tries to convert the bandit Barigaccio. Brandimart does not know why Fortune makes the bandit do a robber's work, since a man like him would not lack other means to live (2.19.38–39). But Barigaccio declines the offer to be reformed: the state, he observes, kills more than he does—and commits much bigger robberies—with impunity. Barigaccio has admitted that he takes what he can from those who are weaker than he is (2.19.41), and Brandimart justly dispatches him. But then the knight excuses himself for not leaving unclaimed the horse that *la ventura* has presented him: it would be crazy and unthinking not to take this gift from Fortune (2.19.48). Boiardo subtly erodes the moral high ground from under the victor to whom the robber's spoils now go.

On the surface of the fiction, the more an object is a meaningless pretext, the more glorious the effort that is expended on its achievement. But

---

[25] Rawski, *Petrarch's Remedies*, 3: 126–27; emphasis added.

beneath this surface, the more an object is an object, the more it may attest to a heroic subject's alienation from his own proper animus. Ranaldo, for example, is liberated from Morgana's realm by Orlando, only to be decoyed into trying to make off with a golden chair. For Ranaldo, Acrasia's Bower has proven less tempting than Mammon's cave. Being poor, he thinks he has a right to be greedy, but the golden object reveals Ranaldo's limits as they are mirrored in the furious, Fortune-like wind blocking his theft (2.9.31–40). Idealistically avoiding dishonor at Angelica's fancy *palazzo*, the knight is subsequently entrapped by an ill fortune that turns into greed for a chair. He too wants a seat at Fortune's table.

4. Fortune versus Force: Fortitude Defying Contingency and Defeat

To answer the question of why Boiardo's knights are such paragons of energy and exertion in a poem that also features Orlando's fruitless attachment to the Fortune-like Angelica, we may wish to ask why the glorious braggarts are so prominent in the poem's fiction: the irrepressible Astolfo near the outset, the volcanic Rodamonte thereafter, and the determined self-starter Mandricardo much later. Why does the story stress so much these characters' readiness to make good upon all challenges to human limits, to put their persons where their braggadochio is by betting hugely on their innate abilities to secure their own glory or satisfaction?

When these imperial egos announce themselves—preposterously, prodigiously, and precociously—it is as if they could only earn their own self-respect by commandeering everyone else's. But the personage they would ultimately intimidate is Fortune herself. "Blow, wind!" Rodamonte blusters, "if you know how / To blow . . . I'm not your slave, and not the sea's / That you can hold me back by force!" (1.6.4). The shameless braggarts contrast with the shamefast Orlando; and yet, contra Orlando's shaming by Fortune, their belligerence is the response of subjects who dare to determine their own fate. "Courage," the narrator asserts, "can conquer everything, / And Fortune lends help willingly / To him who tries to help himself" (2.10.2). But Fortune "has provided no means for [Ranaldo's] escape" (1.9.13) from Castle Cruel, and the monster could surely have caused the knight to cry out in the words of the proverb recorded in Erasmus: "With what a portent"—or rather monster—"fortune has embroiled me!"[26] Per-

---

[26] Adag. II.9.41, "Cuiusmodi portento me involvit fortuna," in *Adages: II.vii.1 to III.iii.100* (1992), *Collected Works of Erasmus*, 34: 106: "The line is taken from a tragedy by the poet Philoxenus [Fr. 11 in edition of Page], who puts into Ulysses' mouth, when

haps courage cannot conquer everything, and thus it is Angelica who lends the unfortunate Ranaldo the help he needs: Crazy Glue chewing gum. The girl has been nothing but trouble up to now, but if there's not much of a paradox in Fortune's favor regularly undoing those to whom it is ostensibly extended, so also the contrary.

Ranaldo, at any rate, has virtuously persevered in adversity, that is, until his fortune should change for the better. He has made do with what fortune he has. And why is Ranaldo such a survivor? His restless independence seems to be part of the answer: he enjoys a kind of freedom from worldly baggage and encumbrance. A fable from Alberti is based on the metaphor of the river of life. It teaches that "Those whom you may think protected by their floats" on the river—the security afforded them by wealth, kingdoms, or status—"are actually in great danger"; much better off are those who swim and hitch rides alternately, knowing "when to pause briefly to wait for an approaching boat or for planks borne by the river, and when to use their great strength to avoid the rocks and fly to shore in glory."[27] The argument seems to favor the *débrouillard* and versatile types in the poem, over the various miserly psychologies so prominent in the interpolated Boccaccian tales. The Terentian "Fortune favors *fortes*" is a popular Humanist adage (*pace* the elder Pliny's fatal appeal to it).

The confidence of the *furiosi* in the "great strength" that Alberti attributes to his swimmers is often undercut by those incidents in the poem in which a charming female betrays a susceptible knight and so subjects him to Ill Fortune. We accept these ladies' somewhat underdeveloped characters because of their participation in the poem's ongoing characterization of the operation of Fortune. "Against great confidence of strength," Petrarch's Reason warns, "Fortune [also] arms *herself* with great strength, often declining an encounter on equal terms in order to show how weak a creature man really is, although he may think he is of the utmost

---

he is imprisoned in the Cyclops's cave, the words 'With what a monster fortune has involved me!' Recorded by Zenodotus [5.45]." For the defiance of circumstance in what has been cited, and as potentially Satanic, cf. Phineas Fletcher's hell-raiser in *The Locusts, or Apollyonists*, Canto II, 17–18: "But yet our forces broken 'gainst the rocke / We strongly reinforce, and every man / Though cannot what he will's, will's what he can / And where wee cannot hurt, there we can curse, and banne. / See here in broken force, a heart unbroke, / Which neither hell can daunt, not heaven appease." (Text from *The English Spenserians*, ed. William B. Hunter [Salt Lake City: Univ. of Utah Press, 1977], 336.)

[27] Leon Battista Alberti, "Fate and Fortune" (the third of the *Three Dialogues*); the quotes are from *Dinner Pieces*, trans. David Marsh (Binghamton, NY: Medieval & Renaissance Texts & Studies, 1987), 23–27.

strength. Thus in silent combat she utterly destroys giant-like men."
"Anything immense labors under its own weight," Reason adds, to remedy
any temptation we might have to trust in our private sufficiency.[28] "We
are barehanded weaklings engaged in an unequal fight with an implacable
foe, who throws us up and down as if we had no weight, whirls us around,
and plays with us, so that defeat would be easier to bear than such continued mockery."[29] Little in Boiardo contradicts this pessimistic assessment of human beleaguerement; thus, Mandricardo's lack of a sword stands
for a more radical emptyhandedness pertaining to us all.

Similarly, little in the poem's military campaigns suggests the furioso's
self-beleaguerement. The illusion of transcendent human strength is not
regularly dispelled on Boiardo's battlefield, despite misfortunes there. The
fairy episodes are different, for they turn on the strength of illusion, and
self-delusion is part of it. But the background for these episodes also includes the world of fortune. The sudden changes in their sequences and
landscapes objectify and externalize otherwise invisible motives and distur-
bances within the characters. These are projected back toward the character from his environment so that any source of animosity or cupidity in his
own psyche is quite concealed from him or us. Indeed, this concealment
is what gives such changes power over his life, changes that reappear in
his world as the effects of Fortune.

Insofar as the sources of a major character's beleaguerement seem external, we might also find them beyond the poem itself: in the Renaissance
politics of Northern Italy, where a city-state is externally defined by other,
rival city-states that threaten to encroach upon its autarchy and its sphere.
Boiardo's Charlemagne, for example, justifies sending Ranaldo to aid the
pagan king Marsilio of Spain against the African invaders of Europe because Marsilio is like a neighbor whose house is on fire (1.4.14). That is
surely the kind of argument that Ferrara would have used to enlist the
papacy's aid against an invasion by Venice. Fielding a Ranaldo or an Orlando on your side would be something like inducing another city-state
into supporting a defense of your own autarchy.

Despite the abundant evidence for the operation of a Machiavellian
politics of Fortune in the poem, the overall narrative shows signs of moving toward a more stable system of relations—a more reliable social con-
tract—based on dynastic marriage. Brandimart's Christianized alliance with

---

[28] Rawski, *Petrarch's Remedies*, 1: 21.
[29] Rawski, *Petrarch's Remedies*, 1: 1.

Orlando, for example, is doubled with his devotion to Fiordelise, which is a conjugal one. Similarly, "Pitiless fortune . . . Could not disjoin so strong a love" as the one engaging Rugiero and Brandamante (3.6.1). The narrator's Boethian hymn to cosmic love applies better here, in fact, than to Orlando's entrapment of Falerina, where the story's real point, as Jo Ann Cavallo suggests, is the implacable force of hate and jealousy, not love.[30] The social and dynastic settlement in the offing, however, does not precipitate narrative closure in Boiardo's actual poem. Boiardo rather depicts coalitions that are formed and dissolved as temporary alliances among selfish interests and personal wills chance to play one restless courtier—which is also to say, one or another court—off against a rival.

Here one feels an audience being offered its own choice in a fictional disguise. Should Ferrara be pursuing the bravura antics of a reapplied feudal style, or should it be cultivating the humanistic substance of the civic virtues? Should the powerful states emerging on the Italian peninsula each attempt to offset their rivals' advantages, or should they propose the common good in the face of a common danger? The poet tells his audience they have come to hear his poem because they are a courteous company interested in the finer things in life, but this in effect means escaping from the instability of their politics and the vagaries of their mercenaries, bankers, allies, and invaders. Yet, the gardens, boats, and blows—the fays, enchantresses, and the mutable narrative line itself—all reflect the operations of the audience's particular society, which is to say, its own, fatal, self-chosen contingency.[31]

---

[30] Jo Ann Cavallo, *Boiardo's* Orlando Innamorato: *An Ethics of Desire* (Rutherford, NJ: Fairleigh Dickinson Univ. Press, 1993), 13–20, 90–95. Cavallo notes the echoes of Boethius's metres on cosmic love (in *Orlando Innamorato* 2.4.2–3) from *De. Cons. Phil.* II, metr. 8 (for which see also Claudian, *De Consulatu Stilichonis*, II.6–29, where love is also Clementia).

[31] The heroic personnel of the *romanzi* seem to reflect not only feudal roles, but the political structures within a given Renaissance romancer's more immediate ken. We have compared Boiardo's view of romance to Machiavelli's view of Italy. Thus, Machiavelli, in chapter 25 of *The Prince*, is half-inclined to believe that an unpredictable Fortune rules all things, but rather than give up on free will altogether, he is prepared to maintain that this foreign power governs half our actions, and leaves the other half to us, or, rather, to our *virtú* in preventing her outrages. He compares her to a torrential stream against which one can take countermeasures. Otherwise, "Fortune . . . exerts all her power where there is no *virtú* prepared to oppose her, and turns to smashing things up where there are no dikes and restraining dams. And if you look at Italy, which is the seat of all these tremendous changes, where they all began, you will see that she is an open country without any dikes or ditches. If she were protected by forces of proper *virtú*, as are Germany,

5. Fortune versus Forcefulness of Interpretation

It is the very concealment of such political meanings from the characters that gives the unpredicability of Fortune such power over human lives. So how, one may ask, has *anyone* developed an insight into what seems to be a general conspiracy?

The answer lies in an interference between a surface vehicle and a more subtextual one, the latter allowing us to reconfigure the narrative more knowledgeably. A citation I owe to Charles Ross's 1976 MLA paper can be useful here.[32] In Chretien de Troyes' *Story of the Grail*, Perceval fails to ask his inevitable questions when he is an uninformed bystander at the quasi-sacramental grail ministrations. Thereafter, a hag comes to Arthur's court to tell Perceval that it's too bad he failed to use his fortune:

> Ah, Perceval, Fortune is bald behind, but has hair in front ... you did not seize Fortune when you met her ... Most unfortunate is he who when the weather is fairer than usual waits for even fairer to come. *It was you, unfortunate man, who saw that the time and the place were right for speech, and yet remained mute.* You had ample opportunity, but in an evil hour you kept silence.[33]

Spain, and France, either this flood would never have wrought such destruction as it has, or it might not even have occurred at all." (After Niccolo Machiavelli, *The Prince*, trans. Robert M. Adams [New York: W. W. Norton, 1977], 70–71).

The knights of Spenser's *Faerie Queene*, to take a very different example of the politicized chevaliers of the *romanzi*, dissemble members of an Elizabethan cabinet, the virtues for which they stand (holiness, justice, etc.) being so many portfolios and ministries within the Queen's government. The knights' quests are the assignments made to deputies and appointees for the administration of the crown's colonies abroad and/or its projects at home. In Boiardo, in contrast, the dukes of Ferrara look like the Dukes of Hazard.

[32] "Boiardo and the Fata Morgana," December 1976, Modern Languages Association meeting, New York City; copy of the paper in possession of the author.

[33] The translation (of lines 4610–83) into prose, from Chretien de Troyes, *Perceval, or the Story of the Grail*, by Roger Sherman Loomis, is taken from *Medieval Romances*, ed. Roger Sherman Loomis and Laura Hibbard Loomis, The Modern Library (New York: Random House, 1957), 3–87; the quote is from pages 80–81. Cf. pages 58–59 (= lines 3202–11, 3243–53): "The youth who had arrived that night watched this marvel but he refrained from asking what this meant, for he was mindful of the lesson which Goremnant gave him, warning him against too much speech, and he feared that if he asked, it would be considered rude. So he held his peace.... The youth ... did not dare to ask concerning the grail and whom one served with it, for he kept in his heart the words of the wise nobleman. I fear that harm will come of this, because I have heard say that one can be too silent as well as be too loquacious. But, for better or for worse, the youth put no question."

Chretien's hag suggests the hero's misfortune, his susceptibility to mischance, but she also *comes to personify it*. With her ugliness and twisted legs, her scourge and her ability to lead a dance, the hag presents an embodiment of Fortune's foul and destructive aspect, and indeed the disaster that Perceval's failure may be causing in the Fisher King's land even as she speaks.[34]

But her speech itself embodies hindsight and recriminations: the hag might be Penitence as well as Misfortune. Perceval saw the grail, but did he in fact perceive that *the time and place were right* for questions? Did he see *the* Grail? Unfortunately for the hag's assertion that Perceval recognized the opportune time for speaking, Chretien has reported that Perceval thought questions were out of season at the time, that he was a child who should be seen and not heard. Similarly, Orlando fails to interpret the image of the labyrinth on Morgana's door: according to Ross, such an entrée announces Orlando's coming failure to attend promptly to advice that will, after several mistakes, enable him to master the interior that the labyrinth represents.

The reader's experience is analogous to Orlando's. Interpretation is impossible without a hiatus or meantime between the positing of a sign and the depositing of its significance. We come to know that Fortune is a ruling goddess in Boiardo's universe only gradually: we would not want to know this, as it were, prematurely. Thus, we plunge into the story to chase Angelica as Venture before we step back from the text to contemplate Morgana as Fortuna. Yet, the information that we have about Angelica finally converts into the interpretation of Angelica's lover Orlando as the plaything of a fortune-driven narrative economy.

Berni's covering moralization explains the Morgana episode this way: "Fate, Fortune, Predestination, Luck [*Sorte*], Chance [*Caso*], *Ventura*, are those things that give great trouble to people."[35] This is right enough for him who runs as he reads, but it can hardly address Boiardo's more particular contribution to the Renaissance revival of the debate between free choice and determinism, a debate that might be symbolized for us by the

---

[34] Burchmore, "The Medieval Sources," 98, reads the rebuke scene in the Conte del Graal as I do, arguing that the hag is a personification. He also notes that "the more explicit allegory of the thirteenth-century Perlesvaus" specifically identifies this hag as Fortune.

[35] "Fato, Fortuna, Predestinazaione, / Sorte, Caso, Ventura, so id quelle / Cose, che dan gran noje alle persone"; Berni, *Rifacimento*, ed. S. Ferrari and G. Nencioni (Florence: Sansoni, 1971), 2.9.2.

double registers on the Schifanoia Palace fresco, with its fixed astrological signs and decans in the middle band, yet with its divine and human activities freely pursued above and below. Initially, the knights are almost blissfully ignorant of, or indifferent to, what controls their lives: specifically Astolfo's magic armor and Ranaldo's magic drink. Ranaldo, in fact, is "scornful of enchantments and all *fatasone*" on principle (2.10.3); "Let him chant his enchanted charms, / Since he won't find a verse that works," he says of the gigantic shapeshifting magician Balisardo (2.9.59). But his repulse of Angelica, like Orlando's infatuation with her, is *also* the product of an enchantment and an enchanted drink. Uninhibited by a superstitious belief in occult powers, Ranaldo has nevertheless not dispelled Fortune's power over his ignorance. His rejection of Angelica may well project a healthy contempt for enchantment and magic, yet this contempt cannot be genuinely critical for he has not examined the sympathies and antipathies operant in his own life. Nonetheless, he has an intimation (at least for a warrior like him) that it's bad luck to be superstitious.[36]

In the activity of the reader, critical reading of the story's wonders and anomalies as riddles and allegories stands in place of the heroes' dispelling of them as enchantments and illusions. What is like gigantic ears that engulf you when they are attached to a noisy threatening ass? Slanderous speech and gossip seem likely answers, though talk radio and satellite dishes also come to mind. But the dukes of Ferrara cannot have worried much about solving such puzzles on the first hearing, even if the marvels had them all ears. Surely they cared more about the knights of the chase and the crack-up, with their total willingness to throw all their persons into every motion, their horses shooting around the field in glorious despite of good morals about restraint, patience, self-control, and interpretive mastery. "There'll be iron and flame and fire and blows," the poet promises: he's bringing on Rodamonte (1.14.1–2). The paladins of romance have returned to us as the heroes of the matinee western, and their mounts as the cars in a James Bond film. But Rodamonte's contemporary counterparts are the *gloriosi* of the World Wrestling Federation—or of a monster truck rally. For he is always a kind of *contender*.

"He / Who hesitates does not strike hard," the poet warns the hesitant *Daniforte* (3.6.18). Yet as the text runs out, Orlando himself becomes

---

[36] This echoes Richard Smullyan, as quoted by Umberto Eco for one of the two epigraphs at the head of his *Foucault's Pendulum*: "Superstition brings bad luck."

unnerved, and he despairs of the greatness of Charles the Great: "Triumphant and victorious, / He made men tremble near and far, / But fortune in a moment took / It all, and he, perhaps, lies slain" (3.7.59). The lady had consoled a frustrated Mandricardo similarly, telling him that "One can't forbid what fortune wants" (3.1.48). But that was hardly any knight's initial premise. "What Fortune wants must be" (2.11.35). Yes, but in that case anyone with a lot of frustrated personal desires or surplus dissatisfaction will want to become his own Fortune. "Never yet / Did fortune fail a baron bold," the swordless Mandricardo affirms optimistically in the penultimate canto of the poem (3.6.48). As Hegel would have said, if the Italian city-states had been more like Boiardo's heroic baronage, "their freedom [would] *not* [have] die[d] of the fear of death."[37]

6. Fortune and Autarchy

> *"Luck's a fool; the door to success is always marked 'Push' "*
> — *The Hand-Book of Harvard University, 1906–07.*

Late medieval Occasion is reinvented as early modern Opportunity when changes in our circumstances, the reverses we suffer, are viewed as ripe for exploitation, rather than as mere occasions for philosophical reflection and passive forbearance. For if it is the pro-active opportunist who attempts the transformation of an individual will—his own—into a general fortune, he might well reason that it is not in our stars, but in ourselves, that we are underlings. "There is a tide in the affairs of men," says Shakespeare's Brutus, urging this new sense of temporal mastery while not admitting that Caesar himself is a decisive embodiment of fortune, and not just another occasion for Brutus to prove that he's not a cowardly failure, dying of the fear of death.

---

[37] Hegel, *Philosophy of Right*, sec. 324: "Peoples unwilling or afraid to tolerate sovereignty at home have been subjugated from abroad, and they have struggled for their independence with the less glory and success the less they have been able previously to organize the powers of the state in home affairs—their freedom has died from the fear of dying" (Hegel's *Philosophy of Right*, trans. T. M. Knox [Oxford: Oxford Univ. Press, 1967], 210). That Hegel may well have Renaissance Italy in mind appears from remarks in his *Philosophy of History*: "Italy . . . had become an object of . . . conquest, and was a prey to the rapacity of the French, the Spaniards, and at a later date, of the Austrians. In fact absolute isolation and dismemberment has always been an essential feature of the character of the Italians in ancient as well as in modern times . . . their culture, the mitigation of their selfishness, reached only beauty but not rationality." (*The Philosophy of Hegel*, ed. Carl J. Friedrich, The Modern Library [New York: Random House, 1954], 134).

Boiardo's characters rarely know the extent to which they may have been their own misfortune, except in some of the interpolated novellae, where the compounding of adversity and the closure of the plots make for new knowledge. But in Manodante's territory Orlando and Brandimart become involved in such a novella themselves. Near the start of this story, the poet says "Fortune never, in the end, / makes [the greedy Manodante]—or any man—content" (2.11.46). Manodante tells Orlando that the Treasure Fay is seeking to entrap the count because he once disdained "some stag with antlers made of gold" (2.12.24). Thus, Fortune is malign, whether one seeks it or slights it. Manodante's son, Ziliante, is a hostage to Fortune, in the form of the lovesick Morgana, who has inveigled Orlando into leaving him her captive. The boy's father, who subsequently succeeds in capturing Orlando himself, wants to trade hostages. He must treat Orlando badly, he tells him, because of his own Foul Fortune and strange befallment (2.12.22). Fortune is controlling *both* their lives. Such knowledge is the beginning of the ability to take charge of one's life, and shortly after the Morgana episode Orlando finds himself in Manodante's prison trying to convert his friend Brandimart not so much to Christianity as to some new and better means for managing their misfortune mutually. The question is, in what way does the Morgana episode itself conduce to the hero's mastery of Fortune?

If the enchanted zones of daemonic force in the *Orlando Innamorato* obey the laws of *projection*—what Boiardisti often mean by "allegory"— then the subject who does not know his own mind will not be able to recognize its effects on his perceptions of his surroundings. He will keep unwittingly encountering his own projections there: what he sees is determined by what he desires and/or dreads. With his perception at the mercy of his projections, he will be led into "an autoerotic or autistic condition in which one dreams a world whose reality remains forever unattainable"; furthermore, "the resultant *sentiment d'incompletude* and the still worse feeling of sterility are in their turn explained by projection as the malevolence of the environment, and by means of this vicious circle the isolation is intensified." These are the formulations of C. G. Jung, written as if to explain a phenomenon like the uncrossable and repeatedly destroyed bridge in Boiardo's Morgana episode (2.8.21–22).[38] But this experience,

---

[38] C. G. Jung, *Psyche and Symbol*, ed. Violet S. de Laszlo (Garden City: Doubleday, 1958), 8; text from Aion, "The Shadow," trans. R.F.C. Hull, ed. *Collected Works*, vol. 9, pt. 2. The passage is quoted for Boiardo and Spenser in Nohrnberg, *Analogy*, 326. Cf.

which traps Orlando in just such a lonely, vicious cycle as Jung describes, also exposes the protagonist to his own recriminations in the person of Penitence, who is a flagellant. Thus, the blows of outrageous Fortune are climactically diagnosed as self-inflicted.

At the center of Boccaccio's *De Casibus*, the opening of Book 3, there occurs an allegorical passage meant to lead us to somewhat comparable deductions. In Boccaccio's parable, Fortune is submitted to violence and fetters, more or less in contradiction to the overall tenor of his treatise, yet in support of what has now occurred to him, that "for the most part," the illustrious "called their adverse fortune down upon themselves." According to the place in question, the author's astronomy teacher, Andalo, was reading to his students a passage that said "Do not blame the stars when the fallen bring about their own misfortune." Supporting his author's point, Andalo himself told a fable about Poverty challenging and outmatching Fortune in a test of strength; Fortune mocks Poverty as Hercules, but Poverty throws Fortune to the ground and pins her there. Then, Poverty explains the ancient mistake of believing Fortune could "raise up and bring both success and failure." Misfortune, it seems, is owed to a different principle. "I wish *on my own* to remove the means of your power from you," Poverty announces to her conquest, and as the victor she imposes her conditions: "I command you to make Misfortune fast to a stake in public and secure him with chains, so that he not only can't go into anyone's home, but also can't go from there—unless with the person who released his bonds. You can send Good Fortune where you want." Miraculously, Fortune "kept her pledge . . . and left Misfortune attached to a post for those only who would release her." Poverty thus takes a lead in giving Fortune the lie, by denying that "all matters, which we foolishly call our own, are in her hands, and therefore subject, at her inscrutable will, to every variety of change and chance without any order therein by us discernible."[39] Andalo's fable is on the way to the opinion expressed by Erasmus: "Such is the force of *Opportunitas*, of Timeliness, that it can turn what is honourable into dishonour, loss into gain,

---

Nohrnberg, *Analogy*, 312–15, for a rehearsal of the Morgana episode in relation to narratives and morals in Spenser. Toward a (Bakhtinian) chronotope for chivalric romance, see Nohrnberg, *Analogy*, 200, 326–28, 763–64.

[39] Giovanni Boccaccio, *Decameron*, II.iii. The previous quotes are from *De Casibus Virorum Illustrium*, III.i. Fortuna reappears in a more Medusan form at the opening of *De Casibus* VI, where she speaks threateningly to the narrator in return for the earlier story he has told at the expense of her power and prerogatives.

Paupertas, Fortune Victrix [Poverty, Fortune's Conqueror]
L. Hachtanus (= Laurens van Haecht Goidtsenhoven),
Microcosmos (Antwerp, 1579), no. 22, p. 22.

Sapiens suprà Fortunam [Wisdom over Fortune]
Florent Schoonhovius, *Emblemata* (Gouda: Burier, 1618),
"EMBLEMA II," p. 4.

S'endurcir aux coups de Fortune
[To harden oneself at the blows of Fortune]
Guillaume de La Perrière, *Morosophie* (Lyon: M. Bonhomme, 1553), no. 56.

Note that the winds blowing on the upright tree
are equivalent to the blows being rained on the downed man.

happiness into misery, kindness into unkindness, and the reverse; it can, in short, change the nature of everything.''[40] Could we but know *when!*

What determines one's fortune? In the Middle Ages, with its earth-bound conception of people as creatures of habit whose identities were determined by birth and by customary offices and obligations, you had to *marry* your Fortune. Win or lose, she is like the foul and fair woman in Chaucer's *Wife of Bath's Tale*, or patient Griselda's tyrannic spouse in the *Clerk's Tale* based on the *Decameron*'s final story.[41] But in the Renaissance, you are quite as likely to rape your fortune, like Malagise seizing Angelica, or to turn it down, like Orlando compelling Morgana. "I judge that it is better to be impetuous than restrained, because Fortune is a woman, and it is necessary to batter and beat her if you wish to keep her down," says Machiavelli, as if drawing his conclusions from Boiardo: "You who pursue the courtier's path (= "di corte . . . la tracci"), / If you don't capture Fortune fast, / She'll fret, she'll turn aside her face . . . Don't cringe before a threatening gaze" (2.9.1). Here Fortune is a shrew that must be tamed, not a hag who has to be accepted.[42]

---

[40] *Sub* "Nosce tempus," in Erasmus, *Adag.* I.vii.70, in *Adages: I.vi.1 to I.x.100* (1989), *Collected Works of Erasmus*, 32: 109. For the iconographic tradition for Fortune/Occasion, see Frederick Kiefer, *Fortune and Elizabethan Tragedy* (San Marino, CA: Huntington Library, 1983), and Lucie Galactéros de Boissier, "Images Emblématiques de la Fortune: Eléments d'une typologie," in *L'Emblème a la Renaissance*, publ. by Yves Giraud (Paris: Soc. d'Édition d'Enseignement Supérieur, 1982), 79–125. For our purposes a pertinant illustration is reproduced in Galactéros de Boissier, "Images Emblématiques de la Fortune," 109, figure 18, from Florent Schoonhovius, *Emblemata* (Gouda: Burier, 1618), no. 11, "Sapiens supra Fortuna" (the caption tells us to compare L. Hachtanus, no. XXII: "Paupertas Fortunae victrix"). Schoonhovius shows a monkish-looking old man mounted over a voluptuous-looking naked lady; she furls Fortune's sail while he ties her down to her wheel.

[41] David Burchmore's University of Virginia thesis identifies Fortuna overtones in the two Chaucerian tales. Griselda's clothing, for example, tends to identify her with Fortune and Misfortune, as well as Wealth and Poverty.

[42] *The Prince*, xv, "The Influence of Luck on Human Affairs and the Ways to Counter It," which here echoes the proverbial *Audaces fortuna juvat timidosque repellit* ("Fortune favors the bold and repells the timid"). Cf. Erasmus on "Fortes fortuna adiuvat / Fortune favours the brave" (= *Adag.* I.ii.45): "The adage advises us to make a strong bid for Fortune; for it is for people who do this that things go well. For Fortune seems to favour that kind of man, but to be inimical to those who dare make no experiments, but for ever hide away in their shells like snails." (*Adages: I.i.1 to I.v.100* [1982], *Collected Works of Erasmus*, 31: 188). For an example of the opportunism referred to here, consider Shakespeare's Bolingbroke in *Richard II*: he has reportedly set sail to reclaim his lands from Richard before the end of the very same scene in which those lands are confiscated. He's left port before the news could have arrived to cause him to embark—there's no delaying *him!* He's jumped the gun to take advantage of the opening of a portal of

Despite a readiness to risk all their force on any and every commitment of their genrous hearts—"animated to conquer or to die" (2.15.1)—Boiardo's knights are not simply embodiments of pure impetuosity. They also exhibit *ambition*, a new dynamic sense of self-serving impetus, even a new kind of *virtú* or heroic style, but also a new kind of personal answerability for one's lot:

> Who curses Fortune, claiming that
> The fault is hers but yours the hurt?
> Occasion comes to us just once. (2.9.2)

Thus, we find in Boiardo a notable Renaissance rendition of a prominent element in subsequent human typology: the new faculty for, and of, self-advancement, which we call opportunism. But energy without self-mastery is blind, and urgency without perspective is brutish; hence all the giants and monsters who emerge in opposition. We also find the concomitant allegories of self-control. The adept management of a mutable existence seems to require a reinvention of prudence: good timing, calculation, and a plan to repossess the power to determine our own conditions. The occasion that comes to us but once is virtually life itself: "The time of life is short," says Shakespeare's Hotspur (*1 Henry IV*, 5.2.82). "To spend that shortness basely were too long." Proper planning against this chance is what the magic books contain, the opposite of the chance merely to go on reinventing Fortune's dismal wheel.

Considered overall, Boiardo's poem mainly prepares its readers for the time of their lives by warning them of frequent reverses and frustrations. But like the *Decameron*, it also presents many fortune-seizing advantage-takers. The enterprising wife, Doristella, for example, when she cuckolded her husband, "tried her *ventura* often, saying 'Heaven helps the vigo-

---

opportunity. "Be his own carver," his uncle York baulks (1.3.144), repudiating this new haste to serve oneself, or to become one's own Fortune. But Richard has given Boling-broke his chance, by himself opportunistically seizing upon his cousin's patrimony at the death of John of Gaunt. And Bolingbroke *precipitates* this fortune: opportunists do their own knocking.

According to the protagonist of George Chapman's *Bussy D'Ambois*, the subject Bussy's preferment by his king indicates a sudden alignment or rachet-like fit between his "good" (or his fortune) and the so-called nick of time: "There is a deep nick in Time's restless wheel / For each man's good, when which nick comes, it strikes: / As rhetoric yet works not persuasion, / But only is a mean to make it work; / So no man riseth by his real merit, / But when it cries clink in his Raiser's spirit" (I.i.134–39). If this clockwork works like clockwork generally, however, the nick in time will come about again: all in due time.

rous' ''(2.26.51). Doristella has opportunistically appropriated a humanist morality of self-improvement, as found in several of Erasmus's *Adages*:

> Plutarch in his "Saying of the Spartans" records that in Sparta even the gods and goddesses are all represented with spears in their hands. . . . They add, he says, a proverb: Set your hand to the work before you appeal to Fortune. Aeschylus, cited by Stobaeus [has this]: "God loves to help the man who helps himself." . . . And so we ought not to be so confident in our efforts that we neglect the help of heaven, nor on the other hand so dependent on that help that we let our own duty go by default.
>
> Aeschylus seems to refer to this in the *Persians*: "Long have I prayed that the gods would bring these things to pass; but when a man makes an effort himself, the god too takes a hand." From the same source is quoted the line "God loves to help the man who helps himself."[43]

The independent Bradamante and Marfisa seem like those goddesses, Venus included, whom the Spartans represented with spears in their hands—and self-determination in their hearts.

The expression in Varro—"God helps those who help themselves"—"indicates that divine help is commonly available, not to the idle, but to industrious men who try as hard as they can," Erasmus also reports in the *Adages*.[44] Thus, one kind of opportunist in the poem is instinctively and endlessly cunning. If she had been more superstitious and moral, the far-from-idle Doristella might have been less slippery and lucky. Thus, Origille, taking advantage of Orlando, "seized—as she knew how—her chance" (2.3.61); similarly, Brunello's thievish eye "seized upon [Orlando's] sword" (2.11.6). Brunello and Origille steal both horse and sword; in the same motions they are also seizing occasion.

Another kind of opportunist also acts effectively, but with more premeditation and care. Thus, Orlando catches and disarms the fleeing Falerina *presto*, and then "grasps the damsel's hair / —The wind has strewn it

---

[43] Erasmus, *Adag.* II.ii.81, "Manum admoventi fortuna est imploranda / Set your hand to the work before you appeal to Fortune" (after Plutarch, *Moralia* 239A), in *Adages: II.i.1 to II.vi.100* (1991), *Collected Works of Erasmus*, 33: 118–19. Cf. the citations above, notes 2 and 42.

[44] *Adag.* I.vi.17, "Dii facientes adiuvant / The gods help those who help themselves" (after Varro, *Res rusticae* 1.1.4), in *Adages: I.vi.1. to I.x.100* (1989), *Collected Works of Erasmus*, 32: 15.

on her shoulders" (2.4.27–28)—as he tries to compel her to disclose the
exit from the garden of Orgagna. "He leads her to a beech / And ties her
tightly to the trunk" (2.4.30); and then he has the presence of mind to
consult his book. This less reckless kind of opportunist is able to control
occasion, rather than be stampeded by it. The well-informed hero shortly
meets a Siren, but he has pre-deafened himself against her charms. Since
this Siren "shows the fair, and the ugly [part] holds hidden" (2.4.36), she
is like Fortune: presentable so long as her glamorous aspect dissimulates
her less attractive one. Orlando pretends to be asleep, and when the Siren
leaves the shore and comes to kill him—at this point she surely is *not* very
attractive—the initiative passes his way and he grabs her by the hair to be-
head her (2.4.38–39).

Fortune springs traps on the unwary and the naively opportunistic
alike: the robber and kidnapper Fugiforca, for example, is surely an experi-
enced occasion-seizer. But he trips as he scampers out of reach, after ignoring a chance to amend: "*fortuna* and his sin caught him" when a brier
snagged both his feet (2.16.58–59). The snatched snatcher is trussed and
shackled forthwith (2.17.8, 22–23). Such a sequence is reversed whenever
Orlando gets himself involved with the treacherous Origille, whom he rescues from being "hung from a pine tree by her hair" (2.11.13). For every
prudent angel who binds up Misfortune, some Angelica-smitten fool insists
on releasing her. Thus, Boccaccio accedes to the truth of Andalo's fable
about our power to fetter Fortune, but he also hears the cries of those who
had loosed Misfortune from his post; they call to Boccaccio in their tor-
ment, thus recalling him to the communication of their stories as exempla
of the malign power of Fortune over human lives.

The garden of the fifth canto in Book 2, which is inspired at the outset
by the love that animates arduous endeavor and universalizes consensus,
is perhaps the one with the most traps, including: a dragon conquered by
Orlando's chastity in the presence of the attractive Origille; the garden's
mistress Falerina preparing a magic weapon to use against the man who
will subvert her domain; the Siren foiled by stuffing one's ears with roses;
an enraged bull; a blinding, predatory bird or harpy; and the malicious ass
with the huge ears already mentioned. As Jo Ann Cavallo explains in her
illuminating remarks on this episode, the perils are the epiphenomena of
the passions and difficulties of a mistress: her raging jealousy, her vicious
spite, and her would-be protectors.[45] And, we may add, her openness to

---

[45] Cavallo, *Boiardo's* Orlando Innamorato, 121–29.

slander: when asinine things are said about the lover, it is the malicious mistress who is all ears. The giants of Daunger, the garden that is virtually a parody of the castle keep in the *Romance of the Rose*, and the Faun hiding her serpent-like snare in flowers and perfumes—*similar, perhaps, / to that which gave Eve the bitter food. / Through grass and flowers the evil streak advanced*[46]—are all part of a courtship or a love affair gone fearfully wrong and terminally bad.

Orlando uses the Sphinx-like Faun's own chain to confine the jealous guardians. But then, in the next canto (Book 2, Canto 6), he attacks the garden's basis, which is a dangerous tree. Why is this tree at the root of the garden's evil? With its deadly golden apples and inverted cone form, it looks like an emblem of avarice or gluttony from Dante's *Purgatory*,[47] but this identification does not make a lot of sense in view of the foregoing. For the ground the tree grows out of is a story that traps dames and cavaliers in the garden *as couples*, not as misers. Thus, the menacing riches of its *cupiditas* imply a double tenor: tantalizing objects, treasures, that are also crushing amorous expectations, pleasures. If the tree is indeed planted in Orlando's own dangerous commitment to fortune, it must be specifically *Fortuna amoris*: for Orlando is rich and unpossessed by greed, but he is desirous and in need—of Angelica. It is Angelica, after all, who sent Orlando on this fool's errand in the first place, to get him out of her way.

Under the umbrella of an earthen humility—that is, humble earth—Orlando barely escapes the chance to die beneath the tree that symbolizes his personal fortune. And though his felling of this life-index lets him free others from the garden's spell, it hardly delivers Orlando himself: from his own humiliating expenditure of spirit on an indifferent idol. For the mission to Falerina's domain only conducts him toward two more projections of his misfortune in being in love with Angelica, namely the domain of Morgana and the persona of Penitence. Morgana is the Treasure Fairy, but

---

[46] Dante, *Purgatory*, trans. Allen Mandelbaum (Berkeley and Los Angeles: Univ. of California Press, 1982), VIII.98–100.

[47] Cf. the emblematic denial of gluttony in *Purg.*, XXII.131–35, 141 ("... a tree that blocked / our path; its fruits were fine, their scent was sweet, / and even as fir-tree tapers upward / from branch to branch, that tree tapered downward, / so as—I think—to ward off any climber ... 'This food shall be denied you' ") with the confession of the avricious Hugh Capet at *Purg.*, XX.43–45 ("I was the root of the obnoxious plant / that overshadows all the Christian lands, so fine fruit can rarely rise from them"), XX.105 ("his *ghiotta* [gluttony] for gold") and XX.115–16 ("What we cry here is: 'Crassus, / tell us, because you know': 'How does gold taste?' ").

Orlando is not a treasure-seeker in her realm any more than he is a miser in Falerina's Garden. Rather, he adventures after the recovery of his own faculty of self-determination.

The sway of treasure in places like Morgana's realm is always a metaphor for the hero's subjection to Fortune. Nonetheless, the pioneering success of Boccaccio's *Poverty* in the management of Fortune is suggestive: Orlando is rich, but he chases after Angelica; Ranaldo is poor, yet he shuns her. The two peers—Roland and Ronald—also exist in an odd, antipathetic relation in other respects. Ranaldo is traditionally a womanizer, randy like his foxy namesake Renyard ("His *ribaldo* is a well known fact," says Orlando at the outset [1.2.25]); but in Boiardo the womanizer wants to have nothing to do with Angelica. Orlando is traditionally much more a Boy Scout, but in Boiardo he nonetheless fancies himself a great lover. Perhaps his older nature overtakes him in the famous bath scene, but it is also possible that he misses his chance because Angelica's application of a vigor-restoring balm or salve actually *unmans* him ("nothing there was seen to grow"; 1.25.39), like a witch's enchantment. Turpine will call Orlando a baboon for missing yet another chance like this one (2.19.50), where two octaves earlier Brandimart is saying that one is crazy to abandon what Fortune offers us (2.19.48). At any rate, *both* Orlando and Ranaldo miss their chance with Angelica, even while each one seems to be in the position occupied by the other. Hints of the hero's impotence, upon the occasion of the bath, imply a warning: he who will not when he may, perhaps cannot when he would.

We note that in the poem overall Orlando is needed to rescue Ranaldo, Rugiero is needed to rescue Orlando, and Angelica is required to rescue both Orlando and Ranaldo; i.e., neither Orlando nor Ranaldo can rescue himself. If they were combined into one character, perhaps such a personage would also become more of his own fortune and owe less to Fortune. Such a mutualization takes place in the case of the friends Orlando and Brandimart, in the story of their surrogacy for each other while in captivity to Manodante. But the dual identity of Ranaldo and Orlando seems permanently unstable; it betokens not only their more or less chronic rivalry with each other, but also makes us think of the continuous war of each with his own alienated fortune.

One's fortune, after all, may only be another name for the successful or unsuccessful assertion of one's personal capacities to seize and realize one's opportunities through the force of one's own character: free persons will hope to overcome the chances of their birth and circumstances, their original allotment of "the goods of fortune."[48] The poem finally treats this issue as a question: Which of two knights more merits the arms of Hector? Should they go to Mandricardo, with his remarkable personal achievement of them, or to Rugiero, with his inherited aristocratic right to them? But the terms are in flux. Mandricardo's Herculean virtue has defeated his poor fortune, albeit Fortune favored and assisted him. And Rugiero's inevitable courtesy and choice of valor have told his blood and high estate as if they were his just desserts and not merely his good fortune.

7. Venture and Virtue

> Nil tribuat Fortuna sibi. sit prospera semper
> illa quidem; sed non uni certamina pugnae
> credidimus totis nec constitit alea castris
> nutatura semel; si quid licuisset iniquis
> casibus, instabant aliae post terga biremes.

Let Fortune demand no tribute for herself. Let her always prosper us, but we did not trust the contest to a single fight, nor was the die cast with all our force to be lost on a throw. Even if unfavorable chance had been allowed, another fleet pressed on behind.[49]

Aristotle's *Nicomachean Ethics* essays a discrimination between true well-being and the mere fortuity of possessing the goods of fortune:

Now if we must see the end [of life] and only then call a man happy, not as being happy but as having been so before [i.e., before his death], surely this is a paradox, that when he is happy the attribute that belongs to him is not to be truly predicated of him because we do not wish to call living men happy, on account of the changes that may befall them, and because we have assumed happiness to be something permanent, and by no means easily changed, while a single man may suffer many turns of fortune's wheel. For clearly if we were to keep pace with his fortunes, we should often call the same man happy and again wretched, making the happy man out to be a "chameleon and insecurely based." Or is this keeping pace with his fortunes quite wrong? Success or failure in

---

[48] Here I am adapting the words of Agnes Heller, *Renaissance Man*, trans. Richard E. Allen (New York: Schocken Books, 1978), 370.

[49] Claudian, *On Stilicho's Consulship*, I, 363–67.

life does not depend on these, but human life, as we said, needs these as mere additions, while virtuous activities or their opposites are what constitute happiness or the reverse.[50]

The constant round of change and undoing in Boiardo's poem can be adduced either to support Aristotle's distinction or to call it into question. The separation of the abiding from the contingent is the theme, but success or failure in life might seem merely to depend on which it is that you reckon your ventures and adventures (or your experience) to have illustrated: whether the happy activities and quality time of virtuous living, or the vagaries of good and bad fortune.

If Orlando is to be read as a protagonist of the traditional, moralized battle in which Virtue *overcomes* Fortune, he is nonetheless only gradually trained as an opportunist of the adept, well-prepared, and occasion-mastering kind. Inside the labyrinthine realm of Morgana (2.9), accordingly, he meets a succession of critical advisements about "ventura." The first one tells the hero it is easy to get in but hard to get out, unless you catch the restless fay whose head of hair is bald in back (2.8.39, cf. 2.9.2). Easy to get into what?, we may ask. Into Virgil's underworld, comes our answer (*Aen.*, VI.126–29), but what is that? Consider Petrarch:

JOY: I have found a gold mine.
REASON: You have discovered an easy way to hell.

"Beware," Petrarch's Reason warns anyone who is made joyful by the possession of riches, "lest you be the one who is being possessed and, in fact, do not hold your riches but are being held by them, and serve them rather than they serve you. You should know that many more are possessed by their wealth than do possess it, and that more often...men belong to their wealth, than their wealth belongs to them."[51] But is this the right warning? The richly endowed Orlando is inescapably romancing the stone, but he does not seem to be attempting to rob Fort Knox. Orlando's appropriation of Morgana's carbuncle looks impulsive and "appetitive," but it does not look like greed for material wealth: the stone proves its value only in its practical use as a lantern (2.8.37), not for its appeal as an idol. Orlando "gets away with it," as Ranaldo will not get away with the chair. Perhaps it pays to be rich. The poor man may be paralyzed by his idoliza-

---

[50] Aristotle, *Nicomachean Ethics*, trans. W. D. Ross (London and New York: Oxford Univ. Press, 1975), I.8.

[51] Rawski, *Petrarch's Remedies*, 1: 164.

tion of wealth, while the rich man may find himself free to dispose of it how he will. For Orlando, Aladdin's lamp is just another lamp.

The stone is got by trial and error, that is through hindsight, foresight, and presence of mind, the three traditional dimensions of prudence. Indeed, "the Count's heart does not care / For such things" as Ariadne's foresighted advice to Theseus on how to escape the "errore' of the labyrinth (2.8.17). This is really the count's first advisement. Impatience has jumped in where Prudence would surely fear to tread ("He thought, 'What am I waiting for? / Were the stream even ten miles wide, / I still would reach the other side!' "; 2.8.23). The second advisement (carved above the *porta* at the bottom of the *tomba*) tells the heedless Orlando to seize Morgana while she sleeps (2.8.38, 37, 39). Seize what? The Main Chance, the major opportunity. By getting himself into the otherworld of Morgana's treasures, Orlando seems to meet an epiphany of a lifelong impetuosity and adventurism. But at the same time he also seems to have gotten into the "tomorrow and tomorrow and tomorrow" of the rat-race that has made human life "a modern ecstasy," in the words of Shakespeare's *Macbeth*. The advice is repeated with a warning, by an anonymous voice that advises the alternative is such long-sufferance that he'll be reputed to be a saint on earth (2.8.44).

The third advisement tells Orlando that strength and persistence conquer in the end, and to dally no more (2.8.55–56). Conquer what? This is a skirmish with fierce Fortune, and the incapacitated damsel who is speaking from her prison implies that fortitude conquers "all things"—except perhaps a workaholic's need to conquer everything.

The fourth advisement instructs Orlando not to wait, for wealth, dominion, honor, and delight all depend on seizing the golden forelock. But now the advice is coming from the Fortune-figure herself, when she's all awhirl, and when it is already too late for Orlando not to start playing catchup. No longer a statue or static icon waiting to be read, Morgana has become a precipitant force drawing the pursuer headlong into unsuccess and the ensuing recriminations, the Penitence or Second Thoughts that accompanied the statue of fleeting Opportunity in Ausonius's epigram.

The fifth and last advisement comes from Penitence herself. Once Morgana has escaped the hero, Penitence advises him to arm himself with patience. Orlando responds that it's a dish for knaves (2.9.7). He dreads incapacity, yet *impatience* goes on making its fatal contribution to Fortune's power over him. Humanist adages and advisements swirl around any proper rereading of this episode's series of events; i.e., one should seize occasion promptly, yet not precipitously, at the most propitious moment. To avoid remorse and self-reviling postmortems, the best advice is *comprime motus*: control commotion.[52] Prudence dictates that one make haste slowly, but also mature one's flight, one's escape.[53] Yet, even when Orlando is in possession of the lock of Fortune twisted in his hand— thanks to his *ventura buona* being willing to grant him a second chance, namely that Morgana should fortuitously turn her head his way (2.9.17)— the crone Penitence warns the count not to trust the fickle fairy Morgana (2.9.19). The last chance to control her seems as virtual and fleeting as the first. Nonetheless, everything depends on Boiardo's hero compelling the medieval Fortune to re-become the classical Occasion originally presented by the figure's iconographic coiffure. Berni's description of Fortune as a "great annoyance," in the encapsulation previously quoted, is probably reductive in a way the episode actually intends.

Orlando missed his original chance to embrace Angelica, yet he also missed his chance *not* to; hence the same missed opportunity is repeated with Morgana. So far as Boiardo's tale is concerned, it is not precisely true that "time past does not return and re-cycle itself back" (2.8.58), or that "Occasion (*Il tempo*) comes to us just once" (2.9.2). The allegory, moreover, is itself a kind of "metanoia," or reconsideration, like Penitence in

---

[52] The phrase from Claudian's *Panygyric on the Fourth Consulship of the Emperor Honorius*, 266, is translated as "subdue occasion" by Sir Thomas Elyot in *The Boke Named the Gouernour*, II.i. In its original context, the words also mean "master thine emotions"; *Claudian*, Loeb Classical Library, trans. M. Platnauer (London: William Heinemann, and Cambridge, MA: Harvard Univ. Press, 1963), 1: 307.

[53] Erasmus's *Adag.* II.i.1, on the "royal proverb" *festina lente*, implies its advice is found in Vergil's *maturate fugam* (Aeneid I.136: "mature/speed your flight"), in *Adages: II.i.1 to II.vi.100* (1989), *Collected Works of Erasmus*, 32: 5. We are arguing that occasion's full symbolism is only arrived at by supplementing its imagery and icons with its axioms and apothegms, and their correctives. Examples may be found in Francesco Guicciardini; his *Ricordi*, Series C, nos. 78–80, argue for the use of procrastination in the face of lack of opportunity. No. 78 includes: "do not rush things madly, wait for the right season." No. 79 adds: "Unless rightly understood, it would be a dangerous proverb that enjoins the wise man to take advantage of the benefits brought by time [e.g., "seize the day"?]. For opportunity knocks at your door just once, and in many cases you have to decide and to act quickly. But when you are in difficult straits or involved in troublesome affairs, procrastinate, and wait as long as you can. For often time will enlighten or free you." *Maxims and Reflections of a Renaissance Statesman (Ricordi)*, trans. Mario Domandi (New York: Harper & Row, 1965), 61–62. The vexed relation of virtue and worthiness to Fortune and opportunity—and the ideal response of flexibility—appears in the same text, Ser. C, No. 31, and Ser. B. No. 52; Domandi, *Maxims*, 49, 109. On rationality versus subjection to fortune, cf. Ser. B, No. 160; Domandi, *Maxims*, 135.

the Greek statue of Ausonius's epigram after that of Posidippus, and it makes us say, with Guicciardini in his *Ricordi*, "Lucky are those to whom the same opportunity returns more than once. For even a wise man may miss it or misuse it the first time. But not to recognize it the second time is to be very foolish indeed."[54] Boiardo's tale, insofar as it is shaped at all, is surely shaped by the recognitive and hermeneutical *return* of one or another of the original, striking opportunities afforded its knights. Thus, Orlando and Ranaldo, regarding the beautiful face of Angelica, might well have hearkened to a later Latin and English emblem of Fortuna or Occasio standing on a sea-borne wheel, "Ne Tenear": "Occasions-past *are sought in vaine*; *But*, *oft*, they wheele-about *againe*."

In his conclusive dealings with Morgana, at least in the present *Innamorato*, Orlando quickly seizes the lock of blond hair blowing from her forehead, holds it tight, and makes her swear by Demogorgon never again to hinder him (2.13.23–29). Orlando has surely reached the same point that was reached in Boccaccio's fable when Poverty dictated her terms to Fortune. He is no longer seizing Opportunity, but squelching Misfortune. Only Demogorgon with his serpentine whips can bring the fays to heel (2.13.27–28), which means, in effect, control the Three Fates: for at the head of Boccaccio's *Genealogy of the Gentile Gods*, the Fates derive from this deity and take their offices from him. However temporarily, then, Orlando is in control of his demiurgical fortune, and is longer merely her whipping boy.

8. Fortune and Wisdom

It may be objected that Orlando gets Fortune's key only in return for leaving Ziliante in captivity. Perhaps he only gets the name for the thing and makes an unwise trade; if so, he has not yet fully mastered his fortune. In a subsequent episode Orlando will chase after an illusion of Charlemagne's

---

[54] *Maxims*, Ser. C., No. 80; Domandi, *Maxims*, 62. For "Ne Tenear," see George Wither, *A Collection of Emblemes, Ancient and Moderne* [1635], Intro. by Rosemary Freeman, Bibl. Notes by Charles S. Hensley, Renaissance English Text Society (Columbia, SC: Published for The Newberry Library, Univ. of South Carolina Press, 1985): Bk. 1, no. 4. The engravings were originally for Gabriel Rollenhagen, *Nucleus emblematum selectissimorum* (Utrecht, 1611? and 1613). Wither adapts Rollenhagen's couplet for the motto, and then expands in his poem: "The first *Occasions*, therefore, see thou take / (Which offred are) to bring thy hopes about; / And, minde thou, still, what *Haste* away they make, / Before thy swift-pac't houres are quite runne out. / Yet, if an *Opportunity* be past, / Despaire not thou, as they that hopeless be; / Since, *Time* may so revolve againe, at last, / That *New-Occasions* may be offered thee."

army in flight; it disappears into a wood and down a spring, which then appears to be a sort of crystal cabinet full of women. "He is thirsty on account of the great heat, and enters the wood in his *mala ventura*" (2.31.44). The fount presents both an escape from defeat and a chance or opportunity for (further) misadventure: Orlando jumps right in, and shortly he's a goner, yet again.

The *aventura istrana* (3.6.57) that gets Orlando out of this captivity, or brings him back to his reason, is told more slowly. The knightly rescuers enter the Naiad's zone through a portal inviting those inclined toward pride, fame, and love to come its way. But the reverse of the legend reads: "Pride and the search for love and honor, / When they control a person's soul, / Propel it forth with so much force / it cannot find the *passo* by which to return" (3.7.13). Cutting down the trees that block the way beyond, Rugiero is seduced into the waters by a laurel nymph; the laurel is the chance to be famous. Gradasso is seduced by a magnificent horse from an ash tree; ash is the wood for spears, the horse is the chance to be victorious. Brandimart avoids these temptations, but he is nonetheless drawn by the amorous water itself; the water is the chance to be embraced. His beloved Fiordelisa tells Brandimart what he should follow, advising that "Courage will conquer everything, / But wisdom has to be its guide." This guide proves to be Fiordelisa herself; she may also be understood as Wisdom, the "mistress of all sciences" (3.7.56), who intervenes to arm her man against the enchantment, and disenchants his friends with the same device.

What this allegory adds to the Morgana episode is obviously the figuration of Wisdom. Fortune was Orlando's guide in Morgana's realm, to judge by the figure of the labyrinth (its denizens being "led by Fortune to the end"; 2.8.16), or by his action of descent after seizing the carbuncle ("as Fortune guided him, / He did not take the right-hand way"; 2.8.34). But at the fount Orlando is freed as much by Fiordelisa as by the questing knight Brandimart. The roses with which she crowns all four knights are the desires that drew them into the waves in the first place, but they are transformed by being recognized. Her role reflects the principle that, in the words of a proposition found in Francisco Suárez, "to the extent that a being participates in intellectuality it will also participate in freedom."[55] That is, Fiordelisa can crown the knights only if the thirst for

---

[55] From *Disputationes metaphysicae*, Sec. 2, #17, trans. George L. Stengren, in *Renaissance Philosophy, Volume 2: The Transalpine Thinkers: Selected Readings from Cusanus to*

fame, power, and erotic and sensual experience are re-read in a reverse mirror, as motions back toward self-knowledge, self-mastery, self-respect, and self-possession. These are the true remedies for Fortune, and they enable us to read the lady as that Wisdom who crowns and mitres her subjects over themselves.

9. Fortune and Freedom

The poem's long discourse on human freedom and personal capacity is made particularly explicit by Rugiero and his tutor Atalante near the middle of Book 2. Atalante warns Rugiero not to leave home and go to war—"your ascendent is too *fell* (*rio*)," "fell" being perhaps Fortune's most frequent epithet. Rugiero can well believe in the heavens' great power over us—if everything is determined, however, he doesn't see that staying home makes any real difference—sooner or later, he'll fulfill his ascendent! Atalante perceives that the youth, who only hopes to "spend an hour with [the troops], then die!," is destined for battle, no matter what objections are put in his way. Having concluded that the heavens and fortune wish to rob the pagan cause of an invaluable asset, he lets Rugiero leave the reservation: "let it happen. It must be" (2.16.36–38, 53).

The seduction of Rugiero into action, away from Atalante's dictates, compels the mage's resignation to impotence in the face of a higher fortune. Likewise, Rugiero's will-to-experience doubles with the poet's overcoming of his own fear of venturing on unprecedented depths. Like the man who first set sail on the ocean (2.17.1), the poet is moving toward the teleological causality of epic. For the young Rugiero is tempted *out* of an imprisoning private world, rather than *into* one, and he leaves on his own power, with an informed will. We cannot think of him as a victim of fortune like Ziliante, the casualty of the strange experiments of Morgana. Rugiero escapes from a closeted or cloistered existence, while Ziliante is detained by one. Having mastered his timing with Morgana, it is *Orlando* who rescues Ziliante, and Ziliante who cannot rescue himself. In contrast to Ziliante, Rugiero is *self*-liberated, by his own commitment to action. Combat offers him the chance to engage with experience definitively, his future fiancée Bradamante included. Thus, the mountain he leaves recalls the one that is placed at such a remove from the stream of Bios, or Life,

---

Suárez, ed. Herman Shapiro and Arturo B. Fallico, The Modern Library (New York: Random House, 1967), 374.

in the Philosopher's dream in Alberti's "Fate and Fortune."

Like the sudden arrival of Angelica at Charlemagne's court in Boi-ardo's first canto, the tempting portals of *aventura* offer to change our life, or help us escape our present circumstances. Yet, they also threaten to deepen our involvement in distractions. When the mail arrives, should we take up those fair tenders from the Publishers Clearing House Sweepstakes, or just pay the bills? In the event, the poem's dubious entrées on wealth, honors, intimacy, celebrity, and that advantageous career move are very short on safe exits. By the end of the text, Orlando has grown wary of such offers: the adventures are inevitably enchanted, he says, which means stacked against him, or somebody like him. In a decisive inward turn, he adds that he no longer trusts even himself (3.7.39). He echoes his earlier identity crisis when he was afflicted by Penitence (2.9.15). Like Don Quixote, he has "risked everything for adventure" (*DQ*, II.66). But in the long run, Orlando's exposure to Fortune has proved disheartening; he speaks out of a Quixote-like *desengāno*, or disenchantment or disillusion with the very "venture" of the work in which he has been so ironically celebrated.

As mortals, Petrarch argues we are continually beset. Mocked by forces quite beyond our control, perpetual beleaguerement is our worldly lot:

> Yet . . . we find a greater cause, or, to be frank, the whole cause, within ourselves. Not to mention all the other things that trouble us, there is our ever present war with Fortune, in which only virtue can make us victorious—that very virtue we willingly and wittingly neglect.[56]

"In reality it is not Fortune that makes a man free, but virtue."[57] The lack of such virtue, then, subjects one to the power of Fortune. Yet, according to a little dialogue of Alberti, Virtue is inevitably on the defensive when confronted by that hostile goddess who is "insolent, proud, domineering, and surrounded by a host of armed followers," and who offers Virtue herself only blows and insults.[58]

Admittedly, not every *aventure* conducts to fame (3.3.19). Nonetheless,

---

[56] Rawski, *Petrarch's Remedies*, 1: 1.

[57] Rawski, *Petrarch's Remedies*, 1: 40.

[58] Alberti, "Second Dialogue: Virtue"; trans. from *Three Dialogues*, in *Renaissance Philosophy, Volume 1: The Italian Philosophers: Selected Readings from Petrarch to Bruno*, ed. and trans. Arturo B. Fallico and Herman Shapiro, The Modern Library (New York: Random House, 1967), 31.

the dispirited peer, whose disappointment we have cited above (3.7.39), is answered by a moving speech of Rugiero. Rugiero gives the text's last discourse on the value of engagement in the face of possible disaster and in despite of the world's constraints on one's freedom and efforts at virtue:

> Rugiero said, "Opinions vary:
> Everyone likes his own ideas.
> Some people say one ought to fear
> Demonic works and fairy spells,
> But if a good knight does his duty,
> He can on no account withdraw.
> He must face every strange adventure,
> And he must never, never fear." (3.7.40)

—*Every* "strana ventura"?, we may pause to ask. The endings of Boiardo's cantos always promise a further chance for distraction, but they also confess to a need for intermission. Rugiero has undertaken Orlando's rescue from the Laughing Stream out of duty, not from desire; so he is already practicing what he preaches. But Rugiero is still young. For older spirits, the time to take a break is also important, and he who hesitates—to do *that*—is as much in need of rescue as Orlando. Speaking to an audience at the end of one of his cantos, Boiardo might pause and say "you have been very patient, now seize your opportunity."

MICHAEL MURRIN

Trade and Fortune:

Morgana and Manodante

Phasis (in Colchis) was to give immediate access to the Caucasus and its mineral wealth. The earliest Greek finds in the area may be local coins of the early fifth century showing the Milesian lion and the Minotaur.[1]

I AM CONCERNED HERE WITH THE INTERRELATION between fortune, in the sense of trade, and romance, an issue raised crucially by Boiardo's Middle Eastern settings, where the heroes and heroines find or inhabit the most wonderful places and have perhaps their wildest adventures. The Middle East constituted a zone truly beyond because it was outside the area of Italian naval and military power. Orlando, Ranaldo, and the other knights travel there on their own and act on their own. They are not colonial warriors arranging local politics for the benefit of a powerful state located somewhere else, and in fact no Westerner could act even as these heroes in such territories.[2] The Mongols and the Turcoman successor states, as well as the Georgians and Armenians of the Caucasus zone, did not normally hire many Western mercenaries. So one wants to know what interest Boiardo and for that matter many earlier poets of aristocratic romance

---

[1] John Boardman, *The Greeks Overseas* (Baltimore: Penguin, 1964), 265.

[2] The hero of *Tirant lo blanc* provides an excellent contrast. All his adventures occur in the known zones along the Mediterranean coasts, and his exploits do have something of a colonial tinge. The romance also mostly avoids the marvelous.

had in these lands, and what such places tell us about romance itself, its social pretensions and fears.

My test case will be Boiardo's most elaborate and perhaps most wonderful set of adventures, those involving Morgana and her strife with Orlando, which also implicate Manodante's family and which the poet prolongs over some twenty cantos.[3] I will not, however, attempt a detailed reading of this sequence. Charles Ross has done that, and many critics have chapters or articles on Morgana in particular. Instead, I will look at the mercantilist implications of the story through some of the classical myths that set up the series and define that interest.

Boiardo signals two classical sources that help to clarify the issue.[4] The first and most important Boiardo indicates initially, when he has Orlando undergo Jason's tests. The story of the Golden Fleece illustrates that heroic and yet dubious side of Mediterranean commerce, which we often call piracy. The second story parallels that of Jason and the Argonauts and may have attracted the poet's attention for this reason. He certainly used Theseus's adventure in the Cretan labyrinth, which he has sculpted prominently on one of Morgana's gates, to develop further the implications of the Argonaut story.[5]

In both stories the hero sails to a foreign land, where he must face what seems certain death in an adventure like the Labyrinth or in a series of tests like those Jason undertakes.[6] A local princess, who falls in love

---

[3] Charles Stanley Ross, "Boiardo's Fata Morgana" (Ph.D. diss., University of Chicago, 1976), 53.

[4] The most profound of the poet's parallels to classical myth does not concern commerce, the one that he makes to the underworld, particularly to Hades as presented in the *Aeneid*. For this series of allusions see Ross, "Boiardo's Fata Morgana," especially 100–3, 126, 132, 145.

[5] Ovid provided Boiardo with abbreviated versions of both stories (*Metamorphoses* 7.1–158, 8.152–235), and Boccaccio mostly presupposes Ovid in his retelling of the stories in the *Genealogie deorum gentilium*, ed. Vincenzo Romano, 2 vols. (Bari: G. Laterza, 1951). See especially GDG 4.11–12.169–71, 10.48–49.519–21, 11.26–27.563–65, 11.29.566–67, 13.25–26.653–56, and 13.64.671.

[6] Neither Theseus nor Jason have much choice either about the voyage or the ordeal beyond the sea. Pelias traps Jason, asking him what he would do if he knew he would be killed by a citizen. Jason replies that he would send the citizen after the Golden Fleece. Pelias then does so, following the warning of an oracle (Apollodorus, *Biblioteca*. 1.9.16). According to Plutarch Theseus, the stranger newly designated heir, though illegitimate, must go to Crete, since the Athenians resent his father, consider him the cause of their troubles, and object that he requires them to lose their legitimate children in the lottery (*Theseus* 17.1–2).

with the hero, gives him the help essential to his success. In the process
she betrays her father and her homeland, and must flee with the hero. He
in turn, being a womanizer,[7] betrays her for another. Jason divorces
Medea to marry the princess of Corinth, and Theseus deserts Ariadne for
Aigle.[8]

Boiardo invents a brilliant inversion of this type of plot. His hero does,
of course, what the others do. He passes Jason's tests with the bulls, the
armed men, and the dragon (*OI* 1.24.17–25.18), and he threads the labyrinth. Yet, as Charles Ross has shown,[9] Orlando does not fit the model of
the hero in this kind of story. It is not just that he lacks the youth and
looks of his classical predecessors. He does not resemble them at all. Instead of a womanizer, Boiardo gives us a courtly lover serving the cold and
distant princess Angelica. When he returns the horn to Morgana's damsel
and rejects the hinted offer of Morgana's love, he says that a man who
does not prize his own lady more than his heart is vile and discourteous
(1.25.16).[10] Finding that this hero will not let her play Medea, Morgana
decides on revenge.[11] The Treasure Fairy cannot imagine that someone
would reject what she has to offer.[12] Her attempts to kill or capture Orlando take up the rest of the sequence.

Falerina, however, does not think Morgana ever had a romantic role
designed for herself. Unlike Aeetes, who set up impossible tests to protect

---

[7] For Jason the womanizer see Boccaccio, GDG 13.26.654–55; for Theseus, Plutarch,
Theseus 29.1–2.

[8] The *Odyssey* has Artemis kill Ariadne on Dia. See G. L. Huxley, *Greek Epic Poetry
from Eumelos to Panyassis* (London: Faber and Faber, 1969), 117. Hesiod introduces the
notion of betrayal and is twice cited by Plutarch (*Theseus* 20.1, 29.2). Boccaccio keeps
the betrayals but changes the names: Phaedra for Aigle (GDG 10.49.521) and Glauce as
an alternate for Creusa (13.26.655).

[9] It is one of the main theses of his dissertation, but see especially "Boiardo's Fata
Morgana," 18, 30, 94, 123–24.

[10] For Orlando as a courtly lover see Andrea di Tommaso, *Structure and Ideology in
Boiardo's "Orlando innamorato"* (Chapel Hill: Univ. of North Carolina Press, 1972), 47–
70. Boiardo had already worked out the characteristics of such a lover for his Tarot cards,
Numbers 1, 3–4 in the *Amore* series. See *Tutte le opere di Matteo M. Boiardo*, ed. Angelandrea Zottoli (Milan: Mondadori, 1944), vol. 2, 706.

[11] Like Ovid's Medea, Morgana collects herbs but then botches a magic potion, when
she transforms Ziliante into a dragon (*OI* 2.13.3–6). See also Ross, "Boiardo's Fata
Morgana," 147.

[12] She is initially defined as the "Fata del Tesoro" at *OI* 1.22.57 and again at
2.12.24. Ross notes that French romance bequeathed three characteristics of fays to
Italian and English romance. They are met, they produce wealth, and they are amorous.
Ross, "Boiardo's Fata Morgana," 37.

his political future, since he had been told that loss of the Fleece meant deposition, and who probably was surprised when Jason showed up, Morgana is aggressive and seeks out candidates. Falerina thinks Morgana wants to destroy people (*OI* 2.7.42–43), and the Treasure Fairy has already killed many.[13] The two readings, that of the damsel of the Horn and that of Falerina, do not necessarily cancel each other out. What Morgana considers aid might be inimical to those who hold other values. The two classical myths help us understand more precisely what she represents and what troubled the poet so much that he had to change the stories so radically.

I begin with the remoter parallel, that of Theseus in the Cretan Labyrinth. Crete is far from the Silk Route, particularly its northern extension that started by the Black Sea.[14] The way Boiardo would have understood the Cretan story then makes it relevant to this inquiry. He probably would have read it euhemeristically. The historical decoding of myth had been popular since the twelfth century,[15] and Boiardo used it in the Prologue to his translation of Xenophon's *Cyropaedia*, where he reproduced Boccaccio's reading of the Hydra of Lerna.[16] Boccaccio in turn pointed to the most prominent of Theseus's historical interpreters, Philochorus, whose reading of the Minotaur he recommended.[17] We know of Philochorus mostly through the summaries that Plutarch gives in his *Life of Theseus*, in which he tries to make historical sense out of early legends about the Athenian hero. Boiardo, of course, probably would not have read this life;

---

[13] Elsewhere Boiardo says that Morgana has a fell nature (*OI* 2.13.4). Jo Ann Cavallo thinks that Falerina speaks in earnest. See her *Boiardo's* Orlando Innamorato: *An Ethics of Desire* (Rutherford, NJ: Fairleigh Dickinson Univ. Press, 1993), 97–98.

[14] For other discussions of the Minotaur story in Boiardo, see my *Allegorical Epic* (Chicago: Univ. of Chicago Press, 1980), 80 and Cavallo, *Boiardo's* Orlando Innamorato, 102, who argues that the same story underlies Ranaldo's adventure at the Rocca crudele, where Angelica plays the role of Ariadne.

[15] Fausto Ghisalberti, "Arnolfo d'Orléans, un cultore di Ovidio nel secolo xii," *Memorie del R. istituto Lombardo di scienze e lettere*, Classe de lettere e scienze storiche e morali 24 (1932): 193–95. Sir James Frazer thought that such readings highlighted a major tendency in Greek religion. See his introduction to Apollodorus, *The Library* (Cambridge, MA: Harvard Univ. Press, 1967), Loeb, vol. 1, xxiii–iv. The Greeks regularly deified human beings. Frazer cites as evidence the fallen at Marathon and Plataea who received heroic honors as late as the second century C.E.

[16] Giulio Reichenbach, *Matteo Maria Boiardo* (Bologna: Nicola Zanichelli, 1929), 71.

[17] GDG 11.26.565. The *Genealogie* was in the Este library, and Duke Ercole used it. The fragmentary 1467 inventory lists two copies (nos. 109 and 113), and it is No. 218 in the 1495 catalogue. Duke Ercole had it in his study in May 1489. See Giulio Bertoni, *La Biblioteca Estense e la coltura Ferrarese* (Turin: Ermanno Loescher, 1903), 222, 242, 262.

therefore, we cannot assume that he saw Philochorus's detailed interpretations.[18] It is the style of reading that counts here.

Philochorus then established a historical reading of the Minotaur for later literary interpreters. For Philochorus, the Cretan Labyrinth was a superjail (*Theseus* 16.1).[19] The Cretans imprisoned Athenian hostages there, held as prizes for the winner in the funeral games of Androgeus.[20] The hostages by themselves could never find their way out. This is the reading Boiardo reproduces on Morgana's royal portal (*OI* 2.8.15-16). Philochorus at the same time euhemerized the Minotaur, who became a Cretan general and athlete named Taurus, who had won all the previous games and whom Theseus had to defeat (*Theseus* 16.1; 19.2-3).[21] Orlando similarly must overcome the giant Aridano, hitherto victorious in all his duels, before he can liberate the prisoners held by Morgana (*OI* 2.7.54-8.12). They in turn know Orlando can free them once they notice that he has reached their underground jail and is still wearing his armor (2.8.48).[22]

The euhemerist reading thus inverts the narrative order of Theseus's Cretan adventure. The hero does not first enter the Labyrinth and then fight. He fights first and afterwards frees the hostages in the Labyrinth. The historicizing reading, therefore, emphasizes not the Minotaur but the Labyrinth and its prisoners, and this, the interpretive order, becomes Boiardo's narrative order. Orlando first kills Aridano and then finds his way through the labyrinth.

---

[18] Guarino of Verona, while he translated some of Plutarch's *Lives* for Borso d'Este in the 1430s (Bertoni, *Biblioteca*, 115), never translated the *Theseus*. His son Battista Guarino nevertheless mentions Plutarch and assumes an allegorical approach to poetry, saying we must "fix our thought rather on the underlying truths which are therein concealed than upon the imaginations in which they are expressed." See *De ordine docendi* in William Harrison Woodward, *Vittorino da Feltre and Other Humanist Educators* (New York: Columbia Univ. Teachers College, 1963), 175. Guarino also thinks one should consult *all* the commentaries when reading an author, Woodward, *Vittorino da Feltre*, 173.

[19] Philochorus asserts this is the Cretan version of the story.

[20] Androgeus was the Cretan prince who won an Athenian athletic competition and was killed.

[21] The Minotaur came into the story early. He appears on a late Minoan sealstone, in a Hesiodic text, and, of course, in the *Theseis*. Huxley, *Greek Epic Poetry*, 118. Huxley cites *Archaeological Reports*, Annual Supplement to *The Journal of Hellenic Studies* (1958): 24 and the *Fragmenta Hesiodea*, ed. R. Merkelbach and M. L. West (Oxford, 1967), 145.

[22] For Theseus as liberator see Boccaccio, *GDG* 10.49.520-21.

Boiardo makes one significant change in his sources, which suggests his own use of the story. He turns a horizontal into a vertical labyrinth and puts all of it underground.[23] Without the *carbone* Orlando would never have made it down the marble stairs, which lead out of the Treasure Chamber (*OI* 2.8.37).[24] They drop more than a mile, and the road is so wicked and twisted that, wandering, a person could die a thousand times. Now if one thinks about such a place that reaches far into the earth and has a maze of passages, and one looks for its realistic equivalent or model, as a euhemerist would, one would think probably of a great mine with its many tunnels, shafts, and pits. Still today in Colorado signs warn tourists not to enter the many deserted mines, with their drop-offs and uncertain floors and ceilings. Many a tourist, unfortunately, pays no more attention to such signs than Orlando did to Morgana's warnings. More to the point, eastern Anatolia and the Caucasus region had many such mines.[25]

In fact, Morgana presides over a giant gold mine. Near the beginning of her duel with Orlando, her damsel tells the hero that Morgana controls the world's supply of gold. She sends it underground to the high mountains, where one digs it out with great effort, as well as hiding it in rivers and inside fountains. She supplies even India. The damsel then adds that her mistress controls silver as well, but she puts the emphasis on gold (*OI* 1.25.5-7). Accordingly and in contradistinction to the other fays and wizards, Morgana does not preside over a magical garden that vanishes at the end of the adventure.[26] Her realm is real. Orlando, though he overcomes Morgana, never thinks of destroying her kingdom, to which she returns in

---

[23] Morgana's royal portal depicts not her own but the Cretan Labyrinth, a structure with identical rooms. Ross shows that Boccaccio in his *Inferno* commentary provides a source for this idea (120–21). The rooms in Morgana's kingdom are not similar, though in the dark the difference vanishes. When Orlando explores the tunnels leading out of the Treasure Chamber, he finds them all completely dark (*OI* 2.8.29).

[24] Elsewhere Boiardo has a similar gem on a helmet light up a tomb (3.2.25). Ross indicates the medieval sources for the *carbone* (105–7). Cavallo, *Boiardo's Orlando Innamorato*, 104 connects the *carbone* to wealth and cites the *Roman de la rose* 1017–126. Stephanus and the anonymous Latin commentator provide a classical parallel (C.E. 630–730). They cite a variant story about the Cretan Labyrinth. Ariadne's crown was a bribe by which Bacchus seduced the princess in *Crete*. Vulcan made it from purest gold and Indian stones, and it lit the way *out* of the Labyrinth. See the *Aratus latinus cum scholiis* in Ernst Maass, *Commentariorum in Aratum reliquiae* (Berlin: Weidmann, 1898), xlii, 192–93.

[25] See the map of Colchis at the end of this essay for the location of this zone.

[26] Dragontina, Falerina, and Atlante have magical gardens.

the end (2.13.29).[27] One can leave a gold mine. One cannot disenchant it. Gold in fact was the lure that drew foreigners to this zone in the first place, and so we come to the quest of the Golden Fleece.

Boiardo's own explanation of the Fleece is astrological. Morgana and the other *fate* serve Demogorgon, who rides the Ram through the sky nightly and punishes any of them who disobey his rules.[28] The Ram in turn, being the lunar house of Mars, presides over the month of March, as it appears in the Schifanoia fresco.[29] Boiardo accordingly dresses Morgana in the colors of Mars: red and white (*OI* 2.8.43).[30] Morgana's armed men rise up crying "War! War!" and instantly challenge Orlando to a fight (*OI* 1.24.54). Gold provokes strife and war. Boiardo thus gives Orlando's adventures a properly heroic, not to say martial, context.

Yet, this whole astrological situation *already* existed in the story of the Argonauts. Apollonius of Rhodes had turned ancient elements of the story into a tight astrological epic,[31] and the Roman poets Ovid and Valerius Flaccus picked up the crucial details. The armed men provide a good example.[32] Ovid would have transmitted this connection to Boiardo, since the armed men in his version come from a "Martius anguis" that fought Cadmus at Thebes (*Meta* 3.32).[33] The god Mars, however, defined the entire

---

[27] She is the Italian predecessor of the mineral queen of the German Romantics who promises wealth to the hero. See especially Tieck's *Runenberg* and Hoffmann's *Mines of Falun*.

[28] Boiardo here reworks Boccaccio, who put Demogorgon inside the earth and had him whip the Erinyes (*GDG* 1, Introduction, 13–15), one reason perhaps why Morgana acts like an avenger and is "fell" (*OI* 2.13.4). For the background see Ross, "Boiardo's Fata Morgana," 172–73.

[29] Richard Hinckley Allen, *Star-Names and Their Meanings* (New York: G. E. Steckert, 1936), 78. The Ram, Mars, and the Moon appear together on a coin of Antiochus of Syria. Hinckley explains that lunar houses were the stages of the zodiac through which the moon passes daily in a circuit of 27–28 days, one of them being Aries or the Ram. *Star-Names*, 7.

[30] Her face when upset shows the same colors, as when she laments over the dead dragon Ziliante (*OI* 2.12.60). See also Allen, *Star-Names*, 79. Botticelli also used red and white for his *Mars and Venus* (c. 1485).

[31] John Kevin Newman, *The Classical Epic Tradition* (Madison: Univ. of Wisconsin Press, 1986), 89–92. Newman draws on the dissertation of his student P. Bogue, "Astronomy in the *Argonautica* of Apollonius Rhodius" (Ph.D. diss., University of Illinois at Urbana, 1977).

[32] The armed men go back to Eumelos of Corinth, the first epic poet of the story (8th century B.C.E.), whom Apollonius quotes when he introduces them. Huxley, *Greek Epic Poetry*, 66.

[33] Rosanna Alhaïque Pettinelli pointed out this Ovidian touch. See her "Di alcune

context for Jason's tests. The Fleece hung on an oak in a grove sacred to
the god (Valerius Flaccus, *Argonautica* 5.629).[34] Just before Jason arrives,
Mars sends a dragon to protect this grove and the Fleece (5.253–55), and
the tests occur in a field sacred to the god, where Jason must sew the dragon's teeth (Ovid, *Metamorphoses* 7.100–2).

Most striking of all, however, is the Ram that Demogorgon rides (*OI*
2.13.27). It is, of course, the Ram with the Golden Fleece that carried
Phrixus to Colchis and later returned to heaven. Boiardo could have found
the story in Valerius Flaccus (*Argonautica* 5.226–28). At Phrixus's death a
flame burned in the sky and the constellation Aries, or the Ram, appeared. Any good astronomy book probably would have given the poet the
same information. Morgana accordingly exists under the zodiacal sign of
the Golden Fleece. Now in classical astrology Aries presides over many
eastern lands: the Hellespont and Propontis or the entrance to the Black
Sea, over Syria, Persia, and Egypt.[35] And this connection leads us to the
historicizing readings of Jason's quest, which Boiardo presents through his
plot rather than by explicit statement.

What was this Fleece for which Jason sailed all the way to the eastern
end of the Black Sea? The coastal cities there had little to offer in themselves but linked visitors with the interior. Behind this coast stretched the
Caucasus Mountains and a highland zone, which the Greeks and the Italians never really controlled and where the Romans managed only an inter-
mittent presence. Strabo tells us that Jason and Medea, on a return trip to
the east, explored this inner zone, in particular Armenia and Media Atro-
patene, and that they even reached the Caspian Sea (*Geographica* 1.2.39;
11.4.8; 11.13.9–10; 11.14.12).[36] Moreover, he also quotes the ancient
poet Mimnermus, who puts Aia, the city of the Golden Fleece, not on the
Black Sea but on the ocean beyond, a location Strabo would have understood to mean the Caspian, which he considered an inlet of the Outer

---

fonti del Boiardo," *Il Boiardo e la critica contemporanea*, ed. Giuseppe Anceschi (Florence:
Leo S. Olschki, 1970), 8–9. The fact that the dragon's teeth in Jason's story come from
Cadmus's serpent is another old part of the myth and survives in a fragment of Eumelos.
Huxley, *Greek Epic Poetry*, 66.

[34] Valerius Flaccus has Phrixus dedicate the Fleece to Mars (*Argonautica* 5.228–30);
Apollodorus has Aeetes do this (*Biblioteca* 1.9.1).

[35] Allen, *Star-Names*, 79, citing Manilius's *Astronomicon*. Manilius is No. 337 in the
1495 inventory of the Este library.

[36] Boccaccio agrees with Strabo. Jason and Medea performed wonders in Asia on
their return visit (*GDG* 13.26.655).

Ocean (1.2.40).[37] Strabo speaks with authority, since he grew up on the Black Sea coast and had an ancestor who governed Colchis (11.2.18). In addition, the Ferrarese could easily have read him. Guarino of Verona translated him into Latin,[38] and the ducal library later had an Italian version.[39] Strabo argues that Westerners visited the area to tap its gold mines, as well as its silver, iron, and copper (1.2.39);[40] modern scholars like John Boardman agree. The Milesians founded Trapezus (Trebizond) and Phasis to open up trade routes into the Caucasus and the high steppe mostly because they wanted minerals.[41] Strabo explains that the Fleece itself refers to gold panning (11.2.19). The Soanes, who hold the heights of the Caucasus, collect gold from rivers swollen by winter rains. For this purpose they use either a perforated crib or a fleece.[42] Presumably, the gold dust collected on the rough surface and coated the fleece.

Western interest in this zone then had been commercial not heroic in the conventional sense. Even a large city-state, Greek or Italian, at best set up trading stations near the area, but none of them commanded the resources to conquer the inner zone, which successfully resisted or thwarted long-term penetration even by great powers like the Roman, Byzantine, and Ottoman Empires, or Safavid Iran (1501–1736). This situation may help to account for the fact that Jason in some versions of the Argonaut legend loses much of his heroism and even verges on an antihero. Ovid certainly shifts the interest away from Jason to Medea. He barely speaks of the voyage to Colchis or any adventures Jason had alone and instead be-

---

[37] Strabo cites here two passages from the *Nanno* of Mimnermus. For all three passages from this work that concern Jason, see J. M. Edmonds, ed. and trans., *Elegy and Iambus with the Anacreonta* (Cambridge, MA: Harvard University Press, 1954), vol. 1, fragments 7 and 8.

[38] In *De ordine docendi* (1459) Guarino's son Battista says his father had recently translated Strabo, Woodward, *Vittorino da Feltre*, 171. Guarino of Verona ran his Studiolo from 1429–59. Cavallo, *Boiardo's* Orlando Innamorato, 4.

[39] No. 447 in the 1495 inventory. The Este, however, lacked the Greek original as of 1470. See Giulio Bertoni, *La biblioteca Estense e la coltura Ferrarese*, 259, document 14.

[40] He also puts Aia, the city of the Golden Fleece, on the River Phasis and so close to the later Greek colony (*Geographica* 1.2.39).

[41] Boardman, *The Greeks Overseas*, 247–48, 250.

[42] Strabo also locates the Temple of Leucothea, which Phrixus founded and which had his oracle, in the Moschian country, a highland behind Phasis. No lamb is ever sacrificed there. The temple once was rich, but in Strabo's time it had been plundered (11.2.17). Boccaccio gives a more generalized reading of the Golden Fleece, equating it simply with wealth (*GDG* 13.26.656).

gins with Medea, to whom he gives a long soliloquy. Next by her magic she guarantees that Jason runs little risk in the tests, which we watch, at least momentarily, through her eyes. Back in Thessaly she again does everything, collecting the herbs for the potion that rejuvenates Aeson and arranging Pelias's death through a deliberately botched magic brew.[43] Boiardo takes over from Ovid the herb collecting, the potion, and the botched transformation when he has Morgana turn her lover Ziliante into a dragon (*OI* 2.13.4–6). Strabo describes one situation that goes even further than Ovid (*Geographica* 11.13.9–10). In Media, Medea and Jason wore the same kind of clothes so that she could occasionally substitute for Jason in public, going out with her face veiled. The Argonaut story with its obsession with gold and the potential commercialism of its setting tends to pull the hero away from heroism.

Boiardo explores this commercialism in the dialectic he develops between Morgana, who supplies raw gold, and the family of Manodante, which exploits it. Leodilla says her father has so much gold and silver that the sun and moon do not behold such wealth anywhere in the world (*OI* 1.21.49).[44] Later, Orlando and Brandimarte meet the king, enthroned above a hall, which is covered with strange figures of gold and silver, carved and set in enamel or glazed (2.11.54–55). And it is this family that provides Morgana/Medea with a suitable unheroic Jason, the beautiful and refined eighteen-year-old Ziliante the blond, who cries when Orlando leaves him behind in Morgana's kingdom.[45] His sister, however, provides the most instructive example. As Ross has shown, Leodilla both begins and ends the theme of wealth and desire.[46] The rich king's daughter has rich lovers, one of whom is named Ordauro (*aurum*, gold), cannot resist gold balls (*OI* 1.21.62–67),[47] and runs off with her first husband's

---

[43] Ovid, of course, has his own reasons for his antiheroic reading of the story. The *Metamorphoses* regularly undercuts heroic scenes and stresses instead the role of women and victims. Eumelos may have introduced Medea to the story of the Argonauts so as to create a link between Corinth and Colchis, Huxley, *Greek Epic Poetry*, 64–65. The various Homeric references to the Argonauts do not mention Medea, Huxley, *Greek Epic Poetry*, 60. Reichenbach lists Ovid as one of Boiardo's unquestioned sources. See his *"L'Orlando innamorato" di M. M. Boiardo* (Florence: "La nuova Italia," 1936), 83.

[44] Ross, "Boiardo's Fata Morgana," 21; Cavallo, *Boiardo's* Orlando Innamorato, 111 n. 21.

[45] *OI* 2.9.28–29; 2.11.48; 2.13.20–22.

[46] Ross, "Boiardo's Fata Morgana," 21, 28.

[47] Murrin, *The Allegorical Epic*, 69.

wealth.[48] She last appears like Lollia Paulina, so covered with jewels that she lights up the family feast (2.13.46).[49] Leodilla also illustrates the deeper psychological issue involved: that of concupiscence or desire. One night she stays awake, waiting for her rescuer, Orlando, to stop snoring, get up, and make love to her (1.24.14–16). She wants both a lover, preferably young and good-looking, and treasure, just as the mistress of treasure finds such a lover, albeit a reluctant one, in one of Leodilla's brothers (2.9.22).[50]

We have already seen in this sequence that Orlando, as long as Angelica or Origille are absent, cannot be tempted by offers of love. He is even more impervious to the lure of wealth. On this issue there are no exceptions. He hardly notices Morgana's stag with the golden antlers (*OI* 1.22.59). As Ranaldo complains, when Orlando criticizes him for trying to carry away a gold chair from Morgana's treasure chamber, Orlando already has a huge assured income, both from Charlemagne and the pope (2.9.34).[51] Yet, his criticism also misses the point. The members of Manodante's family also control great resources but cannot resist wanting more. Orlando, presumably with a smaller income, nevertheless has no desire to increase it. For him chivalry is enough.[52]

Orlando's own explanation for his lack of interest sets up the rationale behind Boiardo's juxtaposition of his adventures in Morgana's realm with that of the Argonauts.[53] He tells the damsel with the horn that whoever wants to acquire silver and gold wants toil without end. The more one

---

[48] *OI* 1.22.13; 1.22.19; 1.22.48.

[49] On Lollia Paulina see Ben Jonson, *Volpone* 3.7.194–96: "A diamond would have bought Lollia Paulina, / When she came in like star-light, hid with jewels / That were the spoils of provinces."

[50] Ross argues that whenever Morgana appears, love and avarice are juxtaposed, "Boiardo's Fata Morgana," 118. He accordingly reads her labyrinth as a psychological emblem of a person trapped within desires, "Boiardo's Fata Morgana," 122–23.

[51] According to Ranaldo, Orlando has so many castles and towns, and is count of Blaye and lord of Aglante or Angers. The episode of the chair both explains why Ranaldo ends up in Morgana's jail and yet exists in a moral realm beyond that assumed in Manodante's circle. It was not desire of wealth that led him to Morgana's, but a wish to avenge his fallen comrades (*OI* 2.2.19). Even the gold chair he wants for others (2.9.32). See Ross, "Boiardo's Fata Morgana," 109.

[52] This analysis should be sufficient to refute Antonio Franceschetti's argument that one knight could be substituted for another in a particular adventure. See his *"L'Orlando innamorato" e le sue componenti tematiche e strutturali* (Florence: Leo S. Olschki, 1975), 164–65.

[53] Murrin, *The Allegorical Epic*, 66–67.

acquires, the less one is content because whoever has more wants more. The traveler who follows such a road struggles but never reaches the desired goal, for such a way is infinite (*OI* 1.25.14–15).[54] Orlando thus refuses to chase the stag with the golden antlers, an interminable affair that Morgana presents as the reward for his passing Jason's tests (1.25.10–11).

Boiardo illustrates Orlando's argument twice-over in his plot. Leodilla, of course, provides a perfect example, but so does the stag with the golden antlers, which is really Morgana's symbol. It never stays in one place but flees away.[55] It searches the earth and never finds a captor (1.25.9). It is *the* emblem for the endless pursuit of wealth. It must run forever, and the pursuer will never catch it.

At the same time, endlessness is precisely the appeal many modern critics see in the *Orlando innamorato*.[56] One adventure generates another in an unending series, a quality long considered the mark of Arthurian romance, as in Dante's celebrated expression: "Arturi regis ambages pulcerrime" ("the most lovely winding paths of King Arthur"; *De vulgari eloquentia* 1.10.2).[57] Dante probably got his phrasing from Virgil and Ovid, who both use *ambages* to describe the Cretan Labyrinth.[58] Ovid's phrasing is particularly suggestive: "et lumina flexu / ducit in errorem variarum ambage viarum" ("[Daedalus] leads the eyes to error by the twisting winding of the various ways"; *Metamorphoses* 8.160–61). In other words Mor-

---

[54] Cavallo shows that Orlando here argues a Boethian position. *Boiardo's* Orlando Innamorato, 100–1.

[55] The inscription over the gate to Morgana's meadow describes the fay in just the same way (*OI* 2.8.39).

[56] To give just a few examples. In 1969 Domenico de Robertis spoke of an "opening to the infinite." See his "Esperienze di un lettore dell' *Innamorato*," *Il Boiardo e la critica*, 208. Six years later Antonio Franceschetti remarked that by the end of the poem one remembers the endlessness of its adventures, "*L'Orlando innamorato*," 161. He then went on to say Boiardo's fantasy is inexhaustible, "*L'Orlando innamorato*," 166. More recently the late Peter Marinelli claimed that the *Innamorato* resists closure and its actions have no ending; see his *Ariosto and Boiardo* (Columbia, MO: Univ. of Missouri Press, 1987), 76, 189.

[57] I cite from the text edited by Pier Vincenzo Mengaldo in the *Opere minori* (Milan and Naples: Riccardo Ricciardi, 1979), vol. 2. Marianne Shapiro translates this phrase as "the lovely digressions in the fables of King Arthur" in her "*De Vulgari eloquentia*": *Dante's Book of Exile* (Lincoln: Univ. of Nebraska Press, 1990), 57. The word *ambages*, however, means winding and twisting paths, and Jean Frappier rightly connects the phrase to the interlace technique of the Vulgate *Lancelot*. See "The Vulgate Cycle," *Arthurian Literature in the Middle Ages*, ed. Roger Sherman Loomis (Oxford: Clarendon, 1967), 318.

[58] *Aeneid* 6.29: "Daedalus ipse dolos tecti ambagesque resolvit."

gana's labyrinth in some sense mirrors the plot. Marinelli expresses this self-reflexiveness quite well, using the moral categories just discussed: "The poem projects itself at once as an extravagant comic work of immense, unquenchable, impossible desiring."[59] The desire that leads people to Morgana's has an arc similar to the desire bringing readers to the poem.

The comparison to Arthurian romance helps to clarify both Boiardo's achievement and his dilemma. Endlessness had especially characterized Grail romances, particularly Chrétien's *Perceval*, which generated so many continuations.[60] At one point in the original fragment, the romance explodes as Perceval vows to find the Grail and the Lance; Girflez, to go for a set of duels at Chastel Orguelleus; Kahedin, to Mount Dolorous; fifty other knights leave for adventures; and Gawain entangles himself in a whole series of quests (*Perceval* 4685-746).[61] At this point the *Perceval* reaches a kind of mathematical infinity. At Morgana's, Boiardo in fact uses the mystery technique of narrative, which the writers of the various Grail stories had made their defining characteristic. The hero experiences his adventures directly, often without subsequent explanation, and the reader knows little more than the hero. Orlando had a guidebook for Falerina's Garden but has nothing to help him at Morgana's but his enemy's warnings. The Grail romances, however, had a mystical rationale for their mystery technique and interlaced structure, for the Grail brought infinity to the center of the story.[62] When Boiardo, however, substituted love of a lady for love of the Grail, he secularized the mode and at the same time made it liable to undesirable parallels like the pursuit of wealth.[63] Angelica like Morgana is a *very* rich lady. So the poet had to deal with the mercantile parallel somehow. He does so through the Morgana

---

[59] Marinelli, *Ariosto and Boiardo*, 37.

[60] The 1495 inventory of the Este library includes a French Grail romance (No. 445), and, of course, the *Tavola ritonda* and the Vulgate *Lancelot* both included quests of the Grail.

[61] Gawain vows to help a maiden beseiged in Montesclaire but is diverted to Escavalon to answer Guinganbresil's challenge. There he is required to search for the Lance, but another set of adventures leave him awaiting a joust with Guiromelanz, as the fragment ends. I cite from *Le roman de Perceval ou le conte du graal*, ed. William Roach (Geneva: Droz, 1959).

[62] Gregory of Nyssa in his *Life of Moses* best expresses the theology of an endless mystical pursuit. See *From Glory to Glory: Texts from Gregory of Nyssa's Mystical Writings*, ed. and trans. Herbert Musurillo (New York: Charles Scribner's Sons, 1961), 81–82.

[63] For the connection of Angelica to the Grail, see Charles Ross's introduction to his translation of the *Orlando innamorato* (Berkeley: Univ. of California Press, 1989), 21.

sequence, in which he exorcises the ghost of a heroism devoted to gain, the story of the Golden Fleece, that epic celebration of a treasure hunt. While it might be acceptable and even desirable for a warrior to be a lover, he could not double as a merchant. He had to resist the temptation to betray his code for marvelous riches. Those susceptible to this lure found their long journey turn into a closed labyrinth, at the bottom of which yawned yet a deeper pit from which Morgana herself could not rescue them (OI 2.8.52; 2.9.24–25).[64]

Yet, the figure of the labyrinth only partially solved the poet's problem. It showed well how wrong desire could create windings and circles without end, but the Middle East offered a different kind of endlessness, one well described by Eduardo Saccone when he said that Angelica ruptures the closed, known world in the *Innamorato* and opens a vast imaginative space into which she draws Orlando, far from home.[65]

The labyrinth offers a negative view of endlessness, a pit like Dante's hell, circling downward. The positive view stresses the horizontal, the long caravan routes that went east from the Black Sea and seemed endless by European standards. They led to and through a land of wonders, mostly the Mongol world system and its successor states, best revealed by Marco Polo.[66] Such a zone now offered much besides gold—silk, gems, and spices—and could not but attract romancers, since the marvelous formed part of the conception of the genre. The *Orlando innamorato* is but the latest in a long line of such stories taking well-known heroes east.[67] Yet, most of the people who actually visited this zone did not do so as warriors. They might go as diplomats like Carpini, as missionaries like William of Rubruck, or as merchants like the Polos, who bought and sold precious

---

[64] Milton picked up the idea and has Satan worry about a worse and lower hell beneath the one in which he already suffers (*Paradise Lost* 4.76–78).

[65] Saccone, "Osservazione su alcuni luoghi dell' *Innamorato,*" *Modern Language Notes* 86 (1971): 52–53.

[66] The Este library had a Latin copy of Marco Polo, No. 62 in the 1467 inventory, No. 319 in that of 1495. Bertoni notes that Borso d'Este gave to the Countess Strozzi Marco Polo in 1457, *Biblioteca,* 56.

[67] Boiardo has his heroes follow known caravan routes to the East and back. Orlando and Astolfo follow the steppe route beyond the Don and turn southeast through Circassia, where Orlando fights the Sphinx. On the way back Orlando and Angelica follow the southern version, traveling south of Armenia through Persia, Mesopotamia, and Syria to Beirut (OI 2.19.51–52). See my *Allegorical Epic,* 76.

stones.[68] Mostly it was merchants. By the time Marco Polo returned from China, others were already going out,[69] and the Italians for some time had a trading colony in Tabriz.[70] And here was the difference. The Italians could not protect such a community by military force. There they could only act as merchants at the mercy of the local government. The merchants had found and could visit lands more wonderful than knights could ever see.

Merchants unfortunately do not belong in romances, and Boiardo never leaves in doubt the aristocratic pretensions of his poem. He himself was a minor aristocrat, who grew up in the family castle at Scandiano and served as captain for the Este both at Modena (1480–82) and at Reggio (1487–95).[71] The proems and ends of his cantos define, as Durling has shown, a closed and refined aristocratic circle.[72] The poet imagines an audience on his same social level and one that shares the same values. He surrounds Morgana, on the other hand, with unchivalric characters. He substitutes for the Minotaur the giant Aridano, who comes from bad blood and commits low-class deeds (*OI* 2.7.42). He drags a woman away by the hair and whips her incessantly (2.2.11–12, 15–16). He fights not with lance and sword but with a club (2.2.17). His bridge is designed to force his opponents to approach him on foot, since the little gate at the middle will not allow a horse to pass (2.2.14). His whole mode of operation is anti-chivalric, but he is not alone among Morgana's servants. Penitence drives Orlando to a lower-class scuffle. She whips him the way a housewife would chase dogs out of her kitchen (2.9.9). Orlando in turn tries to punch and kick her (2.9.10–12).

The poet works out the issue still more elaborately in the running contrast he makes between Orlando and the members of Manodante's family, who have genuine social pretensions but lack a proper code of conduct. The one hero of the family illustrates the difference, as he moves away

---

[68] Frederic C. Lane, *Venice: A Maritime Republic* (Baltimore: Johns Hopkins Univ. Press, 1973), 81.

[69] Lane, *Venice*, 81, 129.

[70] Luciano Petech, "Les marchands italiens dans l'époque mongole," *Journal asiatique* 250 (1962): 560–62, 565, 568–70.

[71] Giulio Reichenbach, "Matteo Maria Boiardo," in *La letteratura italiana: i minori* (Milan: Carlo Mazzorati, 1961), vol. 1, 668–70.

[72] Robert M. Durling, *The Figure of the Poet in Renaissance Epic* (Cambridge, MA: Harvard Univ. Press, 1965), 92–93, 98–103, 107–10. Marinelli argues, however, that the proems to Book 1 are mostly popular but agrees that those to Book 2 are courtly, *Ariosto and Boiardo*, 17–19.

from the values involved in his birth name, Bramadoro (2.13.36–37), to those of his new name, Brandimarte. He starts as a hero prone to the vices of a family he does not know he has but tries to follow Orlando and learn the high chivalric code. Like his sister Leodilla he suffers from concupiscence. The orphan cannot resist chasing the stag with the golden antlers (1.22.59–61) and is later seduced and jailed by Morgana (2.8.36). Rescued by Orlando, he in turn frees his rescuer, appropriately at a border castle controlled by his family (2.11). He next converts to Christianity under Orlando's tutelage (2.12.13) and substitutes for him in the family jail. After the family reunion he leaves the Isole lontane once more to follow Orlando (2.13.52–53). He and his siblings illustrate an important point in the *Innamorato*. High position and wealth do not necessarily make one a proper aristocrat, at least not by the chivalric standards that originated in northern France and were transmitted through the romances, themselves a French invention. That code had no place for trade and commerce; neither does Orlando, its major exponent.

In cultural terms one could argue that Orlando represents in an idealized and sometimes comic form the values maintained at the Este court. Older literary historians regularly stressed the medievalism of Ferrara. Antonia Benvenuti lists some of the most prominent ones: De Sanctis, Panizzi, Carducci, Weise.[73] I would add to her list Symonds among the English. The poet himself through his compliments to family connections of the Este includes in his charmed circle the Gonzaga of Mantua and the House of Aragon in Naples.[74] But what of the other side of the dialectic? What of rich Manodante and his links to the Treasure Fairy? Why is Boiardo obsessed with these mercantile issues and what relevance do they have to the Italian scene?

A look at Manodante's capital city helps to answer these questions. Damosyr or Damogir has some peculiar characteristics. While it has a suitably Persian-sounding name and a sea that in its physical dimensions resembles the Caspian,[75] it is still an invented place in a way that Albraca

---

[73] Antonia Benvenuti, "Tradizioni letterarie e gusto tardogotico nel canzoniere di M. M. Boiardo," *Giornale storico della letteratura italiana* 137 (1960): 535–37. De Sanctis considered Boiardo's poetry anachronistic in the fifteenth century, another way of calling it medieval.

[74] Brandimarte provides the link, since he sees the Este story on the loggia of the serpent-fay (OI 2.25.42–49), and the marriage tent celebrates the House of Aragon (2.27.52–60).

[75] Murrin, *The Allegorical Epic*, 76, n. 68. Boiardo also says that Damosyr is in the ocean (OI 2.11.46), a location that makes sense if he followed Strabo and regarded the Caspian as a gulf of the outer ocean. See the map that Horace Leonard Jones, editor and

or Falerina's Garden is not. Behind Albraca is a real place, the city of Bukhara, and behind Falerina's Garden are all those gardens with rich pavilions built by Muslims and Mongols, so different from Italian palaces.[76] The Caspian unfortunately never had a rich city on its shores and does not have many islands. The ones it has could never support a city like Damosyr.[77] So what could the poet be thinking of?

He imagines a rich city built amidst islands at the north end of a partially enclosed sea or gulf. It controls at least one military outpost far to the south, where Balisardo traps Ranaldo and other knights, a fort conveniently close to Morgana's mine (*OI* 2.2.32). All this fits reasonably well Ferrara's overbearing neighbor to the north, with the Caspian doubling for the Adriatic and with its system of fortified outposts designed to secure trade routes and tap sources of wealth. The Venetians would have appreciated the location of Manodante's fort so close to a gold mine.

I am not interested here in an allegorical reading of Damosyr as Venice, since Boiardo's analysis could apply as well to Genoa, the other commercial republic with colonies in the east.[78] Rather, I wish to argue that in Damosyr and Morgana's kingdom, taken together, Boiardo attacked a system alien to his own. He exorcised, however, a very dangerous ghost.

It was cities like Venice with wealth based on Levantine trade and citizens like Marco Polo that made the Middle East so dazzling. Now a romancer needed marvels; they came with the genre. The poet could hardly ignore, therefore, the zone of greatest wonder, yet at the same time he had to fit the East into a chivalric perspective and reject its mercantile allure, even as he gloried in its palaces, gardens, mines, and treasure.

One wonders, however, how successful Boiardo's exorcism was. Did he solve his problem or only mask it? Who were the true heroes? The courtiers he addresses or merchants like the Polos or Giovanni Loredan, equal to the Polos perhaps in courage but not in fortune? Having already visited

---

translator, includes in vol. 1 of *The Geography of Strabo* (Cambridge, MA: Harvard Univ. Press, 1969), or the map of Charles Ross, reproduced in the Oxford edition of his translation of the *Orlando innamorato*, xxxvi–vii.

[76] Murrin, *The Allegorical Epic*, 75, 77–78.

[77] Astrakhan above the Volga delta did become a major transit center a century later, but even then it was more a trading post than a great city.

[78] It is interesting, however, that even Franceschetti, who rejects any allegorical interpretation of the *Innamorato*, makes an exception for the Morgana sequence, "*L'Orlando innamorato*," 168. His own stance has not convinced subsequent critics at least on this continent. Ross, Cavallo, and I all assume there is much allegory in the *Innamorato*, and Marinelli claims that Boiardo brought allegory into Carolingian romance, *Ariosto and Boiardo*, 30, 45.

China, Giovanni set out in 1338 to open up a way to India, following the northern caravan route and then going south at the Pamirs and across the Hindu Kush. In India his party pleased a cruel prince, and they bought pearls. He died, however, near Ghazna on the way out, and others in the party also died before they reached home. Loredan's father-in-law insisted that his young sons pay him not only his loan but also his share in the profits.[79] A moral tale warning against greed or a story of great, if unrewarded, heroism?

[79] Petech, "Les marchands italiens," 559; Lane, *Venice*, 139. This was in 1338.

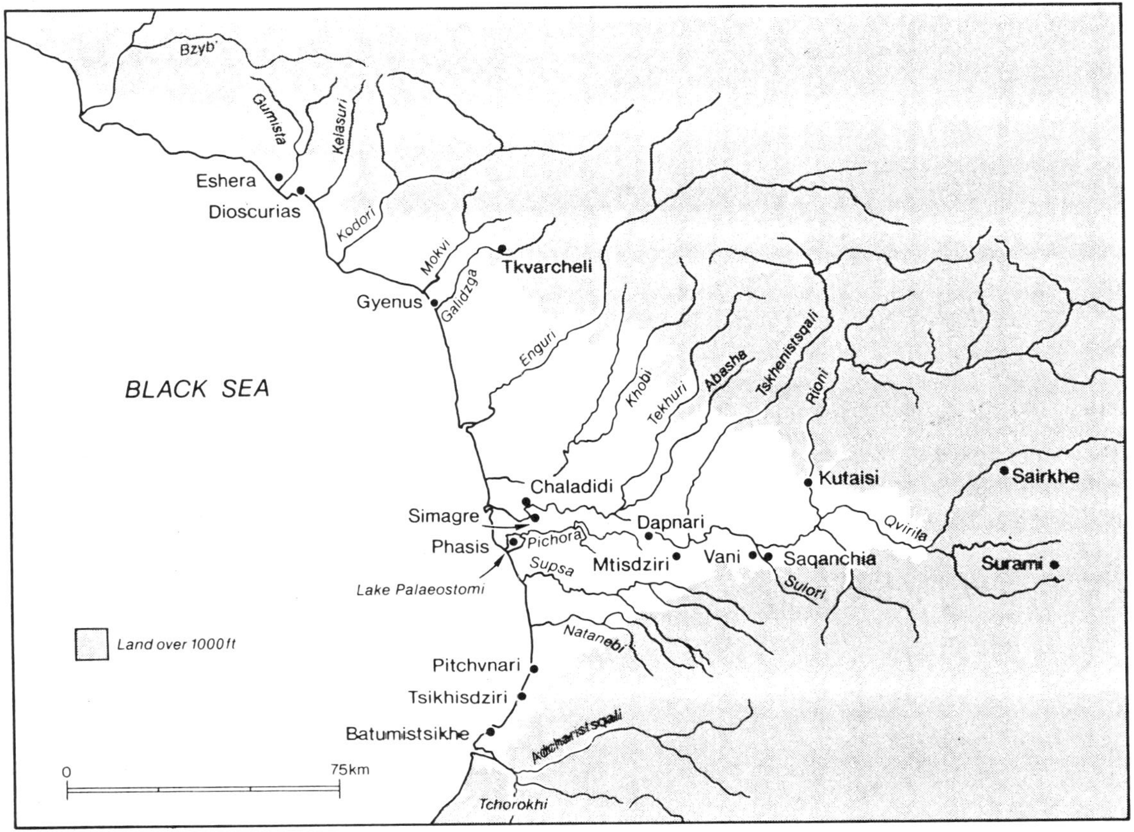

Colchis in the Greek period.

JO ANN CAVALLO

Denying Closure: Ariosto's Rewriting of the *Orlando Innamorato*

CRITICS HAVE POINTED OUT BOTH Ariosto's close attention to detail as he picks up the threads of Boiardo's poem and the importance of the *Innamorato*'s third book for much of the material of the *Furioso*. Peter Brand, for example, speaks of the "extraordinary thoroughness with which [Ariosto] continues the intricate web of Boiardo's action," and Neil Harris rightly says that it would be hard to even imagine what the *Furioso* would be like without the existence of Book 3 of the *Innamorato*.[1] It is, after all, in this third book that Ariosto finds the quest of Mandricardo for Orlando's sword, the enamorment of Bradamante and Rugiero, the battle between Orrilo and the brothers Aquilante and Grifone, and the desire of Fiordespina for Bradamante—all episodes that begged completion. Ariosto even chose to retell the story of Lucina and the Orco, an episode that did not need completing since Boiardo had stated that Turpin had spoken no more about it. And yet, despite all of Ariosto's attention to picking up the

---

[1] Brand states further: "Rarely is there any conflict between the two narratives: everyone is in his right place, going about his appointed business, and no one is forgotten. It seems remarkable that Ariosto should have picked up so many obscure clues and hints. Clearly he took the continuation of the *Innamorato* very seriously." "Ariosto's Continuation of the *Orlando Innamorato*," *Cultural Aspects of the Italian Renaissance: Essays in Honor of Paul Oskar Kristeller*, ed. Cecil H. Clough (New York: Manchester Univ. Press, 1976), 384. Harris says: "non possiamo minimamente immaginarci cosa sarebbe successo se l'Ariosto avesse dovuto riallacciare il *Furioso* al secondo libro boiardesco," "L'avventura editoriale dell'*Orlando innamorato*," *I libri di* Orlando innamorato (Modena: Panini, 1987), 59.

threads of Boiardo's narrative in general and of Book 3 in particular, two major events of Book 3, the Laughing Stream episode and the Battle of Paris, are strangely ignored. These two episodes, moreover, are not insignificant threads of the earlier poem that could be easily disregarded, but are two of the five principal subjects listed in the epigraph preceding the *Innamorato*'s third book.[2]

Giovanni Ponte and Peter Marinelli have noted that Ariosto does not continue exactly the events of Book 3, citing in particular Ariosto's disregard for the *Innamorato*'s Battle of Paris, but they attribute this to aesthetic reasons. Ponte speaks of Ariosto's superior skill, his "well-reasoned detachment," and finds the Battle of Paris in Book 3 to be a "small matter, because it is so little developed."[3] Peter Marinelli likewise speaks of Ariosto's sense of mastery as well as the "fragmentary" nature of the third book in which Boiardo "had, rather dilatorily, begun to describe the ensuing siege of Paris."[4] They both assume a lack of attention on the part of Ariosto due to a lack of artistry on the part of Boiardo.

The first thing that I would like to clarify is that the Battle of Paris episode was much more developed than a myriad of other threads that Ariosto did choose to pick up. It had become the focal point of the epic action in the closing cantos, and, as C.E.J. Griffiths has noted, it showed "a greater sense of the drama of the conflict than earlier battles scenes."[5] Second, Ariosto's attitude toward these two episodes can hardly be considered inattentive, since he imitates them in the course of his poem. The Laughing Stream, the first trap created by Atalante's magic to remove Rugiero from danger after his departure from the mountain of Carena, provides a model for the *Furioso*'s *castello d'acciaio*, garden of Alcina, and *palazzo incantato*. The Battle of Paris, the culmination of the Asian and

---

[2] The five subjects of Book 3 are listed as: 1) the deeds of Mandricardo; 2) the liberation of Orlando and others (i.e., from the Laughing Stream); 3) the genealogy of Rugiero; 4) the siege of Paris; 5) the vain love of Fiordespina. Giuseppe Anceschi notes that this summary is present in the first extant edition that included Book 3 (printed in Venice, 1506). *Orlando Innamorato* (Milan: Garzanti, 1978), vol. 2, 1093. See also Harris, *Bibliografia dell'Orlando innamorato* (Modena: Panini, 1988–89), vol. 1, 34.

[3] Although Ponte does at one point say that the third book reveals a greater artistic level ("miglior livello artistico") than the first two, he is discussing style rather than the unfolding of events. *La personalità e l'opera del Boiardo* (Genova: Tilgher, 1972), 101–2.

[4] Marinelli, "Shaping the Ore: Image and Design in Canto 1 of *Orlando Furioso*," *Modern Langauge Notes* 103 (1988): 33.

[5] Griffiths, "*Orlando Innamorato*, Book III: An Appreciation," *Italian Studies* 36 (1981): 30.

African invasion of France, is later replayed in the *Furioso* for some twenty-six cantos. As I intend to show below, Ariosto undertook an ingeniously elaborate and almost obsessively systematic strategy of suppression of these two episodes. The reason that Ariosto deliberately slips these two events under the rug is, in my view, that they posed a threat to his continuation on narrative, thematic, and structural grounds. By focusing on this case of supposed *non*-continuity, I hope to redirect the general perception of the relation between the two poems.[6]

Something that the Laughing Stream episode and the Battle of Paris have in common is the presence of Orlando and the absence of Angelica. This essay therefore takes as its starting point the movement of these two characters from Boiardo's to Ariosto's poem, and then goes on to explore the larger context of Ariosto's strategies of suppression and its implications for the fortune of Boiardo's poem as a whole.

Exit Orlando and Angelica, *Orlando Innamorato*

Orlando's journey back toward France with Angelica in the second book of the *Innamorato* is a moment of great irony. He is finally returning to Christendom—not as Charlemagne's paladin, but rather as Angelica's escort. The reader, but not Orlando, is aware of Angelica's motivation: she expects to find in France her own object of desire, Ranaldo. Underscoring the ridiculousness of the situation, all of Orlando's actions from Albraca to France just serve to further humiliate and degrade this former Carolingian warrior. While "Commotion grips the Christian lands" (2.17.3) and "They all beleaguer Charlemagne / With fury, from each part of earth" (2.17.4), Orlando is depicted sneaking out of Albraca by night with Angelica, Brandimarte, and Fiordelisa to avoid battle. When the enemy troops catch up with them the following day, Orlando finds "his mind greatly disconcerted" (2.18.19) and allows Brandimarte to defend

---

[6] It may very well be that Ariosto's "erasure" of these episodes is what led retrospectively to a general dismissal of the third book on the part of subsequent readers. Griffiths, in fact, notes his surprise to find what he dubs "a conspiracy of silence" among critics with respect to Book 3: "It was difficult to find references of any kind to Book III and where they did occur they were often disparaging and seldom appeared to be used in any significant measure to illustrate general statements about the poet or his art," "*Orlando Innamorato*, Book III," 27. Marco Praloran has more recently studied the Battle of Montealbano at the end of Book 2, but not in connection with Ariosto, "La battaglia di Montealbano nell'*Orlando innamorato*: analisi di alcune tipologie del discorso epico," *Schifanoia* 3 (1987): 29–43.

them all single-handedly while he goes on ahead with—or rather, be-tween—the two ladies as though they were offering protection to him. Then, when Orlando and the ladies chance upon a group of Laestrygo-nians at mealtime, the paladin forgets all else and runs on in mad haste, leaving the ladies to follow behind: "When he sees this, he spurs his horse / With all his force to join the group" (2.18.35). If he had read and re-membered his Homer, Orlando would have perhaps been more cautious; instead, not only does he fail to see any danger, but he does not pay atten-tion when he overhears their intentions to eat him. A Laestrygonian knocks him out with just one blow on the head, and they remove his armor and poke his entire body looking in vain for a tasty morsel ("un buon boccone") before he regains consciousness. Since the ladies were still on horseback when Orlando was struck down at the table, they are able to turn and flee. This is the exact opposite of the situation in the *Odyssey* in which, upon reaching a harbor, the leader Odysseus escapes because he had chosen the exposed position of the flagship out of a sense of responsi-bility, whereas the rest of the fleet, anchored in the supposedly safe basin, becomes easy prey for the Laestrygonians. In Boiardo's text, Orlando's sword does eventually prove too much for the club-bearing man-eaters. He cuts them all into literally bite-size pieces (no piece of their bodies is left larger than a nose[7]), and then he actually sits down at their table in order to enjoy a meal. Only after all the cooked heads, arms, and feet on the table in front of him make him lose his appetite does he remember the ladies. He manages to find and rescue Angelica while Brandimarte in the meantime defeats the warriors from Albraca and then saves Fiordelisa. Thus reunited, they once more head off to France, but one stanza later they encounter a ship already weighed down with cargo on its way to a joust in Cyprus, and they decide to join in. During the tournament, Or-lando flees in fear when he hears the false news that Gano is plotting against him and that he is about to be captured. Upon arriving in France, he fights against his cousin Ranaldo over the possession of Angelica, and only suspends the fight when Charlemagne offers her as prize to whichever of the two is most successful against the Saracens.

Even though this competition formally places Orlando once again within the ranks of the French army, his misplaced motivation prevents him from giving his best for the Christian cause. As if to highlight Or-

---

[7] "Che non si trova né pezzo né fetta / De alcun, che morto al campo sia rimaso, / Qual sia maggior che prima fosse il naso." (2.18.49)

lando's moral deficiency, Boiardo ascribes to him defective thinking. When Orlando finds that Agramante's troops have arrived from Africa, he joyously thanks God for sending Agramante to destroy France. He thinks God has acted as his go-between, setting up a total Christian defeat so that he can enter at the last moment and by his prowess win the girl:

> Happy at that, the baron bold
> Lifted his joyous face to heaven,
> Saying, "O God on high, you send
> Swift help and aid where there is need!
> Because (if I am not deceived)
> King Charles will lose, Ranaldo too,
> And when each peer has met defeat,
> I'll be invited to the rescue!
> "I will regain—by valiant deeds—
> The love of one I love so much." (2.29.37–38)

It gets worse. While the Christians and the Saracens "played back and forth along the field, / Now on the run, now in pursuit" (2.30.50), Orlando is hiding in the woods and actually praying for a Christian defeat: "And [he] prayed to God devoutly that / That holy flags and *fleurs-de-lys* / Of King Charles's troops would meet defeat" (2.30.61). The devoutness of his attitude contrasts with the sacrilegious nature of his prayer. This shockingly shameful behavior makes it clear to the reader that Orlando will not be able to defeat the Saracens (and destroy Biserta as foretold) while still under the spell of a Saracen princess. When Feraguto recognizes Orlando by his traditional inisignia ("He saw at once a quartered blazon"; 2.31.7), the reader grasps the incongruence between Orlando's outer appearance and his inner state.[8] Feraguto's chastizing of Orlando's inactivity sends him back to the field of battle where, thanks to Atalante's magic, a false vision of Charlemagne's army in retreat leads him to the enchanted waters of the Laughing Stream.

At the Laughing Stream, Orlando is liberated by his friends, Brandimarte and Fiordelisa, with the help of Rugiero and Gradasso. This episode, set in between the Battle of Montealbano and the Battle of Paris, represents a turning point for Orlando. The enamoured knight had previously

---

[8] Sobrino recognized Orlando by his quartered shield as well, alerting the reader to the fact that Orlando has just recently returned to wearing his traditional identifying insignia (2.29.42).

emerged from adventures, traps, or enchantments only to fall back under Angelica's spell—the pattern occurs repeatedly in the episodes of the Sphinx, the Cyclops' cave, Dragontina's palace, Morgana's underwater realm, and Manodante's Islands Far Away. Indeed, in the latter two cases Boiardo draws attention to this pattern with added insistence, deliberately contrasting Orlando's eros-driven decision to head east to seek out Angelica with the duty-motivated behavior of the loyal paladins who head west toward France (see 2.9.46–47 and 2.13.51). It is only after emerging from the Laughing Stream that Orlando, as if waking up from a dream, deliberately sets out to help Charlemagne and has no thought of the enchanting Saracen princess.

Orlando's liberation from the Laughing Stream and return to Paris is also set up as a turning point in the epic battle between Christians and Saracens. While Orlando is trapped in the fountain, the Christians are headed toward a calamitous defeat. The Christians have been pushed back from Montealbano to Paris, and countless knights and kings have been either killed or captured by King Marsilio (3.4.48). The fate of the Christians is undoubtedly at its lowest point as Orlando, freed from the fountain, approaches Paris only to find the city in a river of blood (3.7.55). While still on the slopes outside the city, Orlando follows the lead of Brandimarte and together they begin to turn the tide. They first send King Marsilio fleeing, and then proceed to liberate their fellow Christians and to appropriate an abundance of weaponry from nearby tents (3.8.21–22). This band of one hundred knights enters Paris. Griffiths notes how desperation slowly gives way to determination and unity of purpose in the people of Paris, even in the women and children.[9] Not coincidently, Orlando is once again recognized by his insignia, and now Charlemagne, in pointed contrast to the earlier chastizing speech by Feraguto, openly rejoices with "every man" over the return of this prodigal son and the renewed hopes for victory:

> When those in town behold his quartered
> Shield, a cry rises from the wall.
> And Charlemagne is given word
> Of the Count's presence on the plain
> And the deliverance of the Christians,
> In hand-to-hand fight, from the pagans.

---

[9] Griffiths, "*Orlando Innamorato*, Book III," 30.

> Don't ask me if the emperor
> Rejoices when he hears the news.
> Every man has a sparkling heart
> And wants to sally out to war. (3.8.42)

Orlando's quartered shield was suggestive of the Christian cross, and the colors red and white were said to symbolize charity and chastity. Given that Orlando, after falling for Angelica's charms, left Paris in the disguise of dark vermilion, fought in Albraca under the crest of a winged Cupid and then of a tree, and later used the insignia of a volcano in Cyprus (2.20.49), this is the first moment in the poem since the opening canto of Book 1 in which Orlando is a Christian paladin in both spirit and appearance.

As the strongest knight of Christendom, Orlando appears destined for a final match-up against the strongest of the pagans, Rodamonte. This African warrior, whose literary precedents are principally Turnus (for his rage) and Mezentius (as despiser of the gods), is given genealogical roots in Nimrod (also cited for his ambition and *superbia*). Before the two knights ever meet in battle, Rodamonte makes the Christian victory conditional upon the presence of Orlando, thus paving the way for an epic encounter between the two of them (2.15.30). They first come face to face in Montealbano, where their "frightful duel" was announced at the close of a canto (2.24.66). The following canto opened with the two cavaliers "Who'll wreck this world and then the next" (2.25.1) moving toward each other. Their confrontation is described in epic, even cosmic proportions: "When their swords met, it seemed the sky / Opened, and thunderbolts collided" (2.25.6). The battle is temporarily interrupted when Orlando is knocked unconscious and Bradamante steps in to challenge Rodamonte for having earlier unchivalrously killed her horse (2.7.10). When Orlando regains consciousness (2.29.27), he must wait his turn before approaching Rodamonte. It is, tellingly, not until after Orlando's recovery from the Laughing Stream's spell and his entrance into Paris that the two heroes meet up once again and resume their battle. Boiardo first describes Rodamonte's raging fury (3.8.25–30), and then narrates how Orlando prevents him from entering Paris by landing him in a moat (3.8.31). Yet, Orlando temporarily loses consciousness after being struck by the spire of half a tower (3.8.31), and the battle is again suspended. Soon after, however, as Orlando is chasing pagans with Brandimarte (3.8.49), we find that Rodamonte has been following Orlando. The two knights become locked together in a chiastic verse at the point in which they resume their battle:

"Rodamonte solo e solo Orlando" (3.8.50).[10] It is at this precise moment that Boiardo decides to switch topics. He tells the reader that either because of the people praying in Paris or some other hidden fate, a fierce storm, an earthquake, and the setting sun put an end to the fighting for that day. Boiardo perhaps meant to recall the model of the *Aeneid,* in which, just when Aeneas and Turnus meet at the end of Book 11, night falls and postpones their combat. In any event, with the entire eighth canto dedicated to the martial activity in Paris, one can well imagine that Boiardo wanted to shift the narrative from "armi" to "amore" before going on to depict the epic struggle of the two knights. Indeed, the next canto opens with the romance adventure of Bradamante and Fiordespina. The poem is interrupted definitively in 3.9.26, before the full consequences of Orlando's new self can be played out.

Angelica, in the meantime, has been entirely absent from Book 3. She was last seen early in 2.21.21 when Charlemagne placed her under the care of Duke Namo pending the outcome of the competition between Orlando and Ranaldo, and she was last alluded to (albeit indirectly) in 2.30.61 when Orlando is hiding in the woods and praying for a Christian defeat.

Enter Angelica and Orlando, *Orlando Furioso*

Peter Brand has noted that the opening stanzas of the *Orlando Furioso* explicitly announce Ariosto's intention to continue and complete Boiardo's poem by naming the same subjects and in the same order as Boiardo did in his proem to Book 3: 1) Agramante; 2) Orlando; 3) Ruggiero.[11] Ariosto then leaves aside Agramante and Ruggiero in order to zero in on Orlando. Yet, rather than pick up with Orlando's epic battle against Rodamante in Paris, he recalls instead the return of "Orlando [...] innamorato" to France in the company of Angelica in Book 2 (1.5–7). In his commentary to the *Furioso,* Simone Fornari noted that Ariosto thereby inscribes the title of Boiardo's poem into his opening verses.[12] I would

---

[10] Griffiths notes that in the Battle of Paris, Boiardo's attention is focused very much on the exploits and reactions of individuals, of Charlemagne, Orlando, and Rodamonte in particular. "*Orlando Innamorato,* Book III," 29.

[11] Peter Brand, *Ludovico Ariosto: A Preface to the* Orlando Furioso (Edinburgh, Great Britain: Edinburgh Univ. Press, 1974), 53. See *OI* 3.1.3 and *OF* 1.1, 1.2, and 1.4. For easy reference, all citations of the *Furioso* follow the canto and stanza numbers of the 1532 edition. I cite from the Italian edition by Marcello Turchi (Milano: Garzanti, 1974) and from the English translation by Guido Waldman (Oxford: Oxford Univ. Press, 1974).

[12] Fornari notes: "la diligentia del poeta quando in questo primo verso lo cita

point out as well Ariosto's choice to focus on an event that predates the Laughing Stream and Battle of Paris episodes and represents a particularly low point in Boiardo's ongoing degradation of Orlando's character.

Ariosto alludes to Orlando's prior action in Boiardo's poem by referring to him as he who: "per lei [Angelica] / in India, in Media, in Tartaria lasciato / avea infiniti ed immortal trofei" ("had for her sake left countless immortal trophies in India, in Media, in Tartary"; 1.5). Rather than re-calling the names familiar to readers such as Albraca or Orcagna, Ariosto has listed three vast territories: India, Media, and Tartary. Although the repetition of the preposition "in" gives the sense of a concrete list, the places named only create a sense of vagueness. Moreover, the use of the superlative *infiniti* (countless) in the following verse makes the claim for a great number of Orlando's love deeds without actually naming any of them. Fornari defines *trofei* as "certe imprese gloriose, che poneva in alto colui, che vinto havesse il nemico," but he must not find any examples in the *Innamorato* since he illustrates the term with an event taken from the *Furioso*.[13] Most critics and commentators from the sixteenth century on seem perfectly content to repeat the vagueness of the original verses, sup-plying synonyms for the vast territories and the superlatives rather than at-tempting to locate the references. Mario Santoro, for example, refers to Orlando's "numerous and grandiose undertakings ("numerose e grandiose imprese") done for love of Angelica in the most diverse parts of the world ("nelle terre più diverse del mondo")."[14]

Antonio Franceschetti does attempt to locate the "infiniti trofei" to which Ariosto alludes: "[A]nd they would be the heroic actions around Albraca, the destruction of Falerina's garden, the liberation of Morgana's prisoners, and so on."[15] He thus ends the sentence implying the exis-tence of other episodes that apparently do not come to mind as readily. To my knowledge, no additional episodes could fit this description. Moreover, already the final example, that of the liberation of prisoners from Mor-gana's realm, turns out not to be a deed done out of love. On the con-

---

dicendo 'Orlando inamorato'," *Spositione . . . sopra l'Orlando Furioso* (Florence: 1549; vol-ume 2, 1550), vol. 2, 80.

[13] Fornari, *Spositione*, 80.

[14] Santoro, "Il Proemio del Furioso," *Ariosto e il Rinascimento* (Naples: Liguori, 1989), 33–38.

[15] Franceschetti, "Appunti sull'Ariosto lettore dell'*Innamorato*," *Atti del convegno internazionale dei Lincei per Ludovico Ariosto* (Rome: Accademia Nazionale dei Lincei, 1975), 107.

trary, Orlando had specifically renounced his "vano amore" for Angelica before undertaking the episode, and he is motivated instead by his love for Ranaldo and his sense of duty and justice. Indeed, it is because he has renounced his love as "amor vano" that he is successful in the adventure.[16] That would leave the episodes of Albraca and Orcagna. But Orlando's adventure in the garden in Orcagna, although initially undertaken out of love of Angelica, actually begins only after Orlando has forgotten Angelica in his all-consuming desire for Origille, and then learned that controlling his passion was a requisite for success in the adventure. The infinite and immortal trophies come down to the extended episode of Albraca.[17] There, however, Orlando's most memorable deed was his victory over Agricane, which cannot be seen strictly in terms of a "trophy" won for Angelica since she is immediately forgotten and replaced by God once the knights realize that Agricane's wound is fatal. Some of Orlando's other actions at Albraca are hardly commendable: he defends the treacherous Truffaldino, he aims to kill his cousin Ranaldo, he loses his sword and horn to the trickster Brunello, and he fails to achieve sexual arousal when Angelica bathes him.[18]

Ariosto then speaks of Angelica as: "Quella che dagli esperi ai liti eoi / [Orlando] avea difesa con sì lunga guerra" ("the damsel, whom he had defended so constantly all the way from the Hesperides to the shores of Sunrise"; 1.7). The spatial markers *esperi* and *eoi* take even further this process of amorphization of Boiardo's text. From the sixteenth century to the present, commentaries do not go beyond providing a definition of the terms.[19] Ariosto will use the same strategy later on in the first canto when he says that "Orlando la [i.e., Angelica] guardò *sovente* / *da morte, da disnor, da casi rei*" ("Orlando had frequently saved her from death and outrage and all manner of evils"; 1.55). While the repetition of the preposition *da* (as earlier with "*in* India, *in* Media, *in* Tartaria") suggests the

---

[16] For more on this, see my *Boiardo's* Orlando Innamorato: *An Ethics of Desire* (Rutherford, NJ: Fairleigh Dickinson Univ. Press, 1993), 96–113.

[17] In fact, Ariosto does use the term India when referring to Albraca in 3.69 and 8.62.

[18] Boiardo's tongue-in-cheek praise of Orlando was belied by the narrative itself in which love led him from one disaster to another. Indeed, being in love increased the number of Orlando's *tests*, but certainly not of his accomplishments ("Né tante *prove* più mai fece Orlando, / Quante nel tempo che de amor se accese"; 2.4.3). Ariosto pretends to ignore Boiardo's irony and take the narrator's praise seriously.

[19] For example, one simply reads "Da l'Occidente à l'Oriente" in the text edited by Clemente Valvassori (Venice: Giovanni Andrea Valvassori, 1553).

tangibility of a list, the nouns could not be more vague. Ariosto thereby opens the poem by creating the illusion that the *Innamorato* consisted of a long series of adventures in which Orlando gained glory through his love for Angelica. At the same time, he refrains from providing a minimum of detail that would allow the reader to recall any of the episodes of the previous poem beyond Orlando's return to France with Angelica.[20] The competition between Orlando and Rinaldo over Angelica will then provide the starting point for a more detailed summary.

In formal terms, a more general summary in stanzas 5–7 is followed by a more specific summary in stanzas 8–10. In each set of three stanzas, the end of the stanza does not correspond to the end of the sentence, thus propelling the reader forward without a pause.[21] A reader who did stop to compare Ariosto's summary to the action of the *Innamorato* would find that Ariosto has mixed old and new material. While the Battle of Monte-albano took place in the *Innamorato*, Angelica's flight from Duke Namo's tent to the woods did not (1.9–10). By weaving the new material into the fast-paced summary, however, Ariosto gives the impression that Angelica's escape had already taken place.

Ariosto, in fact, chose to depict Angelica in a way that could have sounded familiar to his readers. In Book 4, Canto 9, of Agostini's 1505 continuation, Angelica appears as she flees from Namo's tent into the woods, where she encounters a knight. The knight is Ferraù, who stops fishing for his helmet and tries to rape her, and is then hindered by Gri-

---

[20] Michael Sherberg comes to a similar conclusion with regard to Ariosto's treatment of the character Rinaldo, remarking that Ariosto "seems to want to keep his readers on the defensive, so that they will not feel confident enough about their own knowledge of the two texts to question his own motives or methods," *Rinaldo: Character and Intertext in Ariosto and Tasso*, Stanford French and Italian Studies 75 (Saratoga, CA: Anma Libri, 1993), 21.

[21] The unwarranted period at the end of stanza 9 may have been added by an editor since Ariosto regularly neglected punctuation. The point is that the sentence clearly spans the two octaves. Although characteristically in the *Furioso* the end of the stanza coincides with the end of a sentence, stanzas 5–7 and 8–10 of the *Furioso* are stylistically set up to be read without pause. Enrico Carrara has noted this hurriedness: "Il poeta ha fretta di iniziare il suo racconto [...] e la fretta del poeta si esprime mediante quel traboccare del periodo sintattico oltre i confini dei periodi ritmici delle stanze; quasi il poeta non avesse tempo di concedersi la pausa che suole porsi al termine di ciascuna di queste. Non credo che nel poema ci sia un séguito così coerente di stanze ove non finisca anche il periodo, come in questo principio," "Dall'*Innamorato* al *Furioso* (Niccolò degli Agostini)," *Studi petrarcheschi e altri scritti* (Turin: Bottega d'Erasmo, 1959), 283.

fone, Aquilante, and Malagise.[22] This scene, however, is no more than an expedient means of removing Angelica not only from Namo's tent but from the poem itself. She is quickly submerged in an enchanted underwater realm early in the following canto and left there for the rest of Book 4.[23]

While Agostini seemed eager to rid his narrative of Angelica, Ariosto not only backtracks to the last time Angelica is seen in the *Innamorato* in order to mark the starting point of his continuation, but he then proceeds to reinvent the past so as to make her the focal point of the opening canto. Other characters are subsequently introduced as parts of her story. Sacripante, left by Boiardo as a victim of enchantment in the Laughing Stream, appears inexplicably to resume his courtship of Angelica. Ranaldo, who in the *Innamorato* was about to find an "alta ventura" of an apparently Breton type, is also used in the reintegration of Angelica into the story. Ferraù's sudden appearance increases the number of Angelica's suitors to three and also brings the reader back to the opening of the *Innamorato* in which Boiardo had depicted three rivals wandering through the forest in search of her: "Or son tre gran campioni alla ventura" ("Now three great barons seek adventure"; 1.2.29). Moreover, two of the three *cavalieri erranti* are the very same as in the opening cantos of the *Innamorato*. The third, Sacripante, has replaced Orlando.

Before the reader has a chance to realize it, what began as a fast-paced summary has become the rewriting of the poem from Angelica's perspective. As Angelica flees the site of the battle into the woods, Ariosto likewise aims to transport the reader's mind away from the epic war of the final cantos of the *Innamorato* and to replay the romance events of the poem's opening.[24] Indeed, romance adventure rather than epic battle will

---

[22] Agostini's fourth book was first regularly printed bound together with Boiardo's three books. See Harris, *Bibliografia*, vol. 1.

[23] She resurfaces in Agostini's subsequent continuation of several years later.

[24] Sangirardi, considering the *Furioso*'s opening canto as a case of "iperboiardismo," notes the stylistic similarity of the two poem's opening cantos: "La concertazione del primo canto dell'*Innamorato* si segnala infatti, come quella del primo del *Furioso*, sia per il ritmo concitato dell'azione e la rapidità dei cambiamenti di scena, sia per un effetto comico di 'cumulo' che produce la somiglianza tra i singoli episodi, che sono quasi tutti episodi di scacco e frustrazione," *Boiardismo ariostesco: presenza e trattamento dell'*Orlando Innamorato *nel* Furioso (Lucca: Pacini Fazzi, 1993), 42. Angelica falling asleep on the grass, the appearance of the ghost of Argalia, the duel between Rinaldo and Ferraù, as well as the proposal to suspend it in order to follow the fleeing damsel all bring the reader back to the beginning of the *Innamorato*. Brand also notes that the *Furioso* returns to the beginning of the *Innamorato*, although he sees a different motivation: "The effect, then, of Ariosto's opening canto for his contemporary readers must have been to recall

take up the narrative space for most of the first thirteen cantos.

Although Ariosto repeatedly evokes Orlando's love of Angelica in the opening stanzas of Canto 1, he does not actually introduce the character into the narrative until well into the eighth canto. When Orlando does appear, it is also by way of Angelica. His name is first mentioned in Canto 8 in connection with the dramatic situation of a naked Angelica tied to a naked rock ("nudo scoglio"). Ariosto surreptitiously includes Orlando in Angelica's story by stating that if he had only known of Angelica's danger, he would have risked a thousand deaths to seek out her "angelici vestigi." Since the reader is still caught up in the suspense of Angelica about to be devoured by the Orca, this assertion is likely to slip by unquestioned. But Ariosto does more than second guess Orlando's state of mind in the passage: he inserts into a dependent clause a bit of false information regarding Orlando: "ch'era per ritrovarla ito a Parigi" ("he had gone to Paris in search of her"; 8.68).[25] Since this passage precedes the actual appearance of Orlando in the *Furioso*, one can only assume that his travel to Paris to find Angelica occurred in the *Innamorato*.[26] Yet, Orlando returned to Paris on only one occasion in Boiardo's poem, and that took place immediately upon his release from the Laughing Stream when erotic desire was the furthest thing from his mind. Nor can *a Parigi* be taken to mean more generally his return *to France*, since he returned to France in the company of Angelica—not in order to find her. This single false statement was perhaps intended to get the reader's memory off balance before the more outright rewriting of Orlando's history in the ensuing octaves. In the 1532 edition, Ariosto will add verses in Canto 12 that both support this attitude and echo Orlando's words at the opening of the

---

the opening of the *Innamorato*, the pursuit of Angelica. It was, no doubt, a happy memory for them and a promising augury of coming enjoyment. But more than that, it brings the wheel of the beloved stories full circle—after all these adventures we are back where we started, with the eternal pursuit of beauty, eternally elusive." "Ariosto's Continuation," 378.

[25] The act of a knight returning to Paris to look for Angelica would not have struck the readers as entirely unfamiliar since in Canto 2 a hermit maliciously sent Rinaldo back to Paris to search for her.

[26] Ariosto craftily follows the two non-locatable verses on Orlando with two more verses about Rinaldo and Ferraù that refer to actual events. Commentaries of the *Furioso* are conspicuously silent when it comes to the first two verses, but then go on to locate for the reader the passages to which Ariosto refers when mentioning Rinaldo and Ferraù. They stop short of saying, however, that there is simply no source for the first two verses. See, for example, the explanatory notes by Lanfranco Caretti and Emilio Bigi in their editions of the poem.

Innamorato. On that occasion, Orlando had said he was resolved to seek out Angelica's face "sin che lo trovo, e per state e per verno, / e in terra e in mare, e in cielo e nello inferno" ("through summer and through winter, till / I've covered land, sea, heaven, hell!"; 1.2.26). Ariosto expands this into the statement that Orlando:

> non avria, per Angelica cercare,
> lasciato o selva o campo o stagno o rio
> o valle o monte o piano o terra o mare,
> il cielo, e 'l fondo de l'eterno oblio.
>
> would not have left a single wood,
> field, pond, stream, valley, hill, plain,
> land, or sea unsearched, nor even
> the heavens or the pit of eternal oblivion. (12.3)

Orlando first appears in the poem in 8.71 following Ariosto's reference to him in the verses cited above. Various scholars, beginning with those of the sixteenth century, have felt the need to account for such a late entry.[27] The reason most often given for Orlando's Canto 8 appearance is Ariosto's desire to create a symmetry between Orlando's entrance into the poem, his descent into madness, and the recovery of his wits. Yet, this supposed symmetry does not exist in the early editions of forty cantos in which Orlando's entrance was equally late. In fact, it is not even applicable to the final edition. Orlando's search for Angelica begins in 8, he goes mad in 23, and he recovers his wits in 39. There are fourteen cantos between 8 and 23, while there are fifteen cantos between 23 and 39. Brand attributes the delaying of Orlando's entrance to the need to treat the characters who had been left behind at *Innamorato* 3.8.[28] This could perhaps have accounted for Orlando's late entrance, but *not* for the rewrit-

---

[27] Giovan Battista Pigna, for example, begins by noting the oddity: "Pare tutta via strano che di Ruggero à dire s'habbia principalmente; & che da Rinaldo & da Ferraù si cominci; & che similmente si lasci Orlando." The first reason he gives is the constraints that Boiardo's text had placed upon Ariosto as continuator: "è stato forza da Rinaldo & da Ferraù incominciare per rispetto d'Angelica, in che finiva il precedente componimento." But Boiardo had clearly not ended the *Innamorato* with Angelica, and so Pigna offers another reason, now shifting the responsibility from the plot of the *Innamorato* to the precedent of classical epic: "Et benche altrimenti introdur si potesse l'amor di Angelica; pure fu cosi in tal modo posto per esservi l'essempio dell'Iliade, la quale ha la prima attione fatta appunto in simil guisa: essendo ella una contesa tra Achille & Agamennone per conto di Chriseide." *I Romanzi* (Venice, 1554), 78.

[28] Brand, "Ariosto's Continuation," 378.

ing of his history that follows. The delay, I would like to argue, is part of Ariosto's strategy to defamiliarize readers with Orlando's most recent history in Boiardo's poem before attempting a complete rewriting of it in his own.

In *Furioso* 8, Orlando appears alone at night in his bedroom. The time is ostensibly a few hours after the storm that interrupted his battle with Rodamonte. Orlando thinks back to the competition over Angelica, and he regrets that he had given in to Charlemagne's wishes. Even this scene is rewritten from a different perspective. Whereas in *Innamorato* 2.21 there had been immediate obedience to Charlemagne's wishes, from the retrospective viewpoint of the *Furioso*, it appears as though Orlando had made a calculation before acting.[29] But more is at stake. The very fact that Angelica—rather than Rodamonte—is the object of Orlando's thoughts at this crucial moment reintroduces his earlier romance infatuation at the expense of his later epic recovery. The rewriting of the competition scene serves to bring *Innamorato* 2.21 to the forefront of the reader's mind while Ariosto conveniently turns attention away from the narrative thread that he is ostensibly picking up (i.e., *Innamorato* 3.8).[30]

Ariosto further draws attention away from Orlando's epic battle against Rodamonte by the very introduction of him in the guise of a forlorn lover alone at night in his bed ("La notte Orlando alle noiose piume..."). Although technically this bedroom scene follows the Parisian battle of Book 3, thematically it transports us back to the very opening of the *Innamorato* when Orlando was likewise engaged in a bedside monologue. Various aspects of that earlier scene are repeated, including his concern over Angelica's possible loss of virginity and the thought of suicide ("Morte me donarò con la mia mano," 1.2.24 versus "con le mie man mi toglio / la vita," 8.78). After the monologue, Ariosto replays Orlando's surreptitious departure from Paris. In both texts, Orlando leaves under the cover of darkness ("la notte scura," 1.2.27 and "mezza notte," 8.86). He dons his armor ("veste l'armatura," 1.2.27 and "Di piastra e maglia, quanto gli bisogna, / tutto guarnissi," 8.84), having changed his traditional insignia ("la insegna del quartero," 1.2.28 and "l'onorata insegna del

---

[29] Franceschetti notes that this scene has been retrospectively modified, but he attributes to Ariosto a different motivation. "Appunti," 107.

[30] Brand notes that the introduction of Orlando in Canto 8 is speeded up stylistically, *Ludovico Ariosto*, 147–48. Sangirardi as well notes the eliptical character of the passage and the "brusca e inconsueta accelerazione ritmica del racconto ariostesco," *Boiardismo ariostesco*, 41.

quartiero," 8.85) for a disguised one: in Boiardo it is dark red (1.2.28) and in Ariosto it is black (8.85). He mounts Brigliadoro (1.2.28; 8.84); he is silent ("tacitamente," 1.2.28 and "tacito," 8.86); and, finally, no one either knows of his departure nor accompanies him ("Non sa de lui famiglio, né scudero," 1.2.28 and "né di scudiero alcun servigio volse," 8.84).[31]

Thus, although Ariosto appears to pick up Orlando's storyline at the point Boiardo had left it (3.8), Orlando's thoughts go back to the competition of 2.21, and Orlando's actions take the reader back even farther, to his departure from Paris in 1.2. This movement back in narrative time from 3.8 to 2.21 and 1.2 not only erases the new role Orlando had assumed by the end of Boiardo's poem, but it also privileges two central moments in the *Innamorato* in which the spotlight was on Orlando's erotic subjection to Angelica. These are, tellingly, the very same two moments that Ariosto privileged in his treatment of Angelica in the opening cantos. Her initial appearance in *Furioso* 1 stemmed from events surrounding the competition of *Innamorato* 2.21, and the ensuing narrative in which she was pursued by various suitors imitated *Innamorato* 1.3. In this way, then, both Angelica and Orlando are made to replay their tale of unrequited love across the expanse of the *Innamorato* at the moment in which they reappear in Ariosto's continuation.

Ariosto must still account for the fact that Angelica had been absent from Orlando's thoughts from his emergence from the Laughing Stream to the end of the *Innamorato*. Using the conceit of the flames of passion burning more fiercely in the dark of night than during the day, Ariosto attempts to explain away—and then, in a second breath, to deny—Orlando's loss of interest in Angelica at the *Innamorato*'s end:

> La donna sua, che gli ritorna a mente,
> anzi che mai non era indi partita,
> gli raccende nel core e fa più ardente
> la fiamma che nel dì parea sopita.
>
> His lady returned to haunt his mind
> —not that she had ever been absent from it—
> and stoked up to a new incandescence the fire
> which during the day seemed to have waned. (8.72)

---

[31] Parallels between the two scenes have been noted by Pio Rajna, *Le fonti dell' Orlando Furioso* (Florence: Sansoni, 1975), 207.

This is yet another rewriting of Orlando's state, but Ariosto here can
defend himself by calling witness to none other than Boiardo who in the
Amorum Libri had announced a return to poems of love in this way: "Tornato è meco Amore, / anci vi è sempre e mai non se partio" ("Love has
returned to me, / indeed has always been with me, not gone"; Ballata
12).[32] Ariosto thus uses the poet-lover of the *Amorum Libri* to contradict
the story told by the narrator of the *Orlando Innamorato*.

But to rewrite the history of Orlando and Angelica in the latter part of
the *Innamorato* was not an easy task nor one that Ariosto took lightly. He
also needed to account for the fact that Angelica was not mentioned at all
in the latter part of Boiardo's poem. He attempts to do just that in the
verses that immediately follow those quoted above:

> Costei venuta seco era in Ponente
> fin dal Cataio; e qui l'avea smarrita,
> né ritrovato poi vestigio d'ella
> che Carlo rotto fu presso a Bordella.

> She had come with him to the West
> [from Cathay; and here he lost her,
> nor did he later find any vestige of her
> now that Charles was defeated near Bordeaux]. (8.72)

The first two verses recall that Orlando accompanied Angelica to the
West and then lost her. The next two verses, however, which are gram-
matically dependent on the previous ones, are intentionally misleading: by
telling us that Orlando could not find any trace of Angelica, Ariosto turns
an acknowledgement of her absence into the claim that Orlando had actually been actively looking for her. The "vestigio d'ella" that could not be
found may even ring familiar to the reader. But it does not belong to any
passage in the *Innamorato*'s third book; rather, it merely echoes the "angelici vestigi" that, as Ariosto had declared a few octaves earlier (8.68),
Orlando would have risked a thousand deaths to find.[33]

In order to rewrite the histories of Orlando and Angelica without internal contradictions, Ariosto also had to rewrite the histories of the char-

---

[32] *Amorum Libri: The Lyric Poems of Matteo Maria Boiardo*, trans. Andrea di Tommaso
(Binghamton, NY: Medieval & Renaissance Texts & Studies, 1993), 255.

[33] There is also perhaps an echo from Boiardo's second eclogue: "le sue vestigie a
seguitar elice," in *Tutte le opere*, ed. Angelandrea Zottoli (Milan: Mondadori, 1936–37),
27.

acters who found themselves at the two sites where Orlando had been: the Laughing Stream and the city of Paris. The next section examines Ariosto's painstaking effort to weave the stories of these other characters into the fabric of the *Furioso* as he made the Laughing Stream and Paris seemingly disappear from Book 3. (Rewriting the history of Angelica did not present Ariosto with this problem: since she had not appeared in Book 3, she was not in contact with any other characters.)

Ariosto's Erasure of the Laughing Stream

The Laughing Stream episode brings together several characters besides Orlando. The first of these to appear in the *Furioso* is Sacripante. Boiardo had deliberately left him in the depths of the enchanted fountain. Ariosto brings him into the first canto of his continuation in a way that avoids recalling his most recent history in Boiardo's poem. While the reader's attention is still focused on Angelica's escape, an unidentified knight appears out of nowhere. Ariosto dwells on the uncertainty of his identity and the consequences this has for Angelica: "Se gli è amico o nemico non comprende: / tema e speranza il dubbio cor le scuote" ("whether he be friend or foe she could not tell; her doubting heart was assailed by hope and fear"; 1.39). He is seen from Angelica's point of view, and his lament over Angelica's supposed loss of virginity further keeps the attention focused on the Saracen princess.

Like Angelica, we are curious to know his identity, and, once that is revealed (in the typical Breton fashion with the phrase "Se mi domanda alcun chi costui sia"), our curiosity may be sufficiently satisfied to allow us to continue without asking where he was last in Boiardo's poem.[34] Just in case, however, Ariosto quickly explains how he got to be where he is now:

> Appresso ove il sol cade, per suo amore
> venuto era dal capo d'Oriente;
> che seppe in India con suo gran dolore,

---

[34] Sangirardi talks about Ariosto's technique of "straniamento," which consists of introducing Boiardo's characters "con tattiche stranianti, sottoposti ad una metamorfosi che, gradualmente o improvvisamente fatta rientrare, produce un effetto di sorpresa destinato ad accompagnare e potenziare il piacere dell'agnizione," *Boiardismo ariostesco*, 45. In this way, Sangirardi continues, "il modello è occultato nel momento stesso in cui è esibito, portato in scena sotto un travestimento che sarà rimosso solo retrospettivamente," *Boiardismo ariostesco*, 47. But in the case of those connected to the Laughing Stream, there is no retrospective correspondence.

> come ella Orlando sequitò in Ponente:
> Poi seppe in Francia che l'imperatore
> sequestrata l'avea da l'altra gente;
> per darla all'un de' duo che contra il Moro
> più quel giorno aiutasse i Gigli d'oro.
>
> Stato era in campo, e inteso avea di quella
> rotta crudel che dianzi ebbe re Carlo:
> cercò vestigio d'Angelica bella,
> né potuto avea ancora ritrovarlo.
>
> For love of her he had come out of the East
> to where the sun sets, for in India he had learned,
> to his great sorrow, that she had followed Orlando to
>   the West;
> then in France he had learned how the emperor had
>   set her apart,
> promising her as the prize to whichever of the two
> yielded greater assistance to the Golden Lilies.
> He had been in the field of battle, he witnessed the
>   rout
> of King Charlemagne. He had gone in search of
> fair Angelica, but so far he had been unable to find
>   her. (1.46–47)

This summary, however, does not correspond to the narrative of the *Innamorato* where Sacripante, at the bottom of the Laughing Stream, never heard the news of the competition between Ranaldo and Orlando or of Carlo's defeat at Montealbano. By using these two events in the explanation of Sacripante's history, Ariosto reinforces them in the reader's mind (they were already the focus of the opening summary), and then he uses them to jump ahead to Sacripante's supposed search for Angelica. Moreover, this description of Sacripante's search contains the same words and even rhyme scheme that Ariosto will later use to refer to Orlando: "né *ritrovato* poi *vestigio* d'*ella* / che *Carlo rotto* fu presso a Bor*della*"; 8.72; italics mine. When the reader encounters these verses seven cantos later, chances are that the situation would sound familiar enough—and vague enough—to allow for the possibility that Orlando had indeed at some earlier point before Canto 8 been searching for Angelica.

Ariosto's suppression of Sacripante's imprisonment in the Laughing Stream contrasts with the way Niccolò degli Agostini had handled the situation. In the opening canto of *Orlando Innamorato* Book 4, Sacripante is found in the enchanted palace of the fairy Falerina. In order to avoid contradicting Boiardo's poem, Agostini is quick to inform the reader that Sacripante had left the Laughing Stream ("de li fu fora uscito"; 4.1.58) before encountering Falerina.

Agostini uses this same episode to pick up the threads of Rugiero and Gradasso's story as well, thus bringing together in the poem's first enchanted site three characters who had been under the Laughing Stream's spell. Agostini imagines that the dwarf who appeared just after the emergence of Rugiero and Gradasso from the fountain has led them to Falerina's palace.

Ariosto may have been able to pass over in silence the latest whereabouts of Sacripante in the *Innamorato*, but he clearly needed to pick up the adventure of Rugiero, progenitor of the Estense dynasty. He nevertheless finds a way to bring Ruggiero into his narrative while avoiding a direct link to Boiardo's poem. He distances the reader from the adventure itself by turning it into a second-hand account by an utterly minor character of the *Innamorato*, Pinabello.[35] As part of his own tale of woe in which he lost his beloved, Pinabello mentions a battle that Ruggiero and Gradasso waged against an unidentified knight outside a castle. There is no indication that this is the place to which Boiardo's dwarf had led them as they left the Laughing Stream. In fact, Ariosto can avoid references to the *Innamorato* altogether because the character Pinabello knows nothing of the state of the heroes either before or after the unsuccessful battle he witnessed. Ariosto does not fill in the gaps, nor does he supply us with any information about the nature of the castle or the reasons for its creation at this point. It is only at a later moment that Bradamante finds out that the knight on the flying horse was Atlante who created the castle to keep Ruggiero from death in France, and that the many knights and ladies imprisoned there were entertained with earthly pleasures (4.32). The function of this new castle, then, turns out to be identical to that of the Laughing Stream. Yet, by the time this functional link has been revealed, Ariosto has already established much more overt, descriptive links to another site from the *Innamorato*: Atalante's original hiding place in the North African mountain of Carena. Both Boiardo's "mur di vetro" ("crystal wall";

---

[35] Traditionally a member of the Maganza clan, Pinabello is mentioned only twice in the *Innamorato*: Boiardo first identifies him with the Maganza (1.2.51) and then shows Astolfo unhorsing him (1.3.16).

2.16.17) and Ariosto's "castello d'acciaio" are inaccessible to outsiders. There is no sign of any path leading up to either of the sheer mountain cliffs. In addition to the description of the locus, key narrative elements, such as the reappearance of Brunello and the spell-breaking ring of Angelica, link the *castello d'acciaio* to Atalante's original hiding place and elide the closer links that the episode has to the Laughing Stream.[36]

Later in the poem, when Ariosto names all of Atlante's various ruses to remove Ruggiero from danger, he leaves the Laughing Stream out of the list. Referring to the *palazzo incantato*, he says:

> Questo era un nuovo e disusato incanto
> ch'avea composto Atlante di Carena
> [....]
> Dopo il castel d'acciar, che nulla giova,
> e dopo Alcina, Atlante ancor fa pruova.
>
> This was a new and unusual piece of magic
> devised by the wizard Atlas
> [....]
> The steel-girt castle had proved useless,
> so had Alcina; here he was, trying something else. (12.21)

One cannot claim that Ariosto here meant to refer only to events in the *Furioso*, since elsewhere in the poem Ariosto systematically lists together episodes from both the *Innamorato* and the *Furioso* without any differentiation. Moreover, the explicit reference to Atlante as "of Carena" calls to mind his original hiding place in the *Innamorato*, and makes the absence of the Laughing Stream all the more suspicious. After all, it is the Laughing Stream rather than the mountain of Carena that serves as the prototype for the other adventures in Ariosto's list. At Carena, although a magic wall prevented others from discovering the site, Rugiero was not the victim of any illusion and was free to leave when he desired to join Agramante. Atalante's Laughing Stream, on the other hand, is an enchanted fountain of sensual delights. Although Atalante originally designed the fountain to protect Rugiero by trapping his opponent Orlando, Boiardo describes how Rugiero fell victim to the fountain as well.

The Laughing Stream introduces a new "character" who will play a

---

[36] For links between the "muro di vetro" in the mountain of Carena and the "muro di acciaio," compare OI 2.3.27–28; 2.16.7 and OF 2.43–44; 4.12–13. See also Rajna, *Le fonti*, 113.

larger part in Atlante's *Furioso* traps: a flying horse. In the *Innamorato*, Gradasso all too willingly mounts a horse that takes him flying through the air out of control before finally dropping him down into the magic fountain of sensuous desire.[37] In Ariosto's *castello d'acciaio* episode, it is Atlante who first rides the flying horse in order to defeat his opponents, but at the episode's conclusion, the horse takes an unwary Ruggiero up in the air out of control and then drops him down onto Alcina's island, another ruse devised by Atlante. Ariosto has simply substituted Ruggiero for Gradasso and expanded the trajectory.[38] Rugiero was, moreover, already familiar with flying horses in Boiardo's poem. He tells Bradamante that his childhood experiences in the mountain of Carena included hunting "grifoni e pegasei, benché abbiano ali" ("gryphons and pegasi with wings"; 3.5.37).

The final two characters present at the Laughing Stream are its heroes, Fiordelisa and Brandimarte. They are the prototypes of a positive, reciprocal love that is contrasted to Orlando's irrational and illusory desires. They also present a picture of knowledge (Fiordelisa) and action (Brandimarte) working together. After the many vicissitudes of the first two books, they marry in 2.27.52 and remain together in the final cantos of Book 2 and in all of Book 3. Given their overall importance in the *Innamorato* narrative and their central role at the Laughing Stream and Paris,[39] Ariosto's treatment of them is tellingly scant. The first mention of either of them is Brandimarte's departure from Paris to seek Orlando. In this way, Ariosto removes him from the epic space and launches him into the forest of romance at the very moment he is introduced into the narrative. Rather than recall Brandimarte's recent exploits in Paris, the scene is reminiscent

---

[37] This situation may allude to Gradasso's unbridled desire for fame. Fulgentius says of another flying horse: "The winged horse Pegasus signifies fame because fame is 'swifter in growth and more changeable than any other evil' " (*Aen.* 4.174–75), "The Exposition of the Content of Virgil according to Moral Philosophy," in *Fulgentius the Mythographer*, trans. and intro. Leslie George Whitbread (Columbus: Ohio State Univ. Press, 1971), 70.

[38] Ariosto also modifies a few details to deliberately differentiate his flying horse from that of the Laughing Stream: he invents a mythological framework, he states that it is a natural rather than enchanted animal, and he calls it by a different name, hippogriff. Rajna devotes seven pages to tracing the hippogriff's literary precedents from the classical Pegasus to the *Innamorato*'s Baiardo and Rabicano, yet the flying horse that transports victims to the very first trap set up by Atalante escapes his attention. *Le fonti*, 114–20. More recently, however, Giuseppe Anceschi has noted with regard to the horse at the Laughing Stream: "Dunque, l'ippogriffo è già qui," *Orlando Innamorato* (Milan: Garzanti, 1978), vol. 2, 1202 n. 9.

[39] Having reached Paris, Fiordelisa remains outside the action while Boiardo focuses on Brandimarte and Orlando's entrance into the battle.

of his earlier departure from Albraca in search of Orlando (2.2.36). He then becomes trapped in Atlante's enchanted palace where he follows false visions of Fiordiligi. This combines two characteristic but earlier situations in the *Innamorato*: his entrapments in enchanted prisons (of Dragontina and Morgana) and his searches for Fiordelisa.

Brandimarte's wife does not appear in the *Furioso* until Canto 24, when she is introduced as "Fiordiligi / Che dell'amante suo cerca i vestigi" ("Fiordiligi, searching for some trace of her lover"; 24.53). She, too, is made to replay earlier scenes in the *Innamorato*. Her situation specifically recalls her own account of how she followed Brandimarte after he left Albraca in search of Orlando (2.13.9).[40] Thus, the introduction of both Brandimarte and Fiordiligi into Ariosto's continuation repeats their earlier exits from Albraca rather than recalling their actions in the third book of Boiardo's poem. Throughout the *Furioso*, they are made to replay their wanderings in search of each other, which occupied the early part of the *Innamorato*. They do not get together at all until Canto 31 and then are separated shortly thereafter and only reunite in Canto 35.

Ariosto finds more subtle ways to keep the focus away from their adventure at the Laughing Stream and Brandimarte's participation in the Battle of Paris. Since these were the two principle events that followed their marriage, Ariosto avoids mentioning that they are married for quite some time, referring to Brandimarte as Fiordiligi's "amante" or "amador" (24.53, 29.43, 31.59, 31.61, 31.75, 31.76, 31.78, 35.33, 35.35). Although Fiordiligi does refer once to Brandimarte in her own speech as "il mio signore" (35.36), her interlocutor Bradamante will follow the lead of the narrator rather than of Fiordiligi, referring to Brandimarte as "tuo amante" in her answer (35.39). It is only after they meet and lose each other and are about to meet again in Canto 35 that Fiordiligi refers to Brandimarte for the first time as her husband: "mio signore e mio marito" (35.58). Thus, after ignoring the characters themselves for several cantos, Ariosto chooses to ignore the three latest events of their story (i.e., their marriage, their liberation of Orlando at the Laughing Stream, and the Battle of Paris) in order to repeat the separations and searches that characterized them throughout much of the earlier poem.

And yet, when Fiordiligi and Brandimarte do finally team up, they set

---

[40] "Con superchia fatica e maggior tedio / Cercato ho Brandimarte notte e giorno, / Né a ritrovarlo è mai stato rimedio" ("With great fatigue and greater care / I searched for Brandimarte, day / and night, but nothing could be learned"; 2.13.9).

out to do exactly what they did in the final cantos of the *Innamorato*—to help Orlando regain his wits. Although the honor of rescuing Orlando will go to Astolfo, this couple in the end comes tantalizingly close to replaying their earlier role of a husband and wife liberation team. Fiordiligi is the character who has the most privileged information regarding Orlando's state of insanity and consequent actions: her first lengthy appearance in the poem follows the account of Orlando's madness and, more specifically, of the discovery of his arms. She not only knows of his *pazzia*, but she also witnesses two duels that result from it: the tragic duel between Mandricardo and Zerbino over Orlando's arms and the farcical bout between Orlando and Rodamonte at the perilous bridge. It is she who spreads the word of Orlando's madness to everyone who is not his enemy so that, of all those she tells, one may set out to purge his brain ("fin che si purghi il cervello"; 31.46).

Brandimarte becomes involved in the search for Orlando as well. When Fiordiligi informs him of Orlando's state, his immediate departure in search of his friend is contrasted with Rinaldo's earlier decision to postpone Orlando's rescue in order to continue his battle against the Saracens (31.49). Recalling, perhaps daringly, the determination of Brandimarte to find Orlando that had earlier led him and Fiordelisa to the Laughing Stream, Ariosto tells us:

> Brandimarte, che 'l conte amava quanto
> si può compagno amar, fratello o figlio,
> disposto di cercarlo, e di far tanto,
> non ricusando affanno né periglio,
> che per opra di medico o d'incanto
> si ponga a quel furor qualche consiglio,
> così come trovossi armato in sella,
> si mise in via con la sua donna bella.
>
> Brandimarte, who loved the count as much
> as one can love a comrade, a son, or brother,
> was disposed to search for him and (refusing
> no toil or danger) to see what he could do,
> by dint of medicine or magic; to infuse some
> sense into his mad mind. (31.64)

Yet, before the reader can even begin to recall their joint liberation of Orlando at the Laughing Stream, Ariosto is quick to dispel any such possibility here. In the very next stanza Brandimarte and Fiordiligi arrive at

Rodomonte's perilous bridge, and within ten stanzas Brandimarte is defeated and sent to Rodomonte's prison in Biserta. Thus, their search for Orlando ends in failure just after it has begun. Moreover, Ariosto has patterned their adventure at Rodomonte's perilous bridge not on the Laughing Stream episode but on their adventure at Dragontina's palace. This not only nullifies the progress that they had made in the course of their adventures, but it keeps the reader's focus on the earliest part of Boiardo's poem. At both Dragontina's palace and Rodomonte's bridge, Fiordelisa witnesses her beloved, after a show of arms, become the helpless prisoner in a potentially eternal prison. In both cases she manages to save him from the worser fate of death, earlier by urging him to do what Dragontina wanted of him and now by pleading with Rodomonte to imprison rather than kill him. The parallel is furthered when we hear that she must search for "Rinaldo paladino" (31.77) or another valiant champion who can liberate him. In the *Innamorato*, Fiordelisa had encountered precisely Ranaldo and led him to Dragontina's realm. They arrived, however, too late since Brandimarte and Orlando had already left for Albraca. In the *Furioso*, Bradamante replaces her brother Rinaldo as Fiordiligi's champion. While in the *Innamorato* eight cantos passed in between Ranaldo's encounter with Fiordelisa and their late arrival at Dragontina's vanished palace, Ariosto has Fiordiligi and Bradamante arrive at Rodomonte's perilous bridge without further ado. Indeed, in the verse immediately following Bradamante's "Andiamo" ("Let's go"; 35.40), we find that they have already arrived. In Boiardo's poem, on the way to Dragontina's palace, Fiordelisa had told Ranaldo the tale of Tisbina, Iroldo, and Prasildo, which we later find to be a true story when its protagonists appear in the main narrative. Ariosto's Fiordiligi tells Bradamante a story as well, but whereas Fiordelisa's novella was new to the reader, here it is the already familiar tale of Isabella, and the reader does not hear Fiordiligi's version of it (35.41). Ariosto, moreover, continues the relation of Fiordiligi to the female protagonist of the novella. Fiordelisa told the tale of a woman who changed lovers, and she hinted at her own momentary attraction to Ranaldo. Fiordiligi tells the story of a woman who preferred to join her husband in death rather than to take another lover. Although we do not know it at the time, this novella foreshadows Fiordiligi's own willed death in the tomb of Brandimarte.

Ariosto's use of the *Innamorato* continues. Despite Bradamante's rapid and decisive victory over Rodomonte, Fiordiligi still does not recover Brandimarte, who has in the meantime been sent as prisoner to Africa. As in the *Innamorato*, Fiordiligi must resume her search. That their reunion finally occurs at Biserta is significant, since this is the very place where they had been blown off course on their way to rescue Orlando and where they had learned of his entrapment at the Laughing Stream (as Brandimarte explains in 3.6.56). Yet, Ariosto makes sure that the reader will not begin to recall that earlier episode and expect them to cure Orlando here as well. Following Brandimarte's defeat to Rodomonte and prior to Bradamante's subsequent victory over him, Ariosto announces Astolfo's mission to recover Orlando's wits and recounts his voyage to the moon to secure them. Once Orlando's liberation by Astolfo has been established, Ariosto proceeds with Fiordiligi's story. Tellingly, in the same stanza that he takes leave of Astolfo in the company of St. John, Ariosto jumps back to Fiordiligi, picking up the story at the same place he had left off, although now telling it from the perspective of Bradamante (35.31).[41]

Once Astolfo has been designated as the liberator of Orlando by an authority no less than God himself, and Ariosto has moved away from the imaginative space of Boiardo's poem through Astolfo's voyage to the moon, the presence of Fiordiligi and Brandimarte during Orlando's recovery is not likely to receive much attention by the reader. Yet, Ariosto links Orlando to the couple by alternating the account of his discovery with a summary of their history. First Astolfo, Brandimarte, and others spot a nude man (39.36–37). Before he is identified, Ariosto stops the narrative to tell of Fiordiligi's various travels in search of Brandimarte. He even includes a reminder of Brandimarte's kidnapping by Bardino and his childhood at the Rocca Silvana. Thus, in the crucial moments just prior to Orlando's recovery of his wits, Ariosto takes pains to recall both Fiordiligi's most recent past in the *Furioso* and Brandimarte's most distant past in the *Innamorato*. Needless to say, in this way he keeps the attention away from their most recent past in the *Innamorato*.

In the end, Ariosto assigns an instrumental role to both Fiordiligi and Brandimarte in the recovery of Orlando's wits. Of all Orlando's companions present in the recovery scene, it is naturally Fiordiligi who first recognizes Orlando: "Fiordiligi mirò quel nudo in fronte, / e gridò a Brandimarte: —Eccovi il conte!—," ("Fiordiligi scrutinized the naked man's face and cried to Brandimart, 'It's the count!' "; 39.44). In the *Innamorato*,

---

[41] The narrative technique of this episode itself is quintessentially Boiardian in structure. See Marco Praloran, "*Meraviglioso artificio.*" *Tecniche narrative e rappresentative nell'Orlando Innamorato* (Lucca: Pacini Fazzi, 1990), 19–20.

she is the one character knowledgeable of both places (e.g., Dragontina's palace, Falerina's Garden, the Laughing Stream) and people (e.g., Tisbina, Marfisa). Her first positive act of the *Furioso* is, after all, to recognize the arms of Orlando dispersed on the ground (24.56). The fact that her identification of Orlando (—Eccovi il conte!—; 39.44) is recounted even before that of Astolfo, which is similarily rendered in direct discourse (—Eccovi Orlando!—; 39.46), suggests Fiordiligi's chronological precedence as liberator.[42] Brandimarte's presence is essential as well, since he is the one knight who succeeds in holding Orlando down while the others are pushed away: "Non fa però che Brandimarte il lassi, / che con più forza l'ha preso a traverso" ("But Brandimart, who had a tighter hold, he could not shake off"; 39.50). As I mentioned earlier, this couple represented in the *Innamorato* the cooperation between knowledge (Fiordelisa) and action (Brandimarte) put to use for the good of others. Ariosto continues these roles: Fiordelisa represents knowledge when she recognizes Orlando, and Brandimarte represents action when he succeeds in holding him down so that Astolfo can force him to inhale his *senno*.

Ariosto prepares us for this momentous event to the utmost by having St. John come on stage and tell Astolfo that the madness and recovery were by the will of God. Boiardo, on the contrary, does not tell the reader ahead of time that Orlando's liberation from the enchanted fountain will restore his identity.[43] Nonetheless, there are so many aspects of Orlando's recovery at Biserta that recall the Laughing Stream episode that, in my view, it is nothing less than an elaborate rewriting of this "suppressed" event. While the *Innamorato* couple were given instructions for rescuing Orlando by a seer ("indovino") in another continent, Astolfo gets instructions for recovering Orlando's wits from a saint in another dimension. Just as Brandimarte and Fiordelisa needed the participation of others at the time of the rescue, Astolfo could not have made Orlando inhale his wits without the help of others, first and foremost Brandimarte. At both the Laughing Stream and the shores of Africa, Orlando is brought to his senses by supernatural means. Consequently, there is no inner struggle

---

[42] Ariosto then undermines this chronological precedence by stating that Astolfo recognized Orlando at the same time as Fiordiligi if not sooner.

[43] He even opens Book 3 suggesting that Orlando will be headed for more amorous disasters. Of course, it is possible that Boiardo meant to delay Orlando's recovery until a later point and thus did not originally intend for the Laughing Stream to take on the significance that he then gave to it as Book 3 proceeded. Yet, given the playfulness of the *Innamorato*'s ironic narrator, he may not have wanted to ruin a good surprise.

toward virtue. We know he is cured because he thinks of his duty to Charlemagne rather than acting like a beast. In both cases, moreover, the past is referred to through the simile of a dream. Upon their recovery from the Laughing Stream, Orlando and the others are: "Come om che sogna e se sveglia di tratto, / Né può quel che sognava ramentare" ("like men who wake up suddenly / And can't remember what they dreamed"; 3.7.37). After Orlando inhales his wits at the shores of Biserta, he is:

> Come chi da noioso e grave sonno,
> ove o vedere abominevol forme
> di mostri che non son, né ch'esser ponno,
> o gli par cosa far strana ed enorme,
> ancor si maraviglia, poi che donno
> è fatto de' suoi sensi, e che non dorme

> As one who, in a heavy, oppressive sleep,
> has been seeing horrible shapes of monsters
> who do not and cannot exist, or has dreamt
> of having committed some gross enormity,
> lingers in wonderment when sleep is ended
> and he is once more master of his senses. (39.56)

Ariosto's simile is more elaborate, but Orlando's state of mind is surprisingly similar. In neither case does Orlando have a clear recollection or full understanding of his period of mental depravity.

The two scenes are also parallel in the overall architecture of the respective poems. Although Ariosto moves Orlando's recovery from the outskirts of Paris to the outskirts of Biserta, in both cases this event leads to his immediate involvement in the ongoing war and to a decisive swing of the tide of the fighting in favor of the Christians. Both Orlando's liberation from the fountain and subsequent attack on Paris *and* Orlando's recovery of his wits and subsequent attack on Biserta are linked structurally by occurring within the same canto (3.7 and 39 respectively). While Orlando was earlier in the company of his liberator Brandimarte, now he is teamed up with his liberator Astolfo. The knights do not fight side-by-side, but they are treated by each poet as the two principle players.

Why did Ariosto assign to Fiordiligi and Brandimarte a secondary role with respect to Astolfo? Besides the fact that giving prominence to this couple would have recalled too closely the earlier liberation scene, there are thematic reasons as well. While Fiordelisa and Brandimarte represented positive reciprocal love in the *Innamorato*, Astolfo in the *Furioso* has

been freed from erotic love altogether. He is therefore a more fit representative of the inner state at which Orlando needs to arrive in order to
return to his traditional role.[44]

The Original Battle of Paris, *Orlando Innamorato*

The Battle of Paris in the *Innamorato* is the culmination of the war between the Christians and Saracens that Boiardo carefully prepares in the
course of Books 2 and 3. At the opening of Book 2, the African king
Agramante, spurred on by Rodamonte's own desire for conquest, decides
to invade France. Rodamonte precedes Agramante and heads for France at
the opening of 2.6; he lands at Monaco in the same canto. In 2.17.3
Gradasso from *Levante*, Marsilio from *Ponente*, and Mandricardo from *Tra-
montana* are all set to converge on Christendom. We hear of Marsilio's
siege of Montealbano in 2.22.38, and Rodamonte and Feraguto head there
to join him. They enter the battle at the end of 2.23, at the same time as
Charlemagne. Agramante lands near Tortosa in 2.29.23 and joins in the
Battle of Montealbano as well. To add to the growing crescendo, Mandricardo heads west in 3.1 to avenge the death of his father Agricane, and he
enters the Battle of Paris in 3.8. In fact, in 3.8.15 Mandricardo is depicted
scaling the walls of Paris with Agramante, Rodamonte, and Feraguto, representing the forces of Asia, Africa, and Spain combined.

On the part of the defending Christians, preparations for battle begin
in 2.6.19 when Charlemagne warns Duke Amone to guard Montealbano
in Ranaldo's absence. Ranaldo's journey back west to Montealbano is announced in 2.9.48, although the reader is warned that "the story's long,
the voyage far." We find that Otachier has also assembled an army to
head into France at Charlemagne's request (2.14.11). Ranaldo is made captain of the troops and they arrive at the border of Provenza in 2.14.16. At
the moment in which Boiardo announces the return of Orlando and
Brandimarte, he explicitly states his plan of pulling together the various
strands of his romance narrative into one substance:

> però che il conte Orlando e Brandimarte,
> mi fa bisogno di condurli in Franza
> acciocché queste istorie che son sparte
> siano raccolte insieme a una sostanza.

---

[44] Although Orlando is married to Alda, he is nevertheless traditionally represented
as chaste and free of passion.

> And Brandimarte and Count Orlando
> Force me to transfer them to France,
> So that these stories, now so scattered,
> May be united, may be gathered. (2.17.38)

This announcement also suggests that the arrival of these two knights into the battle will be a crucial step in moving toward the epic finale. By 3.8, all the poem's major characters have gathered in France.[45] The exception is of course Marfisa, who is still chasing Brunello around the globe, but she would have eventually reached him in Paris where he is to be found among Agramante's troops (see 2.19.15). We also know that Grifone and Aquilante are headed to Paris as well, although at the poem's interruption they are still fighting Orrilo and the Cocodrilo in a battle instigated by their fairy guardians precisely in order to detain them on their journey to epic. Although the Christian victory would have been more than a canto away in narrative time, it was certain to occur (2.1.19).[46]

By focusing on the epic movement of Boiardo's poem, we can see that he was adhering to the basic structure of the Italian epic circulating in Northern Italy as *cantari carolingi*. In the popular fifteenth-century *La Spagna* (based in turn on the Franco-Venetian *Entrée d'Espagne*), Orlando deserts the Christian camp at midnight after an affront from Charlemagne, and his absence prolongs a war against Marsilio by several years. Orlando's fellow paladins leave Paris in search of him, and all undertake various adventures in the East before they finally meet up with each other. They return to the West together, and their arrival saves Charlemagne and Christianity from destruction by the Saracens.[47] The *Innamorato*, like *La*

---

[45] Rodamonte, Feraguto, Orlando, Marsilio, Agramante, Charlemagne, Ranaldo, Rugiero, Bradamante, Mandricardo, and Gradasso all converged at Montealbano, and Brandimarte and Fiordelisa are included in those numbers after the shift from Montealbano to Paris.

[46] I do not mean to imply that the poem itself was almost over. While Orlando is beginning to fulfill his epic role within Paris, the two founders of the Estense dynasty appear to be taking over as heroes of the romance genre. Ranaldo, too, while chasing Baiardo, had stumbled onto an *alta ventura* (3.4.40) in the Ardennes wood. Once the main characters have arrived in France, there is nothing to prevent them from being temporarily transported away on the road to adventure. But they can just as easily be brought back into the epic battle when needed.

[47] Franceschetti notes particular points of contact between the *Innamorato* and *La Spagna*, including Orlando's nighttime departure from Paris. See *L'Orlando Innamorato e le sue componenti tematiche e strutturali* (Florence: Leo S. Olschki, 1975), 146, 250–54.

Spagna, follows the structure of the traditional Italian Carolingian epic.[48] The recognition of the Battle of Paris, then, is crucial because it brings the poem's movement full circle and confirms the *Innamorato*'s overall epic structure.

Ariosto's Erasure and Rewriting of the Battle of Paris

For most of the first thirteen cantos, Ariosto creates the impression that the Battle of Paris has not yet begun. In Canto 1, he depicts expectation rather than action by avoiding any reference to an ongoing battle and noting instead that Carlo is merely *expecting* a siege (1.25). When Rinaldo arrives in Paris in Canto 2, Charlemagne dispatches him immediately to England. Just as Rinaldo is rushed out of Paris by Charlemagne ("Carlo il manda allora allora, / né pur lo lascia un giorno far dimora"; "Charlemagne chose that moment to send him, without conceding him even one day's respite"; 2.26), so the reader is ushered immediately back out of Paris by the poet. Ariosto then proceeds to defer the fighting for several cantos. Not until Canto 7 does he allude to Charlemagne and Agramante:

> Stava Ruggiero in tanta gioia e festa,
> mentre Carlo in travaglio ed Agramante,
> di cui l'istoria io non vorrei per questa
> porre in oblio

> Thus did Ruggiero bask in every sort of pleasure,
> while toil was the lot of Charles the Emperor
> and of Agramant the King: I should not wish
> to forget their story (7.33)

These verses appear to announce a jump from the Alcina episode to

---

He also has determined that Boiardo used *La Spagna* "minore" from a Ferraraese manuscript, *L'Orlando*, 244. Praloran notes the similarity of adventures in the Orient, "Maraviglioso artificio," 23. Rajna states that *La Spagna* was one of the most prized and popular books in the Estense library, *Le fonti*, 20.

[48] Pio Rajna gives the following general outline: "Un barone della corte di Carlo [...] lascia la Francia, e va errando sconosciuto per la Pagania. Là compie ogni sorta di prodezze [...]. Intanto di Francia si partono altri baroni per andar in traccia del compagno. Nuove avventure, nuovi pericoli. Essi giungono appunto in tempo per campare l'amico; e quindi insieme, dopo aver battezzato città e regni, ritornano verso l'Occidente. Per solito il ritorno è sommamente salutare alla Cristianità, giacché serve a dissipare gli eserciti sterminati, che qualche fiero Saracino ha condotto nel frattempo sotto Parigi." *Le fonti*, 14–15.

Charlemagne in Paris. Yet, once Charlemagne and Agramante have been evoked, their story is immediately put on hold once again while Ariosto takes the reader back to the Alcina episode by way of Bradamante. Although Ariosto claims that he would not like to make us forget ("porre in oblio") Charlemagne's story, this very statement allows him to delay the continuation of that story even longer and makes it even more likely that the reader will forget it.

In 8.21, Ariosto breaks off his narration of the Alcina episode. He does not, however, return to "Carlo in travaglio ed Agramante" as promised earlier. Instead, he turns to Rinaldo in Scotland and England, where preparations are being made to enter France. This supports the impression that the battle is still in a state of preparation. Then, rather than allow the troops to reach France and thus return to Charlemagne's story via Rinaldo, Ariosto changes the topic after only nine stanzas (8.21–29). Thus, a movement toward Charlemagne has been announced and then averted twice in two successive cantos. This time Ariosto defends his abrupt shift by evoking the principle of *varietas*. Comparing himself to the "buono / sonator" ("good musician") who "spesso muta corda, e varia suono" ("will select different strings, fresh harmonies"), he claims that Angelica came to his mind while he was intent on telling Rinaldo's story (8.29). Critics have often noted this passage as an example of Ariosto's declaration of his adherence to the technique of *entrelacement*. Yet, the fact that Ariosto felt the need to draw attention to his technique at his particular moment may signal that something else is at stake. The passage, in fact, involves a double-defense: Ariosto first defends his right to shift topics by noting the *varietas* required of a competent narrator/musician, and then he defends this particular switch by blaming the character Angelica for having provoked it.

Ariosto does not refer directly to any events from the *Innamorato*'s Battle of Paris until 8.69. Then, disregarding the carefully constructed swing of tide in *Innamorato* 3.8, Ariosto openly declares that if the storm had not arisen, Christendom would have been vanquished on that very day:

> e se non che li voti li ciel placorno,
> che dilagò di pioggia oscura il piano,
> cadea quel dì per l'africana lancia
> il santo Impero e 'l gran nome di Francia.

> Were it not that God accepted the Christians' prayers
> and flooded the plain in a murkey downpour,

> the Sacred Empire and the mighty name of France
> would that day have fallen to the African
> spears. (8.69)

Moreover, he turns one of the possibilities that Boiardo had used to account for the coming of the storm—the prayers of the Parisians—into a compelling scene in which the actors are now no less than the Emperor Charlemagne and God the Creator:

> Il sommo Creator gli occhi rivolse
> al giusto lamentar del vecchio Carlo;
> e con subita pioggia il fuoco tolse.

> The Almighty Creator turned His eyes
> to the just lament of the old emperor,
> and dowsed the fires in a sudden rainstorm. (8.70)

Yet, Boiardo had left Charlemagne rejoicing at Orlando's return (3.8.42). The French king would have hardly picked this moment to ask for divine intervention to stop the fighting.

To confuse matters more, although Ariosto had consistently given the impression that a battle had never taken place in Paris, at this point he tells us that Agramante had been attacking Paris for an indefinite number of days before the day of the storm. This does not, however, match the events in the *Innamorato*. In Boiardo's poem, Orlando had arrived to defend Paris on the very day that Agramante had begun his attack on the city. This increased the urgency of the situation and the importance of Orlando's arrival. Ariosto's modification makes the day of the storm just one of many. It becomes noteworthy only retrospectively for God's intervention to save Christendom from impending doom. In this way, the day of Orlando's arrival has been turned by Ariosto into the day of his departure. Moreover, if it is true that Agramante would have destroyed Paris had it not been for the storm, then one would expect him to return to fight the following day. Instead, Ariosto tells us that he waited from the end of October through the entire winter and until the spring before resuming his attack.

The mention of the storm in Canto 8 does not lead, in any event, to the continuation of the Battle of Paris, but, as noted above, serves only as a pretext for introducing Orlando and at the same time for removing him from the scene. This pattern of evoking Charlemagne in Paris only to delay his actual appearance in the poem is continued yet again two cantos later. Ariosto announces that he will return to Charlemagne via Astolfo, but only after telling first Ruggiero's and then Astolfo's story:

> Prima di lui [i.e., Ruggiero] che se n'andò in buon
>   punto,
> e poi dirò come il guerriero inglese
> tornasse con più tempo e più fatica
> al magno Carlo ed alla corte amica

> He set off, and first I shall tell of his adventures.
> Afterwards I shall relate how the English knight,
> on a longer and more arduous journey,
> made his way back to Charlemagne,
> and to the court where his friends were. (10.68)

Shortly thereafter, Ariosto once again evokes Charlemagne's story while keeping us distant from Paris itself. Ruggiero's flight on the hippogriff takes him past Rinaldo and the allied troops on their way to France, and he stops to hear the review of troops. The fact that we have not been introduced to the troops already assembled in Paris, but are forced to focus on troops that are on the march, reinforces Ariosto's projection of the entire battle into the future.

The *Furioso*'s depiction of the Battle of Paris does not begin until Canto 14—a remarkable lag considering that this event forms the background of the poem's principle action. Ariosto first reviews the troops of Marsilio and Agramante (OF 14.11–27). This review, which has been called "un'esibizione di competenza boiardesca" for its use of *Innamorato* material,[49] gives the impression, however, as in the case of the earlier review of Rinaldo's army, that the battle has not yet begun. In classical epic, as well as in the *Innamorato*, the review of troops typically precedes a battle.

Mandricardo is then introduced to Agramante as though the two were now meeting for the first time: "Era venuto pochi giorni avante / nel campo del re d'Africa un signore" ("Now a few days earlier a prince had come to the camp of the African sovereign"; 14.30). Ariosto supports his statement that Mandricardo had just arrived on the scene with a two-stanza introduction highlighting earlier moments in Boiardo's poem (14.30–31). However, in the *Innamorato* the two men had not only met

---

[49] Sangirardi, *Boiardismo ariostesco*, 227.

but also fought together. Indeed, they last appeared in the poem as Mandricardo had broken through the Christian ranks to rescue Agramante single-handedly:

> Ma sopra tutti Mandricardo è quello
> Che fa diffesa e mena gran flagello
>   Sol fu lui che Agramante riscosse
> Per sua prodezza e 'l trasse di travaglia.

> But Mandricardo is the one
> Who most effectively defends.
>   Alone he rescued Agramant
> And with his strength saved him from peril.
>   (3.8.47–48)

The reader also encounters Rodomonte for the first time in the poem in Canto 14 after the review of troops. He is introduced through a past history that is, however, completely new to the reader: "fu in Africa mandato da Agramante, / onde venuto era tre giorni inante" ("[he had been sent to Africa by Agramente, from where] he had returned only three days earlier"; 14.25). It is uncharacteristic of Ariosto to summarize action that never took place.[50] It would have been even more uncharacteristic of Rodamonte to have returned to Africa at the command of Agramante just when the Saracen forces were—according to Ariosto's own claim—on the verge of annihilating Christendom. No mention at all is made of the battle with Orlando left suspended at the close of 3.8.[51] On the contrary, the two knights seem to be separated by a time warp. While Orlando is introduced apparently a few hours after his battle against Rodamonte had been suspended due to the storm, Rodamonte has spent various months in Africa. At the same time, Ariosto was evidently well aware of the temporal incongruence that such a distancing of the two heroes would create. He technically avoids contradiction by inserting a jump in Orlando's narrative

---

[50] In fact, it only happens when there is a good reason, as in the case of Angelica and Sacripante discussed earlier.

[51] Ariosto was so successful in erasing the battle that Giovanni Ponte is alone in noting that the epic duel between Rodamonte and Orlando was omitted: "A conferma del distacco ariostesco dal Boiardo si pensi alla rinuncia nel *Furioso* a concludere quel grande duello Orlando-Rodomonte (nel pieno della loro forza e della loro volontà) che nell'*Innamorato* era stato impostato e sospeso ben due volte (II.25.2–11; 29.27–28; III.8.50)," "Boiardo e Ariosto," *La Rassegna della letteratura italiana* 79 (1975): 173 n. 9. In my view, however, there is neither "distacco" nor "rinuncia."

a few cantos before he introduces Rodomonte. Orlando, Ariosto tells us, wanders for several months searching for Angelica until spring (11.81–82). And the two are kept apart in time and space as the poem continues. Since Orlando was whisked out of Paris immediately after his introduction into the poem in Canto 8, Rodomonte's sudden arrival on the scene in Canto 14 allows him to reign supreme as the uncontested hero of the Battle of Paris for quite some time. Ariosto's battle tellingly combines elements from Rodamonte's arrival in France in *Innamorato* Book 2 and Agricane's lone attack of Albraca in *Innamorato* Book 1.[52] In both earlier episodes, as now, Orlando was absent.

Yet, just as Orlando's recovery of his Carolingian identity resurfaced in a new form, so the battle between Orlando and Rodamante reoccurs in a new setting. We are far from the epic dimensions of the Parisian battle when the two heroes eventually meet up. Their short and definitive confrontation will take place, in fact, in the most typical setting in the forest of romance—at a bridge over a river. Their battle recalls a previous one from the *Innamorato*, but, as one can well imagine, not one taking place in an epic context. As Orlando and Rodomonte struggle, they seem to hug each other and they both fall into the water ("[Orlando] cader del ponte si lasciò riverso / col pagano abbracciato come stava. / Cadon nel fiume e vanno al fondo insieme"; 29.47). This replays the scene between Orlando and Aridano at the entrance to Morgana's underwater realm:

> E così seco, come era abracciato,
> Giù nel gran lago se profonda armato
> [. . . .]
> Ché gionse con Orlando insino al fondo.
>
> And thus—in that embrace—with him,
> Down through the deep pool, armed, he swims.
> [. . . .]

---

[52] Rajna links OF 14.100–2, 100–3, 109–10, and 111–12 to OI 3.7.10, 7, 14, and 12–13 respectively, *Le fonti*, 245. In his edition to the *Innamorato*, Anceschi found additional similarities between OF 14.129 and OI 3.8.30, OF 16.29 and OI 3.8.42, and states more generally that the *Furioso*'s siege of Paris, beginning in 14.65, imitates the description of the attack on the city in OI 3.8, 1217 n. Griffiths also notes that Ariosto had Boiardo's description of the war in Book 3 in mind when he wrote his own version of it, citing in particular Rodomonte's exploits in Paris, "L'*Orlando Innamorato*, Book III," 29 n. 8.

He had reached bottom with the Count.
(2.7.61–63)[53]

Having lost their humanity because of disillusions in love, the two knights do not even recognize each other.[54] The battle between Orlando and Rodamonte has undergone a radical displacement and a degenerative transformation, but the very fact that it takes place at all reveals both Ariosto's memory of that struggle in his predecessor's poem and the desire on his part to both suppress and complete it. Orlando will not be given the honor of achieving a victory over Rodomonte, however, even in his animal state of raw strength. That privilege is reserved for Ruggiero, in the final duel that recovers the epic dimension that the *Furioso*'s bout between Orlando and Rodomonte deliberately lacked.

Ariosto's suppression of Boiardo's Battle of Paris requires various shifts of time: 1) Ariosto begins Angelica's story, and indeed the poem itself, by going back in time to the announced competition between Ranaldo and Orlando, thereby effacing the events that took place after that point and giving the impression that the Battle of Paris recounted in *Innamorato* 3.8 had not taken place. Moreover, throughout most of the first fourteen cantos he gives the sense that Charlemagne is still only expecting a siege; 2) Ariosto picks up Orlando's story just a few hours into the future of the first day of fighting in the Battle of Paris, which was interrupted in 3.8.52; 3) in order to reduce the importance of that day, Ariosto tells us that a battle had indeed been going on in Paris for an indefinite number of days; 4) Mandricardo is introduced as having just arrived a few days ago; 5) Ariosto brings Rodomonte into the narrative at the same time as Mandricardo, but telling us that he had just spent several months in Africa.

In conclusion, the Battle in Paris was the climax of what Boiardo had announced as: "La più stupenda guerra e la maggiore / Che racontasse mai prosa né verso" ("The largest, most amazing war / Attempted yet in prose or rhyme"; 2.29.1). If Ariosto goes to such lengths to erase both Orlando's return to his role of paladin in Book 3 and the epic battle that ensued,

---

[53] This phrasing is repeated by Fiordiligi in her account to Ranaldo: "Poi narrò che lo vide giù dal ponte / abbracciato cader con Rodomonte" ("She went on to describe how she had seen him fall from the bridge clinging to Rodomont"; 31.45).

[54] Carrara notes a parallel between their situations: "A ben guardare vi è un certo parallelismo tra le sventure amorose di Rodomonte e di Orlando [. . .]. Le due maggiori figure eroiche, le degne antagoniste dell'epopea ariostesca, sono ora di fronte: ma in quali atteggiamenti!" "Dall'*Innamorato*," 360, 367.

there is a good, practical reason. On a thematic level, Ariosto certainly could not claim to write "cosa non detta in prosa né in rima" ("what has never before been recounted in prose or rhyme"; 1.2) if he could not find a basis for Orlando's sinking into madness through excessive love. On a structural level, Orlando's return to Paris in time to save Charlemagne was a definite move toward closure that needed to be erased and then rewritten only once Ariosto's own poem had begun to move toward closure. As David Quint states quite simply with reference to the *Cinque canti*: "The nature of sequels is to open up the endings of the works they follow."[55] Remembering how eager the Ferrarese courtly society had been to hear more tales of Orlando "innamorato," it is not at all surprising that Ariosto would want to ignore its signs of completion in order to begin anew. What is remarkable, perhaps, is that his suppression of this last segment of Boiardo's poem was so systematic and so successful that it led readers to view the ending of the *Innamorato* from the perspective of the *Furioso*.

---

[55] Introduction, *Cinque canti / Five cantos*, trans. Alexander Sheers and David Quint (Berkeley and Los Angeles: Univ. of California Press, 1996), 4. Here Quint was making the point that the *Cinque canti* make the *Orlando Furioso* seem incomplete in retrospect. Yet, he does not say that the *Furioso* does the same thing to the *Innamorato*. On the contrary, elsewhere he has said: "The *Furioso* is a sequel to the *Innamorato* with a difference: it imposes an ending upon the open-ended narrative of the earlier poem," "The Figure of Atlante: Ariosto and Boiardo's Poem," *Modern Language Notes* 94 (1979): 80.

ROMANCE

WERNER GUNDERSHEIMER

"*Io ben comprendo la vergogna*":
The Faces of Shame in the *Orlando Innamorato*[1]

MANY SCHOLARS HAVE THOUGHT THAT Matteo Maria Boiardo left the *Orlando Innamorato* incomplete out of grief or anxiety at the French invasion in 1494. That opinion nicely reflects the nationalist and irredentist premises of earlier critical writing. Yet, it seems to take adequate account neither of the Ferrarese stance toward the French invasion, the powerful social and cultural bonds between the Este state and the French court, nor of Boiardo's own language and history. The poem's final stanza, while indeed topical, conforms to the standard formulae for leave-taking, which the poet used to sustain what might be called the illusion of orality.[2]

---

[1] The research for this article was facilitated by a machine-readable version of the poem created and distributed by the Oxford University Computing Service. The author wishes to thank David Robey and Marco Dorigatti, of the Faculty of Medieval and Modern Languages, Taylor Institution, Oxford University, for making this resource available to scholars, and Jo Ann Cavallo first for bringing it to my attention, and then for providing an MS-DOS-based copy for my use. Charles Stanley Ross helpfully confirmed my hunch that it would be possible to study shame in the *Orlando Innamorato*, and generously started me off with a few examples. Helpful suggestions came from several colleagues, especially Patricia Staeblein Harris, Cynthia Lewis, Gail Kern Paster, and Lee Vedder. Any mistakes, however, are mine.

[2] For a recent example of this approach, see Patricia Parker, *Inescapable Romance: Studies in the Poetics of a Mode* (Princeton: Princeton Univ. Press, 1979), 34: "The *Orlando Innamorato* breaks off when the jarring noise of real war intrudes upon the delights of amorous adventure." By way of contrast, Neil Harris also sees the Venetian War of 1482–84 as the principal agent of change in Boiardo's morale (*Bibliografia dell' "Orlando Innamorato,"* II (Modena: Edizioni Panini, 1991), 39–44. On Boiardo's literary antece-

The poet-figure frequently tells his audience that for one reason or another, he must suspend the narrative, but that he'll be back. These are precisely the elements of 3.9.26: the poet-figure will return "poco a poco" ("by and by") to tell his audience all the rest ("Racontarovi il tutto per espresso").[3] Boiardo's reference to the French is mild, especially when compared to Petrarch's famous lyric "Italia mia," which Machiavelli used to such powerful effect at the end of *Il Principe*.[4] The poet-figure even makes it clear that the Gallic presence had not heretofore kept him from his craft of versifying: "Mentre che io canto ... Vedo la Italia tutta a fiamma e a foco / Per questi Galli." Nor, I suggest, would their continuing presence have long silenced his muse, had it been as active after 1483 as it had obviously been before.[5] Sadly, Boiardo's death rendered permanent what would have been a temporary silence. In celebrating Boiardo's life and commemorating his accomplishments on this quincentenary, let us not inadvertently belittle him by conceding that his poetic voice would have yielded to a mere military campaign, however distasteful the outcome. Even if, as I believe, his reference to the French as sowing destruction "con gran valore" is ironical, one finds none of the indignation, wounded pride, outrage, or sense of shame here that emerges in Petrarch or Machiavelli.

Interestingly, however, Boiardo was no stranger to these emotions. However aristocratic his personal demeanor or omniscient and Olympian his poetic stance in the *Innamorato*, Boiardo had a deep understanding of the affects, and used that knowledge to great poetic effect. Recent scholarship has begun to reevaluate, and more fully appreciate, this poet's intellectual seriousness. As a result of the work of Michael Murrin, Jo Ann

---

dents, and in particular some of his sources, the best recent work is R. Alhaïque Pettinelli, *L'immaginario cavalleresco nel Rinascimento ferrarese* (Rome: Bonacci Editore, 1983), chapters 1–2.

[3] The standard work for the representation of the poet within Renaissance epics is Robert M. Durling, *The Figure of the Poet in Renaissance Epic* (Cambridge, MA: Harvard Univ. Press, 1965). For the narrator of the *Innamorato*, see especially 92–111.

[4] The poem is the sixteenth canzone. Machiavelli knew Petrarch's poems and letters well, and quotes from them in many places.

[5] It is important to recall that both of Boiardo's major literary works, the *Amorum Libri* and the *Orlando Innamorato*, were substantially completed and the latter work published by the time of the War of Venice-Ferrara (1482–84). Only the nine cantos of Book 3 were written later. The lyric poems collected in the *Amorum Libri* first appeared in print in 1499, but they circulated in manuscript beginning no later than 1477. A fine modern edition, with facing English translation and notes, has now been published by Andrea di Tommaso (Binghamton, NY: Medieval & Renaissance Texts & Studies, 1993).

Cavallo and others, we are less likely to accede to the standard view that "The *Innamorato* has all the energy, irony and fantasy of its most famous successor, and lacks only Ariosto's intangible sense of a higher significance underlying the entertainment,"[6] or that "what Boiardo begins as a carefree entertainment Ariosto integrates into his vision of human nature."[7] As Cavallo has shown, these conventional views needed correction from several different standpoints, and as a consequence of her work we can now approach the poem as, to some extent, a moral essay, a work of sustained allegory, a verbal tapestry of interlaced meanings and messages, a site of significant and powerful characterization, and a sustained meditation on the typologies of love.[8]

Strangely, it has taken nearly half a millenium to arrive at this level of insight into an accessible, even translucent, text. Perhaps the problems critics have had in seeing Boiardo whole are a legacy of the opacities of Francesco Berni's filtration system, a kind of arch, Renaissance Bowdlerization *avant la parole.*[9] The role of Lodovico Domenichi in the process was surely analogous.[10] In any event, now that we are actually reading Boiardo—Charles Ross has deprived even Anglo-Saxon readers of the last possible excuse for not doing so!—the thesis of the poet's underlying moral and intellectual seriousness ought to invite an ongoing process of confirmation and elaboration.[11] This essay is devoted to a first sally at carrying

---

[6] R. Andrews in J. R. Hale, ed. *A Concise Encyclopedia of the Italian Renaissance* (London: Thames & Hudson, 1981), 53.

[7] C. P. Brand, "Ariosto's Continuation of the *Orlando Innamorato*," *Cultural Aspects of the Italian Renaissance. Essays in Honour of Paul Oskar Kristeller*, ed. C. H. Clough (Manchester: Manchester Univ. Press, 1976), 385.

[8] Jo Ann Cavallo, *Boiardo's* Orlando Innamorato: *An Ethics of Desire* (Rutherford, NJ: Fairleigh Dickinson Univ. Press, 1993), esp. 156–60.

[9] H. F. Woodhouse, *Language and Style in a Renaissance Epic: Berni's Corrections to Boiardo's "Orlando Innamorato"* (London: The Modern Humanities Research Association, 1982) carefully and sympathetically analyzes Berni's methods and goals, without denying (or fully assessing) the consequences for Boiardo of having been largely superseded by a rewrite man. While Berni appreciated some of Boiardo's moral concerns, it seems clear that later generations of his readers imputed those concerns to Berni alone. See also E. B. Weaver, "The Spurious Text of Francesco Berni's *Rifacimento* of Matteo Maria Boiardo's *Orlando Innamorato*," *Modern Philology* 72, no. 2 (1977): 111–31.

[10] See Di Tommaso, *Amorum Libri*, 6–7, and the various editions of the poem as redone by Berni and Domenichi that are listed in the definitive bibliography by N. Harris, *Bibliografia dell'Orlando Innamorato*, 2 vols. (Modena: Panini Editore, 1988–91).

[11] M. M. Boiardo, *Orlando Innamorato.* Translated with an introduction and notes by Charles Stanley Ross (Berkeley and Los Angeles: Univ. of California Press, 1989). All quotations and translations from Boiardo are taken from this edition, unless otherwise

out that test of seriousness in relation to a single word—*vergogna*. Shame, after all, is a complex if universal emotion, which until relatively recently only rarely attracted serious and sustained attention, even from the psychotherapeutic community.[12] It figures prominently in the *Commedia* and, as one might expect, occurs in memorable and important ways in the epic tradition.

Yet, few if any earlier literary representations of *vergogna* prepare the reader for its central role in the moral economy of the emotions in the *Innamorato*, nor for the frequency with which it is invoked, nor the richness and variety of its functions in the narrative. Shame constitutes a recurrent theme, a verbal, thematic, and behavioral motif that seems to reflect a profound interest in this emotion on the part of author and readers alike. Boiardo's characters inflict shame upon themselves and others; they internalize shame and manifest it in their gestures and physiological responses; they accept it and reject it, talk about it and experience it in silence, overcome it and succumb to it. Wherever they turn, shame is there—in war, in love, in public, in private, in men, in women. Time and again, this affect has to be reckoned with.

How pervasive is Boiardo's interest in his characters' willingness to shame others and experience shame themselves? A few rough statistics may be helpful. The *Innamorato* is comprised of sixty-nine cantos. The word *vergogna* appears in forty-seven of them, or over seventy percent. You can find it in twenty-three of the twenty-nine cantos in Book 1, twenty of the thirty cantos in Book 2, and nine of the nine cantos in Book 3. At least eighty-five instances of the word occur in the course of the poem, more than any other affect tabulated, including guilt (*colpa*), which appears only thirteen times.[13] For purposes of comparison, Boiardo refers to

---

stated. Ross used the standard Italian edition of the *Innamorato*, ed. A. Scaglione, 2d ed. (Turin: UTET, 1963). I have occasionally translated a passage anew when a more literal rendering seemed appropriate.

[12] See the notes and bibliography to my "Renaissance Concepts of Shame and Pocaterra's *Dialoghi della Vergogna*," *Renaissance Quarterly* 47, no. 1 (spring 1994): 34–56, and the following studies by D. L. Nathanson, M.D.: *Shame and Pride: Affect, Sex and the Birth of the Self* (New York: Norton, 1992); "The Shame/Pride Axis," *The Role of Shame in Symptom Formation*, ed. H. B. Lewis (Hillsdale, NJ: Erlbaum Associates, 1987), 183–204; *The Many Faces of Shame*, ed. D. L. Nathanson (New York: Guilford, 1987).

[13] Nathanson, *Shame and Pride*, 19, explains the difference: "Shame often follows a moment of exposure; what has been exposed is something that we would have preferred to keep hidden, usually something of an intimate and personal nature. Although it can be handled or diminished by laughter, anger, or withdrawal, shame always speaks about our inner self rather than our actions."

jealousy (*zelosia*) eleven times, and pride (*orgoglio*) in about forty places.[14] Vast quantities of tears are shed throughout the poem, with ample justification, yet tear-words (*lacrima, lacrime, lacrimosa,* etc.) appear in only forty-five places, about half of the tally for shame. Whatever this may mean, it is clear that we have here an interesting phenomenon: the abundant presence of an emotion that (because we know it so well) we all try to avoid in daily life, but which the poet found uncommonly appropriate to his own understanding of human nature.

Boiardo's characters sometimes seem to have stepped out of the pages of *The Waning of the Middle Ages*, and it is surprising that Huizinga did not find a way of working a few of them into his portrayal of late medieval people, which itself derived almost exclusively from literary sources. Like Huizinga's classic but now superseded constructions of what he took to be actual people, Boiardo's fictive heroes, heroines, villains, and villainesses functioned at high levels of emotional intensity. Superhuman in their military and amatory affairs, their emotional world was also characterized by extreme states. Quick to laugh or cry, they do so with an awesome plenitude. Formidable in rage, passionate in love, inconsolable in grief, they act out their feelings with such manic intensity that the moments when they sit or lie down and talk things over seem like tiny oases of rationality in their (literally) epic struggles. If the world were a gigantic kindergarten for hyperactive adults, these people would be strong candidates for early admission. Like children, their emotions are close to the surface, and they are not shy about the primal urges that drive them on. In constructing his characters' experiences of shame, however, Boiardo writes of this affect with a naturalistic grasp that sets him apart from earlier writers of the romantic epic.

That is to say that Boiardo's people, in relation to shame, are something quite different from walking (or riding) emblems designed to illustrate the virtues or dangers of the emotions. Rather, they are fictive per-

---

"Often shame is confused with guilt, a related but quite different discomfort. Whereas shame is about the *quality* of our person or self, guilt is the painful emotion triggered when we become aware that we have acted in a way to bring harm to another person or to violate some important code. . . . Whenever we feel guilty, we can pay for the damage inflicted."

[14] Interestingly, the adjectival form of *zelosia,* (*geloso*), is not found at all in the *Orlando Innamorato*. I have recently addressed some aspects of the late Renaissance understanding of jealousy in Italy in " 'The Green-Eyed Monster': Renaissance Conceptions of Jealousy," *Proceedings of the American Philosophical Society* 137, no. 3 (September 1993), 321–31.

sonages who embody and actualize the affects in ways that the poet may have observed closely, and has certainly represented carefully. His treatment of shame strongly supports this distinction. For example, shame is typically manifested through several involuntary physical reactions, notably the blush, the averted gaze, the attempt to shrink away or cover up, and what Darwin called "confusion of mind."[15]

Almost like a modern novellist, Boiardo knows all about these responses. Thus, his characters commonly blush in expression of their shame. When the wizard springs a trap on Orlando, he reacts with shame to his captivity:

> Vermiglia avea la faccia come rosa
> Il conte Orlando per cotal vergogna;
>
> Count Orlando's face was red as a rose
> Because of such shame. (2.9.35; my trans.)

When King Manodante captures Orlando, planning to trade him for his son who is being held prisoner, he, too, professes shame for his lack of chivalry:

> A benché di vergogna io sia vermiglio,
> Pensando ch'io te fo mal capitare,
> Sapendo che tu merti onore e pregio;
>
> I turn bright red from my embarrassment [*vergogna*].
> I know you may be harmed—I think
> You merit honor.

Nevertheless, the king reconciles himself to his shame, realizing that he can accomplish the release of his son only by acting in an unchivalrous manner. Similarly, when King Manodante recognizes his own unworthy conduct as compared to Orlando's magnificent service to him, he erupts in a royal flush ("per vergogna e nel viso vermiglio"; 2.13.35). Later, Ranaldo learns that he had been rendered insensible and almost thrown off his horse by Feraguto. Such is his shame at this news that "Tutto nel viso divenne vermiglio" (2.24.50).

Other victims of shaming experiences also avert their gaze in a similarly involuntary acknowledgment of the trauma. When Leodilla tells Orlan-

---

[15] See Gundersheimer, *The Green-Eyed Monster*, 39 n. 13.

do her story, she explains how she appropriated the appearance of shame
in addressing her father:

> fingendo la faccia vermiglia
> E gli occhi quanto io pote vergognosi,
> Con quel parlar che a pianto se assomiglia,
> Nanti al mio patre ingenocchion mi posi.
>
> Making my face look very red,
> Trying to make my eyes seem modest [ashamed],
> Speaking so that I seemed to weep,
> I kneeled before my father. (1.21.55)

This passage seems especially suggestive, involving as it does feigned
shame, the ability actually to affect an affect.[16]

While castigating Aquilant and his associates, Ranaldo shames them by
asking them how they could bear not to avert their gaze:

> Come poteti gli occhi al celo alciare
> De vergogna, o vedere vi lasciati,
> Sendo tra gli altri si vituperati?
>
> How can you lift your eyes to heaven
> When you've been so disgraced [shamed] and scorned?
> How can you let yourselves be seen? (1.23.29)

As for Orlando, he has to deal with shame from the very first canto, when
Angelica makes her entrance:

> E talor gli occhi alla terra bassava
> Ché di se stesso assai si vergognava.
>
> He cast his eyes upon the ground
> For he was so ashamed [about himself]. (1.1.29)

Orlando's shame here, as elsewhere, comes from his inner life. Unlike Folderico's wife, who proclaims herself unashamed at having cheated her husband (1.22.11), Orlando would never do anything shameful, yet he is very
quick to experience shame.[17] It is he himself, not others, who senses this

---

[16] Fooling a parent, from Isaac and Jacob to, say, *Goodbye, Columbus*, would be a rich
theme for literary research.

[17] *OI* 2.2.4: "Ben stima lui che non seria fuggito / Mai per vergogna per nulla
maniera."

shame at his own susceptibility to the tormenting feelings of the lover, and who therefore experiences feelings ranging from mere embarrassment to loss of self-esteem to actual mortification.

Physical, or corporeal, shame may occasion blushing or aversion of the gaze, but it also tends to produce an attempt to cover or conceal the body. Boiardo uses *vergogna* to identify sexual or bodily shame, and is well aware of the instinctual responses to this sense of exposure. Thus, when Fiordelisa needs to have her birthmark verified, Brandimarte clears the room:

> É fatto gli altri tuor di quel cospetto,
> Pero che Fiordelisa avia vergogna,
> La fece avanti á loro aprire il petto,
> Onde più prova ormai non vi bisogna.
>
> He moved the others out of sight—
> Since Fiordelisa was so ashamed—
> And made her expose her breast in front of them,
> They needed no more proof than that. (2.27.30;
>   my trans.)

Such bodily or sexual modesty also occasions a wish for darkness, which among its other benefits conceals the marks of shame. Orlando feels this when, having rescued a seductive lady, he waits for night to fall:

> Mille anni pare á lui che asconda il sole,
> Per non avere al scur tanta vergogna;
> Perchè, benche non sappia dir parole,
> Pur spera di far fatti alla bisogna.
>
> The sunset seems a thousand years
> Darkness will leave him less embarrassed [ashamed].
> He hopes to do the deed, although
> He does not know the words to say. (1.29.48)

Without this cover, a person may be immobilized, like Mandricardo who is ashamed to emerge from a fountain where he is skinny-dipping:

> così ignudo non so che mi fare,
> Che mi ritiene alquanto la vergogna.[18]

---

[18] The incident ends well for Mandricardo, for his blond woman companion envelopes him in her tresses, takes him to her tent, and in the course of their dalliance, "pur scrive Turpin verace e giusto / Che il paviglion crollava intorno al fusto"—a nice

> Naked like this I don't know what to do,
> Shame is holding me back somewhat. (3.1.33;
>   my trans.)

At moments of acute shame, people typically undergo what Donald Nathanson has called "a cognitive shock, a period of time during which we are unable to think clearly or plot effective action."[19] Boiardo fully understood the power of shame to incapacitate, for he creates several situations in which characters are sufficiently confused that they are unable to respond to the demands of the moment. At one such moment of embarrassment, Orlando is "immoto," "sbigottito." Even giants are not immune, as when Ranaldo tries to get at one by breaking through a door:

> Il gran gigante se vede confuso,
> Tema e vergogna il fanno dubitare.

> The monstrous being seems confused
> And falters out of fear and shame. (1.9.32)

When Origilla recognizes Orlando, she finds herself speechless, and feeling, as we might put it, like death warmed over:

> Ben se credette alora de morire;
> Pallida viene ed abassa la fronte,
> E per vergogna non sa che se dire.

> She truly believed herself about to die;
> Turned pale and turned her face away,
> And from shame knew not what to say. (2.11.17;
>   my trans.)

When people talk about being mortified, they are generally talking about shame, an affect that can so rapidly and drastically undermine self-esteem that one seems to feel as bad as, or even worse than, being dead. That feeling, fortunately transitory most of the time, can be very powerful. The passage just quoted illustrates Boiardo's awareness of the existential linkage between shame and death, but he uses this observation with powerful results in several other places. In 1.2.26, a weeping, lovesick, depressed Orlando rouses himself from his lethargy with the thought that

---

instance of a Renaissance double-entendre that has survived into modern Italian slang.

[19] "Understanding Shame," in *Directions in Psychiatry*, 1989.

"per vergogna non voglio morire." When Ranaldo realizes that he has fought Marfisa all day without success, "He dies from shame, he feels disgraced" ("Mor di vergogna e pargli aver gran scorno"; 1.19.265). For Agramante, shame is more painful than death itself:

> Perchè avea di vergogna un tal sconforto,
> Che avria pena minore ad esser morto.
>
> He was so discomposed by shame
> He'd have hurt less had he been slain. (2.17.37)

Astolfo expresses a similar aversion to the prospect of shame when the frightful Grandonio turns to attack him. Though pale with terror, "He'd rather die than be put to shame" ("al morir più che a vergogna é dato"; my trans.)

If shame is worse than death for the chivalrous knight, he (or she) will go to considerable lengths to avoid it. Marfisa fights harder and talks tougher than almost anybody in the poem. For her, the slightest sign of weakness is shameful. At one point, she threatens to destroy a citadel by kicking it down, saying that she would be ashamed to use her sword ("avea vergogna di adoprarvi il brando"; 1.20.42). The possibility that *men* might perceive in her some weakness drives her to new heights of violence in combat:

> vergognata se stima e vilissima
> E che beffando ogni om dietro gli rida,
> Se tutto il mondo à more non disfida.
>
> She'd think herself disgraced and shamed
> And mocked by men behind her back
> Unless she dared the world to death. (1.34.1)

In that respect, Marfisa resembles other characters who try to escape the pervasiveness of shame, which must always be a potential presence on the field of honor. Ranaldo, having accidentally given the appearance of cowardice, addresses his remonstrances to God, believing that his reputation is in ruins: "Io son sempre in eterno vergognato"; a few stanzas later, he returns obsessively to the theme: "Questa vergogna ha l'onor mio coperto"; 1.5.48–50). Like the blush that covers the face to the roots of the hair, shame in Boiardo's striking image spreads itself over the candid face of honor.

Shame comes to Boiardo's characters in all sorts of military situations.

A knight has to worry about it when obliged to contend with people of lower status, with unarmed commoners, and especially with women. Provocative and threatening though she is, Brandimarte refuses to fight an unarmed Marfisa, feeling:

> Chè à ferire una dama disarmata
> . . . parea vergogna è grande iscorno.

> To hit an unprotected maid
> Seemed shameful—a disgrace!—to him. (2.19.9)

Even Orlando considers himself obliged to torture a woman on one occasion (2.4.30) to elicit some information. While he recognizes that his behavior is justified, that his action comes, so to speak, with the territory, he is shamed: "Mia sera la vergogna e tuo il dannaggio," he avers, and proceeds to do nasty things to her. For a good Christian knight, even a situationally necessary breach of code provides sufficient cause for shame. Some characters are less susceptible to shame, or better at rationalizing their actions, just like real people. For example, Ranaldo can't afford to be so easily ashamed; when he needs something, he takes it:

> Perch'io mi stimo che'l non sia vergogna
> Pigliar la robba, quando la bisogna.

> Since I believe it's no disgrace [vergogna]
> To take things when there's need for them. (2.9.35)

Ranaldo is the exception. Most knights shame quite easily. They can even be mortified through purely symbolic means. A Boiardan trickster named Aridano achieved this by hanging the captured weapons of certain knights upside down, purely to shame their owners:

> . . . l'armi di ciascun barone
> Ne' verdi rami d'intorno distese.
> Roverse le avea poste quel fellone,
> Per far la lor vergogna più palese. (2.9.43)

Such inversions were part of the semiotics of public life in Renaissance cities, as Edgerton's work on *pitture infamanti* and Davis's analysis of charivaris have shown.[20] Still, one welcomes from a great literary work further

---

[20] S. Y. Edgerton, *Pictures and Punishment: Art and Criminal Prosecution during the Florentine Renaissance* (Ithaca: Cornell Univ. Press, 1985), documents numerous instances of

evidence regarding secular rituals of humiliation.

The shame under discussion here is altogether different from the Germanic *schame* (the source of our word), which, according to Aldo Scaglione, played a vital role in the medieval chivalric epic. In such works as Wolfram von Eschenbach's *Parzifal, schame*—in the sense of "others' rights and needs" or what we might call deference—is enshrined among the qualities essential to a good knight. These include a good many more familiar traits like courtesy, compassion, generosity, humility, beauty, nobility, moderation, good breeding, leadership, and mastery of arms.[21] This courtly shame, a virtue related to humility and a proper sense of the limits of one's status in a social hierarchy, has some strong ties with shame seen as an affect, a powerful innate capacity to experience one's own inadequacy. *Vergogna* in the *Innamorato* is in fact frequently triggered by some real or imagined breach of code. However, as we have seen, it may also come from other directions, such as the perception or belief that one is in some way a loser.

The poet, in fact, seems to understand that the experience of shame is not only personal, but may also be contextually determined. For example, no knight would ever look forward to losing a battle, but there are opponents so mighty that to be killed by such people would be a cause for pride, not shame. When Ranaldo prepares to fight Gradasso, he proclaims:

> Non mi sera vergogna cotal sorte,
> Anci una gloria aver da te la morte.
>
> There'll be no shame in such a fate,
> Just glory, being slain by you. (1.5.10)

Boiardo of course had other plans for him anyway, but the attitude itself seems significant. Conversely, victory over an unworthy opponent can induce shame. Ranaldo's observation offers a particularly clear instance of

---

criminals hanged in effigy upside down, and explores the meaning of such representations. Unfortunately no examples of this public art survive, but in modern times this genre underwent a gruesome renaissance of its own when the actual body of Mussolini was hanged upside down in a public setting. For the ritual inversions practiced in early modern charivaris, see N. Z. Davis, *Society and Culture in Early Modern France* (Stanford: Stanford Univ. Press, 1975), chap. 4; she explores analogous phenomena in her essay "Women on Top," chap. 5.

[21] *Knights at Court: Courtliness, Chivalry, & Courtesy from Ottonian Germany to the Italian Renaissance* (Berkeley: Univ. of California Press, 1991), 158. The list, with minor deletions, is Scaglione's.

the way in which characters in this poem reveal a reflective self-awareness of their abilities to embrace shame and hold it at bay.

The contextuality of shame also appears as a national trait. When Ranaldo fights Rodamonte, the Saracen warrior tries to disable Baiardo, Ranaldo's horse, whereupon Ranaldo tries to shame him:

> Non ti vergogni, perfido, ribaldo,
> Ferir del brando à si digno animale?
> Forse nel tuo paese ardente e caldo,
> Ove virtute e prodezza non vale,
> De ferire il destriero é per usanza;
> Ma non se adopra tal costume in Franza.

> Ranaldo said, "False Saracen!
> You were not born of noble blood!
> Treacherous lout, aren't you ashamed
> To strike a precious animal?
> Maybe in your hot, burning land
> Where neither virtue counts nor worth,
> Your custom is to hit a horse,
> But that's not what we do in France!" (2.14.48)

Rodamonte brushes away this shaming rhetoric in words of contemptuous and profane dismissal:

> La usanza vostra non estimo un fico,
> Il peggio che io so far, faccio al nimico.

> I don't give a fig for the way you do things,
> The worst I know how to do, I do to my enemy.
>   (2.14.50; my trans.)

Despite this candid, matter-of-fact exposition of cultural difference, Ranaldo continues to regard Saracens as an inferior people (2.24.50), and that is understandable since they live outside the normative code through which shame and pride, unworthiness and self-esteem are mediated to the Christian knight.

Matteo Maria Boiardo might have understood the moral relativism implicit in the 1960s' saying "Different strokes for different folks," but his characters would have taken it literally. True to their chivalric origins, they act out their extraordinary feats on the field of battle and in the bower of Venus. In so doing, they vent their extravagant passions with a finely aestheticized naturalism. For behind and above them, moving them about for an urbane, sophisticated readership of Renaissance courtiers and ladies, we can discern the shadowy figure of a great puppeteer, an archly knowing courtier, keenly observant of human nature and behavior in all its protean complexity. If, as Durling has argued, this poet works to provide *diletto*, it is a delight in a dilated view of men and women in their essential roles of love and work.[22] To his "dolce compagnia," Boiardo offers if not a tapestry at least a cartoon in the Renaissance sense, a thoughtful and nuanced *disegno* of the minds and hearts of his masterfully sketched humanity.

---

[22] On the concept *dilatio* and its applicability to the European epic (in senses far more technical than that used here), see Patricia Parker, *Inescapable Romance*.

MANUELE GRAGNOLATI

Love, Lust, and Avarice:
Leodilla between Dante and Ovid

LEODILLA IS A FAMOUS EXAMPLE OF A "malmaritata," an unhappily married woman. She appears in the *Orlando innamorato* for the first time in 1.20-10, where she is saved by Brandimarte and Orlando from three giants. In order to avoid her marriage with old Folderico, she had challenged him to a race. But Leodilla was defeated because her avarice forced her to stop in order to catch three heavy golden apples. She had then betrayed her husband with young Ordauro and had tried to escape with him, but was caught by Folderico and eventually kidnapped by the giants. After being rescued, Leodilla meets her beloved Ordauro and leaves with him.

When Leodilla appears many cantos later in her father's castle (2.13.46–49), Boiardo recalls the details of her story as he is about to introduce the episode of Doristella, the other famous "malmaritata" of the poem. This episode, also based on *Decameron* 2.10, replays several features of the earlier story. For instance, both girls are rescued by Brandimarte from the dangers incurred when they attempted to betray their husbands to whom they were married against their will. Both girls tell their stories in the form of a versified *novella* constructed with the same narrative technique;[1] both turn out to be long-lost siblings of major characters: Leodilla discovers that she is the sister of Brandimarte while Doristella the sister of

---

[1] See Marina Beer, "Alcune osservazioni sulla novella nell'*Orlando Innamorato*," in Riccardo Bruscagli and Amedeo Quondam, eds., *Tipografie e romanzi in Val Padana fra Quattro e Cinquecento* (Modena: Panini, 1992), 146, 150, and n. 14.

Fiordelisa, Brandimarte's beloved. Both stories end with the return of the girl to her father's castle and with the celebration of values fundamental to Boiardo, namely friendship, family (represented by the discovery of familial bonds) and religion (represented by conversion to the Catholic faith). But one difference between their stories is striking. While Doristella marries—the importance of this moment is emphasized by the fact that her marriage is celebrated together with that of her sister Fiordelisa to Brandimarte—Leodilla appears alone at the castle of her father Manodante. Boiardo leaves her in 1.25.22 and does not say whether she marries Ordauro, or even whether she continues her relationship with him. This ambiguity, due to the uncertainty of her marriage, is all the more significant if we think of the value marriage has in the medieval tradition as an instrument of the redemption of the Fall and as a legitimization of carnal love.[2]

As Jo Ann Cavallo points out, the links between the two episodes based on *Decameron* 2.10 situate Leodilla and Doristella along a spectrum of positive loves, which Brandimarte and Fiordelisa exemplify to a greater extent, and Ruggiero and Bradamante to an ideal one.[3]

While Cavallo suggests that Leodilla is "less deserving than Doristella" of a fully happy ending due to the avarice that led her to her mismatched marriage and to her fickleness shown by her attraction for Orlando,[4] I would go further and argue that Leodilla, in a certain way, represents an exemplary contamination of avarice and lust. Focusing on the passages from Ovid and Dante that are important sources of the episode, my analysis will suggest that Boiardo uses the character of Leodilla to reflect on the inherent affinities between lust and avarice. These two elements, as we

---

[2] Antonio Franceschetti, regarding Leodilla, speaks of "nessuna conclusione né in bene né in male," and says that, at the end of her adventures, the girl is "nel punto stesso, si direbbe, in cui erano iniziate le sue peripezie," *L'"Orlando Innamorato" e le sue componenti tematiche e strutturali* (Florence: Olschki, 1975), 90–91. For the value of marriage in the Middle Ages, see George Economou, "The Two Venuses and Courtly Love," in Joan Ferrante, George Economou et al., eds., *In Pursuit of Perfection: Courtly Love in Medieval Literature* (Port Washington: Kennikat Press Corp., 1975), 17–19; and Giuseppe Mazzotta, *The World at Play in Boccaccio's "Decameron"* (Princeton: Princeton Univ. Press, 1986), 125–26. See also Jo Ann Cavallo, *Boiardo's* Orlando Innamorato: *An Ethics of Desire* (Rutherford, NJ: Fairleigh Dickinson Univ. Press, 1993), 146. For the importance of marriage in Boiardo, see the comment to the sixth eclogue in Guido Mazzoni, "Le ecloghe volgari e il Timone," *Studi su Matteo Maria Boiardo*, ed. Naborre Campanini (Bologna: Zanichelli, 1894), 335–41.

[3] Cavallo, *Boiardo's* Orlando Innamorato, 130–36.

[4] Cavallo, *Boiardo's* Orlando Innamorato, 134.

will see, are closely related and intersect continually. Nevertheless, I will consider them separately in the interest of clarity.

The first time Leodilla appears, she is next to a "tesoro" (1.20.20), a fact which immediately establishes a connection between the girl and wealth. In the following canto, when Brandimarte is wounded, Leodilla demonstrates a singular familiarity with an "erba soprana"—the same "sovereign herb" mentioned again at the end of her story (2.13.49)—that has special characteristics and is compared to gold and silver:

> By the day's light it looks like *gold*;
> It seems to scintillate at night.
> The flower of this wondrous plant
> Is red, its root like *silver*, white. (1.21.40)[5]

With the first words that Leodilla says in the poem, she presents herself as the daughter of the king of the "Isole Lontane" and insists on the wealth of her father:

> The King of Islands Far away,
> My father, gathers the world's treasure.
> His hands hold so much *gold* and *silver*,
> No horde beneath the moon holds more.
> The sun shines on no greater riches,
> And I was heir to all of this. (1.21.49)

In the next two octaves she repeats herself and draws attention to her own riches:

> I was the daughter of a king,
> Beautiful, happy, rich in things— (1.21.50)

> Intelligence had spread abroad
> Of my old father's massive wealth. (1.21.51)

In the course of the poem, Boiardo never stops emphasizing Manodante's wealth, as though abundance of money were the only characteristic of the "Isole Lontane":[6]

---

[5] Quotations from the *Orlando Innamorato* are taken from the bilingual edition of Charles Ross (Berkeley and Los Angeles: Univ. of California Press, 1989). Italics are mine.

[6] See also 2.13.10, where Manodante is defined as "a great and powerful king."

> An old king, Manodante, lives
> At Damogir, across the ocean,
> And he has gathered greater wealth
> Than any mind can contemplate. (2.11.46)
>
> They reached the royal palace—its
> Richness unequaled in the world. (2.13.45)

The insistence on the incredible wealth of Leodilla's father serves both to emphasize Leodilla's avarice and to deny her a justification for what will soon appear as one of her most marked inclinations. I would even suggest that her very connection to the wealthy kingdom of the "Isole Lontane" is the origin of Leodilla's avarice.[7] Wealth and insatiable greed are connected elsewhere in the poem, right from the opening stanzas in which Boiardo states:

> And as it happens to great lords
> Who only want what they can't have,
> The greater obstacles there are
> To reaching what they would obtain
> The more they jeopardize their realms,
> And what they want, they cannot gain. (1.1.5)

A link between wealth and avarice, also emphasized by references to Dante's *lupa* and its insatiability, is established again in the description of the door of "Ricchezza" in Medusa's garden where Riches and Avarice sit side by side:[8]

---

[7] It does not seem casual that Brandimarte, Leodilla's brother, was originally called Bramadoro ("greed of gold"): the change of his personality, which is reflected in the change of his name, may be due to the fact that the child is kidnapped and taken to Rocca Silvana. Here, nature, which is represented by the name of the place, might have purified the child from the influences of the father's castle, though not completely. The significance of the name "Bramadoro" is pointed out by Charles Ross, "Angelica and the Fata Morgana: Boiardo's Allegory of Love," *Modern Language Notes* 96 (1981): 13. n. 4. In 1.22.57–61 Brandimarte, who has not listened to Leodilla's words because he is too concentrated on Fiordelisa (1.21.70), follows Morgana's deer. This animal represents wealth and does not seduce Orlando, who is always immune from the sin of avarice (1.25.13–16). On this aspect, see Beer, "Alcune osservazioni," 157–58.

[8] For my analysis it is interesting to note that in Freud's interpretation Medusa represents the emblem of the threat of feminine seduction (Sigmund Freud, "Medusa's Head," *Sexuality and the Psychology of Love*, ed. P. Rieff [New York: Collier, 1963], 212–13). For the interpretation of Medusa as the expression of threat both sensual and rhetorical, see John Freccero, "Medusa: The Letter and the Spirit," *Dante: The Poetics of Conversion*, ed. Rachel Jacoff (Cambridge, MA: Harvard Univ. Press), 1986, 119–35. Dante already links

> But at the door that's opposite
> (Where you'll leave) you'll find Riches sits,
> Hated, though no one dares to say it—
> She does not care; she mocks all men,
> You must give her a piece of branch:
> That is the only way to pass,
> For next to her sits Avarice—
> Though she has much, for more she asks. (1.12.36)[9]

As we will see, this connection between having much and desiring more is emphasized in Orlando's famous speech to the "fata del lago" in 1.25.14. It should not be surprising, therefore, that the very rich Leodilla, the daughter of the wealthiest man on earth, is so attracted to wealth and treasure.

At the beginning of the tale, the reader sympathizes with Leodilla, who had just taken such devoted care of Brandimarte that Boiardo uses the adverb "dolcemente" twice (1.21.39 and 48). When she speaks of her marriage and says that she had to choose between two candidates, her attraction to the young and beautiful Ordauro seems perfectly understandable, even though it is difficult to interpret her "shame" (1.21.53). But the reader's sympathy fades when Leodilla says that, in an attempt to avoid marriage to the old Folderico, she trusted in her wickedness ("malizia") and made a "hard and cruel" request. She convinced her father to enact a "law" stating that whoever wished to marry the girl must defeat her in a race: the winner would marry Leodilla as his prize, but the losers would be punished by death. The explicit model for this scene, as has been noted, is the myth of Atalanta and Hippomenes as told by Ovid in *Metamorphoses* 10.560–707.[10] What has not been noted, however, is the way in which Boiardo invites a comparison with this text. He even uses the Ovidian text in the construction of his character's name. "Leodilla" is a

---

avarice and *eros* in *Paradiso* 9.127–42, when in the heaven of Venus, Folquet de Marselha condemns the avarice of the clergy.

[9] "Ma a l'opposita porta, ove hai a uscire, / Ritrovarai sedersi la Ricchezza, / Odiata assai, ma non se gli osa a dire; / Lei ciò non cura, e ciascadun disprezza. / Parte del ramo qui convienci offrire, / Né si passa altramente quella altezza, / Perché Avarizia apresso lei li siede; / Benché abbia molto, sempre più richiede."

[10] For instance, see Giulio Razzoli, *Per le fonti dell'"Orlando Innamorato"* (Milan: Albrighi, Segati e C., 1901), 84; Giulio Reichenbach, *L'"Orlando Innamorato" di M. M. Boiardo* (Florence: La Nuova Italia, 1936), 62–74; Ross, "Angelica and the Fata Morgana," 13.

possible reference to the fact that the Ovidian narrative ends with the metamorphoses of Atalanta and Hippomenes into lions. An analysis that reconciles the two texts is, therefore, indispensable for a more complete understanding of the episode in the *Orlando Innamorato*.[11]

Several of Boiardo's variations with respect to the Ovidian narration are of great importance. First and foremost, Atalanta decides to enact the cruel law because she is trying to protect herself from the oracle predicting her death should she marry (*Met* 10.564-66). Leodilla, on the other hand, uses the same cruel conditions in an attempt to pursue her infatuation for Ordauro. Ovid underlines the confused psychological condition of Atalanta, who loves Hippomenes and thus does not know what to do (*Met* 10.636-37). Because of this uncertainty we can excuse the fact that the girl stops to gather the first two apples. But Ovid wants to emphasize further her lack of responsibility by having Venus help Hippomenes. If it were not for the goddess who forces—"coegi" in line 676 is quite strong—Atalanta to take the third apple (that the goddess herself renders even heavier), Hippomenes probably would have lost the contest. Venus explains:

> And obliquely into a side of the field, returning whence she would lose much time, with all his youthful strength he threw the shining gold. The girl seemed to hesitate whether or not she should go after it. I forced her to take it up, and added weight to the fruit she carried, and so impeded her equally with the weight of her burden and with her loss of time. (10.674-78)[12]

The contest of Leodilla is different; despite her obvious wealth and her calculating intelligence, she is attracted by the gold and moves toward it impetuously:

---

[11] Francesca Battera has considered the sources of Leodilla's episode, particularly the Ovidian myth of Atalanta and a novella from the *Libro dei Sette Savi* ("Per una lettura di *Orlando Innamorato* I, xx–xxii," *Studi e problemi di critica testuale* 34 [1987]: 85–103). Battera connects Leodilla with avarice on the basis of Boccaccio's interpretation of the Ovidian myth in the *Genealogie* and Berni's "translation," but does not consider the fact that Boiardo deliberately invites a comparison with the Ovidian story. I am analyzing the implications of this comparison.

[12] "Inque latus campi, quo tardius illa rediret, / iecit ab obliquo nitidum iuvenaliter aurum. / an peteret, virgo visa est dubitare; coegi / tollere et adieci sublato pondera malo / inpediique oneris pariter gravitate moraque." I quote the Latin and English texts from Ovid, *Metamorphoses*, trans. Frank J. Miller. Second edition, revised by G. P. Goold (Cambridge, MA: Harvard Univ. Press, 1984), 112–13.

> But when he saw that I would pass,
> He quickly from his purse withdrew
> A polished apple made of gold.
> Enchanted by that gilded fruit
> I chased it, leaving my pursuit.
>
> That material is so beautiful
> It leads most of the world astray.
> The slippery, round apple rolled,
> And I had trouble catching hold,
> And when I did, he threw the next
> And still ran on in front of me,
> But tiring now, so that at once
> I seized the apple and caught up. (1.21.62–63)[13]

After grabbing the two apples, Leodilla is determined not to turn back again for any reason:

> I told myself, "I must be sure
> To turn back now for nothing else.
> I won't swerve one inch for the world—
> I want no husband who is old." (1.21.64)

But when Folderico throws the third apple, the girl is dazzled by its splendor. She stops thinking and avidly grabs the treasure and thereby loses the race:

> That's what I said within my heart.
> I raced, my hopes almost fulfilled,
> When that old, treacherous criminal
> Threw the third apple from his purse.
> Its splendor was so dazzling that,
> Although the race had no time left,
> I ran to snatch the globe, and so
> Never again caught Folderico. (1.21.66)[14]

---

[13] "Come lui vide che a passarlo andava, / Un pomo d'oro lucido e polito / Fuor della tasca subito cavava; / Io, che invaghita fui di quel lavoro, / Lasciai la corsa e venni al pomo d'oro. / Ché quel metallo in vista è si iocondo, / Che la più parte del mondo disvia; / Et era sì volubile e ritondo, / Che de pigliarlo gran fatica avia. / Io presi il primo, e lui gettò il secondo, / Fuggendomi davanti tuttavia, / Dove ebbi assai fatica, et ad un ponto / Questo pigliai et ebbilo ancor gionto."

[14] "Così parlava meco nel mio core, / Alegra, già vicina alla speranza, / Quando il

The rewriting of the myth of Atalanta demonstrates how "in his use of
the works of Ovid or Boccaccio or the *Roman de la rose*, Boiardo consistently shapes his own narrative to remove some of the features that made
these earlier texts morally ambiguous."[15] There are no ambiguities in the
Orlando Innamorato episode; gone are Atalanta's extenuating circumstances
(her love for Hippomenes and divine intervention) that attracted the sympathy of the reader. The personal responsibility of Leodilla and her blinding avarice become even more clear if we remember that at the beginning
of her speech she tells Brandimarte and Orlando that her story is exemplary of how "others / Suffer strange shifts of Fortune too." (1.21.49). In contrast with Brandimarte's previous—and justified—reference to "ruthless
Fortune" (1.21.44) and "wicked Fortune" (1.21.46), Leodilla has little
with which she can rebuke Fortune. Her story reveals both her inconsis-
tency and her failure to recognize her own responsibility, a failure that is
also typical of the characters of Dante's *Inferno* and is a sign of her conversion manqué.

At this point it will be useful to consider the description of the apples
thrown by Folderico and the spell they cast on Leodilla. As can be noted
from the passages cited above (1.21.62–66), all the attention is placed on
the exterior aspects of the glittering apples and on *sight*—the sense characteristic of narcissistic love that unites *eros* and self-love[16]—as the sense
that is involved and subsequently overcome. Although the starting point
is Ovidian, as twice Ovid defines the apple thrown by Hippomenes as
"nitidum" (*Met* 10.666 and 675), Boiardo amplifies the motif of the brilliance and brightness of Folderico's golden apples that are "lucid[i] e po-
lit[i]," "in vista . . . iocond[i]," "sì volubil[i] e ritond[i]," and of a dazzling
splendor. Later, Boiardo will use the same words to describe the golden
apples of Orgagna's garden. In that episode, which shows the necessity of
using reason to control the senses, Orlando defeats various female monsters with the help of a book, and then must cut down a tree of golden
apples in order to destroy the garden. These apples, too, are described with
an emphasis on the sense of sight. The tree is "bella da riguardare oltra
misura" (2.5.6) and in describing the fruit and the trunk Boiardo reuses

---

vecchio malvaggio e traditore / Il terzo pomo della tasca lanza; / E tanto me abagliò col
suo splendore, / Che, benché tempo al corso non me avanza, / Pur venni adietro e quel
pomo pigliai, / Né Folderico più gionsi giamai."

[15] Cavallo, *Boiardo's* Orlando Innamorato, 10.

[16] Cavallo, *Boiardo's* Orlando Innamorato, 39–41.

the adjectives with which he had described the golden apples in the Leodilla episode:

> Di *vaghe pome d'oro* è tutto adorno;
> Queste son grave e *lucide e rotonde*,
> E son sospese a un ramo piccolino:
> Grande è il periglio ad esser lì vicino.

> Pretty, gold apples grace the tree,
> Heavy and round and radiant,
> And they hang from a slender branch
> And menace people who come near. (2.5.7)

> Il tronco da lì in gioso è sì *polito*,
> Che non vi salirebbe anima data.

> The trunk, from branches down, is smooth,
> So no soul born of man could climb. (2.5.9)

The complementary readings of Michael Murrin[17] and Cavallo allow
a complex interpretation of the episode and, above all, allow us to see a
combination of the sins of lust and avarice in the golden apples in Orgagna's garden. As Murrin points out, avarice is represented by the golden
ass with the serpent-tail that guards the door made of precious gems, while
the peacock-lady represents sight, the sense that is involved in all the appetites and especially characterizes avarice. Orlando, instructed by the
book, knows that he must not look at the bird and has little difficulty killing it as he is never tempted by the sin of avarice. Murrin shows, through
the conflation of the figure Eris/Iris (who represents the splendors of
wealth and at the same time its dangers), the connection of the peacock-
lady to the figure of Juno. He argues, therefore, that the golden apples,
which set in motion the Trojan War and which conclude the episode of
Falerina's Garden, hold the connotation of avarice. Cavallo, on the other
hand, examines the biblical intertexts in order to emphasize the necessity
of reason as controller of the senses; she analyzes the three monstrous figures (the siren, the harpy, and the faun) as manifestations of female intrigue and of the dangers of sensuality, linking the tree of the golden

---

[17] Michael Murrin, "Falerina's Garden," in *The Allegorical Epic: Essays in its Rise and
Decline* (Chicago: Univ. of Chicago Press, 1980), 53–85.

apples with the tree in the garden of Eden.[18] One last confirmation of
the contamination of lust and avarice represented by Orgagna's golden
apples—and therefore the identical golden apples in the Leodilla episode—
is the fact that just as the apples remind us of Juno and thus of avarice,
they also remind us of Venus, the goddess who won Paris's apple, and of
the sensuality and *eros* she represents.

If, then, Leodilla's avarice is the cause of her defeat in the competition
and of her subsequent marriage to Folderico, we can say that the extremely rich girl does not learn from her mistakes. In the second part of her novella, Leodilla recounts that, after having deceived Folderico, she took her
husband's treasure and left with the very rich Ordauro:

> The rest was serving girls and grooms,
> All ambling slowly, all unarmed.
> We had a caravan of camels
> Carrying food and gold and silver.
> Everything, every treasure chest,
> That ancient, evil man possessed
> With little danger we'd removed
> When I came through the tunnel's gloom. (1.22.48)

Boiardo thereby suggests that if the two greedy lovers had not had the burden of the stolen treasure that forced them to move slowly, they could
have escaped without being caught by Folderico. Avarice punishes Leodilla for the second time, and her responsibility for her own downfall is emphasized by the contrast with the sources that Boiardo uses in the construction of the second part of the novella, Plautus's *Miles Gloriosus* and a
novella from the *Libro dei sette savi*, which both contain a happy ending.[19]

Boiardo's attitude toward wealth and riches in this episode concords
with his statements elsewhere in the *Orlando Innamorato* as well as in the
Timone. Humanistic moral philosophy taught that the magnanimous soul
must be above the attraction of wealth and dignity.[20] Boiardo seems to

---

[18] Cavallo, *Boiardo's* Orlando Innamorato, 90–95.

[19] For these sources, see Colbert Searles, "The Leodilla Episode in Bojardo's *Orlando
Innamorato*," *Modern Language Notes* 17 (1902): 406–11; and Battera, "Per una lettura di
Orlando Innamorato."

[20] See Georg Weise, *L'ideale eroico del Rinascimento e le sue premesse umanistiche*
(Naples: Edizioni Scientifiche Italiane, 1961), 1: 213–15, where one can find statements
by Guarino of Verona ("id esse fortis et magnanimi sprevisse divitias") and Coluccio
Salutati ("Magni quidem et preclari animi est non desiderare divitias, sed maximi con-

move toward a more earthly conception of money, in the sense that he acknowledges its positive value: he does not condemn wealth per se but,
rather, the excessive greed for wealth and the attempts to attain it. The
subsequent ideal is the aristocratic conception of measure, of *aurea medio-
critas*, a use of money controlled by reason.

In the poem, the discourse is dialectic and contrasts Orlando to Ranaldo and Brandimarte. After the success in the first two tests of the "fata del
lago," Orlando is invited to hunt Morgana's deer, which Morgana promised would give him infinite wealth. Not only does the knight immediately
refuse, but he also emphasizes, through a reference to Boethius and Dante,
his disinterest toward wealth:[21]

> —Dama, non mi grava
> Avermi posto a rischio de morire,
> Però che di periglio e di fatica
> L'onor de cavalier sol se nutrica.
>
> Ma l'acquisto de l'oro e de l'argento
> Non m'avria fatto mai il brando cavare;
> *Però chi pone ad acquistar talento,*
> *Lui se vol senza fine affaticare;*
> *E come acquista più, manco è contento,*
> *Né si può lo appetito saziare;*
> *Ché qualunche n'ha più, più ne desia:*
> *Adunque senza capo è questa via.*
>
> Lady, I don't care
> That I have run the risk of death,
> Since weariness and perils are
> What feed the fame of cavaliers.
>
> But to win gold or silver, I
> Would never have unsheathed my sword,
> *Since those who set their minds on wealth*
> *Are working at an endless labor.*

tempsisse"; "nichil est tam angusti tamque stricti animi quam amare divitias, nichil ho-
nestius, nichil magnificentius quam contemnere si non habeas, sed si habeas, ad liberali-
tatem mugnificentiamque conferre").

[21] For the references to Boethius's *De consolatione philosophiae*, see Cavallo, *Boiardo's
Orlando Innamorato*, 100–1.

They're less content the more they get—
They never can be satisfied.
Those who have much want only more,
And there's no end to such a road. (1.25.13–14)[22]

An analysis of the Dantesque intertext of Orlando's words allows a more thorough comprehension of avarice and the spiritual condition of restlessness that it implies. Known as Dante's canzone of avarice, "Doglia me reca ne lo core ardire" depicts the "mad desire" that pulls the "avaro" to run after what will never give him satisfaction:

> Corre l'avaro ma più fugge pace;
> oh mente cieca, che non pò vedere
> lo suo folle volere
> che'l numero, ch'ognora a passar bada,
> che 'nfinito vaneggia.
> Ecco giunta colei che ne pareggia:
> dimmi, che hai tu fatto,
> cieco avaro disfatto?

The miser runs, but peace flees faster: oh blind mind, whose mad desire cannot see that number, which it seeks always to pass,

---

[22] Ranaldo's attitude is different from Orlando's. After being rescued along with other knights by Orlando from Morgana's realm, Ranaldo tries to leave with a chair of pure gold, which he plans to use to pay his soldiers. Orlando rebukes him and says that "era viltate / a girne carco a guisa di somiero"; Ranaldo answers contrasting a realistic utilitarianism to his cousin's aristocratic contempt for things he does not need: "I know a friar / Who used to preach, and his job was / To tell the good of abstinence. / He easily showed this with words, / But he had such a bulging paunch, / One step was all that he could launch! / Your words are like that friar's—false. / You preach precisely as he does, / Who praises fasts, his body filled, / Whose only prayers are for his geese. / King Charles rewards you lavishly, / And you're provisioned by the pope. / You've towns and castles numberless: / You're count of Blaye, lord of Anglant! / I'm poor! I hardly own one hill!— / Montalban's all I have on earth! / Sometimes I've got no food unless / I go and earn it on the plain! / When luck or something come my way, / I help myself with both my hands, / Since I believe it's no disgrace / To take things when there's need for them"; (2.9.33–35). Franceschetti (L'"Orlando Innamorato," 120) notes that here "all'utopistico ideale si contrappone così la realtà quotidiana e il senso pratico della vita, e proprio il diverbio fra Ranaldo e Orlando sulla sedia d'oro ci sottolinea che il poeta è molto più partecipe e sentimentalmente legato a quest'ultima che al primo." This conception, at the same time, serves to emphasize Leodilla's avarice: Leodilla is, as the poet often reminds us, extremely rich and therefore has no justification for her excessive attachment to money.

stretches to infinity. Now here is the one who makes us all equal:
tell me, what have you done, blind undone miser? (69–70)

The same concept is expressed in *Convivio* 3.15.9:

> In questo errore [di "sempre desiderare e non compiere mai suo
> desiderio"] cade l'avaro maladetto, e non s'accorge che desidera sì
> sempre desiderare, andando dietro al numero impossibile a gi-
> ungere.

> And into this error falls the cursed miser, and he does not realize
> that he desires himself always to desire, going after the number im-
> possible to reach.[23]

As Teodolinda Barolini points out, Dante here underscores the common
ground of all concupiscence. In particular, Dante constitutes an important
precedent for Boiardo's construction of the character of Leodilla, because
"Doglia mi reca" links carnal desire to desire for wealth: both are immoderate and excessive, and both are condemned to insatiability. This conception condemns the forms of desire that are far from reason ("ragione") and
measure ("misura") and connects them with each other, foreshadowing
the *lupa*, the all-embracing model of cupidity and insatiability of the *Commedia*.[24]

---

[23] I quote the English translation of both passages from Teodolinda Barolini, "Dante
and His Lyric Past," *The Cambridge Companion to Dante*, ed. Rachel Jacoff (Cambridge:
Cambridge Univ. Press, 1993), 31. Another passage from the *Convivio* is exemplary of the
restless condition to which desire can lead, when it is addressed in the wrong path:
". . . l'anima nostra, incontamente che nel nuovo e mai non fatto cammino di questa
vita entra, dirizza li occhi al termine del suo sommo bene, e però, qualunque cosa crede
che paia in sé avere alcuno bene, crede che sia esso. E perché la sua conoscenza prima
è imperfetta, per non essere esperta né dottrinata, piccioli beni le paiono grandi, e però
da quelli comincia prima a desiderare. Onde vedemo li parvuli desiderare massimamente
un pomo; e poi una donna; e poi, più procedendo, desiderare uno augellino; e poi, più
oltre, desiderare bel vestimento; e poi lo cavallo; e poi una donna; e poi ricchezza non
grande, e poi grande, e poi più. E questo incontra perché in nulla di queste cose truova
quella che va cercando, e credela trovare più oltre. . . . Ne la vita umana sono diversi
cammini, de li quali uno è veracissimo e un altro è fallacissimo, e certi meno fallaci e
certi meno veraci. E sì come vedemo che quello che dirittissimo vae a la cittade, e compie lo desiderio e dà posa dopo la fatica, e quello che va in contrario mai nol compie e
mai posa dare non può, così ne la nostra vita avviene: lo buono camminatore giugne a
termine e a posa; lo erroneo mai non lo aggiugne, ma con molta fatica del suo animo
sempre con li occhi gulosi si mira innanzi." (4.12.15–19)

[24] Barolini, "Dante and His Lyric Past," 29–32; and "Guittone's 'Ora parrà', Dante's
'Doglia me reca,' and the *Commedia*'s Anatomy of Desire," *Proceedings of the First Inter-*

The *Timone* allows an even better understanding of Boiardo's meditation on avarice and desire. The poet explicitly expresses the ideal of the
golden mean that refuses both the ascetic distance from the world and the
excessive and lustful attachment to material goods.[25] Richeza and Ausi-
lio's speeches, in the second act and at the very end of the play, respectively, are two clear examples of the moral principle of measure and reason
as the guides of life:

> Ora tu intendi lo effecto importuno
> De le due extremitate, et io non lodo
> Né quel né questo, e biasimo ciascuno;
> Ma solamente con color me aprodo
> *Che sano usar misura temperata*
> *E son discreti*; e con questi mi godo,
> Quai non mi tengon troppo riserrata,
> Ni me lasciano andare in abandono
> Usandomi a bisogni dislegata.

Now you can understand the negative effect of both extremities. /
I praise neither this nor that, but condemn both. / I can only be
with those people / who can use temperate measure / and are discrete. I enjoy myself only with those / who do not enchain me too
much / nor leave me in abandon, / using me without control according to their needs. (2.1; my trans.)

---

national Dante Seminar, Princeton, October 1994, ed. Robert Hollander (Florence: Le
Lettere, 1998). In "Doglia mi reca," for instance, the misers are characterized precisely
by their "dismisura": "Come con dismisura si rauna, / così con dismisura si distringe"
(85–86). The same way, the sinners of the circle of avarice and prodigality in the *Inferno*
are both unable to use "misura" ("Tutti quanti fuor guerci / sì de la mente in la vita
primaia, / che con misura nullo spendio ferci"; 7.40–42) and restless ("ché tutto l'oro
ch'è sotto la luna / e che già fu, di quest'anime stanche / non potrebbe farne posare
una"; 7.64–66). On the other hand, as we will see, it is reason that allows love to be
virtuous rather than lustful, human rather than bestial. For the reference to the she-wolf,
la "bestia sanza pace," as an example of restless cupidity in the *Commedia*, see *Inf* 1.49–
58 and 98–99 ("mai non empie la bramosa voglia, / e dopo 'l pasto ha più fame che
pria") and *Purg* 20.10–12.

[25] With respect to Lucian's model—whose completely different message underlines
the bitter acknowledgment that men appreciate only he who is rich—the changes in the
Timone suggest Boiardo's ideal of discretion and balance. See Marcello Aurigemma, "Il
Timone di M. M. Boiardo," *Il Boiardo e la critica contemporanea*, ed. Guiseppe Anceschi
(Florence: Olschki, 1970), 29–60; Lienhard Bergel, "I due *Timone*: Boiardo e Shake-
speare," *Il Boiardo*, 73–80.

> El giovane fia tratto da prigione;
> Più prodigo non fia, ma liberale,
> Spendendo e dispensando *cum ragione*.

May the young man be rescued from prison; / may he be not prodigal anymore, but liberal, / spending and dispensing with reason. (5.6; my trans.)

Leodilla, then, represents exactly the opposite of Boiardo's ideal of measure; through the construction of this character and of her adventures the poet exemplifies the negative consequences of avarice. Turning to the other element that characterizes this figure (her attachment to senses, her lust), we see its manifestations the moment she meets Ordauro.[26] Her attraction to him is based only on sight and is solely physical. It does not imply any sort of spiritual quality:[27]

> Intelligence had spread abroad
> Of my old father's massive wealth,
> And tidings of my lovely face
> (I can't say whether true or false)
> Had led two lovers in one day
> To ask for me: old Folderico,
> Aged over sixty, *and Ordauro,*
> *Forelock to toe a handsome blond.*
>
> Each man was rich, of noble blood,
> But Folderico was thought wise,
> A prophet of such subtle ways,
> He was compared to Heaven's God.
> *Ordauro had more manly force,*
> *For he was big and strong of limb.*
> I never took advice back then:
> I spurned the old and chose the young.
>   (1.21.51–52)[28]

---

[26] Regarding Leodilla, Franceschetti speaks of a dimension of "assoluta e totale sensualità," *L'"Orlando Innamorato,"* 89.

[27] With the fact that Leodilla realizes she is driven only by senses—to the extent that she consciously rejects the "antiveder tanto sotile" and the "consiglio" of "sagio" Folderico; 1.21.52—it is maybe possible to explain her "vergogna," which would otherwise remain unexplained, that the girl feels in choosing Ordauro and that pushes her to devise the strategy of the competition (1.21.53–54).

[28] "Era la fama già sparta de intorno / Della ricchezza del mio padre antico; / E nomi-

When Leodilla is held by Folderico in Altamura, she seems to suffer more from the fact that her senses are not satisfied in bed than from being separated from her beloved Ordauro:

> I'd been provided with a wealth
> Of jewels and gold and all delights—
> Except the pleasures had in bed:
> I wanted better ones and more.
> The old man, who suspected, wore
> His key at all times on his belt,
> And he became so jealous, he
> Would not have not been believed, if seen. (1.22.16)

When Ordauro, as is narrated in the second part of the novella (1.22.10-55), finally manages to enter Altamura and to meet Leodilla, their relationship is exclusively physical, an aspect on which Boiardo insists:

> Ancora esser mi par nel paradiso,
> Quando rammento come io lo baciai,
> E come lui baciomme nella bocca;
> Quella dolcezza ancor nel cor mi tocca.

> I still think I'm in Paradise
> When I remember how I kissed him
> and how he kissed me on the mouth:
> That sweetness still affects my heart. (1.22.24)

The description of their intercourse has a problematic connotation: by encapsulating the lovers' kiss within the ironic reference to paradise and to the episode of Casella in the *Purgatorio* ("che la dolcezza ancor dentro mi suona"; 2.114), Boiardo forces the listener/reader to link the expression "lui baciomme sulla bocca" with the famous passage from the circle of lust in *Inferno* 5.136: "la bocca mi baciò tutta tremante." Leodilla's citation of Francesca invites the reader to connect her with the adulterous figure and

---

nanza del mio viso adorno, / O vera o falsa, pur come io te dico, / Menò due amanti a chiedermi in un giorno, / *Ordauro il biondo* e il vecchio Folderico; / *Bello era il primo dal zuffo alla pianta,* / L'altro de li anni avea più de sessanta. / Ricco ciascuno e de schiatta gentile; / Ma Folderico sagio era tenuto / E de uno antiveder tanto sotile, / Che come a Dio del ciel gli era creduto. / *Ordauro era di forza più virile,* / *E grande di persona e ben membruto*; / Io, che a quel tempo non chiedea consiglio, / Il vecchio lascio, e il giovane me piglio."

therefore with lust.[29] The reference to Francesca is so explicit that it does not disappear in the next octaves but rather echoes throughout the episode:

> Allora il suo parlar vidi esser vano,
> Con quel piacer che ancor nel cor mi serbo.
> Noi cominciammo il gioco a mano a mano;
> Ordauro era frezzoso e di gran nerbo,
> Sì che al principio pur mi parve strano,
> Come io avessi morduto un pomo acerbo;
> Ma nella fin tal dolce ebbi a sentire,
> Ch'io mi disfeci e credetti morire.
> [. . . .]
> Più fiate poi tornammo a questo gioco,
> E ciascun giorno più crescìa il diletto;
> Ma pur il star rinchiusa in questo loco
> Mi dava estrema noia e gran dispetto;
> E il tempo del piacer sempre era poco,
> Però che quel zeloso maladetto
> Me ritornava sì ratto a vedere,
> Che spesso me sturbò di gran piacere.

> I learned the those were empty words,
> With pleasure that my heart still holds.
> We started playing hand to hand,
> Ordauro of great strength, impatient,
> And it seemed strange to me at first,
> As if I chewed a bitter apple,
> But by the end it felt so sweet,
> I thought I'd die, and I dissolved
> [. . . .]
> We many times renewed our game,
> And every day the pleasure grew,
> But being trapped inside that room
> Was getting on my nerves at last,
> And pleasure always went too fast

---

[29] For another use of *Inferno* 5 in the *Innamorato*, see Rebecca A. Mechanic, "In Pursuit of Earthly Justice: The Albarosa Episode of Boiardo's *Orlando Innamorato* as a 'Positivization' of *Inferno* V," *Canadian Journal of Italian Studies*, forthcoming.

> And pleasure always went too fast
> Because that cursed, suspicious man
> So often came to check on me,
> He was a frequent interruption. (1.22.26–28)

Though it is certainly true that Leodilla's desire is rewarded and she is finally enjoying her lover, Boiardo insists on the reference to *Inferno* 5, as if he did not want to let us indulge Leodilla and Ordauro's intercourse too much. He is not condemning physical love per se, but he wants to underscore the lustfulness of this particular relationship. "Con quel piacer che ancor nel cor mi serbo" is a new reference to *Purgatorio* 2.114, but "piacer" replaces "dolcezza" and recalls Francesca's speech in *Inferno* 5.104–5: "mi prese del costui piacer sì forte, / che, come vedi, ancor non m'abbandona." Not only is "piacer" repeated several times, but the line "Più fiate tornammo a questo gioco" is a further reference to *Inferno* 5.130–31: "Per più fiate li occhi ci sospinse / quella lettura."

Leodilla is so overcome by sensual pleasure that for a while she seems to subordinate her avarice and expresses only joy in the satisfaction of her senses:

> That sweetness made me think I'd die.
> From then, I cared for nothing else.
> Let others search for power or wealth
> Or seek renown throughout the world;
> The smart ones want their pleasure first,
> To live delightful, happy lives.
> May those who work for fame or things
> Ignore this—and the loss be theirs! (1.22.27)[30]

Above all she feels like dying:

> Ma nella fin tal dolce ebbi a sentire,
> Ch'io mi disfeci e credetti morire.
>
> But by the end it felt so sweet,
> I thought I'd die, and I dissolved. (1.22.26)

---

[30] "Io credetti morir per gran dolcezza, / Né altra cosa da poi stimai nel mondo. / Altri acquisti possanza o ver ricchezza, / Altri esser nominato per il mondo. / Ciascun che è saggio, il suo piacere apprezza / E il viver dilettoso e star iocondo; / Chi vole onore o robba con affanno, / Me non ascolti, et abbiasene il danno."

The combination of death and the verb "disfarsi" was already used by Guido Cavalcanti in the famous canzone "La forte e nova mia disaventura"; "disfarsi" is repeated three times (lines 2, 4 and 25) and expresses the consequences of the tragic Cavalcantian conception of love and knowledge as based on senses and leading to death. "Morte" as the consequence of this conception of love is theorized in a line of "Donna me prega,—per ch'eo voglio dire," which is the philosophical version of Cavalcanti's tragic poetic mode: "Di sua [di "amore"] potenza segue spesso morte"; (line 35). It is the key-word of the imagery of Cavalcanti and concludes also "La forte e nova mia disaventura": "Io pur rimagno in tant'aversitate / che, qual mira de fòre, / vede la Morte sotto al meo colore"; (lines 29–31). Through Leodilla's "Cavalcantian" words, Boiardo expresses the danger of connecting love with senses and not with reason.

Moreover, in a passage so overtly marked with the intertext of *Inferno* 5, the image of love as death recalls also Francesca's famous statement that "Amor condusse noi ad una morte" (*Inf* 5.106) and, therefore, Dante's condemnation of "peccator carnali" in the "bufera infernal che mai non resta" (*Inf* 5.31) of the circle of lust. If we remember that for Dante, "carnal sinners" are those who place reason beneath passion, "che la ragion sommettono al talento" (*Inf* 5.39)—the same "talento" to which Orlando refers in his speech in 1.25.14—we can better understand the complexity of Leodilla's episode. Her immoderate greed is far from reason, just as her love is driven only by the search for physical pleasure. Leodilla continues to refer to this "piacere" that seems to be destined to renew itself forever without ever being satiated (1.22.28). In "Doglia me reca," which is an important step in Dante's meditation on desire and which displays an earlier conflation of lust and avarice, Dante points out the error of those who call love what is mere bestial appetite ("chiamando amore appetito di fiera"; 142), and believe love to be outside the garden of reason ("e crede amor fuor d'orto di ragione"; 147). Without realizing that the discriminant between lust and love is the use of reason and measure, i.e., the qualities that render us human rather than bestial, Leodilla confuses mere desire deprived of reason with true love. This "appetito di fiera" even echoes, perhaps, in her leonine name.

Leodilla's love for Ordauro is based primarily on sight and senses. The pleasure that it gives is primarily physical and never completely fulfilling. Its characteristics are expressed through the intertext of *Inferno* 5 and are similar to those that derive from self-love.[31] Leodilla seems to be think-

---

[31] Even though Leodilla's words in 1.22.26 refer to the physical pleasure of inter-

ing only about herself and is more interested in the satisfaction of her own senses than in the construction of her love for Ordauro. It should not be surprising, therefore, if fidelity is not one of her most striking virtues.

After the narration of the second part of her novella, we find Leodilla with Orlando (1.24.12). This scene further highlights that Leodilla's desire for physical pleasure is as endless as her greed for wealth. While they are looking for Brandimarte, who had left to follow Morgana's deer, Orlando and Leodilla, who "da esser assalita dubitava / e forse non gli avria fatto contrasto," spend the night together. But the paladin does not touch her:

> Orlando stretched along the grass
> And did not move until first light;
> Fast asleep, he snored constantly.
> The damsel did not rest at all
> But stayed awake in disbelief
> That such a valiant cavalier
> Could be so hard of heart that he
> Took no delight in lovemaking. (1.24.15)

Boiardo ironizes the angry reactions of the girl, who would have no problem betraying Ordauro with Orlando. As her senses have not been satisfied, she is so mad that she becomes intolerant of Orlando and she barely supports his presence:

> She found the Count a disappointment,
> And, in the clear light of the morning,
> She climbed his steed, disconsolate.
> If she had known where she could turn
> She would have willingly gone off,
> But she was lost, as I have said,

---

course and not to the infatuation based in illusion found in the courtly love tradition, it is meaningful that Boiardo employs the verb "disfarsi" to indicate the consequences of Leodilla's love for Ordauro: together with the verb "consumarsi," it expresses the negative effects of *eros*, which explicitly refers to the contemplation of courtly lyric tradition and denotes the presence of self-love activated through sight, as in the case of Fiordespina, Silvanella, Angelica, Ranaldo, Narciso, or Ferraguto. For a detailed description of this love, see Cavallo, *Boiardo's* Orlando Innamorato, 41. Francesca expresses the negative consequences to which the misuse of this very same lyric tradition can lead. See Teodolinda Barolini, *Dante's Poets: Textuality and Truth in the "Comedy"* (Princeton: Princeton Univ. Press, 1984), 3–14.

> So she stayed, quiet and depressed.
> The Count asked her the cause of this.
>
> She answered him, "Your snoring kept
> Me up all night. I haven't slept.
> Besides that, I have got this itch...." (1.24.16–17)

The adjective "malinconiosa" ("depressed" in the English translation) underlines the importance that Leodilla—who feels "pizzicare"—attributes to the satisfaction of her senses. The adjective is suggestive because it explicitly recalls the figure of Bartolomea in *Decameron* 2.10, which is, as we have seen before, one of the main sources that Boiardo uses for the construction of the character of Leodilla: there, Boccaccio refers to the "grave malinconia della donna," due to the fact that Ricardo does not sleep with her.

Regarding the interconnection of the motifs of lust and avarice, it is interesting that after this dialogue Orlando begins his "sterile" adventures following Jason's model, because throughout the poem the theme of the Argonauts is connected to avarice.[32] During this adventure Leodilla continues to be angry with Orlando, wishes the defeat of the paladin and even says that he, who has saved her life, is the most cruel man in the world. Boiardo's irony emphasizes the absurd behavior of the girl, who is made ungrateful by lust:

> Everyone listen to me now:
> The Count's example plainly proves
> No woman shows you gratitude
> If you don't water her green flower! (1.24.44)

Leodilla goes so far as to say that she would leave if the "fata del lago" were not forcing her to stay. We can wonder why Boiardo wants the girl to stay if she will leave Orlando very soon anyway. Maybe because, in this way, Leodilla—who is not only still very attached to the senses but probably has also not yet overcome her greed—has the opportunity to hear Orlando's speech on wealth (1.25.17) and to learn from him what her personal experiences have not been enough to teach her. By comparing Leodilla's words when she is overcome by sensual pleasure and seems to forget about money (1.22.27) with Orlando's speech, it is possible to see how Leodilla's pseudo-philosophy, which is soon contradicted by her behavior,

---

[32] See Murrin, "Falerina's Garden," 67.

is less a conscious rejection of avarice and its dangers than an invitation to enjoy the pleasures of life at one's disposal.

Some time later the two characters meet Ordauro, with whom even the so easily seduced Orlando is happy to leave the girl he perceives as a "heavy burden." Orlando further highlights Leodilla's lust, as the reference to the nettle recalls the girl's itch during the night that she spent beside the paladin:

> The Count said, "If she's yours, she's yours.
> I will not quarrel over her.
> Take her, and take off! By Macone,
> She's like a nettle in my neck.
> I'll thank you for your courtesy
> If you'll relieve me of this nuisance.
> Go with her anywhere you please,
> As long as you don't come with me." (1.25.20)

In spite of his habits, Orlando does not desire Leodilla probably because the girl is strongly connected to avarice, by which the hero is never tempted in the course of the poem.

We do not know whether Leodilla has learned Orlando's lesson or not, because we leave the girl with her lover—whatever their relationship might be—and we find her alone many cantos later (2.13.46) in her father's castle. In the *Orlando Innamorato* the meaning of events only comes in retrospect and Leodilla's episode can be fully understood only by comparing it to Doristella's variants. Doristella's marriage is the final recognition of her love for Teodoro, while Boiardo's silence concerning the final events of Leodilla's relationship with Ordauro—so that we do not know whether she marries—underlines her responsibilities and faults. While Doristella has no active involvement in her marriage with Usbego, Leodilla has the chance to marry Teodoro but wastes it because of her attachment to money. While Doristella falls in love with Teodoro gradually and also on behalf of his inner qualities ("Andando e ritornando a tutte l'ore / di quanto dimorammo in quel paese, / mi piacque sì, ch'io fui presser d'amore, / veggendol sì ligiadro e sì cortese"; 2.26.25), Leodilla is immediately and uniquely inflamed by Ordauro's appearance; she would even betray him with Orlando. Further, the fact that she appears for the last time among the riches of her father's castle wearing "so many gems" that "the feast was lit by just their splendor," is a sign that she has not yet overcome her attachment to money (2.13.46). On the contrary, her brother

Brandimarte—formerly Bramadoro—goes back to his father's castle where the recognition scene takes place, only to leave the castle with Orlando.

I have suggested that Boiardo treats Leodilla ambiguously because she represents a singular contamination of avarice and lust. Not only does she exemplify the common ground of insatiable desire far from reason but, in a certain way, Leodilla's exclusively sensuous love for Ordauro is a form of avarice. In desiring him, she is concerned mainly with herself and the satisfaction of her desire. In particular, the rewriting of the Atalanta myth and the connections with Falerina's Garden allow Boiardo to join these two sins in the golden apples. Further proof of the conflation between lust and greed is Ordauro, the object of Leodilla's lustful passion: when he first appears, he is presented as "Ordauro il biondo" (1.21.51), a sort of gold squared ("OR d'AURO"), if not cubed ("il biondo").[33]

When the Leodilla episode is considered in light of both intertextuality and Boiardo's whole corpus, the negative treatment of her character is evident and recalls the poet's conception of desire. On one hand, her greed is endless and far from reason, to the extent that she cannot control it. On the other hand, her love shows some likeness to the *venus in malo*, i.e., with a love founded solely on sight and physical attraction. Such love is based uniquely on the senses and has an easily interchangeable object. It is a neither generous nor altruistic feeling, a self-love, lustful and therefore, in the poet's high conception of love and its power, greedy. Boiardo is fully aware that wealth and physical love are important and valuable, but they should not be the only aim of one's action. Desire, wherever it is addressed, has to remain under the control of reason and measure: otherwise, like the miser of "Doglia me reca" and Leodilla during the race, one runs but never wins.

---

[33] The meaning of the name Ordauro is noted by Ross in the annotated index of his edition of the *Orlando Innamorato* on page 883.

CHARLES ROSS

Damsel in Distress?
Origille's Subjectivity

THE ORIGILLE STORY, which occurs in the twenty-ninth and final canto of
the first book of Boiardo's *Orlando Innamorato*, is one of those "literary
fantasies" of impersonation, imposture, geometrical pairs, and lost identity
that Stephen Greenblatt, in his essay "Psychoanalysis and Renaissance
Culture," identifies as "a peculiarly *Renaissance* story."[1] It seems worthwhile, as we go about the work of recovering Boiardo, to consider Origille
and the events surrounding her not, as critics usually have done, as just
another example of misogyny, but, following Greenblatt's cue, as a chapter
in the development of Western conceptions of identity and subjectivity.

Probably every period of history has regarded eccentricities of character
as markers of individual identity. Origille, who is constantly referred to as
perfidious and a traitor and who outwits three lovers, her father, and, on
three separate occasions, Orlando, represents a recognizable type of deceptive female. It is tempting, in considering why Origille behaves as she
does, to seek out earlier traumas of oppression and repression that may
have molded her personality. But Greenblatt posits that this temptation to
psychoanalyze Renaissance literary characters, although strong, should be
avoided.

The problem is not simply that in many Renaissance stories, because
there is no childhood narrative to examine, we have practically no infor-

---

[1] Stephen Greenblatt, "Psychoanalysis and Renaissance Culture," *Learning to Curse:
Essays in Early Modern Culture* (New York: Routledge, 1990), 239.

mation with which to work. Rather, we are misled by a deceptive similarity between psychoanalysis, "a brilliant hermeneutical system centered upon stripping away layers of strategic displacement that obscure the self's underlying drives," and an older "conception of a person as a theatrical mask secured by authority."[2] Renaissance culture placed an unusual stress on proper names and property (including the body) to define people. According to Greenblatt, an increase in record-keeping, particularly during the reign of Henry VIII in England, contributed to this cultural phenomenon, but the political bureaucracies of Italy were no less advanced in the fifteenth century, when—to recall, for example, one of Jacob Burckhardt's arguments for the appearance of individuals during the period—the despots of Italian city-states issued passports and required innkeepers to report the names of travelers.[3] By contrast, a modern conception of personality tends to go beyond character types to locate personal identity within the psyche. Freudian psychoanalysis searches beneath layers of defenses and neuroses to uncover one's essential being.

Renaissance literature tempts us to psychoanalyze because modern theories emerged from, and are therefore akin to, this Renaissance correspondence between identity and property. But psychoanalysis lacks applicability because of the different nature of Renaissance subjectivity. "Subjectivity," Katherine Mauss writes, "is often treated casually as a unified or coherent conception when, in fact, it is a loose and varied collection of assumptions, intuitions, and practices that do not all logically entail one another and need not appear together at the same cultural moment."[4] Even if we can identify "highly developed forms of interior experience" during the Renaissance, according to Paul White, it does not follow that we may impute "twentieth-century models of selfhood on a culture."[5]

Greenblatt's solution suggests that Renaissance literature reflected the cultural equation of individuality with property by telling stories about appropriated or lost identity. At the same time, it posits the Renaissance as a time when modern conceptions of character and subjectivity were beginning to emerge. What I suggest is that this moment between old and new,

---

² Greenblatt, "Psychoanalysis," 142–43.

³ Jacob Burckhardt, *The Civilization of the Renaissance in Italy*, trans. S.G.C. Middlemore (New York: Phaidon Press, n.d.), 6.

⁴ Katherine Eisaman Mauss, *Inwardness and Theater in the English Renaissance* (Chicago: Univ. of Chicago Press, 1995), 29.

⁵ Paul White, "Theater, Religion, and the History of the Early Modern Subject," unpublished paper, Shakespeare Association of America conference, Washington, D.C., March 1997.

between a status society and a new subjectivity, occurs midway in Boiardo's story of Origille. The first half of her story is her history, a story narrated to Orlando by a knight named Uldarno. The second half represents her present in the poem, beginning when Orlando rescues her from a tree from which she hangs by her hair, then allows her to accompany him on road of errantry.

Most of her story occurs in Canto 29 of Book 1, a canto unified by the common theme of stolen or missing identity. The first half is told in terms of theatrical masks—or, since Boiardo's genre is chivalric romance, escutcheons on armor and signs of knighthood. The second half strikes a more modern chord, as Orlando slowly discovers Origille's perfidy, while at the same time discovering himself. Each part uses a different but otherwise common literary motif to establish the theme of stolen or missing identity. The first half, in which, as Greenblatt says in reference to Shakespeare, Boiardo "voiced, texted, and deepened" the Renaissance cultural interest in "identity as property,"[6] turns on the presence of a strange custom, a typical feature of chivalric romance. In the second half, Origille slowly exposes Orlando, stripping away his warrior identity to give him a glimpse of his—and her own—inner identity. The resulting dyptich shows us two sides of Origille. She is perfidious, a traitor, a hypocrite, and a seductress whose behavior is allusively suggestive of a Venetian courtesan. But she is also a powerful individual presence, an object of passion, a woman whose invisible inwardness undermines social networks, one who turns oppression into self-expression, who moves from the confinements of her father's house to the free wanderings of the chivalric landscape. Origille's hanging from a tree by her hair, at the point where the two parts intersect, is the very image of subjection, the picture of a damsel in distress. Boiardo's revelatory mirrors and allegories—what James Nohrnberg, in an essay in this volume, calls "projections"—then turn her subjectivity, in the narrow sense of her oppressive plight, into a surprisingly sympathetic portrait of a complex female subject.

I

When Orlando first finds Origille hanging by her hair from a tree, her story is told to him by a knight named Uldarno, himself condemned to death for assuming, at Origille's behest, another knight's identity. For the law of Bactria, where Origille lives, specifically condemns to death knights

---

[6] Greenblatt, "Psychoanalysis," 141.

who wear the armor and markings of others. Such a law characterizes a status society, where identity is a form of property and individuality is a matter of external differentiations. Nonetheless, as the narrative unfolds, displaying the harsh effects of the law, its social premises are also undermined. So confusing are the names of the players in Origille's social life that it appears that Boiardo has constructed an almost reductio ad absurdum of the concepts of property and identity.

The sheer involution of the story told by Uldarno tests the definition of identity in Bactria. Uldarno's story involves three lovers, a brother, a bad man, and an unscrupulous father. People die in Bactria for misappropriating identity, but the spellings and sounds of names like Oringo, Locrino, and Corbino are so similar that one can almost understand the anxiety to keep them separate. Oringo is the bad man who killed Corbino, Origille's brother. Uldarno and Locrino are Origille's lovers, and in the story Uldarno dresses up to look like Oringo, while Locrino assumes the arms of Origille's third lover, Ariante. (Ariante also had the inside track with Origille's father to marry her, on condition he defeat Oringo.) While the real Ariante is meeting the false Oringo, actually Uldarno, the false Ariante, who is Locrino, meets the real Oringo. Fired by love, young Locrino manages to defeat the bad Oringo and deliver his prisoner to Origille's father. He in turn offers Locrino his daughter, even though he realizes Locrino is not Ariante, with whom he had contracted for Oringo's head (*OI* 1.29.27). The father accepts an imposter when it suits his purposes.

Origille *originates*—there may be a paranomasia in the Italian—each imposture. She convinces Uldarno to dress like Oringo. She tells Locrino to assume the shield and crest insignia, two gold horns on green, of Ariante. Although love is the root of all evil, corruption of identity contributes to further crimes when Locrino wrongfully agrees to yield his prisoner (the real Oringo, who had killed Corbino, the son of Origille's father). The hatred of Origille's father can be explained by the loss of his son and heir, although this is unstated, as well as the presumption that his daughter Origille could not substitute for a lost son. Oringo's murder of Corbino also fits the pattern of lost identities: like the three lovers he is sentenced to death not so much for killing Corbino but because Corbino was young and had not established himself, while Oringo was "di gran fama" (*OI* 1.29.33). Origille's father escapes punishment because the cultural equation of property and identity excuses a complicitous party whose status society seeks to maintain.

In her work on inwardness in the Renaissance, Mauss identifies hanging as the proper penalty for one who transgresses a social hierarchy (it happens to Horatio in Thomas Kyd's *Spanish Tragedy*).[7] When Orlando first finds Origille, she is hanging by her hair. Uldarno, one of four knights assigned to guard her, calls her an "anima prava," a "falsa damigella," and accuses her of "malizia" (*OI* 1.28.53–54). But the evidence of Origille's treachery, as Uldarno relates it in the first half of the canto, can also be read as signs of her subjectivity. As Uldarno speaks, Origille screams, and Boiardo seems sympathetic to the problem of women who seek to make themselves heard. Her screams and tears suffice to give her an individual presence and induce Orlando to release her.

No single interpretation accounts for her position. From among various possibilities her individuality emerges. Origille is not just a false damsel, but one who defines herself by flouting society. Her threat to the social order of Bactria is symbollically presented in the story: she manipulates men into abandoning their armorial signs, into disguising themselves as others, undermining the hierarchies of society.

She suffers accordingly. It is significant that Uldarno also says Origille is said to be twisting in the wind the way she used to twist the promises she made to her tortured lovers. Her situation, Cavallo notes, is a Dantesque *contrapasso*, a punishment appropriate to her crime.[8] But Uldarno's interpretation of her punishment disguises its purpose under the law of Bactria, to torture her with something worse than death (*OI* 1.29.34–35). Uldarno compares Origille's conceit in her beauty to that of a peacock spreading its tail "beneath the sun for men to praise" (*OI* 1.29.5).[9] Origille's hair is, therefore, a sign of vainglory, as in the traditional picture, which Michaelangelo included in the Sistine Chapel, of the biblical Absalom caught by his hair in a tree.[10] But Origille's hair also signals something about her relation to society. The ultimate authority of Bactria never appears in person. There is no prince to mete out justice, as say, in a Shakespeare play where Theseus or Prince Escalus issues decrees. Instead, the law operates anonymously, and for that reason more effectively since there is no recourse, no way to argue circumstances as excuses.

---

[7] Mauss, *Inwardness*, 59.

[8] Jo Ann Cavallo, *Boiardo's* Orlando Innamorato: *An Ethics of Desire* (Rutherford, NJ: Fairleigh Dickinson Univ. Press, 1993), 14.

[9] The gender confusion of the bird may be traced to Ovid's *Metamorphoses*, where the Cyclops calls Galatea "vainer than a praised peacock" (*Met* 13.802).

[10] D. W. Robertson, Jr., *A Preface to Chaucer* (Princeton: Princeton Univ. Press, 1962), 385, illustration 115.

The social order is fixed and rigid.

The ambiguous image of Origille hanging in the wind should cause us to consider an interpretation that goes against the surface grain of her story. The strict law of Bactria sentences her to a horrible fate not because she deceives lovers, but because she tampers with the local cultural investment in personal identity and property. In a similar scene in the prose *Lancelot*, one of Boiardo's main sources for Arthurian motifs, Yvain finds a damsel hanging by her two braids from an oak tree.[11] He releases her and defeats the knights who guard her. Yvain then learns that the woman suffers because she once helped Gawain seduce the daughter of the king of North Wales. To Yvain's mind she is innocent of wrong. But there is enough ambiguity in the French story to make a case that Gawain's seduction was a form of treachery to which the hanging damsel contributed. Origille duplicates the ambiguity if not the details of this portion of the prose *Lancelot*.

The hypocrisy Uldarno accuses her of is also, in Mauss's view, a strong sign of inwardness. The type appeared in later religious tracts, where, as Mauss shows, "the hypocrite's realization of his internal resources seems profoundly subversive."[12] For Machiavelli, hypocrisy, inwardness, and invisibility toward others undermine social networks and the kinds of identity that can be founded upon networks. What Mauss calls the "sinister interiority" of hypocrites, magicians, con men, and whores "competes with and undermines another kind of identity, founded upon the individual's place in the social hierarchies and kinship networks."[13] Despite Uldarno's oral narrative, Orlando openly declares that nothing she could have done justifies her cruel punishment, and after defeating Uldarno and three others who have been assigned to guard Origille, he saves her despite her reputation.

Boiardo's written text, as well as Orlando's rescue, challenge the oral tale told by Uldarno to discredit Origille. According to Walter Ong, writing displaced the old feudalism of personal loyalty and enhanced the individual sense of the people otherwise trapped in community.[14] And over the centuries of their development, romances recorded the displacement

---

[11] *Lancelot-Grail: The Old French Arthurian Vulgate and Post-Vulgate in Translation*, ed. Norris J. Lacy (New York: Garland, 1993), 296.

[12] Mauss, *Inwardness*, 40–41.

[13] Mauss, *Inwardness*, 40.

[14] Walter Ong, *The Presence of the Word* (Minneapolis: Univ. of Minnesota Press, 1981), 54.

of what Ong calls the "orally organized world."[15] Within the *Innamorato*, characters sometimes read and sometimes listen. Although we must keep in mind that the humanist Boiardo had a healthy ability to disbelieve what he read—the *Innamorato* itself is a prank based on a manuscript by Turpin—nonetheless, readers in the *Innamorato* usually learn things as they are: the meaning of the sphynx, for example; the truth about Trufaldino; the layout of Falerina's Garden (*OI* 1.5.76, 1.13.29-46, 2.5.4). People who listen do so to learn the truth but tend to remain sceptical. One's identity depends on what one says as well as what one hears.[16]

---

[15] Ong, *Presence*, 54.

[16] Anomalies in the telling of a story further signal the presence of the identity theme. It is almost a Boiardan device. For example, Uldarno tells the story of Origille, with its rapidly mentioned and jingling cast of characters, in the compressed style Mary Ellen Lamb, in *Gender and Author in the Sidney Circle* (Madison, 1990), 87–90, identifies with male narrators in Philip Sidney's *Arcadia*. In contrast to men, women usually tell lengthy stories. In the *Innamorato*, Boiardo calls attention to this gender imbalance after Fiordelisa relates the longest sustained narrative interpolation in the poem—the story of Tisbina, Prasildo, and Iroldo that she tells Ranaldo (*OI* 1.12). Boiardo quips that those who find this story too long may skip part and "just read half of it" (*OI* 1.12.90). Although it seems incongruous to suggest skipping half a story one has just been through, Boiardo's remark also raises the issue of gender in several ways that impact our understanding of Origille. First, as Vladimir Nabokov liked to say, you can never read a work of art, only reread it, in order to appreciate the meaning that emerges from its patterns (Vladimir Nabokov, *Lectures on Literature*, ed. Fredson Bowers [New York, 1980], 3). That seems to be the real point of the narrator's remark at the end of Fiordelisa's long story to Ranaldo, that Boiardo expects his readers to be re-readers. Uldarno's story, however, with its confusing cast of characters, remains difficult even on rereading, suggesting the problem of the identity-obsessed social system that confronts Origille. Later in the book, Fiordelisa meets a woman who will turn out to be her sister. Hearing Doristella tell a story about a lost little girl, kidnapped by the sea in Liza as she was when small, Fiordelisa interrupts, only to have Brandimarte silence her: "Now Fiordelisa interrupted / To ask who that maid's mother was, / But Brandimart, who wished to listen, / Turned around, gave a little grin, / And said, 'Good Lord! Let her go on! / I'd like to hear, if you don't mind.' / And Fiordelisa, who loved him, / Fell silent, and she spoke no more."; *OI* 2.26.23. Brandimarte, known since his first appearance for his courtesy in love, never treats Fiordelisa so rudely elsewhere, although in his defense, his grin betrays a self-consciousness of the gendered silence he imposes on Fiordelisa, or his own premonition that the story will reveal Fiordelisa's lost identity.

In terms of Boiardo's plot, then, it seems no coincidence that Brandimarte's brusque behavior occurs when Fiordelisa is about to learn her identity, as when Orlando listens to Uldarno, and Fiordelisa listens to Doristella. Doristella's story does not suffice to demonstrate identity: Fiordelisa must actually meet her parents and discover an identifying stain on her breast, while Orlando must experience Origille's treachery for himself. Boiardo's written text, and Orlando's rescue, therefore challenges the oral tale told by Uldarno to discredit Origille. One seeks one's identity by listening closely, but only some sign—a written text or a birthmark—can offer proof.

Origille's screams and her rescue by Orlando tacitly remind us how the story Uldarno tells unwittingly reveals a world of female confinement and ritual silencing. Claudia Hermann claims that "woman ... has long since learned to respect not only the physical and mental spaces of others, but space for its own sake, empty space. It is because she needs to maintain a protective distance between herself and the men she has not chosen."[17] Origille's trickery and deceit may be read as her way of creating this protective distance in a closed society. Origille operates almost exclusively within the confines of her father's house. The plot she weaves for Uldarno even involves her having him arrested so that she can visit him in the prison her father maintains in his house. Origille's constraint is so thorough that Uldarno himself does not question her plan to meet her, for love-making, in her father's prison. When Orlando finds her, her plight symbolizes her position in society: she is confined, and those who vituperate and torture her deny her subjectivity. Her screams are her self-expression; her tree is her space. But when released by Orlando, Origille escapes from Bactria's hierarchies into the free space of romance landscape, the plain where knights and ladies wander *errando*.

II

When Orlando carries her away, she is able to put real distance between herself and a society that treats her as property. Romance space offers a release like the denouement of drama. In fact, the plot of Origille's story probably derives from Plautus's *Casina*, a play, familiar to the humanist Boiardo, about a man who disguises himself in order to have sex with a slave girl. Origille is no slave girl, but her behavior, like that of many of Boiardo's enchantresses, echoes a class of women whom we are increasingly recognizing as entreprenurial individuals: the courtesans, for which Venice and Ferrara were famous.[18]

---

[17] Claudine Hermann, from "Les coordonnées féminines: espace et temps," trans. Marilyn R. Schuster, abridged in *New French Feminisms*, ed. Elaine Marks and Isabelle de Courtivron (New York: Schocken Books, 1981), 168–73; quoted by Dawn Green in her unpublished paper titled "Representations of Space as a Metaphor for the Self in Vittoria Colonna and Gaspara Stampa."

[18] The most obvious courtesan in Boiardo's poem is the woman who spends the night with Mandricardo in a room adorned with fine silks, white sheets, orange blossoms, and mechanical birds (*OI* 3.1.65). Rome was unsurpassed for courtesans, but the Veneto was well known too. See Paul Larivaille, *La vie quotidienne des courtisanes en Italie au temps de la Renaissance (Rome et Venise, XVe et XVIe siècles)* ([Paris]: Hachette, 1975).

Our understanding of Origille's subjectivity increases if we recognize that Origille operates like those courtesans who surely impressed their patrons with their sense of self because they required guile and ability to operate successfully in a society that simultaneously encouraged and demeaned them. Origille's control over her lovers, who lose themselves and become powerless before her, resembles the accounts of the noblemen who, despite their high birth, felt unable to live without, for example, Adriana Sorvignan, a late sixteenth-century courtesan profiled by Guido Ruggiero.[19] Courtesans, in turn, were under the constant threat of gang rape and having their faces slashed if they angered their clients;[20] perhaps this is why Origille steals Orlando's sword the second time she deceives him. But they also, in exceptional circumstances, developed their own identities, their own voices. In her study of the Venetian courtesan Veronica Franco, Margaret Rosenthal shows how Franco developed her own poetic voice in the literary wars of Venice. Wooed by the king of France at one extreme and robbed blind by her household servants, for ten years Franco added poetry to her other accomplishments as she struggled to maintain herself in careful opulence. Her balancing act could not last. No courtesan could outlive her beauty and her luck. She made out her will twice while young, and in a letter to the mother of a daughter who wanted advice on entering the profession, pointed out the dangers of disease. Attacked by the Inquisition, Franco was reduced to poverty by age thirty-six. It seems to fit the pattern that we last see Origille ill—and abandoned.[21]

Origille's story gives narrative form to a process of social change that Italy witnessed during the Renaissance: later women poets of the sixteenth century like Veronica Franco, Gaspara Stampa, and Vittoria Colonna found a voice in their writing that gave them identities. Origille does not write poetry, like Franco or Stampa or Colonna, but she does something similar. As she rides away from Bactria with Orlando, she lies to him, "with smooth words and a smiling face" (*OI* 1.29.47). It is her conversation, her words—not anything physical—that rouses Orlando's passion.

Just as Origille makes the Count love her by "talking of many things"

---

[19] Guido Ruggiero, *Binding Passions: Tales of Magic, Marriage, and Power at the End of the Renaissance* (New York: Oxford Univ. Press, 1993), 30.

[20] Margaret Rosenthal, *The Honest Courtesan: Veronica Franco, Citizen and Writer in Sixteenth-Century Venice* (Chicago: Univ. of Chicago Press, 1992), 38, 147.

[21] There are no other cases of illnesses in the poem. For Franco and the visit of Henry III, see also Larivaille, *La vie quotidienne des courtisanes*, 112–23.

(*OI* 1.29.48), so the narrative form of romance operates as a form of wish-fulfillment. There is perhaps no more common image in Boiardo's own *Amorum libri* than the loops of gold—the "duri lacci"—that snare a lover, the loops being the blond hair of a woman.[22] Normally the male lover is bound by the loops of gold. But Boiardo's romance image prefigures the usage of later women poets, notably Gaspara Stampa, where we see that the woman is bound by the same "duri lacci" that binds men. The lyric theme of the release from bondage of a woman by Love occurs in Stampa's poem "S'avien ch'un giorno Amor a me me renda," in a passage cited and translated by Green: "Ed io, cantando la mia libertade, / da cosí duri lacci e crudi sciolta, / passeró lieta a la futura etade" (While I, my liberty so gaily singing released from bondage harsh and cruel, shall go with springing step into my future state). Orlando acts out this lyric when he releases Origille from her own hair. She is then free to wander in romance space, free to be herself, for better or worse.

III

Women in Renaissance stories are usually defined by their relationships to men. Once outside Bactria and given an opportunity to meet someone beside her rescuer, a figure who may be as oppressive as the parental house she left, Origille proves that she is not constitutionally unfaithful, for she falls in love with Grifone. First, however, she is forced to ride Orlando's horse with him. Origille, as usual, makes the best of what is really another form of confinement. As she rides with the Count, she fires his passion. Orlando's physical longing for Origille is so out of keeping with his character as a chaste knight and devoted servant of Angelica that Giulio Reichenbach, the most important mid-century Boiardo scholar, proclaimed the event marked a breakdown in Boiardo's art, revealing Boiardo's failure to create a psychologically consistent character. Orlando's passion for Angelica is never physical in the poem, so much so that even when she bathes him, in imitation of classical maidens, he remains unaroused ("crescere in alcun loco non mostrava"; 1.25.39). According to Reichenbach, the Origille episode remains superfluous to the main story and damages the otherwise consistent portrait of Orlando as an apostolic warrior, the de-

---

[22] See, for example, poem 82 ("laci d'oro"), but also 20 ("catena d'oro"), etc., in *Amorum Libri: The Lyric Poems of Matteo Maria Boiardo*, trans. Andrea di Tommaso (Binghamton, NY: Medieval & Renaissance Texts & Studies, 1993).

fender of the faith. Boiardo tries to excuse his lapse by claiming that it is no wonder Origille lights Orlando's fire ("lo incese del suo amore"; *OI* 1.29.46): she is so maliciously beautiful that even "If she could love a thousand men / A day, her smiles would fool each one."[23] Yet, even Reichenbach admitted that the canto is well constructed: the woman who specializes in making men abandon their external, armorial bearings also causes Orlando to forget his self-defining love for Angelica.[24]

The theme of lost identity connects both halves of what might be considered the Origille dyptich in Canto 29, and continues every time Orlando meets Origille in the *Innamorato* (as well as everytime Origille appears in the *Furioso*). As he rides with Origille toward the end of the canto, Orlando waits impatiently for night to fall. But when the two finally dismount, Origille distracts the Count with a trick. She points to a nearby stone edifice and tells him that if he climbs its thirty steps and looks inside at what resembles a pool of water ("a guisa di fontana"; *OI* 1.29.50), he will see a vision of heaven and hell. When Orlando reaches the top of the rock, which is inscribed with letters of gold, Origille steals his horse. As she rides away, Orlando realizes he has been duped. He reads the letters on the rock and learns that it is the tomb of Nino, who founded the city Nineveh. Descending, he sets off on foot, as Boiardo concludes the canto and the first of the three books of the *Innamorato*.

No critic has yet offered an explanation for the hollow rock that Orlando peers into. In pastoral poetry, features of the landscape reflect psychic situations, as when rain and ice indicate a shepherd's frustration in love. And it is a feature of romances that castles, magic gardens, and rings usually operate as external indicators of the personalities of those characters who come in contact with them. Like prisms, these marvels reflect dif-

---

[23] "E se in un giorno avesse mille amanti, / Tutti li beffa con dolci sembianti," *OI* 1.29.45.

[24] "In questa figura così compatta e coerente non v'è che un solo errore psicologico, che non si riesce, nonostante tutte le sottigliezze, a superare: ed è il suo innamorarsi di Origille, che non si verifica prima o dopo l'amore per Angelica, ma contemporaneamente ad esso, anzi proprio mentre Orlando, appena partito da Albracca, è in cammino per compiere la straordinaria impresa che la sua dama gli ha imposto. Deve essersene accorto anche il Boiardo, perché si sforza di conestare la situazione con ogni espediente: mettendo a riscontro da una parte un uomo del tutto inesperto nelle cose d'amore e di carattere aperto, franco, leale, dall'altra una donzella maestra in ogni astuzia, e per di più di estrema bellezza. . . . Così la situazione stridente viene in parte sanata, e noi ci accigniamo con minor distacco ad assistere ai ripetuti inganni di Origille, e alle ripetute riconciliazioni e ricadute di Orlando" (Giulio Riechenbach, *L'Orlando Innamorato* [Florence: Nuova Italia, 1936], 131–32).

ferent aspects of different characters, according to how they are viewed. As Greenblatt suggests, it cannot be supposed that Boiardo's purpose was to peel back the layered defenses that conceal or defend the modern subject. Instead, like the artists who decorated the Schifanoia palace, Boiardo created symbolic art for a sophisticated audience that could be expected to seek its hidden meaning.

It is easy enough to find something negative to say about Origille's manipulation of Orlando at King Nino's tomb. Nino's wife Semiramis leads the lustful in the second circle of Dante's *Inferno* (*Inf* 5.58), as Boiardo knew, making Origille, at first glance, a type of such a lawless woman. But it is also possible to suggest that Origille used this stereotype to play on the Count's own lustful desire when she sent him climbing. The thirty steps that lead up Nino's tomb to the vision of heaven and hell may be read at least two ways. Cavallo glosses them as an inverted reference to Dante's choice of the thirtieth canto of *Purgatory* for the appearance of Beatrice, a figure whom Angelica imitates to a certain extent. But it may be more significant that "to give a thirty-one" was a slang expression in the Veneto for gang-raping a prostitute. The number occurs in the first canto of the poem, when we are told that thirty knights are drawn before Orlando in the lottery for who will first fight for Angelica (*OI* 1.1.58). Thirty names are drawn before Orlando hears his: he is thirty-first, the sad soldier at the back of the line. Now, thirty steps lead Orlando up King Nino's tomb, where he realizes that Origille, now no victim, has tricked him.

What does Orlando see when, at Orgille's direction, he looks into King Nino's tomb? The fountain-like rock of King Nino's tomb recalls the Narcissus myth as it appears elsewhere in the poem. At the Laughing Stream, for example, Orlando sees dancing maidens in the water, a projection of his own desire (*OI* 2.31.45). In Canto 29, while gazing into the mirroring tomb, Orlando suddenly recognizes his situation. He thinks he is a champion, but inside the real Orlando he is a fool. He cannot control his passion for Origille, but instead of requiting him she steals his horse, the chivalric equivalent of unmanning him. Of course, Orlando is notoriously obtuse in Boiardo's poem. He learns no lesson—in fact, he falls for Origille two more times. Instead, it is we, Boiardo's audience, who recognize how the fountain-like tomb of heaven and hell, in good Renaissance fashion, holds up the mirror to Nature and reflects the lives of Boiardo's characters.

When Orlando looks at the tomb, he sees not only his own reflection but the culmination of Origille's deception. For if the vision in King

Nino's tomb is an expression of Orlando's self-deception, it is also her own image that Origille lures him to gaze at. Because romances rely on external representations of inner life, their plots often consist of thematic and duplicative structures observable by a thinking audience, although not perceived by the narrative participants. The *Innamorato* is a book about deception and fraud, from Galafrone's plot to send Angelica to fool Charlemagne's knights to Orlando's belief that Ranaldo only pretends not to love Angelica. Origille's apparently simple exterior—the traitress, the deluder of men—fits this pattern of deception. Orlando sees heaven and hell; that is, he learns that Origille is more complex than he expected.

Her other adventures reveal the extent of her personality that was warped by the customs of Bactria and allegorically mirrored in King Nino's tomb. These adventures must be read in the context of Boiardo's complex plot, and therefore several critics have commented that Origille figures the false side of Angelica.[25] For example, Orlando finds Origille as he journeys to Falerina's Garden. He has been maliciously sent there by Angelica, who hopes that he will perish in the enchantments of the place and so not threaten the life of Ranaldo, whom she loves. Cavallo tightens the parallel by noting that both women have crafty, wicked fathers and brothers who sadly die young. Angelica has many sympathetic moments. By the same token Boiardo's art also gives Origille a more rounded character. Boiardo mentions briefly that the enchantress Falerina has constructed a false garden in order to take revenge on Ariante and "his lying wench" Origille (*OI* 2.5.19). The story is left untold, but the situation recalls the motif of Morgan le Fay's Val Sans Retour.[26] Morgan constructed her enchantment out of anger against two lovers and included a chastity test that can only be met by a knight who has never been unfaithful to his lady. Orlando meets a similar test at Falerina's Garden, where he must be chaste three days to defeat the dragon at the first gate. Because Origille tricks him into gazing into Nino's tomb, he misses his chance to make love to her. But because he has not made love, he is ready to countenance Falerina's spell. Origille's behavior, so maligned by Uldarno, actually assists the Count.

It is a rule of narrative construction that evil opponents will improve

---

[25] Antonio Franceschetti, for example, regards Origille as a projection of Angelica, who actually deceives Orlando more times than Origille does, although only Origille is called "falsa" (*OI* 1.28.53), "traditrice," and "dama ria" (*OI* 2.12.5).

[26] *Lancelot-Grail*, 305.

the moral status of even a questionable character. Compared to Falerina and her deathtraps, Origille is merely a tease. Her early refusal to make love after igniting the hero redounds to his benefit, saving him for Angelica and creating the grounds for his success against the more intricate marvels of Falerina's Garden. When Origille frees herself from Orlando, she steals his horse, an integral part of a knight's sense of self; but then, Orlando has not been himself since he first fell for Angelica, and Origille is really only normal in her disinterest in the squint-eyed, truant Count. Her moral stature increases further when she associates herself with a decent knight, Grifone. She falls in love with the young knight, and he with her, at the Bridge of Roses, when she explains how she comes to own Orlando's steed by making up a story about Orlando's death.

Unlike Orlando, who misses his first chance with Angelica and Morgana, Origille seizes her opportunities. She and Grifone are both doomed to be fed to Falerina's dragon, when Orlando once again rescues her. James Nohrnberg in this volume argues that Orlando's release of Origille is an unbinding of her bad fortune. Still later, Origille is said to seize her chance when Orlando rescues her once again, this time from the devouring dragon of Falerina's Garden (*OI* 2.3.61). She makes her own Fortune. Even without her many other signs of inwardness, that alone would make her a fit subject for Boiardo's romance.

Origille typically appears in the rest of the *Innamorato* only when she is trapped, first by a stream that requires a ferry to cross, then in King Manodante's prison, lastly by illness. Having met her in Bactria and then the Bridge of Roses, the Count encounters her on a third occasion, this time as he travels to King Manodante's realm. On his way he finds her quarreling with a ferry woman. The cause of the quarrel is not mentioned, but it must be that the ferry woman does not want to waste time with a damsel. The ferry woman's task is not to transport a woman cross a river (*OI* 2.11.15), but to lure knights into the vicinity of Balisardo, Manodante's agent, who captures them because Manodante has put out a search for Orlando. Orlando takes Origille under his care. They board the ferry and travel downstream to Damogir.

The association between Origille and Orlando's identity continues in Manodante's realm. Smitten with passion, Orlando reveals to her his plan to disguise himself so that he might manage to rescue Manodante's son Ziliante without interference from Manodante, who intends to capture Orlando because the fata Morgana will release Ziliante only in exchange for the Count. (Manodante's treachery recalls that of Origille's father, who was also willing to trade his honor for his son.) Having learned that Grifone, whom she loves, is among the knights in Manodante's prison, Origille reveals Orlando's identity to Manodante and wins freedom for herself and Grifone as her reward (*OI* 2.12.7).

We see Origille only once more in the poem, briefly at Blancherna, where she is said to be too ill to accompany Grifone to the Cyprus tournament. Cyprus is the island of Venus, and in Boiardo's story the place is also a trap: Orlando departs surreptitiously with Angelica when warned of a false plot against him (*OI* 2.20.38–40). By not going there, Origille avoids meeting Angelica. Once again she does good, if inadvertently, as her absence spares Orlando from having to face the two women in his life at once. Then, in a touching conclusion to her story, Grifone waits till she is well enough before leaving her, "not without laments" (*OI* 2.20.8). Even by the narrow terms of Renaissance narrative, where a woman's identity is dependent on her knight, Origille sheds the stigma of treachery that one society gives her in order, however briefly, to show herself capable of finding a new life.

IV

We may conclude that Origille, her paranomasiac homeland of Bactria, and her romance wanderings constantly raise questions of identity: that of Uldarno, the knight who tells her story and whom she caused to assume a false identity; that of Orlando, who forgets himself with a new woman; and that of Origille herself. How to account for the contrast between her claim to subjectivity and the social, and generally male, mold into which Origille is cast as a deceiver? Under the despots of Renaissance Italian city-states, wrote Burckhardt, "people were forced to know all the inward resources of their own nature."[27] People became individuals because they behaved differently, because they traveled, because they chose their own dress. Italian princes, moreover, unlike those in the north of Europe, were not dependent on an aristocracy that believed itself "the only class worth consideration," but selected talent from every grade of society. The nobility "were forced in social intercourse to stand upon their personal qualifications alone."[28] Origille is no conformist, or she would never have been punished in Bactria. She chooses her suitors' disguises and manipu-

---

[27] Burckhardt, *Civilization*, 7.
[28] Burckhardt, *Civilization*, 28.

lates a complex plot. A hypocrite and traitor from the point of view of Ul-darno, Origille leaves the oppression of Bactria for the wider world and adventure with Orlando. Even when rescued, she continues her independent ways, rejecting Orlando and falling in love with Grifone.

Her story continues in Ariosto's *Orlando Furioso*, but Ariosto flattens her character. Recovering from her illness, she finds a new lover, Martano, and fools Grifone into thinking they are brother and sister. But her lover Martano not only pretends to be her brother, he then steals Grifone's armor. Where Boiardo voiced the connection between identity and property by telling the story of how she induced her lovers to pretend they were not themselves, Ariosto tests that connection, as Greenblatt puts it, and deepens it. The result is a darker picture of society. Gone is Boiardo's delicate story of jingling Corbino and Oringo, erotic horse rides, and the place that Shakespeare's Athenian workers in *A Midsummer Night's Dream* will call King Ninny's tomb. Boiardo secretly knows that Origille is a clever courtesan in disguise.[29] But Ariosto the narrator—not one of her disgruntled lovers—openly calls her a "puttana" (*OF* 16.18). Ariosto's Martano steals Grifone's armor and identity until Grifone manages to recover his reputation and insignia. There is nothing symbolic about Martano's punishment for violating the culture's conception of identity: he is flogged to the point of death (*OF* 18.93). By contrast, Origille's hypocrisy and treachery seem a valid response to a society that fails to credit her as a person. As Boiardo tells the tale, she hangs her by her hair not only as a torture, but for pity: a sign of her social plight.

---

[29] Boiardo surprises us by his sympathy for the plight of women, as when Doristella, for example, complains about the misfortune of being born a woman: "Macone does not want / Me to pursue his law and rule, / Since he created me a woman, / Born in the world with such ill luck / That birds, beasts, every animal / Lives freer, with less grief than me"; *OI* 2.26.27.

HUMANISM AND LITERACY

JOHN McMICHAELS

Double Vision: Boccaccio's *Filocolo* in Boiardo's *Orlando Innamorato*

JUST AS THE *TESEIDA* OFFERED BOIARDO a precedent for his own story of arms and love, I would argue that the *Filocolo* provided him with a presentation of the theme of *caritas* or spiritual love.[1] Boiardo's extensive use of Boccaccio, in my view, stems from an unorthodox Christian belief they shared, in which human beings on earth create their own Hell or Purgatory, depending on whether they live in a world of false illusion or clear sense of truth. The false vision creates a dualistic world view, causing human beings to love others only as objects or to demonize them as something alien and evil, whereas true vision allows one to see others as autonomous beings. Boiardo uses Boccaccio's *Filocolo* to develop narratives in which false seeing, based on a false doubleness, gives way to a unifying, Christian vision of inner spiritual truth. This "double vision," involving two different kinds of seeing, informs the basic conflicts in both works. In the *Filocolo* Florio and Biancifiore are on an upward, spiritual pilgrimage, as they change from seeing only with the eyes to a deeper insight. Similar-

---

[1] Although there are no records of Boiardo's private library in Scandiano, Bertoni notes that there was a copy of the *Filocolo* in the Estense Library in Ferrara. It was one of the best libraries in Italy in the fifteenth century, and Boiardo had free access to it throughout his life. Moreover, there is a direct presence in the *Orlando Innamorato* of Question Four of Book Four of the *Filocolo* (which is also used in Book X of the *Decameron*) in Fiordelisa's novella of Tisbina, Prasildo, and Iroldo, the first novella of Boiardo's poem. In this way Boiardo acknowledged his debt to Boccaccio and advised the knowing reader that his imitatio has Boccaccian significance, in this case the upward spiral of friendship and courtesy.

ly, Brandimarte and Fiordelisa in the *Orlando Innamorato* are on an upward journey from sensual love to *caritas*, which is divine love. Boiardo's representation can be seen as a commentary on and a validation of Fiammetta's answers to the nature of love. Further, Boiardo creates episodes in the *Orlando Innamorato* that closely parallel events in the *Filocolo*. Indeed, Boccaccio's vision of love, as presented in the *Filocolo*, becomes a major intertext for Boiardo's poem.

Some critics of Boccaccio, as well as those of Boiardo, have judged that they wrote only to entertain. Boccaccio has suffered this judgement mostly on the basis of the *Decameron*. Studies of Boccaccio, including those of Robert Hollander, Janet Smarr, and Victoria Kirkham, have illuminated the allegorical significance of the *Decameron* in light of his other works, including the *Filocolo*.[2] Similarly, contemporary scholarship on Boiardo, such as the work of Michael Murrin, Charles Ross, and Jo Ann Cavallo, has shown a Boiardo of serious intent.[3] My own contribution, based on their work, involves a new reading of Boiardo's view of love, through Fiammetta's definitions of true and false love, to show that Boiardo has used Boccaccio's allegorical novel in episodes that have not been interpreted allegorically before, and that these episodes, like those commented on by Murrin and Cavallo, have political as well as personal consequences.

In the *Innamorato*, Boiardo uses Brandimarte and Fiordelisa, the true lovers, as a foil to the mad love of Orlando for Angelica, showing that true love, though rare, can exist. Further, the true love of Brandimarte and Fiordelisa, like the love of Florio and Biancifiore, has political ramifications: no acts are merely private.[4] The higher love of both couples in-

---

[2] Robert Hollander, *Boccaccio's Two Venuses* (New York: Columbia Univ. Press, 1977), Janet Levarie Smarr, *Boccaccio and Fiammetta* (Urbana: Univ. of Chicago Press, 1986), and Victoria Kirkham, *The Sign of Reason* (Florence: Leo S. Olschki, 1993).

[3] Michael Murrin, *The Allegorical Epic* (Chicago: Univ. of Chicago Press, 1980). Charles Ross's introduction to the translation of *Orlando Innamorato* (Berkeley and Los Angeles: Univ. of California Press, 1989), 19–27. Jo Ann Cavallo, *Boiardo's* Orlando Innamorato: *An Ethics of Desire* (Rutherford, NJ: Fairleigh Dickinson Univ. Press, 1993).

[4] Michael Murrin was perhaps the first to observe Boiardo's extensive political allegory. In "Falerina's Garden," chapter 3 of *The Allegorical Epic*, Murrin discusses the "deranged psychology" of Falerina as tyrant and "victimizer" and the effect on her "political state, which murders instead of protecting its citizens" (57). The love a ruler should have for her people is turned to wrath (62) or, as with Morgana, to greed. Murrin cites Boccaccio's *Teseida* as a source for Boiardo. My own argument, of course, turns to the *Filocolo*, in which wrath and greed are two versions of the same thing: love as utility, which is always hate, as Fiammetta points out, because it involves treating people as objects to be used, which turns to wrath when they will not obey; it is love of material

spires harmony and community among those able to accept their friendship, whereas the selfish, concupiscent "loves" of others cause only destruction, discord, and war.

In the *Filocolo*, when the questions of love are put to Fiammetta, Queen of the May, only her answer to Question Seven provides a key to the moral focus of the story. The seventh question of thirteen, it is the central question both numerically and philosophically.[5] Question Seven is asked by Caleon: "Gracious queen, I desire to know if every man, for his own well-being, ought to fall in love or not. And I am moved to ask this by the various things seen and heard and maintained by the varying opinons of men" (4.43).[6] Because she knows that Caleon loves her, Fiammetta replies, "It is necessary for us to speak against that which we follow with desire" (4.44). That is, she knows it is not a hypothetical question but a real one demanding a true answer, not just an answer within the framework of assumptions of the game itself.

Thus, Fiammetta is forced to deconstruct the game. She explains that "love takes three forms, and through these three all things are loved" (4.44). Fiammetta calls the first kind divine love, the love that makes the world go round, literally. Fiammetta says that we can all participate in this "honest love," which ought to be practiced as a matter of habit, virtue being, as Aristotle says in the *Nichomachean Ethics*, acquired only through habitual practice. This divine love is practiced through seeing the hand of

---

objects, a perversion of love into greed. Murrin extends the political allegory beyond the fairy tale world of Boiardo into his episodes of clashing armies, the world of the giant warrior Rodamonte, who wants to own the whole world or destroy it, so consumed is he by avarice and wrath. Murrin comments on the way "violence spreads and grows" in the descending spiral of horror at Boiardo's Castle Cruel (71). In her *Boiardo's* Orlando Innamorato, Jo Ann Cavallo develops Boiardo's political allegory further, particularly in the contrasting novelle of Castle Cruel and the story of Tisbina, Prasildo, and Iroldo, her sixth and seventh chapters. Cavallo emphasizes the political allegory of the downward spiral of Venus *in malo* at Castle Cruel, where evil increases geometrically until it is annihilated, consumed by its own wrath (55–56). Whereas, in the story of friendship and Venus *in bono*, genuine love expands arithmetically and, theoretically, forever, creating positive personal and political results. Cavallo (64) points out that Boiardo got the Tisbina, Prasildo, Iroldo story from Boccaccio's *Filocolo* (4.4) and from its later reworking in the *Decameron* (10.5). I am indebted to both Murrin and Cavallo as I seek to follow a related argument in a new direction.

[5] Seven as Diana's number represents chastity, not just as virginity or celibacy but as faithfulness. Kirkham, *The Sign of Reason*, 29.

[6] All references to the *Filocolo* are from the translation by David Cheney with Thomas G. Bergin (New York: Garland, 1985); the Italian text: *Filocolo*, ed. A. E. Quaglio, *Tutte le opere* (Milan: Mondadori, 1967).

God manifest in all of his creatures including one's fellow man. Fiammetta continues, "The second is called love of pleasure, and this is what we are subject to. This is our deity [in the game of love we are playing]" (4.44). It is not true love. It is the realm of Venus and Cupid, which if truly named is called "lust." To follow the god of love is to enslave oneself and the beloved. The third kind of love is also false and is more dangerous and destructive than the second. Fiammetta says this kind of love is based on "utility." It is the power to use people and things. In fact, it treats people as things to be owned, manipulated, or destroyed.[7] To Fiammetta, this kind of love is really hate. It is also a form of greed. Thwarted possessiveness provokes irrational anger.

Fiammetta's Question Seven becomes the allegorical center of the *Orlando Innamorato*. Boiardo as reader picked up on the importance of this question and wove an answer to it into the tapestry of his poem. There are four episodes in the *Orlando Innamorato* that show Boiardo's gloss on Boccaccio's *Filocolo*, both in the similarity of the episodes and by directly engaging Fiammetta's answers concerning true and false love: 1) Ranaldo's horrifying experience at Castle Cruel; 2) Fiordelisa's novella of Tisbina, Iroldo, and Prasildo in Book 1, Canto 12 and its continuation in Canto 17; 3) Orlando's rescue of Brandimarte and others from Morgana's realm in Book 2, Canto 8 and subsequent events with King Manodante at Damogir in Book 2, Cantos 9–13; and 4) Brandimarte's feats at Febosilla's palace and Liza in Book 2, Cantos 25–27. The first two are covered at

---

[7] To better understand Fiammetta, we may turn to the *Teseida* and look at Boccaccio's gloss to Book Seven. In the *Teseida*, we find that this third kind of "love" is not love but greed. Boccaccio's gloss places this false love not under Venus but under Mars. It is about power: acquisition, ownership, and control:

> For an understanding of this it should be remarked that in every man there are two principal appetites. One of these is called the concupiscible appetite, whereby man desires and rejoices to have the things which, according to his judgment—whether rational or corrupt—are delightful and pleasing. The other is called the irascible appetite whereby a man is troubled if delightful things are taken away or impeded, or when they cannot be had. (*Teseida*, 196)

This is derived from Plato, Book 4 of the *Republic* and *Phaedo*, and also from Aristotle's *Nichomachean Ethics*. It shows that the result of denial of things desired is of two types, both vicious. Possessive love denied causes anger and fear, leading to intrigues, discord, cruelty, and merry madness. Boccaccio means by "merry madness" the attributes of a person who "rushes furiously to his undertakings with an impious soul and with noise and with pomp" (*Teseida*, 198). The above passages are taken from *Teseida*, trans. Bernadette McCoy (Sea Cliff, 1974); the Italian edition: *Teseida*, ed. Alberto Limentani, *Tutte le opere* (Milan: Mondadori, 1964).

length in other studies of Boiardo's connection to Boccaccio.[8] Therefore, I will deal only with the latter two episodes.

In Book 2, Cantos 8 and 9, Boiardo presents an adventure that shows a failure to practice or even to understand genuine love or *caritas*. In the realm of Morgan the Fay, Orlando seizes the fairy by the forelock. Morgana (who represents both Fortune and Riches), is forced to give her key to Orlando, and he is able to release Ranaldo and others held captive, including Brandimarte. So far so good. But there is a problem. In order to gain Fortune's key, Orlando agrees to allow Morgana to keep Ziliante, a handsome young man whom Morgana keeps as a love slave. Ziliante means nothing to Orlando. To him, Ziliante is a nobody, and Orlando sacrifices him to free the others. As subsequent events will show, however, treating a human being as a pawn has a spiritual cost that goes beyond the individual who perpetrates it. Denying a person's humanity can have serious political consequences. It is not politically astute. Since one can never be sure who is important and who is not, it is politically expedient to show friendship and kindness to all. Since this is a lesson Boiardo derives from the *Filocolo*, we ought to return for a moment to Boccaccio's text.

In the *Filocolo*, there are several examples of Florio being mistreated as a nonentity when, dressed in humble garb as "Filocolo," he goes on a pilgrimage to restore a "love cut short" by the abduction of Biancifiore. The most revealing example of the political danger of which I speak occurs in Book 4 when the Admiral, who guards the virginity of the enslaved Biancifiore as she waits in a tower to be transferred to the Sultan's harem, secretly falls in love with her and longs to possess her with that "love" which is hate, as Fiammetta says. Visiting the tower to relieve a bout of melancholy by gazing upon Biancifiore, the Admiral is outraged to discover her asleep with Florio, who has married her in a ceremony of their own and has made love to her. The attitude of the Admiral immediately changes to hate as the burning anger of jealousy over his lost possession clouds his mind. The Admiral reviles her as a "whore" and orders that the two lovers be burned at the stake (4.126). But Mars, along with Florio's true friend Ascalion and a magic ring from Florio's mother, saves the pair. Realizing that his forces cannot succeed, the Admiral sees reason and con-

---

[8] See Cavallo, *Boiardo's* Orlando Innamorato, chaps. 6, 7, 14, and 15. Cavallo connects Brandimarte and Fiordelisa to the *Filocolo*'s Florio and Biancifiore (pp. 143–44), but she does not take into account the two episodes considered here, points which, in my view, are central to an understanding of both the role of Brandimarte and Fiordelisa in the *Orlando Innamorato* and of Boiardo's relation to Boccaccio.

cludes that the gods are displeased with him for attempting to destroy them. He says, "I did wrong in condemning the two young people to a foul death without having full information about them. What do I know of who they are?" (4.145). By condemning to death two unknown and supposedly unimportant young people, the Admiral has incurred the wrath of gods and men.

Under a sign of peace, the Admiral approaches the victorious knights and repents his unreasonable cruelty (4.147). But the Admiral does not know the full extent of his vicious blunder until Florio says he is the son of the king of Spain. The Admiral realizes that Florio is his own nephew and that he has almost succeeded in murdering his sister's only child and the heir to the throne. He cries, "Oh, cursed be my impulsiveness! Alas, why did I not recognize you before that hasty command?" (4.152). He uses lack of recognition to justify his vile deed and chastises Florio for not telling him sooner. He says, "Your hiding of your name and keeping yourself from me when you came here made me employ this base cruelty toward you" (4.152). His love for the young couple is not disinterested; rather, he has the highest interest "at stake," as it were. At least now that he knows Florio and Biancifiore are "family," he treats them with extreme courtesy, arranging for them an official wedding and a huge celebration in the very meadow that had just been a bloody battlefield. Yet, Boccaccio's point here is that "if only I had known" is no excuse. Since one never knows, one ought to treat all men and women as brothers and sisters because it might turn out to be so. Politically speaking, this is the only safe course. Whether the Admiral ever learns this lesson is never made clear.

Boiardo uses this lesson of the political consequences caused by lack of *caritas* in his representation of both Orlando and King Manodante. Orlando's decision to allow Morgana to keep Ziliante is almost disastrous. In her Hell of Riches, Morgana looks on Ziliante as her private possession, but Ziliante is the son and heir of King Manodante of Damogir. Morgana's selfishness is upsetting a whole realm. The king puts out a dragnet to capture Orlando and trade him to Morgana in return for Ziliante. Brandimarte frees Orlando from the dragnet, and they go to Damogir to attempt to release all the knights captured, including Astolfo and Ranaldo. They plan to go to King Manodante incognito and fool him by pretending to capture "Orlando" for the king. The plan works until the perfidious Origille betrays them, and Orlando and Brandimarte are imprisoned by the king, who does not know which of the two is Orlando (2.12).[9]

---

[9] All references to *Orlando Innamorato* are from Ross.

While they are imprisoned, Orlando explains the Christian faith to Brandimarte, who immediately converts. As with Fiordelisa earlier, Brandimarte has been a Christian in spirit for a long time. To charity and hope he now adds Christian faith. Immediately, he offers to insist that he is Orlando so that the real Orlando can escape.[10] Orlando at first refuses to allow Brandimarte to suffer for him, but he finally agrees when Brandimarte threatens to return to "paganism." Orlando is freed by King Manodante, who keeps Brandimarte with him, thinking Brandimarte is Orlando, until the king can exchange him for Ziliante. Unfortunately, Astolfo, a captive there also, blurts out that Brandimarte is not Orlando, and King Manodante in a fury orders Brandimarte to be quartered alive (2.12.56). Brandimarte is chained in a tower to await execution.

Meanwhile, Orlando frees Ziliante from Morgana's clutches and returns with him, along with Fiordelisa and Bardino, who had kidnapped Brandimarte as a child and sold him to the King of Castle Wild. King Manodante's joy at the return of Ziliante is eclipsed by the revelation of Bardino that the prisoner in the tower whom the king is about to execute is really his elder son Brandimarte. King Manodante orders the prisoner brought before him and, after determining that he is indeed "Bramadoro," the kidnapped son, the king weeps and says:

> My dearest son,
> My son, what can I ever say
> For jailing you so miserably?
> We have to follow what God wants.
> There's no undoing what's been done. (2.13.43)

Brandimarte and his father reconcile, and Orlando converts the king and his whole court to Christianity.

Thus, all's well that ends well. However, since as the king says, "There's no undoing what's been done," what if the king had quartered Brandimarte alive? Or as in Boccaccio's *Filocolo*, what if the Admiral had succeeded in burning his nephew and Biancifiore at the stake? When King Manodante says, "We have to follow what God wants," he seems to mean there is no arguing with destiny; God arranged it so that he almost killed

---

[10] Boiardo borrowed the escape plot from Plautus's comedy, *The Captives*. He conflates the comedy's plot with Boccaccio's *Filocolo* to show the mechanism or psychology by which a father could end up unwittingly enslaving, torturing, and imprisoning his own son. In a similar way, an Ovidian lover, lost in carnality, might eventually end up sleeping with his own daughter, an unknown child of his past lusts. Such unwittingly behavior is culpable because of the pattern it creates.

his own child out of ignorance. In light of Boccaccio's point about the Admiral, perhaps Boiardo means something else by the king's statement: Boiardo shows that "following what God wants" means treating all men as you would your son or your nephew because you never know. *Caritas*, as Boccaccio indicates and Boiardo reiterates, thus becomes the operating principle of human life. This underlying point may not be immediately apparent to the reader any more than it was to the Admiral or King Manodante. To read the deeper level in Boccaccio and Boiardo, one must lift the veil of allegory.

The *Orlando Innamorato* shares with the *Filocolo* the idea that failure to see this higher kind of love and to practice it results in a pernicious sort of "double vision," the universal human tendency to see duality rather than unity. It is the tendency to see the "other" as object or enemy. The perceiver cannot be redeemed from a dualistic form of seeing without the intervention of what might be called "grace." The episode in the *Filocolo* in which Boccaccio presents the intervention of divine grace occurs when King Felix has hardened his heart once again to his son Florio and Biancifiore. The couple hopes to return to Spain with their newborn son, but before they will return, Florio requests that Felix and his whole kingdom convert to Christianity as Florio and Biancifiore have done in Rome. Throughout the story, Felix has rejected Florio and Biancifiore, refusing to see them as anything but pawns to his will. Although Felix claims to love his son, his actions look more like hate. Boccaccio refers to the story of Pisistratus found in Dante's *Purgatorio* when his wife, mad with fury, insists on killing a young man who out of love for their daughter has embraced her in public. Pisistratus responds, "What shall we do to those who wish us harm / If we take vengeance upon those who love us?" (*Purgatorio*, XV, 104–5). Felix remains as intractable as ever. Choosing to reject Florio's offer of reconciliation and conversion, he vents his rage at the absent Florio, cursing the day his son was born and still plotting ways to kill Biancifiore (Boccaccio 5.78). Rather than love them, Felix casts them in the role of the "other," demonizing them and hating them.

At this point, Felix is visited by a dream vision in which God gives him a political message:

> I am he who can do all things, and whose equal is not to be found, and in whom your son and his wife and his companions newly believe. And if you do not graciously accede to his wishes, I shall make him rule in your presence, whether you like it or not, for as long as his life shall last, since no one can exceed that limit, and

I shall make you live so long that you will see his death. After this, the rebellion of your barons will be made apparent to you, and before your eyes they will take away your rule bit by bit, despite your opposition. . . . You will die shamefully and be an abomination to all the world. (Boccaccio 5.80)

Felix has a clear choice for the first time in his life: he can exert his will and continue to demonize his own son, destroying his kingdom in the process, or he can repent of his wrath, convert to Christianity, and rule over a peaceable kingdom to be passed on eventually to his son and grandson. Felix chooses the unifying vision. Florio and Biancifiore return with their child and eventually complete the pilgrimage to Campostella begun by Biancifiore's father Lelio and mother Giulia.

Boiardo's "take" on Boccaccio's story is an episode that begins in Febosilla's palace, which is the second episode that I will explore in this paper. As Fiordelisa and Brandimarte admire the frescoed walls of the courtyard, the couple is privileged to see in the frescoes an *ekphrasis* of the entire history of the Estense, Boiardo's patrons and dukes of Ferrara. The dynastic theme depicted here, which will be transferred to Rugiero and Bradamante, is presented to their worthy prototype, Brandimarte and Fiordelisa (2.25).

Then, Boiardo goes on to provide an allegorical scene that encodes a secret message for all would-be dynasts. It is the same message Boccaccio gave to Felix: embrace the "other" or perish. Earlier in the *Filocolo*, Boccaccio stated, through Ascalion to the Admiral, "Truly the wrath of the gods is earned by whoever refuses peace and prefers war, when a just peace can be established" (Boccaccio 4.148). Choosing discord over peace when peace is possible is pernicious mischief. In his own version of Boccaccio's insight, Boiardo presents this message of reconciliation through narrative adventure rather than direct statement.

In Boiardo's story, Brandimarte and Fiordelisa are locked into Febosilla's palace, the doors having disappeared when Brandimarte killed the protean giant serpents. With them is Doristella, whose obsessively jealous husband, also slain by Brandimarte, had incarcerated her there to keep her from her lover. Doristella tells them the only way to get out of the castle is for Brandimarte to kiss whatever pops out of a nearby tomb they have to open. Brandimarte replies with bravado, "I'll what? A kiss? . . . Is that all? Nothing else to do?" (2.26.5). But when they open the tomb, a dragon rears its ugly head. Brandimarte reaches for his sword to slay it, but Doristella makes him stop, saying that if he kills it, they will be stuck in the palace until they die. Brandimarte must kiss the serpent.

Brandimarte suddenly lacks confidence. He cannot believe he is being asked to do this: "You see those teeth? / And you want me to kiss that face? / Its form is so malicious that / I'm frightened just to look at it" (2.26.9). He wonders why he should kill himself by attempting such a stupid feat. Doristella calls him a coward and questions his faith. Finally, Brandimarte must put his newfound Christian faith to the test and perhaps have his face bitten off, or stand there in a melancholic funk until they all die. Will he do the deed? Yes. No. He waivers. Brandimarte at the Crossroads of the Pythagorean Y is faced with one of life's crucial decisions.[11] He may have other chances, but this is one of those moments of decision that leads upward along the right-hand path or downward to the left along the path to perdition. Brandimarte kisses the serpent. It turns into a beautiful woman, the fairy Febosilla, who after living a thousand years turned into a dragon, as fairies are wont to do from time to time. As she then explains, she had to remain in this condition until she was kissed by a brave knight. To thank Brandimarte, Febosilla restores his horse to life and enchants his armor, after which Brandimarte, Fiordelisa, and Doristella are able to leave the palace and travel on their way.

Perhaps it seems like a stretch to argue that Brandimarte's kissing a serpent is like Felix's forgiving his son, but I would argue that there is a real connection for two reasons: one is psychological and the other is political. First, from a psychological point of view, Brandimarte in an enchanted castle where he is expected to kiss a serpent or perish is in exactly the same position as Felix in his real castle, where he is expected to embrace the son he has demonized as an enemy. For Brandimarte the demon is presented as a real dragon, the archetypal Other. By kissing it, Brandimarte stops seeing it as the Other, and in fact it ceases to be so. In the same way, when Felix finally embraces his son, Florio ceases to be the enemy. In fact, Florio was never the enemy. That was his father's demonic projection. In both cases, a dualistic view gives way to a deeper unity.

As a "political" act, Brandimarte's kiss of peace has wide-ranging consequences. First, it gets them out of the box they are in. Once they are out of the castle, Fiordelisa discovers that Doristella is probably her sister.

---

[11] Murrin comments on the Pythagorean Y in Landino: "Landino's Aeneas is a hero constantly at the crossroads, choosing between opposed alternatives, often deceptive. The symbol for his situation and for the whole procedure recurs constantly in the *Camaldulensian Dialogues*: the Pythagorean Y, man choosing morally as well as intellectually." Murrin, *The Allegorical Epic*, 46.

They all ride to Doristella's home in Liza, along the way picking up by coincidence the man who kidnapped Fiordelisa as a child and took her to Castle Wild to be raised with Brandimarte. They arrive at Liza and lift the siege of the city by reuniting Doristella with her lover Teodoro. Fiordelisa is acknowledged to be the long lost daughter of the king and queen after some funny business over her birthmark. Brandimarte and Fiordelisa finally wed, as do Teodoro and Doristella. The people of Liza convert to Christianity, and "all of Armenia joined the faith" (2.27.35).

Thus, in their long pilgrimage, Brandimarte and Fiordelisa, the two characters in Boiardo's epic who are patterned after Florio and Biancifiore, are restored to family and kingdom. Later, they journey to Biserta, home of Agramante, near the former site of ancient Carthage. There they spread their tent, fabricated by a Sibyl of Naples and illustrated with pictures of the Twelve Alfonsos, progenitors of the Este from Spain on the distaff side. Again, Brandimarte and Fiordelisa are privileged witnesses to the dynastic theme of the Estense, which becomes the subject of Boiardo's third book of the *Innamorato*. Never finished, the story of Rugiero and Bradamante becomes the main theme of Ariosto's *Orlando Furioso*, in which Brandimarte and Fiordelisa are largely ignored and eventually killed.

To conclude, I would like to suggest that Boiardo's reading of Boccaccio's *Filocolo* represents a deep understanding of Boccaccio's insight into the nature of love, friendship, and social interrelationships as opposed to the "double vision" of greed and wrath. Both Boccaccio and Boiardo present negative *exempla* of false dualities, of false love that is really hate, and positive exempla of genuine love or *caritas*, based on Fiammetta's answer to the question, what is love. Boccaccio's Florio and Biancifiore and Boiardo's Brandimarte and Fiordelisa are on an upward spiritual spiral. More than this, however, Boccaccio and Boiardo each present an allegorical level that presumes there are natural laws or structures that inevitably shape our lives in reaction to our own decisions.

RICHARD F. SORRENTINO

Bella Istoria, Vera Istoria, and Boiardo's Competent Reader

FOR FIVE HUNDRED YEARS NOW, readers have been delighted by Matteo Maria Boiardo's epic-romance, *Orlando Innamorato*, a new variation on the Carolingian legend passed down through various centuries.[1] A putative deviation from the heretofore indisputable authority of Turpin, Archbishop of Rheims, is played out in the hero's decision to abandon the court "per amore."[2] The initiative taken by Orlando, along with the loss of reputation he suffers because of it, are the pretext for a supposed censorship by Turpin. This particular "novella" was not worthy of inclusion in his distinguished Chronicle, or "vera istoria"; hence, the poem's self-definition, in its opening lines, as a "bella istoria."

Yet, the authoritative Chronicle of Turpin is among the many and var-

---

[1] Most readers may know that the *Orlando Innamorato* has circulated in various versions, beginning with the *rifacimenti* of Francesco Berni and Ludovico Domenichi of the sixteenth century. These versions of Boiardo's poem were designed to overcome the linguistic "problems" of the original, composed just before the Florentine standard came into vogue at the beginning of the sixteenth century. The efforts of Pietro Bembo, a strong influence on Ludovico Ariosto's *Orlando Furioso*, were in fact the inadvertent cause of a discomfort with Boiardo's Emilian vernacular; the original poem was thus virtually unread for some two and a half centuries, until the edition of 1830 in London by Antonio Panizzi. For English-speaking audiences, there finally is the full translation by Charles S. Ross (Berkeley and Los Angeles: Univ. of California Press, 1989).

[2] Charles S. Ross, "Angelica and the Fata Morgana: Boiardo's Allegory of Love," *Modern Language Notes* 95 (1981): 20: "Boiardo changed his Carolingian source by transforming Orlando's wrath into excessive love for Angelica."

ied sources of the *Orlando Innamorato*. The epithet "bella istoria" is itself derived from the tradition comprising Turpin's "istoria." The big difference between Boiardo's poem and the free variations based on legendary material, "belle istorie," is in the denial of such origins by an ironic narrator. The poem's readers, possessed of a great sophistication regarding the legend of Roland, could see through the transparent pretense of Turpin's censorship. Therefore, they would go on, reading the poem, as we do today, to discover a significant inclusion of the "vera istoria" in many of its existing versions.

In Boiardo's day, the Carolingian legend had proliferated through various generations of storytelling, from the *chansons de geste* of medieval France to the reelaborations told at Venice, and, later in the fourteenth century, in the narratives known as *cantari in ottava rima*, which circulated in and around Florence.

The readers in the Este court at Ferrara had, on the evidence of extant catalogues of the court library, access to a good number of texts from France, Venice, and Florence, from virtually all the periods and cycles of chivalric narrative.[3] Thus, they might well have been apprised of certain divergences and similarities between the tales told about Roland. What I will now explore is how the divergences between versions of Roland's legend may have been produced by differences in audience; differences existed in the cultures in which variations arose, but also in the level of cultural attainment of recipients. It is evident that the audiences in and around Venice, in the early fourteenth century, had a higher level of cultural attainment than those in and around Florence later in that same century.[4] The contrast between versions of the legend of Roland as told to naive and erudite recipients had long been the case. By Boiardo's time, indeed, those versions of the tale addressed to naive recipients had gained

---

[3] A well-known reference to the Este catalogue can be found in Giulio Bertoni, *La biblioteca Estense e la coltura ferrarese al tempo di Ercole I* (Turin: Loescher, 1903).

[4] For evidence of the period, see Franco Sacchetti's novella no. 114 of the *Trecentonovelle*, ed. with an introduction by Antonio Lanza (Florence: Sansoni, 1993), 231–32. With explicitly scathing irony meant for the storytellers of his own day, Sacchetti tells the story of a blacksmith who, taken to task by Dante for attempting to sing his rhymes in the form of a *cantare in ottava rima*, proceeds to sing the stories of Tristan and Lancelot with no adverse consequences. Yet, at that time, the *cantari* were at the height of their popularity as stories told or sung by minstrels in the town square. At the same time, the *cantari*, along with the chivalric legends that were the best-loved subject matter of the *canterini*, as the storytellers were known, had fallen out of favor with the more learned audience of writers like Sacchetti.

a certain amount of credit even among sophisticated readers, in the form of *cantari in ottava rima.* Originally oral recitations delivered to illiterate listeners in the public square, the *cantari* had lately found their way into the courts of northern Italy in the form of transcriptions and compilations.[5]

Texts known as *La Spagna,* based on an earlier adaptation of Roland's legend known as *L'Entrée d'Espagne,* and *I cantari di Rinaldo da Montealbano* had a wide circulation among naive and learned audiences in the fourteenth and fifteenth centuries. Reading the transcribed texts of *cantari* as well as the long-circulated chivalric romances in *langue d'oil,* along with the intervening versions of the Roland legend in a northern Italian vernacular known as *Francoveneto,* Boiardo's readers could have been aware of certain discrepancies between the texts produced for naive and learned audiences.[6]

What may thus become evident to a competent reader of the *Orlando Innamorato* is a gap in the credibility of Turpin and his "vera istoria." The article of faith that the "istoria" once represented could no longer be the case; centuries of corruption by storytellers and various elaborators in the legend had produced irreconcilable discrepancies. One of many issues that emerges in the *Innamorato* is an assessment of the relative merits of written versus oral means of communication. Boiardo's pose as a storyteller with a "bella istoria," or variation on the "istoria" of Turpin, is the first indication of such a concern. The written source, Turpin's Chronicle, is impeached in favor of the "canto," the oral recitation being carried out by the storyteller. Yet, there is an important irony, detectable in the transparency of the pretense. Boiardo's narrator calls attention both to the written narration and to his written sources at many points of the poem. A reader is thus provided with the means of discriminating between oral and written versions of the legend inherited by Boiardo. The act of reading itself is potentially glorified as the means of such discovery.

Nevertheless, Boiardo's fiction of oral narration is, as part of a written text, constant and sustained, a paradox whose blatancy calls attention to

---

[5] Relevant historical information can be found in Carlo N. Dionisotti, "Appunti su antichi testi," *Italia medievale e umanistica* 7 (1964): 131, and in Domenico de Robertis, "Esperienza poetica del Quattrocento," *Storia della letteratura italiana,* eds. Emilio Cecchi and Natalino Sapegno (Milan: Garzanti, 1964), 4: 437.

[6] For information concerning the texts in *Francoveneto,* see Gunter Holtus, Henning Kraus, and Peter Wunderli, eds., *Testi, cotesti e contesti del franco-italiano* (Tubingen: Max Niemeyer Verlag, 1989).

a further discovery. Within the sustained fiction of spoken narration, there is a return to the sort of naiveté that had marked the listening reception of *cantari*. The reader is thus privy to a "meraviglia," an amazement, peculiar to Boiardo's "bella istoria." After centuries of storytelling in both written and oral form, the poet's simulation of an oral narration constitutes an innovation that would not have been possible in prior times. Paradoxically, the innovation could have been suggested to the poet by the most recent texts to which he and his audience had access, the *cantari in ottava rima* in their written guise. Well aware that the tales told in texts such as *La Spagna* and *I cantari di Rinaldo da Montealbano* were based on oral narrations, Boiardo and his audience were able to detect the signs of an oral narration, intentional and unintentional, in a written text. Boiardo's simulation of spoken narration in a text whose origins are in written sources, which include those very *cantari* texts, is a sign of tribute; his "bella istoria" is the very latest addition to the long history of the legend of Roland and Charlemagne.[7] As the phenomenon of the *cantari* had demonstrated, even poor illiterates could bask in the reflected glory of the legend. For sophisticated readers such as those of the Este court, the reward was something more. Readers of the *Innamorato* could see how the legend's glory continued, even beyond the legend's relevance as an article of Christian faith.

One such reader was Ariosto. The lesson emerging from his continuation of the *Orlando Innamorato*, particularly concerning written and oral means of communication, is the subject of my conclusion.

The long history of the Carolingian legend began with its first recorded text, the *Chanson de Roland*, a text evidently intended for feudal nobles at the top level of cultural attainment in eleventh-century France. In one of the more famous episodes of the poem, the ambush of the Peers and the twenty thousand men of Charlemagne's rear guard is in full cry at the Pass of Roncevaux. After some hesitation, for fear of ruining his reputation, Roland starts to sound his olifant to summon reinforcements. However, Ganelon, the traitor who through an intrigue with the Moorish king of Spain has concerted the massacre, convinces Charlemagne that Roland is not in any danger and that he is using his horn to hunt rabbits. He further

---

[7] The same point is made by Michael Sherberg in "Matteomaria Boiardo and *I cantari di Rinaldo da Montealbano*," *Quaderni d'italianistica* 7 (1986): 166: "Through the poet's precise allusion to his sources, the *Innamorato* becomes a segment in the vaster history of the Carolingian era, the chronicling of which, Boiardo would have us believe, is an ongoing process to which each poet/historian contributes with his work."

reminds Charlemagne of Roland's occasional disloyalty, as when Roland had carried out an unauthorized conquest of the Spanish city of Nobles some time prior to the action of the poem (Digby MS., 1770–84). When Charlemagne and his forces finally do get back to the Pass, following parallel hesitations of Roland and Charlemagne, they are only in time to bear witness to the debacle. Roland, whose temples burst from the strain of sounding his horn, lies dead along with Oliver, Turpin, and the entire rear guard under his command.

In Italy, the story of Roland was continued in a *chanson* known as the *L'Entrée d'Espagne*.[8] At the center of the *Entrée*'s events is the unauthorized conquest of the city of Nobles by Roland, the basis for accusations of disloyalty by Ganelon in the original *chanson*.

Roland, for his insubordination, incites a public rebuke; Charlemagne, in his rage, proceeds to strike the hero on the cheek with his gauntlet. Connotations of Roland's disloyalty are thereby laid aside since, as Nancy Bradley-Cromey says, Charles's public humiliation of the hero is in violation of feudal ethics. Thus, Roland's obligation to his lord, at that point, ceases.[9] In view of the lifting of his duty, Roland has no choice but to desert the camp, which he does late the same night, under a pseudonym and in disguise.[10] For the next fourteen years, Roland will embark on a series of adventures during which he will seem largely forgetful of his prior obligations; but in the end, he will return, hence to meet the destiny reserved for him at Roncevaux. The events of the original *chanson* are not narrated by the author of the *Entrée*, but they may be inferred by the

---

[8] Antoine Thomas, ed., *L'Entrée d'Espagne, chanson de geste franco-italienne publiée d'après l'unique manuscrit de Venise par Antoine Thomas*, Société des anciennes textes Français, vol. 69 (Paris: Librairie de Firmin Didot, 1913). For relevant considerations, see Nancy Bradley-Cromey, *Authority and Autonomy in the Entrée D'Espagne* (New York: Garland Publishing Co.), 1993; Alberto Limentani, *L'Entrée d'Espagne e i signori d'Italia*, eds. M. Infurna and F. Zambon (Padua: Editrice Antenore, 1992). Bradley-Cromey (71) offers some considerations surrounding the issue of a French precursor of the *Chanson de Roland* in which the story of the *Entrée* might have been told. Citing the invasion of Nobles as a thematic core, she makes some careful but positive assertions concerning such a lost text, or texts.

[9] Bradley-Cromey, *Authority and Autonomy*, 43.

[10] In the next century, a series of *cantari* known as the *La Spagna* appeared in Tuscany. Adapted from the events of *L'Entrée*, Orlando (as he became known to his Italian readers thereafter), deserts the camp of Carlo Magno in the wake of accusations of disloyalty by Gano (formerly Geune, or Ganelon in the *chanson de geste*). See Michele Catalano, ed., *La Spagna, poema cavalleresco del trecento* (Bologna: Commissione per i testi di lingua, 1938).

seven-year engagement between the forces led by Charlemagne and King Marsilius, which begins the action of that text.

The *Entrée*, intended for learned audiences like the *Roland*, arose in a different cultural and political environment and at a different period of history, in the first third of the fourteenth century in northern Italy. The political implications of Roland's predicament are indeed conspicuously altered. As I have already noted, Roland's feudal obligations are laid aside with the emperor's public rebuke; in consequence, the emperor's authority is greatly diminished. Much more than the interplay of intricate feudal conflicts that concerned audiences of the original *chanson*, the Italian Trecento audience was much more interested in the relationship between a citizen and his leader. As any reader of Dante's *De Monarchia* could infer, the political situation of Italy of the early Trecento was characterized by an ongoing debate concerning models of good governance.[11] The issue held a special importance for Italians of the time. The decline of imperial authority that followed the death of Frederick II late in the previous century left a power vacuum, which was to confer a good deal of volatility on Italy's fragile communal system. By the end of the fourteenth century, the one-man rule of the *signorie* had replaced republican forms of government in various cities, including Florence.

In the *Entrée*, the shift in the center of authority, from Charlemagne to Roland, was evocative of historical events; Charlemagne resembled the actual weakened emperor while Roland, through his martyrdom, was an idealized figuration of the hero sent by God to redeem mankind.[12]

Religious allegorical connotations are strengthened by the citation of Turpin, the Archbishop of Rheims, by the *Entrée*'s poet. Attributing his voice to Turpin, the reputed author of a chronicle of the events at Roncevaux as well as an eyewitness to those events, the poet was able to claim a historical authoritativeness for his version of events.

Turpin was a powerful influence on many authors of medieval Italy, including Andrea da Barberino, whose *Aspramonte* predates the *Orlando Innamorato* by little more than a mere half-century.[13]

---

[11] Bradley-Cromey, *Authority and Autonomy*, 23–30, 53.

[12] Bradley-Cromey, *Authority and Autonomy*, 26, states that "For the Paduan, Roland becomes the bearer of the word needed for good governance, thus an analogue of the Christ."

[13] Marco Boni, ed., *L'Aspramonte* (Bologna: Commmissione per i testi di lingua, 1951).

However, an intervening phenomenon, known as the *cantari in ottava rima*, was to confer a further influence on the legend. The original audiences of the *cantari* heard the tales recited in the public square. Naive and possibly illiterate, they were poorly informed concerning the earlier legend and probably largely ignorant of the Chronicle of Turpin. The storytellers thus took liberties with the tales of Roland and Renaus (Orlando and Rinaldo as they became known to their Tuscan audiences) in accordance with the demands of their audiences. Like the frescoed figures of Giotto of the early Trecento, and the literary characterizations of Boccaccio, the reputed inventor of the *cantari* of the same period, Orlando and Rinaldo came to resemble ordinary, natural men, at odds with the earlier heroic characterizations. Orlando, for his Tuscan audiences, experiences sudden and violent flare-ups of temper not necessarily related to the greater tale, although certainly suggested by his wrathfulness of earlier texts. He is also endowed with a prodigious appetite, something that might well have been an endearing trait to the tradesmen and merchants who heard the tale recited in the town square.

Rinaldo, formerly a rebel against Carlo Magno, is transformed, by means of a brief but significant interpolation, into a defender of his family reputation. In the opening *cantare* of the tale, he is slandered by Ginamo di Maganza who, in the court of Carlo Magno, claims Rinaldo as his own, bastard son. The hero's drama is thus shifted from that of having to defend himself against imperial encroachments on his feudal interests to having to defend his and his family's reputation against the calumnies of the Maganza clan.[14]

For Boiardo's audience, the *cantari* were good adventure stories, containing scenes of dueling and other derring-do of which they were most fond. Thus, in the fashion of a storyteller surrounded by a naive crowd, Boiardo begins his tale.[15] For Boiardo himself, the *cantari* were arguably the most recent and most pliable model for original and innovative variations. The poet labeled his putative *cantare* a "bella istoria," an epithet taken directly from the *canterini*, as the storytellers were known. He thus succeeded in capturing the attention of serious readers, readers

---

[14] Elio Melli, ed., *I Cantari di Rinaldo da Monte Albano* (Bologna: Commissione per i testi di lingua, 1986).

[15] For considerations concerning the audiences of the *cantari*, see Giovanni B. Bronzini, *Tradizioni di stile aedico dai cantari al Furioso* (Florence: Olschki, 1966), and Maria Cristina Cabani, *Forme del cantare epico-cavalleresco* (Lucca: Maria Pacini Fazzi, 1988).

who would understand the narrator's corrosive attitude toward Turpin and his "vera istoria."

For Boiardo and his readers acquainted with the Roland legend as transmitted in written *chansons*, but also in the prevalently oral medium of the *cantari*, the viability of Turpin's authority could well have been the subject of some dispute. In the *cantari* themselves, his very name had been suppressed in favor of the much more transparent references to the "istoria," the "libro," and the "autore." Naive audiences could thus appreciate the model of authority devised for their own sensibilities. As Boiardo's readers could have realized, the anonymous attributions were also modeled on the much-more learned precedents of Arthurian narrative whose authors referred to a similarly anonymous *conte* among their own sources.

Boiardo's mocking attribution of his story to Turpin is a reference to both sorts of tradition. On one hand, he is recapturing the naiveté of a *cantari* audience by denying his source; the audience of the *Innamorato* will soon discover, in fact, that the poem's sources are many and anonymous, like those of the *cantari* themselves. The poet's audience was privy to a further discovery. Boiardo's simulation of an anonymous source points to the more erudite tradition of the romance, hence a further violation of Turpin's authority. The first clue given to readers may be found in the poem's very title. Orlando in Love, a hero whose enterprises are in the name of love, for the first time in the history of his legend, signifies the poet's inclusion of the Arthurian Cycle, a source of which his audience could have been well aware.[16]

What soon becomes evident in Boiardo's poem is a certain privileging of the text in its written form.[17] Orlando's characterization appears to proceed, in fact, from two great written narratives known to Boiardo and his audience, *L'Entrée d'Espagne*, and Andrea da Barberino's *Aspramonte*. The conflict in Orlando, between individual and communal imperatives, though traceable to the Arthurian Cycle, is most immediately detectable

---

[16] The compilation of incompatible cycles of narrative in the *Innamorato* was first noted by Pio Rajna, *I fonti dell'Orlando Furioso* (Florence, 1897); a more recent critic, Marco Praloran, *Maraviglioso Artificio: tecniche narrative e rappresentative dell'Orlando Innamorato* (Lucca: Maria Pacini Fazzi, 1990), applies Rajna's historicist criteria to a narratological analysis.

[17] According to Giulio Reichenbach, *L'Orlando Innamorato* (Florence, 1938), 23, Pio Rajna chose not to believe that the refined poet of Scandiano would have deigned to include the humble, pedestrian rhymes of the *cantimpanchi* in his poem of Orlando. Thus, it would appear that the positivist Rajna was inclined to take Boiardo's narrator at face value.

in *L'Entrée*. We have already seen how, in that poem, the hero deserts the court of Charlemagne in pursuit of individual initiatives and against his sworn feudal duty. In Andrea's romance, adapted from a number of Franco-Venetian *chansons*, a similar clash occurs.[18] The hero is face to face with Ulivieri, son of Gherardo da Fratta, a sworn enemy of Carlo Magno. Orlando and Ulivieri are not dueling just as the vassals and champions of their respective overlords, but also over a much more personal issue. Orlando is in love with Aldabella, Ulivieri's sister. He thus faces a double bind: in order to win, he would have to kill the brother of his beloved thus to lose her forever; but abandoning the duel would mean losing her as well as disgracing his overlord.

In the end, the heroes are the beneficiaries of a divine intervention. A cloud appears, thus separating the heroes; a heavenly voice exhorts them to cease all hostilities. Orlando and Ulivieri lay down their arms at once. Peace is made at last between Gherardo and Carlo, and the final obstacle between Orlando and his love for Aldabella is thus removed.

In the *Orlando Innamorato*, at least at the beginning, no such tidy resolution is in order. Orlando deserts the court of Carlo Magno as he does in the *Entrée*, to pursue a private interest; as in the *Aspramonte*, his private interests are influenced by his love of a lady. The lady, in Boiardo's poem, however, is no longer Aldabella, but a Saracen princess, Angelica, possibly suggested to Boiardo by the comely daughter of the sultan of Jerusalem in the *Entrée*. Just as he is about to embark on his desertion in her pursuit, Orlando articulates his dilemma: "Veggio il meglio, et al peggio m'appiglio" ("I see what's best. I pick what's worst"; 1.1.31.8).[19]

Boiardo's quotation of Petrarch demonstrates a privileging of the erudite tradition exemplified by the lyric, even despite formal resemblances to a *cantare in ottava rima*.[20] The signal serves as an acknowledgment of the

---

[18] For information on the position of the *Aspramonte* and other Carolingian texts among Boiardo's sources, see Antonio Franceschetti, *L'Orlando Innamorato e le sue componenti tematiche e strutturali* (Florence: Olschki, 1986), 229–60.

[19] The line from Petrarch, cited here from the Ross translation, is from *Rime Sparse*, 264.172.

[20] According to Claudia Micocci, *Zanze e parole: Studi su Matteomaria Boiardo* (Rome: Bulzoni, 1987), 7, ". . . Boiardo è uno dei punti centrali della cultura quattrocentesca, il crogiuolo che unifica, in una visione le cui suture sono sommerse, tradizioni e culture coeve, più decisamente dell'ordinato Poliziano, del visionario Pico." (". . . Boiardo is one of the central points of the culture of the Quattrocento, the crucible who unifies, seamlessly, coeval traditions and cultures, more decisively than the orderly Politian, than the visionary Pico.")

hero's inner conflict as proceeding from written intertexts like the *Entrée*, the *Aspramonte*, and so many others, including the Arthurian romance.[21] Orlando's pursuit of his lady is not unlike the quests undertaken by Lancelot and Tristan in the romances of which Boiardo's audience was quite fond.

What, then, of the *cantari in ottava rima?* The epithet "bella istoria," in the opening lines of the poem, as well as the rhyme scheme of Boiardo's poem, signifies a certain sort of tribute, at least in the first part of the poem. More than anything else, the reader may suspect that the poet is attempting to recapture the inherent "meraviglia" of the recited text, along with its effects on naive listeners. Hearing the story for the first time, the illiterates who heard the *cantari in ottava rima* were conceivably much more susceptible to "meraviglia" than the jaded audiences of the Italian courts, who had heard the same tales told again and again with only slight variations. At the level of metanarrative, Boiardo's inclusion of the *cantari in ottava rima* could well have implied a genuine novelty; up to that time, only readers of Luigi Pulci's *Morgante* could have been privy to a tale whose main source was an essentially oral narration, but whose intended audience was the erudite court nobility of Florence.

Later in the poem, though, it becomes evident that the *cantari in ottava rima* exemplify something further. For Boiardo and his readers, the *cantari*, oral narratives in contrast to the written intertexts, become an important model for the lack of control over verifiability that had come to characterize the transmission of the Carolingian legend in recent years. The issue, hence the prominence of citations of the *cantari*, comes into play near the end of Book 1.

At that point of the poem, there is the famous duel at Albraca between Orlando and Ranaldo, incited by insults drawn from Rinaldo's legend.[22] The legend's unverifiability becomes a real problem when Orlando questions his adversary's heroism, saying that his slaying of the pagan Mambrino, as recounted in the *cantari*, was carried out with the help of the sorcery of Malagise.

Ranaldo cannot acquit himself of Orlando's accusations; his problem,

---

[21] Jo Ann Cavallo, *Boiardo's* Orlando Innamorato: *An Ethics of Desire* (Rutherford, NJ: Fairleigh Dickinson Univ. Press, 1993), an allegorical reading of the poem, provides a thorough rendering of Boiardo's classical and medieval sources.

[22] For relevant insights on this episode, see Sherberg, "Matteomaria Boiardo and *I Cantari di Rinaldo da Montealbano*," 165–81.

on its surface, is the lack of witnesses except for Malagise himself, whose mendacity was the stuff of his legend. Lurking just beneath the surface, however, is Boiardo's critique of the whole tradition of the *cantari*, transmitted by word of mouth and thus inherently unreliable. Malagise becomes the representative of the transmitters of that tradition, the storytellers whose variations could be altered for the sake of appealing to an audience who, in any case, was none the wiser concerning the sources of the tale. Boiardo's readers could infer the doubt cast by the ironic narrator on stories told to ignorant listeners of the public square.

At the same point of the poem, Boiardo the poet is supposed to have conceived of the poem's encomiastic purpose: the hero Rugiero was just about to step onto the stage as the progenitor of the Este dynasty. At that time in Italy, a scurrilous legend was making the rounds. According to certain tales told to naive and erudite persons alike, the ruling Este family were descended from the traitor geste of Ganelon. Boiardo's impugning the entire tradition of the *cantari in ottava rima* may well have stemmed from his intention of stifling the slander. The *Orlando Innamorato*, especially from Book 2 onward, shows distinctive signs of expressing a courtly agenda in whose name the written poem was to have superseded the oral accounts of Este ancestry.

Soon to follow, at the opening of Book 2, were the crucial episodes of Falerina's Garden and the Fata Morgana's underwater realm, whose descent from the written romances is incontrovertible. It is also perhaps no coincidence that, at the opening of Book 2, the *Innamorato*'s narrator lays out the conclusions of his tale. Rugiero, the progenitor of the Este dynasty, would die by the treachery of the Maganza clan, hence to replace Roland as the martyr of tradition. Orlando himself would go on to destroy the invading army of Agramante, thus to emerge the hero of Christendom of his prior legend.

Ariosto: Boiardo's reader

Ariosto's *Orlando Furioso*, the continuation of Boiardo's poem (unfinished because of the poet's death in 1494), addresses the conclusions indicated by Boiardo, particularly concerning the illustrious ancestry of the Este. Dedicating his poem to Cardinal Ippolito d'Este, his then-patron, Ariosto makes reference to the questions surrounding the believability of a "vera istoria" as told by Turpin, by legions of storytellers and, at one point, by his immediate predecessor.

In a passage explicitly evocative of the *Innamorato*, Ariosto stages a meeting of Rinaldo and Gradasso for the purpose of resuming their duel, postponed because of Malagise's trickery in the *Innamorato* (*Orlando Furioso*, 31.95–105). Ranaldo, who had leapt aboard a departing ship in pursuit of the demon Draginazzo in Gradasso's disguise, had been disgraced because of the appearance of cowardice caused by his not having been on the scene at the real Gradasso's arrival shortly thereafter. At first, because of Rinaldo's—Ariosto reverts to the traditional Tuscan spelling of characters' names, hence, Rinaldo, Malagigi, Ferraù, and others—apparent cowardice, Gradasso hesitates, considering him an unworthy adversary. Then, Malagigi comes forward to corroborate Rinaldo's account of events. Ariosto refers to Rinaldo's account as his "vera istoria," one of only two such references in the entire *Furioso* (31.101.4).[23] However, since the story is being corroborated by Malagigi, a known liar and cheat, the allusion is quite hollow; Rinaldo is the victim of an injustice similar to that of his dishonoring in the *Innamorato* and in the *cantari*. Consistently with both his tradition and with the *Orlando Innamorato*, he is the victim of a narrative irony through which the reader alone can detect his true heroism.

From Ariosto's standpoint, which is also that of a reader of a written text, the narrative irony of Gradasso's disbelieving Rinaldo's "vera istoria" comes from both sources. The most immediate source is the *Innamorato*; Boiardo's authority is driven home by the ostensible irrefutability of his written text. Yet, Ariosto tacitly gives credit to the oral texts in which Rinaldo's victimhood had originated, thus casting some doubt on his predecessor and, that is, on Boiardo's privileging of written texts.

What Malagigi's corroboration of the "vera istoria" of Rinaldo shows, in fact, is that a true story may seem false to those who, like Gradasso, are unacquainted with the written text whereby the story can be verified. Gradasso, by his incredulity, shows that he is indeed not familiar with Boiardo's version of events.

Thus, a written text may, under certain circumstances, be refutable evidence on a par with the unreliable oral tradition already taken to task in the *Orlando Innamorato*. Gradasso, being the non-reader he is, goes on to gain a substantial reward, in the form of the long-sought-after prize of Baiardo, even after the horse has taken flight into a cave, in a scene explicit-

---

[23] The other "vera istoria" alluded to by Ariosto is *La Spagna*, in *Furioso* 18.97.2. I am grateful to Amedeo Quondam and the staff at the Istituto di Studi Rinascimentali at Ferrara who graciously allowed me the use of their electronic concordance of the *Orlando Furioso* during the winter of 1991.

ly evocative of the *cantari in ottava rima.* In all extant versions of the legend, Baiardo, following his flight into the cave of Vulcan, from which he had first been ensnared by Malagigi, was never again to be possessed by any man. The appropration of Baiardo by Gradasso is also in violation of the conventions of chivalry, contained in other texts which Gradasso has apparently not read.

Gradasso, a naive recipient who hears Rinaldo's "vera istoria" for the first time in oral form, is entirely entitled to his disbelief; yet, as the action of Ariosto's poem bears out, he is also entitled to pursue the duel with Rinaldo nonetheless. His ignorance of chivalric convention means that he has nothing to fear in terms of personal disgrace. In any case, he shows that he does not take such a threat quite so seriously as a knight who is well aware of the relevant conventions.

Ariosto does not, I think, draw any original conclusions. As we have observed, Boiardo, at least at the beginning of the *Innamorato,* casts his own poem as just one more "bella istoria," a further variation on the already corrupted, and perhaps unknowable story of Roland and Renaus. It was at that same point in the poem that Ranaldo had disgraced himself as a result of his defection from the duel with Gradasso; and so the variation, even while being feigned as the work of some crude and unreliable story-teller, is in reality descended from a tradition fraught with infidelity. Even if Rinaldo, and even Boiardo himself, were telling their version of the truth, who was to vouch for its source?

Ariosto, putting Rinaldo in the position in which we see him in Canto 31 of the *Furioso,* makes no such claim but, on the contrary, proceeds to throw further doubt on the substance of a "bella istoria." Casting the faithless Malagigi as corroborator of a written text, he shows how such a text can nevertheless contain a pack of lies transmitted through unreliable sources; he further shows how, for Gradasso, there are rewards to be gained by virtue of an ignorance of the texts. For Orlando, on the other hand, the reading of texts that include the scrawlings of Angelica and her lover Medoro can lead to the consequences that gave Ariosto's poem its title.[24]

According to Ariosto's narrator, the reader reads at his peril and not

---

[24] See James T. Chiampi, "Between Voice and Writing: Ariosto's Irony According to Saint John," *Italica* 60 (1983): 340–49. Chiampi's reasoning is that Ariosto, through Saint John, expresses the view that poetry in its written form is the symbol of a fallen universe incapable of judging the authenticity of the human voice.

necessarily with the delight promised by Boiardo's narrator to his read-ers.[25] Gradasso's ignorance of written texts is indeed at the base of a cer-tain sort of wisdom; he is free from the conventions that might lead to a neglect of self-interest; in counterpoint is Orlando, whose erudition has led him, in Ariosto's poem, to outright insanity. As in his tradition, Or-lando is trapped in the conflict between communal and individual impera-tives; in Ariosto's poem, he is thwarted by his reading of the textual tradi-tion in which such a conflict had arisen in the first place.

The reader, for Ariosto's narrator, is potentially trapped between con-flicting textual conventions; precisely because the conventions appear on the written page, the reader is liable to the sort of credulity that renders him unable to act in his own self-interest, or even to discriminate between self-interest and established convention.

In reality, as Ariosto, a competent reader of Boiardo, may have been able to infer, Turpin, along with Boiardo's ironic narrator, are just two of many authorities whose versions of history are not any more believable be-cause they are preserved on the written page; nor are the tales told in oral form by a storyteller such as that which Boiardo himself impersonates for much of his poem any less credible, even despite the unverifiability con-ferred by the oral medium. Hence, the reader, regardless of his competence of the legends of Roland and Charlemagne, may be drawn into the skepti-cism such as that which Ariosto envisions for Gradasso. On the other hand, a reader may indeed experience a suspension of disbelief leading to "meraviglia" despite his erudition.

Conclusion: The Competent Reader as Ideal Reader

The Carolingian legend did, over the centuries, assume a didactic purpose; especially in the Italian versions, the hero Orlando became a paragon of Christian heroism, as well as of the sacrifice of self for a greater good. However, for Boiardo, and especially for Ariosto, the new lesson of the

---

[25] Don Quixote de la Mancha, who goes insane from reading chivalric romances, is a case in point. In the same novel the priest and barber of the Don's village, walling in the Don's library decide, at the last moment, to salvage the *Orlando Innamorato*. The bar-ber declares that he is charmed by Boiardo's Italian, but we might also infer Cervantes' tacit absolution of Boiardo from any guilt in having caused the Don's madness. The *Furioso*, on the other hand, is a very likely precedent for the idea of madness incited by excessive reading about chivalry; the Don's inability to distinguish between chivalric con-ventions and reality is quite akin to Orlando's inability to discriminate between conflict-ing textual conventions in Ariosto's tale.

legend may be summed up in two words: caveat lector. Both poets knew that in reality it would be impossible for readers to return to the naiveté of a recipient of the *cantari in ottava rima* in whom a true faith in the heroism of Orlando may be possible, simply by virtue of Orlando's being a Christian.

The transmission of the legend by inherently unreliable oral means, in retrospect, may have been a factor in the vitiation of the message of Carolingian legend. Boiardo proceeds, in his version of the legend, to elaborate on the merits of the written text; like earlier authors of romance, he makes the most of the possibilities of a narrative preserved on paper.[26] Moreover, from the *Innamorato*, the reader is able to infer the advantages of a sustained narrative capable of being followed by a reader, in heightening the drama of which only a written text is capable, of prolonging suspense as in the episodes of Falerina and the Fata Morgana, or of the lengthy and disjointed segment of Ranaldo's story of Book 1.[27]

However, tacitly, and by means of the simulation of spoken recitation, Boiardo's narrator gives at least the impression of an idealized audience sitting before him. Even despite the verifiability conferred by the written medium, Boiardo knows that there is nothing quite so entertaining as the immediacy of the recitation. Speculation varies as to the actual situation of Boiardo's oral delivery of his verses; parts of the poem, such as Astolfo's surprise defeat of Gradasso with Argalia's golden lance, for instance, might have lent themselves to oral narration. Yet, as any reader of Boiardo may realize after reading a few canti, the overall poem requires the concentration of a reader; like later compilations of the *cantari*, which were the form in which Boiardo and his circle read poems like *La Spagna* and the *Rinaldo*, the *Innamorato* largely precludes the immediacy of a listening reception.

Is Boiardo trying to have it both ways? At the beginning of his poem, Boiardo warns his reader against "meraviglia" at hearing the story of Orlando in Love; but also, in some sense, the warning may be understood in

---

[26] Cavallo, in *Boiardo's Orlando Innamorato*, demonstrates that Boiardo, notwithstanding disclaimers by the ironic narrator, was quite interested in conveying in his poem certain allegorical messages contained in the romances, comments on classical literature, philosophical tracts, and other written texts of the Middle Ages. Religious allegory, though having little resonance in the poem's courtly context, lived on in the poem as an underlying driving force of narration, even as it formed the crucial historical backdrop for the adventures of Orlando.

[27] See Marco Praloran, *Maraviglioso Artificio*, for information as to how Boiardo achieves the effect of heightened suspense in the poem's narratology.

terms of a formal consideration. The reader will not be hearing a song; he will be reading a romance. Therefore the reader will be privy to a certain sort of fraud; in part, the narrator of the poem is in bad faith to the extent to which he knowingly draws on an unfaithful tradition. Yet, as a reader may also infer, the narrator initiates a new kind of deceit, quite transparent, in the form of a romance disguised as spoken narration. Ultimately, the discovery by the reader, of Boiardo's fiction of spoken narration, must come through the very act of reading. So, although the pretense of a spoken narration refers, at least in part, to the historical phenomenon of the *cantari in ottava rima*, the glorification of the act of reading is the age-old message of the romance driven home by Boiardo's simulation. The reader is glorified as ideally capable of reading a "bella istoria," hence also to become a part of the "vera istoria" in which the story was told.

MICHAEL SHERBERG

The Promotion of Literacy
in the *Orlando Innamorato*

IN HIS 1965 STUDY, *The Figure of the Poet in Renaissance Epic*, Robert Durling characterizes Boiardo's narrator in a way that today seems fairly self-evident and has become something of a critical commonplace. "In the *Orlando innamorato*," he writes, "Boiardo deliberately attempts—not only in the introductions and endings of his cantos, but throughout—to create the illusion of a series of recitations of the poem."[1] Durling's finding of a consistent narrative stance, that of the *canterino*, weakens against contrary evidence, as Andrea di Tommaso later pointed out. Citing Giulio Reichenbach's study of the poet, published in 1929, di Tommaso argues convincingly that Boiardo's narrator does not recite but reads from a prepared, written text.[2] The posture of a reading narrator compromises the *canterino* pose because it establishes a written text that, as Franz H. Bäuml and Edda Spielmann note, "exists independently of the reader and his memory."[3] The poem thus marks its departure from the oral tradition, which depends instead on a reciter/composer of a fluid text that is subject to as many per-

---

[1] Robert Durling, *The Figure of the Poet in Renaissance Epic* (Cambridge, MA: Harvard Univ. Press, 1965), 92.

[2] Andrea di Tommaso, *Structure and Ideology in Boiardo's* Orlando Innamorato (Chapel Hill: Univ. of North Carolina Press, 1972), 22–30.

[3] Franz H. Bäuml and Edda Spielmann, "From Illiteracy to Literacy: Prologomena to a Study of the *Nibelungenlied*," *Oral Literature: Seven Essays*, ed. Joseph J. Duggan (New York: Barnes & Noble Books, 1975), 66. I am grateful to Leslie Z. Morgan for directing me to this reference, and to Bäuml's work in general.

mutations as there are recitations. This narrator, in other words, belongs to the world of literacy, and so his orality comes from a different place than that of a true *canterino*.

The fact of the narrator's literacy raises another question: whether or not the narratee is, like the narrator, literate. The poem's fictional situation, of a reading at court, does not require a literate audience; rather, its audience is a composite of literates and "quasi-literates," the latter being "*illitterati* who must and do have access to literacy."[4] In its very first line the narrator addresses this audience, though the group's precise configuration varies. At first it appears to be uniquely male, a group more likely to be literate: "You who assemble—lords and knights . . ." (1.1.1).[5] Elsewhere the narratee appears to be singular, though this is likely the work of apocope: "Io vi cantai, segnor. . . ." ("Lords, you have heard my song"; 1.2.1). Elsewhere still the poet modifies his apostrophe to include both women and men: "Come listen—listen graciously— / Ladies, lords, court nobility" (3.1.2).[6] The creation of a plural audience within the text serves Boiardo well, for the group can easily consist of both literate and quasi-literate listeners, ranging from court humanists to other court staffers or citizens who might listen in. Moreover, the projected presence of women in the group would increase the percentage of quasi-literates in the imagined audience.[7] By inscribing listeners within the work, and thus creating a narra-

---

[4] Franz H. Bäuml, "Varieties and Consequences of Medieval Literacy and Illiteracy," *Speculum* 55 (1980): 246.

[5] "Signori e cavallier che ve adunati. . . ." I cite throughout from Matteo Maria Boiardo, *Orlando Innamorato*, trans. Charles Stanley Ross (Berkeley and Los Angeles: Univ. of California Press, 1989). Ross's dual language edition reproduces Aldo Scaglione's edition of the poem, found in *Orlando Innamorato–Amorum Libri*, 2 vols. (Turin: UTET, 1963).

[6] "Venite ad ascoltare in cortesia, / Segnori e dame e bella baronia."

[7] I have no specific data on literacy rates in Ferrara in the late fifteenth century. Data does exist for Florence in 1480, however, where about 28 percent of boys aged 10–13 attended formal schools; see Paul F. Grendler, *Schooling in Renaissance Italy: Literacy and Learning, 1300–1600* (Baltimore: The Johns Hopkins Univ. Press, 1989), 77. It seems likely, especially given the similar cultural developments in the two cities in the late Quattrocento, that literacy rates in both places were fairly comparable. Grendler also records data from Venice in 1587 that shows 26 percent of boys and only 0.2 percent of girls in public schools (46), thus establishing a disparity at least between male and female education, and most likely between literacy rates as well. Grendler himself explains: "Most members of fifteenth-century Renaissance society could not comprehend learned women. Those favorably disposed saw them as prodigies, whereas others viewed them with hostility. . . . Lacking support from the larger world, the majority of . . . Latin learned women discontinued their studies after marrying or entering a female monastery. They

tee whom we may clearly distinguish from his implied reader,[8] Boiardo makes clear that literacy is not a prerequisite for reception of the poem. At the same time, however, the poem itself suggests that literacy carries with it certain advantages that a narratee locked in the world of orality cannot enjoy.

In what follows I would like to demonstrate some of the ways by which Boiardo's narrator promotes literacy. What modern readers have perhaps overlooked in the flood of signs of orality that washes through this poem is the fact that Boiardo fairly consistently couples signs of orality with others that advance literacy. The poem creates this duality in its structure, its specific language, and its themes. And while Boiardo may encourage reading for altruistic motives, it is possible to infer reasons why a broader reading public would redound to his own advantage as well.

Boiardo's readiest encoding of signs of orality and literacy appears in the poem's superstructure, that is, in its division into canti and libri, songs and books. These two terms, the former referring to sound, the latter to a material artifact,[9] segment the poem from its very start, though in general the narrator insists on the division into canti far more than that into libri. References to canti fairly abound, primarily in short-range proleptic or analeptic statements, from one canto to the next.[10] For example, the first

---

had acquired impractical skills for their sex'' (93). Evidence from elsewhere in Europe also confirms much higher literacy among men than women; see Roger Chartier, ''The Practical Impact of Writing,'' in *Passions of the Renaissance*, vol. 3 of *A History of Private Life*, eds. Philippe Ariès and George Duby (Cambridge, MA: The Belknap Press of Harvard Univ. Press, 1989), 111–15.

[8] I am using the terms ''narratee'' and ''implied reader'' as defined by Seymour Chatman in *Story and Discourse: Narrative Structure in Fiction and Film* (Ithaca: Cornell Univ. Press, 1978), 149–50: ''The counterpart of the implied author is the *implied reader*—not the flesh-and-bones you or I sitting in our living rooms reading the book, but the audience presupposed by the narrative itself. Like the implied author, the implied reader is always present. And just as there may or may not be a narrator, there may or may not be a *narratee*. He may materialize as a character in the world of the work. . . . Or there may be no overt reference to him at all, though his presence is felt.'' I find this distinction to be especially useful for the present discussion of Boiardo's narrative strategies, since while the narratee may or may not be literate, the implied reader must be; as real readers, therefore, we may identify far more surely with the implied reader than with the narratee. Our own literacy, and countless other reasons, make it well nigh impossible ever fully to understand the poem's narratee.

[9] From its earliest Latin origins, ''liber'' refers to the material upon which writing takes place: ''liber'' is the bark of a tree and becomes a book by metonymy, since tree bark was used for writing.

[10] I borrow my terminology here from Gérard Genette, for whom prolepsis is ''any

line of Canto 3, Book 1, reads, "Lords, when I left you" ("Segnor, nell'
altro canto io ve lasciai"), a reference to the material of Canto 2. In the
final octave of Canto 3 the narrator refers to "The bloody battle . . . / As
I, next canto [It. 'canto'], will recount"[11]; and he opens Canto 4 by announcing, "The brawl those barons had begun / Was told you earlier in
my song [It. 'cantare']" (1.4.1).[12] This free interchange of "canto" and
"cantare" continues the oral pose as well as suggesting, in an evocation of
the *cantari* tradition, that each canto was destined for reading at a separate
sitting. Invitations such as the one made at the end of Canto 26, "Now,
gentle lords, I'm leaving you, / But if you want to come back, I / Will fin-
ish. Here I leave this duel . . ." (1.26.64),[13] further allude to this situation. A narratee schooled in the oral tradition therefore likely under-
stands these references to the poem's structure, and the preponderance of
Boiardo's references suggests just such an assumption.

Remarks about the poem's division into books, on the other hand,
would not necessarily make sense to a quasi-literate narratee unfamiliar
with the written form of the text. Toward the end of Book 1 the narrator
offers the following prolepsis:

> So instantly King Sacripant
> Was brought to fair Angelica.
> His heart and marrow were on fire
> With great love for that girl, as you
> Will hear in the ensuing book. (1.27.42)[14]

Taken literally, the last line creates something of an adynaton. The contrasting references to the poem as sound, through "odire," (to hear) and
as visual experience, through "libro," cannot here be reconciled except
through metaphor, or better, as catachresis. Indeed, the poem's books are
larger units into which the canti are gathered for the benefit of a reader,

---

narrative maneuver that consists of narrating or evoking in advance an event that will
take place later," and analepsis is "any evocation of the fact of an event that took place
earlier than the point in the story where we are at any given moment." *Narrative Discourse: An Essay in Method*, trans. Jane E. Lewin (Ithaca: Cornell Univ. Press, 1980), 40.

[11] ". . . la crudel baruffa, / Come ne l'altro canto avrò contato. . . ."

[12] "L'altro cantar vi contò la travaglia / Che fu tra' duo baroni incominciata. . . ."

[13] "Or, bei Segnori, io vi lascio al presente, / E se voi tornareti in questo loco, / Dirò
questa battaglia dove io lasso. . . ."

[14] "Così fu dimandato incontinente / Re Sacripante ad Angelica bella. / Questo avea
il core e le medolle ardente / D'amor soperchio per quella donzella, / Come odireti nel
libro sequente."

not a listener. Their existence is wholly irrelevant to a narratee who apprehends the poem sequentially, for whom the work consists of but a series of sounds that die in their moment of enunciation. For the listener the future of this text lies not in reading but in performance, which does not permit study of the poem in its larger units.[15]

When in fact Boiardo's narrator refers to the poem's division into books, he breaches the oral pose, making a reference intended more for implied readers familiar with the poem as visual experience rather than sound. This phenomenon arises in part because Boiardo creates an identity in his poem between the author and narrator, so naturally some slippage occurs between the projected positions of the two. But that registers only when the modern reader imagines the situation of quasi-literate narratees and their limited access to the written text. The difference in the information available to narratees and implied readers, and the fact that in this case at least the reader enjoys greater access than the narratee, may suggest a first skewing in favor of literacy over orality. At the same time, however, the narratee still enjoys advantages that the reader cannot claim,

---

[15] The early division of the *Innamorato*'s first two books into three supports my argument here. Echoing Zottoli, who first made this claim, Giuseppe Anceschi describes the *princeps* as containing sixty canti, with twenty-nine in the first book, twenty-one in the second, and ten in the third (Matteo Maria Boiardo, *Orlando innamorato*, ed. Giuseppe Anceschi, 2 vols. [Milan: Garzanti, 1978], 1: viii). As Anceschi reports, the 1486 edition in fact contains the following rubric at the head of what is today 2.22: "Third book of Orlando inamorato in which are recounted the wondrous adventures and huge battles and the noble death of the paladin Rugiero, and how nobility and courtesy returned to Italy after the construction of Moncelice" ("Libro tercio de Orlando Inamorato ove sono descrite le maravigliose aventure et le grandissime bataglie et mirabil morte del paladino Rugiero e come la nobeltade e la cortesia ritornarno in Italia dopo la edificatione de Monselice"; 2: 922, my trans.). Zottoli's claim, however, again reported by Anceschi (2: 922), that Boiardo must have approved the division since it appeared in an edition published *in vita*, may be questionable, since it relies on certain assumptions about authorial control of printing in the late Quattrocento that are not necessarily valid. In his edition of the poem Aldo Scaglione comes to the same conclusion, all the while making a strong argument against it: "One is right in doubting that it is of Boiardo's hand, because of the inaccuracies contained therein: Rugiero's death and events in Italy after the founding of Monselice—things that are not found at all in the poem; moreover, at 31.48 it is said: 'this book has already taken the breath out of me: you will hear the third some other time': an evident sign that the author made the third book only begin there, and not here. In any event the epigraph must not have been disapproved, given that the edition came out during the author's life" (2: 346, my trans.). For the present purposes, the question of how this rubric came into print is irrelevant; what it establishes is the potential arbitrariness of any division of the poem into books. This becomes especially evident in the second book, where Boiardo's narrator offers a variety of canto proems, each of which could well serve as a proem to the entire book.

and especially that of a "live" performance whose nuances contribute to create meaning, as anyone who has heard Charles Ross read aloud his translation of the poem can attest.[16]

We may infer from the remark about the poem's division into books that the narrator can write; this is one way by which he distances himself from the traditional figure of the *canterino*, heir to and promulgator of an oral tradition, stringer of formulas more than a modern poet. Elsewhere the narrator refers explicitly to his activity, as the poem's author, of writing. The author/narrator's references to writing imply a different sort of compositional process than a *canterino* would undertake:

> Astolfo was freed with the others,
> Everyone had forgotten him,
> Since when he first was sent to prison,
> Rumor spread that he'd been done in.
> He'd always liked to talk a lot
> And made more boasts than I can write. (1.7.38)[17]

Here the poem falls victim—in the Italian—to its own rhyme scheme, and for that we may forgive the poet. Nevertheless, this affirmation of writing removes the narrator from the moment of reading, again remanding him to a prior, off-stage moment of composition. A similar reference to composition comes in Book 2:

> These words were said by Brandimart,
> And others that I don't record.
> He's someone who discourses well
> And always has a quick response. (2.12.29)[18]

As no evidence suggests that the narrator writes down his story as he recites it, the "qui" of "qui non scrivo" ("I don't record [here]") must refer not to the place of enunciation but to a prior place, that of written com-

---

[16] I refer to a "live" performance between quotation marks because in fact no such thing takes place within the fiction of the narrator's reading. Boiardo himself very likely read his poem aloud to court audiences and others, but his narrator, who exists only as a poetic construct, never did.

[17] "Astolfo con quelli altri fo lasciato, / Né se amentava alcun che 'l fosse vivo; / Perché, come fu prima impregionato, / Fu detto a pieno che de vita è privo. / Era lui sempre di parlar usato, / E vantatore assai più che non scrivo."

[18] "Queste parole Brandimarte usava / Et altre molte più che qui non scrivo, / Come colui che molto ben parlava / Et era in ogni cosa troppo attivo."

position. By suggesting a prior moment of composition the narrator furthers the distance between himself and his narratee. Moreover, the activity here mentioned, writing, is one of which many in the listening audience are likely incapable. These allusions all thus partake of a rhetorical strategy aimed at conferring authority upon the narrator, an authority probably achieved in no small part through the association of writing with magic. As Walter Ong has observed, "[w]riting is often regarded at first as an instrument of secret and magic power"[19]; the poem itself confirms this with its many books of magical incantations. At the same time, the narrator further asserts his authority through an ironic attitude toward his characters. By silencing the loquacious Astolfo and Brandimarte, he implies access to more information than he shares, increasing the narratee/reader's dependence on him. The distance separating the author from his material, a gap established fictionally by the references to Turpin's book but which in reality is a natural result of the presence of independent, fixed texts,[20] enables such a stance.

In general Boiardo associates authority with writing. Affirmation of the author/narrator's roots in chirographic culture actually comes very early in the poem, in its third octave, in the initial reference to Turpin, first *auctor* of the *Innamorato* and its primary authority:

> Few people know this story, since
> Its teller—Turpin—kept it hid.
> He may have feared that his account
> Seemed disrespectful to the Count. (1.1.3)[21]

So the narrator not only can write; he can also read, and his power increases thanks to his unique access to Turpin. These lines in fact represent the poem's first assertion of the advantages of literacy: it allows access to texts that can yield new texts. One may wonder whether Boiardo's narra-

---

[19] Walter J. Ong, *Orality and Literacy: The Technologizing of the Word* (New York: Methuen, 1982), 93.

[20] "A further consequence both of the fixity and the independent existence of a fixed text is the fact that it does not necessarily require the commitment of its bearer to its content; the scribe, the reciter, or the reader of a written text can confront that text critically, even ironically. . . . form and content of a written narrative can be manipulated by the writing author or scribe and the reciting reader to a much greater extent than a traditional oral poem by a performing oral poet." Bäuml, "Varieties and Consequences," 249–50.

[21] "Questa novella è nota a poca gente, / Perché Turpino istesso la nascose, / Credendo forse a quel conte valente / Esser le sue scritture dispettose."

tor reads the poem aloud in part in order to grant access to a story that is otherwise available only in writing.

Complementary to the dynamic of orality and literacy in the narrator's own experience is the same duality in the narratee. Just as the narrator can read and write, and reads his poem aloud, so, too, does the narratee hear the poem but would derive significant advantages from being able to read it. Throughout the *Innamorato* references to enunciation and reception predominate in the form of verbs of speech and hearing. Boiardo establishes these patterns in the very first octaves: "Be still, attentive, listen to / The rare events that prompt my song" (1.1.1); "Don't think it strange, my lords, to hear / Orlando *innamorato* sung" (1.1.2); "I mean [It. 'Dico di,' I speak of] Orlando, baron bold" (1.1.3)[22]; and so forth. The narrator's insistence on verbs of orality, and on the moment of enunciation, furthers the fiction of the oral setting and implies an assumption that the audience is rooted uniquely in oral culture. But while literacy may be a secondary skill, given the oral setting of the narration, it nonetheless does emerge as useful. For example, at the end of Canto 12, Book 1, the narrator ironically observes: "This canto has been very long, / But those who loathe its length may skip / A portion. Just read half of it" (1.12.90).[23] Once again the fiction of the oral setting yields to a reference to another place of reception, and to another form, written, of the text. The narratees' exposure to this admonition again suggests an alternate route of access to the text, one they may wish to explore. Reading here offers a clear benefit: readers may skip over material they find tedious, thus escaping the tyranny of the narrator. The instruction to read only half of the canto is of course easier said than done, however, since it comes at its end, after any reader has probably read all eighty-nine of the preceding octaves. But the very incongruity of the suggestion underscores the advantage to be accrued, since it compels narratees and readers alike to stop to consider the advice.

This assertion of the benefits of literacy finds confirmation elsewhere in the poem in broader thematic terms. The most striking, though by no means unique, proof comes in Canto 18 of the first book, in a brief dialogue between Orlando and Agricane. Having suspended their duel, the

---

[22] "State attenti e quïeti, et ascoltati / La bella istoria che 'l mio canto muove"; "Non vi par già, signor, meraviglioso / Odir cantar de Orlando inamorato"; "Dico di Orlando, il cavalliero adatto."

[23] "Or questo canto è stato lungo molto; / Ma a cui dispiace la sua quantitate, / Lasci una parte, e legga la mitate."

two are stargazing, and Orlando reflects aloud on the beauty of God's plan. Agricane responds by recalling—and defending—his resistance to knowledge:

> I have no skill in any science.
> I didn't want to learn when young:
> I broke my teacher's head as payment;
> They couldn't find another one
> To show me books or how to write.
> They all were too afraid of me.
>   And so I spent my early years
> In riding, games of arms, and hunts.
> I don't think that a nobleman
> Should spend the whole day reading books.
> He should develop physical
> Force and the speed a knight requires.
> Learning is fine for priests and scribes:
> I know what I have need to know. (1.18.42–43)[24]

Agricane implies two routes of learning: oral transmission through teachers and written conveyance through books. He offers a typical defense of youth, that it is a time for carefree activity such as hunting and other games. In this, he recalls the young Iulio of Poliziano's *Stanze*, who similarly praised a lighthearted youth dedicated to the hunt,[25] and he enters

---

[24] "—Io de nulla scïenzia sono esperto, / Né mai, sendo fanciul, volsi imparare, / E roppi il capo al mastro mio per merto; / Poi non si puotè un altro ritrovare / Che mi mostrasse libro né scrittura, / Tanto ciascun avea di me paura. / E così spesi la mia fanciulezza / In caccie, in giochi de arme e in cavalcare; / Né mi par che convenga a gentilezza / Star tutto il giorno ne' libri a pensare; / Ma la forza del corpo e la destrezza / Conviense al cavalliero esercitare. / Dottrina al prete et al dottor sta bene: / Io tanto saccio quanto mi conviene.—"

[25] "How much sweeter, how much surer it is / to follow the fleeing beasts in the hunt / through ancient woods beyond trenches or walls / and to espy their lair along a long trail" ("Quanto è più dolce, quanto è più securo / seguir le fere fugitive in caccia / fra boschi antichi fuor di fossa o muro, / e spiar lor covil per lunga traccia!" Agnolo Poliziano, *Stanze per la giostra di M. Giuliano de' Medici*, in Carlo Oliva, ed., *Poesia italiana. Il Quattrocento* [Milan: Garzanti, 1978], I.17, my trans.). While in Iulio's case the devotion to Diana comes at the explicit expense of fealty to Venus, the comparison to Agricane remains valid. Both figures refuse passage to an activity (learning, love) that late-Quattrocento humanist culture has privileged. Their resistance and subsequent punishment do not imply condemnation of the active life, however; rather, both poets appear to suggest that the active life will no longer suffice, that some sort of contemplation, of books or female beauty, must complement it. Castiglione will codify this position in Book 1 of *The*

into an argument about the priorities of arms versus letters that will find resonance in the sixteenth century.[26]

In response, Orlando deploys a far more complex argument to dissuade him from his position.

> Orlando answered, "I agree
> A man's first honors are in arms,
> But learning does not lessen men—
> It adds, like flowers in a field.
> Not to acknowledge our Creator
> Makes you an ox, a stone, a log.
> Unschooled, you cannot well conceive
> The heights of holy majesty." (1.18.44)[27]

The fact that we contemplate God distinguishes us from the rest of the animal, vegetable, and mineral worlds; but full knowledge of God cannot happen without learning, presumably in the two forms that Agricane has mentioned. That the poem supports Orlando's position seems clear for several reasons. First, it is the pagan, and therefore the enemy, who defends ignorance, and the Christian who successfully integrates Agricane's defense of arms and supplements it with an urge to learning. Moreover, as the battle continues the next day, the narrator ridicules Agricane by comparing him not to a hunter but to the hunted: "As in the woods the lion

----

Book of the Courtier. After first arguing that "the first and true profession of the courtier must be that of arms," including the hunt, Ludovico da Canossa goes on to state that "the true and principal adornment of the mind is letters. . . . nothing is more naturally desired by men or more proper to them than knowledge, and it is the height of folly to say or believe that it is not always a good thing." Baldesar Castiglione, *The Book of the Courtier*, trans. George Bull (New York: Penguin Books, 1984), 57, 88–89.

[26] For the Italians, at least, the matter seems to have been settled by the early Cinquecento. In the *Courtier*, for example, no one disagrees with Ludovico da Canossa's assertion of the importance of letters; indeed, Giuliano de' Medici seconds the argument by discussing how the humanist bent of "Monsigneur d'Angoulême," the future Francis I, bodes well for the French monarchy after years of erroneous dedication uniquely to arms: "I believe that just as the glory of arms flourishes and shines in France, so also with the greatest brilliance must that of letters" (Castiglione, *The Book of the Courtier*, 84). Boiardo's Orlando would appear to have served as a good (French) model for the French prince.

[27] "Rispose Orlando: —Io tiro teco a un segno, / Che l'arme son de l'omo il primo onore; / Ma non già che il saper faccia men degno, / Anci lo adorna come un prato il fiore; / Et è simile a un bove, a un sasso, a un legno, / Chi non pensa allo eterno Creatore; / Né ben se può pensar senza dottrina / La summa maiestate alta e divina.—"

roars / After the hunter injures it, / Fierce Agrican with greater force, / Furious, swings his sword once more" (1.19.6).[28] Finally, after Orlando defeats him, the dying Agricane requests baptism, professing his faith in Orlando's religion ("I / Believe in your God"; 1.19.12) and contemplating the very sky that had been the topic of their earlier discussion: "That knight, who was so fierce, now cried / And kept his eyes toward heaven" (1.19.14).[29] Had he lived, he probably would have received the same religious education Orlando later offers to Brandimarte.[30]

As the poem elsewhere makes clear, books often offer the key to knowledge, and failure to read them can lead to disaster. Two types of books populate the *Innamorato*: handbooks with didactic value for problem-solving, and narrative books. Examples of the former include Malagise's little volume of magical incantations, or the book given to Orlando by a palmer, similarly full of instruction: "So please accept from me this book! / Its power is miraculous, / Since every question, every doubt, / Is mentioned and explained in here" (1.5.67).[31] Like most books in the poem, this one has evident material value, a reflection no doubt of its content: the narrator describes it as "bright with enamel, gilt with gold" (1.5.66). Physical characteristics underscore the value of other books as well, such as the important manuscript described in Canto 13 of Book 1. The book hangs from a golden chain attached to an extraordinarily beautiful horse, a horse as beautiful as Baiardo himself. Next to the horse lies a dead girl, and a sign written upon her body promises the horse to the knight who avenges her murder. The narrative is written in blood and, as Boiardo's narrator explains, "That book declared to one who read / The history and mystery / Of that dead damsel on the door, / The means and agent of her murder"

---

[28] "Come rugge il leon per la foresta, / Allor che l'ha ferito il cacciatore, / Così il fiero Agrican con più tempesta / Rimena un colpo di troppo furore."

[29] "Piangea quel re, che fo cotanto fiero, / E tenìa il viso al cel sempre voltato."

[30] Indeed, Boiardo's charge that the Saracen study of arms does not suffice goes to Brandimarte as well: "Brandimart was a Saracen, / But poorly taught and ignorant, / As he was used, since he was small, / To riding and to bearing arms" ("Era quel Brandimarte saracino, / Ma de ogni legge male instrutto e grosso, / Però che fu adusato piccolino / A cavalcare e portar l'arme in dosso"; 2.12.12). In converting his friend, Orlando offers a thorough education: ". . . he recites / To him, first, the Old Testament, / Then tells him how God wished it changed. / He then recites all of the New" ("Prima narrògli il vecchio Testamento, / E poi perché Dio vòl che quel se muta; / Gli narrò tutto il novo a compimento"; 2.12.13).

[31] "Questo libretto vogliolo accettare, / Che è di virtù mirabile e soprana, / Perché ogni dubbioso ragionare / Su queste carte si dichiara e spiana."

(1.13.29).[32] It relates, in other words, how Albarosa, the girl whose corpse Ranaldo has found, had suffered torture at the hand of Trufaldino. Moreover, it tells the story in greater detail than Boiardo's narrator does:

> The book recounted all these things
> More graphically, with other words,
> And there were tragic deeds, and there
> Were also gentle conversations
> Such as two souls in love exchange. (1.13.45)[33]

The fact that Boiardo's narrator synopsizes the tale again suggests his authority over the narratee and reader in limiting their access to information.

The episode further dramatizes the distance that writing creates between the event and its record, while demonstrating the importance of literacy as a means of activating voices after death. Ranaldo confronts a curious situation: Albarosa, while dead, wears a sign written in the first person, inviting and inciting vengeance for her murder: "Who passes here will not live long / Unless he swears to right my wrong! / But if he swears to take revenge, / For I was mightily betrayed, / He'll have that able steed to ride— / Its speed is faster than the wind!" (1.13.25-26).[34] While she is already dead, she—or the person who writes for her—still attempts to control her destiny through carefully deployed rhetorical strategies. The sign both makes a threat and offers a reward, and with what information it does provide it appeals to the knight's sense of justice. Only in a second moment does the curious knight, who has accepted the challenge, learn the details of Albarosa's fate. In remanding the communication of the details to a second moment Albarosa, or her agent, appears to believe that threats and rewards, in their urgency, make better motivators than a prolix tale. Still, her story itself does not deter Ranaldo; indeed, it serves to reinforce his resolve. But the sign and the book both require that Albarosa's avenger be literate or have access to literacy. Unlike many of the *Innamorato*'s intradiegetic narrators who offer an oral account of their past, Albarosa is dead, and literacy therefore offers the only means to keep her story

---

[32] "Quel libro, a chi lo legge, dichiarava / Tutta la istoria e la novella oscura / Di quella dama occisa su la porta, / Ed in che forma, e chi l'avesse morta."

[33] "Narrava il libro tutte queste cose, / Ma più destinto, e con altre parole; / Ché vi erano atti con voci pietose, / E quel dolce parlar che usar se suole / Tra l'anime congionte ed amorose."

[34] "Chi passa quivi, arà di morte stretta, / Se non giura di far la mia vendetta; / Ma se giura lo oltraggio vendicare, / Che mi fu fatto con gran tradimento, / Avrà quel bon destriero a cavalcare, / Che di veloce corso passa il vento."

alive. By marking the ability of the book to transcend the moment of enunciation, Boiardo thus identifies it as an especially potent antidote to fortune, which can take narrators away from us before they can tell their tale.

Reference books likewise can help control fortune, as Orlando discovers in Falerina's Garden.[35] Endowed with a book that exposes the garden's secrets and that will assist him in disenchanting it, Orlando fails to read it at first and is lost: "The Count does not know what to do. / His spirit sags. He is confused" (2.4.19).[36] Later, he remembers having the book: "For now I have remembered this: / Next to my chest there is a text / That clarifies this whole affair" (2.4.31)[37]; he then proceeds to destroy the garden. To these two moments correspond attempts by Orlando to defeat figures of fortune. He first encounters a lady holding a sword, whom he grabs by the forelocks, insisting that she explain how he can get out of the garden. Boiardo's narrator recounts that,

> She shakes all over, frightened, she
> Does not relent because of fear:
> She does not speak. She won't respond.
> The threats of Count Orlando are
> Useless—she will not talk, won't answer.
> No fear of him provokes from her
> The smallest sign that she's concerned. (2.4.28–29)[38]

Shortly thereafter the knight meets a siren, similarly resistant, only this time he defeats her, thanks to the book:

> As loud as possible, she crooned—
> Since she knew nothing else to do—
> But the Count did not hear her tune:
> Too many roses blocked his ears.

---

[35] For a thorough allegorical reading of this episode, but one that does not account for the relationship between books and fortune, see Michael Murrin, *The Allegorical Epic: Essays in Its Rise and Decline* (Chicago: Univ. of Chicago Press, 1980), 53–85.

[36] "Or non sa il conte ciò che debba fare, / E nella mente alquanto se sconforta."

[37] "[—]Or mo di novo mi è tornato a mente / Che in un libretto l'aggio scritto al petto, / Qual mi mostrarà il fatto tutto a pieno.—"

[38] "Lei, ben che tremi tutta di spavento, / Per quella tema già non se confonde, / Anci sta queta e nulla vi risponde; / Né per minaccie che gli avesse a fare / Il conte Orlando, né per la paura / Mai gli rispose, né volse parlare, / Né pur di lui mostrava tenir cura."

> Orlando held her by her hair.
> He dragged her from that lake to shore,
> And cut her head off with the sword—
> So had the book told him to do—. (2.4.38–39)[39]

Orlando's experience in Falerina's Garden proves his point to Agricane: force is not always enough; the successful knight must sometimes rely on learning as well.

Orlando's experience with a book in Falerina's Garden also recalls Ranaldo's encounter with Albarosa's corpse. In that case, the distance between event and text that literacy creates has the effect of keeping stories alive; here, as we witness Orlando's passage from an initial failure to later success, thanks to reading, we see another advantage to literacy. Through these two episodes Boiardo appears to enact the evolution of his own culture as it grows more dependent upon literature. The results he describes signal a clear endorsement of the humanist program, which depends finally upon access to books. From this it becomes ever clearer why Boiardo installs a reading narrator. The figure of the *canterino* has become an anachronism; the text must respond to the new modes of promulgation and reception of texts that coexist with, and have sometimes supplanted, the oral tradition.

To the above-mentioned advantages of literacy that Boiardo suggests, I would add one more: literacy would allow future readers to imitate Boiardo's narrator and read the poem aloud before a group.[40] Such an option presented itself thanks not only to the spread of literacy but also to the evolution from manuscripts to printed books. Indeed, the presence of both early printed editions alongside manuscripts of the *Innamorato* offers an eloquent reminder that Boiardo's age was one of transition in book culture. Moreover, the advent of printing, which took place in Emilia in the very years that Boiardo was writing,[41] may have accelerated the urge to

---

[39] "Lei, quanto più puotea, cantava forte, / Ché non sapeva fare altre diffese, / Ma la sua voce al conte non attiene, / Che ambe l'orecchie avea di rose piene. / Per le chiome la prese il conte Orlando, / Fuor di quel lago la trasse nel prato, / E via la testa gli tagliò col brando, / Come gli aveva il libro dimostrato."

[40] By the late Quattrocento silent reading had established itself, though voiced reading still took place, not just in the formal settings that the poem imagines but among less advanced readers. On the privatization of reading and the development of silent reading, see Chartier, "The Practical Impact of Writing," 124–27.

[41] See Giorgio Montecchi, "La stampa a Scandiano alla fine del Quattrocento," *Tipografie e romanzi in Val Padana fra Quattro e Cinquecento*, ed. Riccardo Bruscagli and Amedeo Quondam (Modena: Franco Cosimo Panini Editore, 1992), 9–28.

literacy, since the proliferation of books would advertise the benefits of reading. The poem's editorial history in fact makes clear that for as much as Boiardo's narrator assumes a reading pose in the poem, the poet himself did at some point envision and realize a plan to make the work available for reading, thus offering a mode and setting for reception that could reproduce or differ from the one enacted in the text itself. His motives for doing so, and for urging his audience to know how to read, may finally relate to the fundamental paradox of his narrator understood as a projection of Boiardo himself. For as much as the narrator may allude to the oral tradition, he is no more a *canterino* than is the poet, nor is this text one of many anonymous Carolingian poems that found typefonts in the late Quattrocento and throughout the Cinquecento.[42] Indeed, this book has an author, one who doubtless yearns to reach readers over time and to preserve the integrity of his text and its authorship. Printing offered this possibility, though Boiardo may never have imagined that printing could be as unstable as the oral tradition he both embraced and eschewed. We know this to be true today, thanks to Francesco Berni and Ludovico Domenichi as well as to recent philological studies of the poem itself.[43] Boiardo surely thought that literacy would give his work some permanence in the form of an audience who could receive it fixed in writing. But—and this is perhaps the final irony in Boiardo's promotion of literacy—as too many chapters in the history of the poem testify, printing finally offered no promise of authorial control, and literacy only enables people to read whatever editions, accurate, rewritten, Tuscanized—that the market, or the library, offers.

---

[42] Marco Praloran reaches the same conclusion on the basis of his (brilliant) narratological analysis of the poem: "Evidently the modes of representation are similar to those of the *cantari* (in this sense there comes into play above all the 'position' of the narrator with respect to the events narrated, the element of 'live recording,' which ties Boiardo's work very clearly with the *canterini*), while also carried out in a much more refined way; but the structure of the plot no longer foresees those pauses, those ellipses (voyages, displacement, rest) that are characteristic of the *canterino* tale which, all told, is traditional and shaped by the narrative schemes (in truth often reduced and banalized) of the late French *chansons.*" "*Maraviglioso artificio*": *Techniche narrative e rappresentative nell'Orlando Innamorato* (Lucca: Maria Pacini Fazzi editore, 1990), 71, my trans.

[43] On Berni, Domenichi, and other interventions on Boiardo's text, see Elissa Weaver, " 'Riformare' l'*Orlando Innamorato*," *I libri di Orlando innamorato* (Modena: Edizioni Panini, 1987), 117–44. On the challenges of preparing a new critical edition of the poem, see Antonia Tissoni Benvenuti, "Il terzo libro, ovvero 'El fin del Inamoramento d'Orlando'," *Tipografie e romanzi*, 29–44, and Cristina Montagnani, "Verso l'edizione dell'*Orlando innamorato*: i testimoni più antichi dei primi due libri," *Tipografie e romanzi*, 45–54.

KATHLEEN CROZIER EGAN

On the Indignity of Man:
The Quarrel between Boiardo
and Pico della Mirandola[1]

IT WAS IN 1486, WHEN MATTEO MARIO BOIARDO was forty-five years old
and probably beginning work on Book 3 of the *Orlando Innamorato*, that
his younger cousin Pico della Mirandola took his *Conclusiones* to Rome
and proposed a public disputation of its theses.[2]

The debate never took place: a commission appointed by Pope Innocent VIII declared seven of the nine hundred theses definitely heretical,
and found six more of them suspect. Most of the theses in question dealt
with Egyptian Cabalist magic and the possible elevation of man to divine

---

[1] A longer version of this essay is the first chapter of my doctoral dissertation, "On
the Indignity of Man: An Essay on Boiardo's *Orlando Innamorato*," Yale University,
1996. I would like to thank Charles Ross and Jo Ann Cavallo for their extremely helpful
editorial suggestions.

[2] According to Panizzi, Boiardo began writing the poem around 1472; see *Orlando
Innamorato di Bojardo; Orlando Furioso di Ariosto; with an Essay on the Romantic Narrative
Poetry of the Italians*, ed. by Antonio Panizzi. 9 vols (London: Pickering, 1830), lviii.
Charles Ross states that Boiardo had already completed much of the first two books by
1480, when Ercole d'Este appointed Boiardo governor of Modena. Boiardo prepared the
first two books for the press in 1482 or 1483 during the height of the Venetian conflict,
which occasioned his outcry at the end of Book 2. His governorship kept the poet quite
busy during the final decade of his life; but we know that he was working sporadically on
Book 3 during this period, and, according to the correspondence of Isabella d'Este,
reading the completed cantos to her and her mother for their amusement. On this see
the introduction to Ross's translation of the *Orlando Innamorato* (Berkeley and Los
Angeles: Univ. of California Press, 1989), 15–18.

status, a subject Pico dwelt upon further in the famous *Oration On the Dignity of Man*, which was to serve as an introduction to the proposed debate. Pico, possessed of the enthusiasm and energy of youth—he was only twenty-four when he made his proposal—wrote a spirited *Apologia* in defence of his orthodoxy, and published it together with part of the *Oration*. The publication of this material only made matters worse, though; and Pico fled to France, only to be pursued, arrested, and imprisoned there for a time before being allowed to return to Italy with French royal letters in his favor.[3] Lorenzo de'Medici consistently and strongly supported Pico's cause, and appealed repeatedly to the pope for Pico's pardon, without success; this pope's reluctance to completely exonerate Pico rang with more than a little injustice, for it was widely known that Innocent VIII had broken a number of his holy vows, including having fathered at least eight illegitimate children.

But in 1492 Pope Innocent VIII was succeeded by Alexander VI, and with this change came a complete reversal of Pico's fortunes. Alexander was quite enthusiastic about Cabalist magic, and thus in less than a year, and only a year before Pico's death, the young philosopher was granted a full pardon. At the same time Pico also received a personal letter from the new pope in which he praised Pico's works, including the disputed nine hundred theses; this letter was printed in all the editions of Pico's works so as to assure any prospective reader that the ideas contained within were fully sanctioned by highest authority.[4] The new pope then had the Room of the Saints in the Vatican painted with a series of Egyptian scenes alluding to the mythology behind the Hermetic works, thought to be written by the prophet Hermes Trismegistus in ancient times, upon whose authority Pico had based most of the magical sections of his theses.

The relationship of a work of art to its native and contemporary culture is of course one of the great issues, if not *the* great one, in art criticism; I have recounted Pico's theological adventure as a way of beginning to suggest in this essay that the several types of relationship between the lives and work of Boiardo and Pico form a small but extremely interesting case study in that subject of both aesthetic and cultural criticism. I believe that the part of Boiardo's poem that he was working on at the time of Pico's dramatic crisis, most notably the tale of Orrilo in Book 3, seems to

---

[3] See Frances A. Yates, *Giordano Bruno and the Hermetic Tradition* (Chicago: Univ. of Chicago Press, 1964), 112.

[4] Yates, *Giordano Bruno*, 114.

take up, to a significant extent, many cultural and religious issues raised by the new humanism; and it does so in a way, as I hope to show, that arguably constitutes a pointed response to the case of Pico and the implications of his thought. Reading the cousins Pico and Boiardo together is, in my opinion, to overhear the most intimate of intellectual arguments, intimate in the way only family quarrels can be: in its immediate response and familiar mockery; in its underlying deep passion, concern for tact, and complicated indirection; and, very importantly, in its ultimate concern for dialogue and corresponding avoidance of any final rupture. The importance of that last concern contrasts tragically to another type of Renaissance family quarrel, which was to place its mark on Boiardo and his son: the quarrel over rights to an inheritance, resolved unjustly by poisoning. It is no exaggeration, I think, to find in these two opposing modes of "argument" a basic paradigm for the opposing heaven and hell of earthly disputes.

Even if Pico and Boiardo were not actually related, we would hardly be surprised to find that Boiardo's poem treated the great spiritual, intellectual, and political issues of the day in ways that resonated with Pico's writing: Pico and Boiardo were near-contemporaries, both aristocrats, both intellectuals, educated in the same tradition, who could hardly do otherwise than address many of the same concerns in their respective, voluminous writings. And, although without documentary evidence of Boiardo's intentions here I can only make a literary case for a Boiardo-Pico debate, I believe the literary evidence points strongly to a Boiardian contest with, if not Pico himself, then a philosophical adversary for all practical purposes indistinguishable from him. Therefore, in order to examine how what I am calling the quarrel between Pico and Boiardo both broadly and specifically disputes man's proper place in the universe and the civic polity, I will begin, first, with a necessarily abbreviated look at Pico's new philosophy, which builds on a line of proto-humanist predecessors extending back to Petrarch, and some of the implications of this new philosophy for the established order of church, state, and individual. I will then outline some of the many connections between Pico's vision of the newly independent individual and the contemporary intellectual enthusiasm for the newly translated corpus of Hermetic writings—which had, like Orrilo in the poem, an Egyptian home and some very prominent crocodiles. Lastly, I will undertake a more extended examination of the especially significant Orrilo episode from Boiardo's poem, where I find that the poet responds with a characteristically imaginative combination of direction and indirection to Pico's views and their dangerous implications. I will suggest that this episode provides for us one important key to this intensely intellectual poem's relation to the culture, history, and intellectual ferment of its surrounding reality.

The first question we must ask for our analysis of the Pico-Boiardo "quarrel" is an obvious one: what was it about Pico's *Conclusiones*, his *Apologia*, and his *Oration* that elicited such antagonism or, conversely, such enthusiasm, in his readers? Generally speaking, the theses that suggested uses of Cabalist magic for religious purposes offended the Church most, especially the one that asserted that Cabalist magic is the best—Pico goes so far as to say the *only*—confirmation of Christ's divinity;[5] Pico spends much of the *Apologia* explaining this thesis. But such theological technicalities are not the most prominent parts of the *Oration*. This work was and still is renowned primarily for the *related* doctrine of the "divinity" of man, for its notion of man as the only earthly being who has no particular assignment in the hierarchy of created things and who therefore can rise at will to the heights of divinity, or sink at will to the depths of animal nature, or even plant nature. Man is unique in this freedom to choose his own nature; and in the *Oration* Pico boldly assigns to God the role of the herald explaining man's nature to Adam:

> We have given to thee, Adam, no fixed seat, no form of thy very own, no gift peculiarly thine, that thou mayest feel as thine own, have as thine own, possess as thine own the seat, the form, the gifts which thou thyself shalt desire. A limited nature in other creatures is confined within the laws written down by Us. In conformity with thy free judgment, in whose hands I have placed thee, thou art confined by no bounds; and thou wilt fix limits of nature for thyself.[6]

Man's free will, then, and not his designation by God for glory, is what sets him apart from the beasts. Man is a "chameleon," and as such can change "color" any time he pleases. Thus, the medieval notion of the cosmos, an orderly hierarchy with each created being in its rightful place, cannot accommodate man, who individually and by his own actions will

---

[5] This is the seventh of the magical conclusions: "Nulla est scientia, que nos magis certificet de diuinitate Christi, quam Magia & Cabala."

[6] Translation by Charles Glen Wallace in *On the Dignity of Man, On Being and the One, Heptaplus* (Indianapolis: Bobbs-Merril Educational Publishing, 1981). For the Latin original, see *De hominis dignitate; Heptaplus; De ente et uno; e scritti vari*, ed. by Eugenio Garin (Florence: Vallecchi Editore, 1942), G.I.104.

determine where he belongs in this order. For Pico, then, man does not behave, or act, in accordance with any predesignated nature; rather, he himself creates and reveals this nature by acting: man's being follows from his doing, and not vice-versa. So the scholastic proposition "operari sequitur esse" is reversed for man; the adage applies to the material world of things, to which man, ideally, is superior.[7] "Fortuna" is thus dealt a crushing blow; man cannot ascribe his failings to mere chance or to being born under an unlucky star, but instead must take responsibility for his own fortunes and misfortunes.[8]

Such a philosophy requires man to be particularly watchful of himself, since he can count on no astral influence to guide him through his life, excuse his wrongdoings, or explain away his ill-fortune. This is a man who must create himself, continually, out of "the center of his unity." No individual can rest assured of his lofty position in the cosmic order; and since every action he takes redefines his being, he must prove himself worthy of his place over and over again throughout his life. Only his death can grant him peace and confirmation of his true nature.

Because of the volatility of the self, one is bound to a course of self-examination during one's sojourn in the material world. This philosophy demands a constant striving towards self-knowledge, for it is through an understanding of the self that one recognizes in the self that divine spark which is unique to man. Pico's somewhat overwrought confidence[9] in the

---

[7] On this subject see Ernst Cassirer, *The Individual and the Cosmos in Renaissance Philosophy*, trans. with an introduction by Mario Domandi (Philadelphia: Univ. of Pennsylvania Press, 1979). See especially chapter 3, "Freedom and Necessity in the Philosophy of the Renaissance," specifically pages 84–85. The volume of essays, *The Renaissance Image of Man and the World*, ed. by B. O'Kelly (Kent, Ohio, 1966) is also helpful.

[8] This last notion is the main thrust of Pico's *Disputationes adversus astrologiam divinatricem*, in which he attacks the notion that the disposition of the stars has any influence on man's activities. Ficino had accepted the idea that the bond that connected the heavens and the earth was a kind of "effluvia," which would directly affect any earthly thing sympathetic to a given star. Pico rejects this idea categorically, first by attacking the method through which previous philosophers had arrived at such conclusions, and then by attacking the conclusions themselves. To be able to accept any true causal connection between the stars and one's earthly fortunes, argues Pico, one must be able to empirically demonstrate and record, step-by-step, the direct influence of some originating cause, and the changes that it effects, right down to the event or state of being of the entity in question on earth. We thus cannot, with any authority or validity, predict the future by looking at the stars unless we have this empirical demonstration, for "Non potest coelum ejus rei signum esse, cujus causa non sit," Pico della Mirandola, *In astrologiam libri* XII.iv.12. fol. 543.

[9] In the later parts of the *Oration*, Pico, who is being hounded by religious

individual's ability to transcend his animal nature by sheer virtue of his unique free will places him at the summit of a long ascent undertaken by the earlier forerunners of the emerging cult of the individual, among whom we can place such thinkers as Petrarch, Manetti, Valla, Ficino, and Alberti.

Each of these artists and thinkers engages the issue of the self and its free will. Although their views and their expressive means diverge widely, they nevertheless form a recognizable line in the development of the Renaissance notion of the Individual and his powers.[10] That notion deserves its revolutionary reputation: in it, Man is no longer a pawn destined to carry out some predetermined plan merely to recite a role already chosen by God; rather, he is a creative being, free to ennoble or degrade his God-given body and spirit on his own. This Man-as-Magus, as Yates calls him, is far less dependent upon placing himself into the constructs of tra-

---

authorities, debates in a mode that sounds distinctly more harried and defensive as he tries to build a wall of classical and biblical authority between himself and the censors.

[10] A very brief survey of this line would note the following: in the fourteenth century Petrarch raised individual self-consciousness and self-obsession to new poetic and ultimately cultural heights, in effect inventing the self as a new poetic subject by cunningly sexualizing (and thus secularizing) the philosophical purity of the Dolce Stil Nuovo; clearly, however, his notion of the will is still heavily Augustinian. Petrarch's innovations were followed (and in some senses, furthered) fifty years later, by Lorenzo Valla's pioneering attempt to define the individual in exclusively *internal* terms. Valla's *De professione religiosorum* addresses the relationship between the individual and God, and focuses on man as a free agent in expressing his faith: piety and religious devotion are located entirely *within* the individual; faith expressed through some *external* conduct is categorically rejected. Like Pico, Valla was considered heretical and had to recant portions of his work. Pico was also influenced by Manetti, whose 1452 *De dignitate et excellentia hominis* has a formal and stylistic schema that Pico followed. Manetti emphasizes the superiority of man over all beasts, but does not go so far as Pico would to maintain that man can, by dint of his own will, actually *become* a divine being; nor does he reject, as Pico does, the idea that man occupies a designated position—a central or superior one—in the existing order of things. Manetti is more concerned with promoting an active civic-humanistic life; in this he resembles Alberti, who, although a typical humanist in his notion of man's ability to control his own fate by exercising his inherent *virtù*, is mainly concerned instead with earthly prosperity and day-to-day efficiency in workday matters. But it is probably Ficino to whom Pico owes the greatest debt for his optimism about man: Yates credits Ficino with the creation of the image of Man as Magus, or magic-wielding Operator on the universe, which Pico took up with such enthusiasm. It was Ficino who translated the Egyptian texts that gave rise to the Hermetic revival initiated by the Neoplatonic Academy in Florence, of which both Ficino and Pico were members; Ficino's humanism comprehends both Alberti's practical good sense and Pico's more mystical ambitions for man. Writing when Boiardo was working on the *Orlando Innamorato*, Ficino claims that man's achievements have brought him into another Golden Age.

ditional religious, social, and political institutions in order to arrive at self-definition than were his medieval predecessors; the very order to which he belongs is, to a certain extent, self-created. It should therefore come as no surprise that the depiction of "Fortuna" in art and literature at this point undergoes a radical transformation: the Middle Ages depicted Fortune most often with a wheel, picking men up and casting them upward or downward entirely at random. This image gives way, in the Renaissance, to one of Fortune as a sailboat, subjected to favorable or unfavorable winds, but with man at the wheel, choosing, wisely or unwisely, how to respond to these random forces, thus attaining some control over his "voyage," or life. And from Pico's point of view, it seems, a superior individual might even transcend the boat itself, and be borne aloft on the wind over which he, as a Renaissance "Magus," has somehow managed to gain control.

At the core of any mysticism is the avoidance—called transcendence—of practical detail, which is replaced by a subjunctive assertion of authority and demand for trust: there is no mysticism without the presence of and belief in a divine authority. But an important inspirational and positive authority for Pico in the *Oration* is Hermes Trismegistus; and Hermes' authority, as it happened, came from a historical error—and was all the more powerful because of that mistake. Pico begins the long march of his ancient authorities with the Apostle Paul and the Patriarch Jacob, but the third great authority he cites is the Egyptian Osiris, who when torn to pieces "gathered the many into one," and so provides a model for Man's ascent to the Bosom of the Godhead.[11]

The Hermetic revival occasioned by Ficino's 1463 translation of the *Corpus Hermeticum* (printed in 1471) had already spurred an interest in all things Egyptian during Boiardo's lifetime, especially among learned humanists and aristocrats, and even before Pico's hyperbolic praise and elevation of Hermeticism to the status of sole guarantor of divine revelation. Hermes Trismegistus, for us only a mythical name connected with certain gnostic revelations and magical treatises, was for the Renaissance a real, historical Egyptian priest who had himself written the texts with which his name is most commonly associated;[12] these texts discuss, in the form of

---

[11] *Oration*, 10.

[12] Notably the *Asclepius*, thought to have been translated into Latin by Apuleius of Madaura, and the *Corpus Hermeticum*, translated by Ficino as *Pimander*, after the first of its fifteen treatises. The *Asclepius* especially describes the religion of the Egyptians.

dialogues, such topics as the Creation, astrology and magic, the doctrine of regeneration, God, man, and nature. Though in fact they were written by various authors in the third century A.D., Renaissance intellectuals accepted the notion, supported by both Lactantius and Augustine, that they were much earlier than Plato.[13] Believing they had found the fount of Greek wisdom, Renaissance men hailed Hermes as a prophet and a sage, and the Egyptian "author" became exceedingly popular.[14] Critical history, with its assessment of sources, was just about to be born; but not quite yet, which made it easy for Renaissance man to read effects as causes.[15] In a similarly inverted way, the new individual was the result, and in many ways the victim, of new and ill-understood forces, mainly economic; but for Pico, that victim looked instead like the master of Creation.

Hermes rapidly became a well-known figure and was often represented in Renaissance art and iconography. The first thing one sees upon entering the Cathedral at Siena, in fact, is the portrait of Hermes Trismegistus on the mosaic pavement that was laid down in the 1480s. And in Ferrara itself, where Boiardo spent so much of his life, Duke Borso d'Este gave over an entire room in his palace to paintings of symbols taken from Hermetic magical principles: the months of the year, the signs of the zodiac, and the thirty-six decans, who were the Egyptian sidereal gods who ruled over the ten divisions of the 360 degrees of the circle of the zodiac.[16]

---

[13] The elements of Greek philosophy they found in these works confirmed their belief that Plato and the Greeks derived their knowledge from Hermetic writings, and not the other way around, as was actually the case.

[14] Proof of Hermes' widespread popularity is plentiful. Indeed, when Cosimo de' Medici first came into possession of a manuscript containing fourteen treatises of the *Corpus Hermeticum* in 1460, he ordered Ficino to put aside the Plato manuscripts, which were assembled and awaiting translation, and to translate this work of Hermes Trismegistus instead, saying "mihi Mercurium primo Termaximum, mox Platonem mandavit interpretandum." (Ficino mentions this in his dedication to Lorenzo de'Medici of the commentaries on Plotinus; see Ficino, 1537.) More manuscripts exist of the *Pimander* than of any other work by Ficino. For more on the general popularity, and limitations, of hermetic ideas in the Renaissance, see *Il mago, il cosmo, il teatro degli astri: saggi sulla letteratura esoterica del Rinascimento*, a cura di Gianfranco Formichetti; introduzione di Fabio Troncarelli (Rome: Bulzoni, 1985). See also D. P. Walker, *Spriritual and Demonic Magic from Ficino to Campanella* (London, 1958).

[15] See Paul Veyne, *Did the Greeks Believe in their Myths?: An Essay on the Constitutive Imagination*, trans. by Paula Wissing, especially chap. 1, "When Historical Truth Was Tradition and Vulgate" (Chicago: Univ. of Chicago Press, 1988.)

[16] For more on Duke Borso's interesting room, see Giacomo Bargellesi, *Palazzo Schifanoia; gli affreschi nel "salone dei mesi" in Ferrara* (Bergamo: Istituto Italiano d'arti grafiche, 1945).

Boiardo would thus have had ample exposure, along with the rest of his contemporaries, to the Hermetic craze that permeated his age. Humanism itself could hardly have had a more prominent position among the various ideologies developed during this period. Indeed, humanism and Hermeticism were hardly separate movements; Ficino and Pico were both strong advocates of Hermetic magic as well as forerunners of the humanist movement. The humanists derived much of their optimism about mankind from Hermetic texts—from the *Asclepius*, before the *Corpus Hermeticum* came to light, and then from Ficino's translation of the latter. The famously elevated opening of Pico's *Oration* was taken directly from the *Asclepius*, which reads:

> What a great miracle is Man, O Asclepius, a being worthy of reverence and honour. For he passes into the nature of a god as though he were himself a god; he has familiarity with the race of demons, knowing that he is issued from the same origin; he despises that part of his nature which is only human, for he had put his hope in the divinity of the other part.[17]

Here is one of the original turns away from "lower" human nature; the idea that man can achieve the divine is a commonplace in Hermetic texts, with powerful echoes as late as Shakespeare's *Hamlet*.[18] The first treatise of the *Corpus Hermeticum* discusses the Creation in many of the same terms that the mosaic Genesis does, but tellingly depicts Adam as a divine being: he falls, but he does so *knowingly*, of his own free will. He is not, like the older Adam of Genesis, punished for wanting to be like God, or for disobedience. It is crucially important for us to note how eagerly the Renaissance thinkers adopted these Hermetic doctrines, finding in them a central confirmation for their rewriting of the Fall and its notions of original sin and the presence of evil. Those conveniently subside, and in their place arises a vision of the individual human will as the leading actor in history: Adam chooses his fate. This idea has an ingenious simplicity, and was viewed wholly positively as an advance in thought from the Au-

---

[17] *Corpus Hermeticum* II, 301–2; in Yates, *Giordano Bruno*, 28.

[18] "What a piece of work is a man, how noble in reason." (*Hamlet*, 2.2). In the fourth treatise of the *Corpus Hermeticum*, Hermes tells his son Tat that since the intellect is drawn from the very substance of God, some men are gods and their humanity is near divinity. If man makes proper use of God's gifts of intellect and the word, he differs in no way from the immortals. This is comparable to Pico's comparison of man to a chameleon—able to evoke his own divine nature and become divine, if he is wise.

gustinian tenets of man's will as defective. Though the later Protestant doctrine of man's total subjugation to his fate, and consequent almost inevitable damnation, might appear wholly opposite to the humanistic one, they are actually the opposite sides of one coin: they share a belief in the absolute primacy of will in the human constitution. For the humanist, that will had to be a will to full selfhood; for the damnationist, that will had to be a will to faith, as the only way out of the human predicament. It is impossible to underestimate what an enormous intellectual change is represented by this passage and the multitude of others like it, which elevate the will—whether angelic or merely stoical—to the place of the central actor in all history. By this step more than any other, the primary focus of European thought moved away from God, and on to Man.

One especially important consequence of the diffusion of Hermeticism, with its associations with ancient Egyptian magic, was that it contributed to a more general familiarity with Egyptian myth and folklore, including the central deity of Egyptian religion, the man-god Osiris. Being a major Egyptian god, Osiris was naturally associated with the Hermetic tradition and with Hermes himself. Traditionally, in fact, Hermes was Osiris's confidential scribe; Osiris held him in high honor and accepted his advice in all matters, even assigning him the role of assistant to Isis, under whose governance he left his kingdom when he departed to teach the world about the planting of crops and vines.[19] Osiris respected Hermes because of his wisdom and ingenuity; Hermes taught men to speak distinctly, named objects that had previously remained unnamed, invented letters, arithmetic, music, sculpture, and astronomy, and instituted the worship of the gods.[20] In fact, he stood for a civilizing force, the same force that Osiris came to symbolize; he was also strongly associated with magic, through the astrological principles outlined in "his" works. Thus, Hermes and Osiris were closely associated both physically, by nationality and by a personal relationship, and spiritually, by what they stood for in the mythological tradition.

The ideas about man advanced in the Hermetic texts are radically optimistic: they describe in Hermes Trismegistus a figure quite similar to Osiris, the god who had lived on earth among men but who had divine powers, who magically came back from the dead, regenerated, reinte-

---

[19] Sir E. A. Wallis Budge, *Osiris and the Egyptian Resurrection* (New York: G. P. Putman's Sons, 1911), 10–11, Diodorus's account.

[20] Budge, *Osiris and the Egyptian Resurrection*, 10.

grated. The Renaissance magus using magical principles derived from the Egyptian Hermetic texts would ideally use the powers he had acquired to good purpose, as Osiris was supposed to have done. Osiris was a natural patron for the new humanist mode of Renaissance thought.

In any event, and quite apart from these added impetuses, Osiris was already a well-known mythological figure for the learned of the period.[21] According to the legend, Osiris is killed and later cut into fourteen pieces by his brother-in-law Typhon,[22] who then scatters these pieces throughout the country. Upon discovering Typhon's perfidy, Osiris's wife and sister Isis travels all over the land in search of her husband's body parts. In one version, Isis buries the recovered pieces separately, and Osiris comes back to life once she has finished burying them all; in another, she herself unites all the pieces with wax and aromatic spices. Osiris, then, has the magical power to reconstitute and revive himself after being dismembered.

Osiris is also traditionally associated with crocodiles. Although in Egyptian mythology it is Sebak who is usually represented as a crocodile, this god was often depicted, both in Egyptian art and in Renaissance emblems, with Osiris or a figure connected with Osiris.[23] In an Egyptian bas-relief at Philae, Sebak is depicted with the mummy of Osiris standing on his back.[24] A sixteenth-century emblem representing "Dii Egyptiorum" shows a human figure with a dog's head standing with one foot on a crocodile.[25] Valeriano's *Hieroglyphica* represents an image of the sun (an emblem entitled "Solis Simulacrum") as a man standing in a boat that a crocodile is carrying on its back. Osiris usually signified the sun; we know he did for Valeriano. And, of course, Plutarch himself attributes to Isis a magical power over crocodiles: when she goes looking for the bits of her dead husband Osiris, she travels in a papyrus boat that no crocodile dares attack.

---

[21] Numerous sources told the story of Osiris and Isis: Plutarch's *De Iside et Osiride*, Diodorus Siculus's *Biblioteca Historica*, Julius Firmicus Maternus's *De Errore Profanarum Religionum*, and Macrobius's *Saturnalia* were all available during the fifteenth century.

[22] Diodorus's version differs somewhat from Plutarch's. According to Diodorus, Typhon was Osiris's brother, and he tore him in twenty-six pieces, not fourteen. Typhon even throws one part into the Nile, just as we will see Aquilante do in the episode we examine below.

[23] See Jane Aptekar, *Icons of Justice: Iconography and Thematic Imagery in Book V of "The Faerie Queene,"* (New York: Columbia Univ. Press, 1969), 91–92. Aptekar discusses the iconography of the crocodile and the crocodile's relation to Osiris in chapter 6.

[24] Apetaker, *Icons of Justice*, 92. The examples that follow are also taken from Aptekar.

[25] The figure is Anubis, Osiris's son and lord of the dead, a title also held by Osiris.

The Hermetic connection to humanism, and the connection between crocodiles and the dignity of man, are the crux of what I take to be Boiardo's argument against these new philosophies, in Book 3's significant tale of Orrilo and the crocodile. Earlier, I noted that Pico's writing suggests the greatest possible revision of the image of Fortuna: not as a wheel, nor even a sailboat with Man at the helm, but as a magical wind controlled by an all-powerful mage. But if Pico himself would endorse that image, as I suspect he would, it is important that we clear our heads from the magical spell of his rhetoric, and remember that he would do so only at the enormous cost of ignoring empirical reality. His idealism sees the best in man; he assumes that magic is not only real, but readily available to us (and at this date in Italy, we cannot hold Pico fully responsible for the possible ill consequences of that belief). But man has other, distinctly unmagical, aspects: so that if we do accuse Pico, less of a misguided supernaturalism and more simply of the unavoidable fault of Youth, it seems to me we surely will have a point, and come closer to understanding Boiardo's place in relation to the delights and excesses of the new humanism. Of course, we too are carried along on the sails of Pico's rhetorical imagination; but as with every type of entertainment or theater, the moment must come when the world will reintrude itself, and we are left to encounter, as best we can, the plain sense of events: the daily tasks of life that, for example, Boiardo handles in his highly mundane correspondence, applying repeatedly for someone's rights to a water supply, petitioning the authorities to drop criminal charges against a friend or acquaintance, or asking that the citizens of his town be allowed to pay their taxes with goods rather than with cash—dealing, to recall a dismissive comment by Pico, with "the workman in the work, and the work in the workman."[26] The nature of such tasks also reminds us that a debate between Pico and Boiardo would be a very old and still familiar one (it goes back at least to Menander): the opposition between the idealistic, but also unrealistic, student, and his worldwise elder and guide. That is to say, thinking of Menander, Plautus, and Terence here can instructively illuminate the mixture of chaffing, irritation, guidance verging on manipulation, and affectionate counter-exuberance that I find Boiardo adopting in his response to Pico and his philosophical school. I want to suggest that, in a tale that turns out to be all about the difficulties of arguing with a Proteus-like trickster,

---

[26] *Oration*, 7. Pico suggests turning from that kind of everyday labor to the leisure of contemplation, so as to be able to "flash on every side with cherubic light."

the Protean artist-aristocrat Boiardo borrows his own artistic voice and technique from the *servus dolosus*, the tricky slave of Hellenistic New Comedy—who also, we ought to remember, knew exactly how to mock the pretensions of the *original* Neoplatonic mystifications and arcana.

Boiardo's dissent is given by the allegorical method, so prized by the Neoplatonists; but in this case it is cleverly turned against them to represent in art a compelling countervision to theirs in philosophy, a warning that their new doctrines were more likely to issue not in the Dignity of Man, but rather in his catastrophic abasement. At the very least, Boiardo suggests, this so-called new freedom had a very high cost, which it was hardly rational to pay, given the short odds of successful transcendence in the chaotic new world, which was equally the consequence of the new freedom. In fact, I find ample evidence in this episode and throughout the poem, so full of violent and deluded characters, to suggest that the *Orlando Innamorato* could just as plausibly be titled, "On the Indignity of Man," so conclusive an answer to Pico does it give.

Near the beginning of Book 3, Grifone and Aquilante are liberated from one of the numerous evil magical realms they have encountered, only to come up against yet another enchantment. As the two knights ride through Egypt, they meet two ladies with two dwarfs; one lady is dressed completely in white, the other all in black. Before actually speaking to the knights, the ladies exchange a few words in a whisper. Their private conversation reveals to the reader that they have foreseen the eventual death of these knights back in France, and that they can and will detain them in Egypt in order to delay fate for a while; for, although one cannot possibly change destiny, "pur se puote il tempo prolungare / E far col senno forza a la fortuna" ("But still one can prolong one's time / And, if one's clever, sway one's fortune"; 3.2.43).[27] Thus, before the episode proper even begins, Boiardo has already evoked Hermes (for the knights are in Egypt) and his magical realm of astrology.

The ladies petition the knights' aid in killing a certain knight named Orrilo, who has been persecuting their realm near the Nile where the villain inhabits a tall tower. Every time a knight or lady attempts to travel through the region, the ladies explain, Orrilo, who was brought to life by means of a magical spell ("nacque per incanto"), captures them and feeds them alive to his crocodile. Of course, the logic of that particular action

---

[27] This and all subsequent quotations are taken from Charles Ross's recent edition of the *Orlando Innamorato* (Berkeley and Los Angeles: Univ. of California Press, 1989).

carried out fully would lead to a generationless world, and so it is metony-mically appropriate that his companion crocodile performs the function of turning fertile territory (archetypally fertile, since it is the Nile environs that are in question) into a wasteland.

Only when Grifone and Aquilante, at the behest of the two ladies, en-gage Orrilo in battle do they actually discover the precise nature of his en-chantment. In short, Orrilo is able to put himself back together again upon being dismembered. When Aquilante slices him in two, the top half simply jumps back onto the lower half, which has remained in the saddle; the two halves rejoin, and the battle continues. When Orrilo's head is cut off, he merely picks it up by the nose and puts it back on. Even when Aquilante throws both his right and left arms half a mile out into the Nile, Orrilo just swims out to retrieve them and comes out whole again. One of the damsels who commissioned them for this enterprise laughs at their efforts—laughter which is important for the tone of the incident— and tells them that "Se in mille parte l'avesti a dividere / E più minuto il tagli che il panìco / Non lo potrai veder del spirito privo: / Spezato tutto, sempre sarà vivo" ("If he were in a thousand parts, / Milled finer than ground millet is, / You would not see his spirit leave. / Even divided thus, he'd live"). Grifone and Aquilante do manage to kill the monstrous croco-dile once Orrilo has unleashed it upon them, but they believe that they have accomplished very little if they do not also destroy Orrilo himself. The episode is broken off with a discouraged Grifone and Aquilante facing a seemingly endless battle; and though Boiardo promises to return to this "impresa" to tell us how it all turns out, his poem ends before we hear an-other word about Orrilo and his crocodile.[28]

The episode actually thematizes one of the poem's most prevalent images—that of the dismembered body—but with a twist: this dismember-ment can go on forever.[29] For unlike the masses who are chopped to pieces in the usual battles, this knight can put himself back together again indefinitely and with ease. Such self-mastery of the ubiquitous destructive

---

[28] In Ariosto's continuation and conclusion of this episode, Astolfo happens on the scene and reads in a book of magic that to kill Orrilo one must pluck out one particular hair on his head; I would find support in that singular detail for an Ariostan under-standing of Orrilo as somehow related to the problems of individualism. In a Gordian moment, Astolfo scalps the knight, cuts all the hair off, and is proclaimed a hero. See *Orlando Furioso* 15.64–92.

[29] I have written about images of dismemberment in chapter 3 of my dissertation, "On the Indignity of Man."

force that overwhelms so many in this poem strongly suggests, I believe, that Orrilo is actually a personification of that mysterious force itself, and as such highly important for our understanding of its nature. Only a diamond can cut a diamond; and that characteristic action is the only way to identify diamonds and thus distinguish possible counterfeits. So Orrilo is "the real thing," the epitome of a certain type of destructive force, these tropes hint; but he is still described as a mere "cavallier": though enchanted, he is not designated a monster, a goblin, or a demon, but a knight, comparable to all the others, but superior in his ability to reconstitute at will. What does he signify, with his magical talent, the lack of which spells doom for so many others in the *Innamorato*?

Boiardo's main direction, I believe, is first of all given by the very deliberate context of the episode at hand. He pointedly locates this episode in Egypt, next to the Nile River; his knight Orrilo, then, is Egyptian. He is enchanted, associated with some kind of mysterious magic unavailable to Grifone and Aquilante in the West. He has as his constant companion a thirty-foot long crocodile apparently, here in the *Innamorato*, an exotic, mysterious creature so unusual that it has to be described before it can be named. Boiardo identifies it thus, saying of Orrilo:

> Tiene una torre in su il fiume del Nilo
> Ove una bestia a guisa de dragone
> Che là viene appellata il cocodrilo
> Pasce di sangue umano e di persone
>
> His tower's by the river Nile
> Where there's a beast just like a dragon
> That feeds on human flesh and blood,
> And it is called the crocodile! (3.2.46)

This beast "che là viene appellata il cocodrilo" is thus a more-than-usually exotic animal. So, Orrilo is an Egyptian who is associated with strange, mysterious creatures and strange, mysterious customs (for this crocodile eats human flesh); and he himself has the unusual magical power to reintegrate his dismembered body parts and revive from what for others would be certain death.

All this suggests, of course, some mysterious, exotic Egyptian god or hero; and most specifically, it outlines the special attributes of the particular god whose history and attributes I reviewed earlier: Osiris. Anyone familiar with even the rudiments of Egyptian mythology—an increasingly large group, as I have discussed—would not fail to note that certain salient features of Osiris were also characteristic of Boiardo's Orrilo. Osiris, like Orrilo, is Egyptian and associated with the Nile and its tremendous powers. He is also strongly associated with dismemberment. Both Orrilo and Osiris live in Egypt near the Nile; both have magical powers; both can reintegrate once dismembered; and both are associated with crocodiles. It seems very likely, then, that Boiardo had an exaggerated parody of Osiris in mind when he created Orrilo and his crocodile; and from the elevated treatment of the Egyptian in the sources available during the Renaissance, there is no doubt that Orrilo-as-Osiris would *have* to be a parody rather than a straightforward imitation, for the traditional Osiris was a *creator* of law and order, not a disruptor thereof. In the mythology, Osiris taught the Egyptians how to sow and reap crops, and put an end to their long-standing practice of cannibalism; Boiardo's Orrilo, on the other hand, disrupts any possible order in the realm he terrorizes, and propagates the spread of a kind of cannibalism by his association with the crocodile who, we are told, "pasce di sangue umano e di persone." Orrilo feeds passersby to his crocodile, unlike Osiris who taught the Egyptians to respect all human life as sacred and to regard man as the image of God.[30]

Why did Boiardo create such a markedly unflattering contrast to his subtext, one that by its point-for-point opposition to the tradition strongly suggests the satirist's hand? What or who is the object of his satire? I find the confluence of this episode's likely date of composition, the two men's family relationship, the prominence of Osiris in the *Oration*, the inverted Hermetic references, and the poetic depiction of a grotesque selfhood in the attributes of Orrilo, all pointing to Pico as Boiardo's likely target. Pico promotes the idea of man as Magus; Boiardo, however, depicts a demonic type of magus using his magic for evil purposes only, dehumanizing and decivilizing the realm in his control, essentially negating the humanistic principles so closely tied to the Egyptian Hermetic texts which he paradoxically represents. Because of its marked ironic links to the Hermetic-humanist intersection, the story of Orrilo inevitably interrogates the enthusiasm of Boiardo's contemporaries for an ideological trend that the poet seems to see not as an advancement and gain, but as instead, to put it mildly, a serious decline and loss. This magical Egyptian religion of Hermeticism may purport to achieve miracles, to make man into a powerful

---

[30] Budge, *Osiris and the Egyptian Resurrection*, xviii. Even the names might support the idea of a satiric inversion: could Orrilo be a punning compound of "Osiris Rio," Wicked Osiris?

magus capable of imitating the gods, of living forever. But this power corrupts, and corrupts exponentially, because its characteristic act is a new kind of self-reflexive metamorphosis: Orrilo always returns to himself! It is an archetypal image for the committed individualist caught in his most characteristic act: a kind of perpetually tautological self-definition, which he commences in response to any critical attack. In the figure of Orrilo, we can see that the power of selfhood, of which he is so sardonic an epitome, corrupts the man who has it, and in turn corrupts the landscape around him, making it literally uninhabitable, savage, and uncivilized. The exaltation of self through the exclusion of all else and all others literally destroys those others, the land, and generation.

How does this power of selfhood work, exactly? The representation of Orrilo as a man who cannot be cut up, whose self is impregnable to every opponent's attack, perfectly figures the problem of debating certain types of ideology: their invulnerability lies in their infinite power of generalization (which is to say, their power to recast all terms into their own terms, for that is in effect what it is to generalize), their almost total lack of any particularity with which debate might grapple. Now, it is indisputably the case that Pico's rhetoric—which I believe the poem to be treating here, however elliptically—is quintessentially protean, general, and non-particular, which are the tendencies, sometimes negative, of the philosophical turn of mind. Pico has the certainty of youth, inexperience, and infatuation, and Boiardo's satiric response rings with a broad experience, a knowledge of life that is mainly figured through the episode's internal observers, audience stand-ins, and guides: the laughing ladies, with their superior awareness of mankind and fate. As I have already suggested, to argue with Pico is to argue with Youth: probably futile, especially at the moment, but nevertheless necessary, and one of the conscientious obligations of Age.

If we take the exordium of Pico's *Oration* and read it critically, we find an encyclopedia of abstraction, generality, and lack of distinctions.[31] Pico

---

[31] See the *Oration*, 3–7. For example, Pico properly begins his work with a citation from an authority. However, his authority is Abdul the Saracen, an either apocryphal or much-fingered source, really the most general of word-of-mouth anecdotal figures who claims to speak the opinion of "the Arabians," as though a consensus obtained among them! Abdul then, who is no one really, is asked by no one in particular, "What thing on, so to speak, the world's stage" did he view as "most greatly worthy"? He answers (or Pico makes him answer) without hesitation, that he views "nothing more wonderful than man." And, in a strange "coincidence" that Pico finds significant, Mercury, in the *Asclepius*, thinks the very same thing.

has no interest in mediated knowledge, it seems, or the weighing of actual differences: he sees the excellence of man as, instead, that he "has nothing of his own. . . . he is confined by no bounds." This distinction, however, etymologically as well as logically also suggests no *bonds*: of kinship, religion, or community, for example. Man is told to "sculpt thyself into whatever shape thou dost prefer," which implicitly connects Pico's thought to the act of metamorphosis. But that metamorphic skill seems less praiseworthy in an Orrilo; and of course, with only himself as a guide, how would any individual recognize himself to *be* (or not to be) an Orrilo?

Thus, the excellence of Man, Pico says, is a matter of protean *will*, and the freest of gifts from a wholly benevolent deity—the One who, as we saw earlier, supposedly gave Adam the free will that he used to choose to seek the Godhead, and fall: "O great liberality of God the Father! O great and wonderful happiness of man! It is given him to have that which he chooses and to be that which he wills."[32]

How does one argue with such a rhetoric, once it has initiated its nearly unbreakable connection to the most motile of our energies, our personal will? For that connection provides a reductive structure of interpretation that is proof, just like Orrilo, against practically any attack; and its strongest weapon is its unvarying orientation to futurity. If you say to Pico, "But so much freedom may very well be used for evil purposes," he will in effect reply, and sincerely believe, "Not if you turn your will to higher things!" Fair enough—except it leaves out practically everything, most notably any real recognition of the facts of history and the existence of other people, and other types of people. This "turn" of Pico's, that is to say, is the opposite of its predecessor in the tradition, the "turn" that finds one of its first and highest descriptions in Augustine's *Confessions*. What Pico's theology lacks, like its Hermetic antecedents, is the Fall; his notion of the will is pre-lapsarian.

---

[32] Pico glances at bad choices, it is true; the will may choose an animal or vegetable existence. But he takes those up, in the oldest debating trick, only to dispose of them before they can be used against him, so that he can get to his real, rhapsodic and celebratory point: he draws a winning picture of the active life, cherubic contemplation, the struggle for heaven, and finally, the achieved rank of angel. These passages are all panegyrics to the triumph of the will: we shall equal the angels "When we have *willed* it, we shall not at all be below them." In fact, for Pico, a man who makes bad choices isn't a man at all: he is merely a bush, or a brute. That certainly elides the problem of evil with a neat trick of *a posteriori* redefinition; but it can hardly satisfy even the lightest skeptical intelligence, let alone an intelligence like Boiardo's.

Since Pico's answer to any objection is always the same—we must perfect our will—it does not matter where you attack him, "take him apart,"
as debaters still say. In the future, the pure realm of intention, he is always
the whole, unmarked, and unwounded creature of his imaginative vision.
That vision is powerful and intoxicating, but as though Christ had returned from the tomb without the stigmata! No wonder the Church, at
least before it too had caught the Hermetic fever, could not abide Pico.

But the consequences of a Piconian avoidance of consequence would
have to be, in reality, catastrophic: we are not in Eden anymore. The will,
in marked contrast to Pico's characterization of it, is our balkiest part.
And in the perpetual lag between our thought and our act, between our
personal knowledge and the whole case, between our own appetite and the
appetites of others—can lie death, destruction, or madness. If Man alone
could have stopped those, he would have, surely; that he has not means,
to Boiardo, that he cannot. To delude oneself instead, as Pico does, that
he has not yet done so, but is *about* to, is simply a recipe for destruction
(because reality ignored will always, eventually, send in its bill). Invoking
Osiris, Pico thinks himself his spiritual descendant, bringer of civilization;
to Boiardo, who sees their moment in history with the clarity of one who
has lived and had great responsibility for the well-being of others, he is
more like Orrilo, bringer of catastrophe. And in fact, the indirection with
which the older poet makes the point, the actual humor (almost slapstick)
with which he deploys the tale, are very much the best of ways to respond
to those who are wholly "convinced." If Pico could see himself in Orrilo
and laugh, along with the two ladies, he would already be saved from his
intellectual error.

That hopeful note, however, does not diminish the size of the mistake:
the ultimate goal of Orrilo's effort and talent, his Will and Imagination is
a kind of aggressive return into himself, which strongly suggests the way
that individualism leaves the question of an individual's worth perpetually
begging, because of the unavoidable paradoxes of self-awareness and self-
judgement. Surely the fact of Orrilo's definite enchantment with regard to
his shape, yet pointed avoidance of even Pico's first principle of metamorphosis—to change from one's human nature to that of an angel, or even
possibly to animal or plant—suggests that Boiardo has also used his Nile
setting to hint at a kind of riddling or jesting variation on the great mythic tradition of Oedipus, which had poetically raised questions about the
course of our lives and therefore their value. I find his version rather mischievously and metaleptically invoking, as it were, a now ossified and re-

dundant Sphinx, the ponderous Egyptian version whose no-longer-dan-
gerous question is already asked and answered. Boiardo sees a new phenomenon on the high road; the humanists' remarkable apostles somehow
resemble Orrilo, because at every challenge (that is, question, debate, or
criticism), he and they all automatically enact the same uncritical, untem-
poral answer: "Man"! Which of course is Pico's response, his unvarying
solution to the riddle of existence.

In the course of their rather absurd struggle, Grifone and Aquilante,
with good old-fashioned chivalric valor, manage to destroy the cannibalis-
tic crocodile and thus arrest that particular scourge. But they are unable to
kill the magician himself. His power is greater than theirs, and their religion is not sufficiently active, perhaps, to outdo that of Hermes. Boiardo
points to what is lacking in Grifone and Aquilante's moral code when he
has them discuss the success or failure of their mission purely in terms of
personal glory; this shows, in fact, that they share the disease of selfhood
with Orrilo. Their encounter with the "magus" seems to have brought a
latent problem to the surface: the spell remained unnoticed until it was
too late to ward off its effects. This makes almost a definition of evil magic, and furnishes another sign that Orrilo resides on the demonic side of
Hermeticism.

The knights have already killed the crocodile; thus, at least, no one
else will be eaten alive even if Orrilo does continue to challenge every
passerby. But Grifone and Aquilante want to kill Orrilo as well—not, apparently, to save lives, but to be able to boast of their achievement:

> Grifon verso Aquilante ragionava:
> —Se questa bestia fosse ancora viva,
> Quale abbiam morta con affanno tanto,
> Di tale impresa non avremo il vanto.—
>
> Disse Aquilante: —Io non so certo ancora
> Che onor ce seguirà questa aventura;
> Far non so io tal prova che mai mora
> Quella incantata e falsa creatura.
>
> Grifon said to Aquilant,
> "All that we have to show in this
> Business is one dead beast—which was
> Hard to kill (if, in fact, it's dead)."
>
> "I'm not sure," Aquilante mused,

> "That this adventure leads to fame.
> I don't know what to do to slay
> That spurious, enchanted man." (3.3.18–19)

Thus, by one of his favorite narrative tactics, the suspended or inconclusive tale, Boiardo throws the moral puzzle back to the reader: if the pursuit of fame is no motive for the kind of excellence that alone can overcome false philosophy, what strategy would be effective?

Great art is always as much a matter of pointed omissions, invitations to deeper thought, as it is of any actual surface or statement. Remembering this, we can see the "effective strategy" take shape by contrast to the tropes Boiardo foregrounds here. Taking our bearings from this episode, the motive for the kind of excellence that alone can overcome false philosophy has to be the desire to defend truth, to take just action, guided by traditional and communal norms and authority; in other words, to have reasons for action exactly the opposite to those seen here in the two knights. The significantly individualistic failure of Grifone and Aquilante to understand what could be their own proper motivation is one of the innumerable signs of the larger social breakdown that forms so much of the matter of *Orlando Innamorato*, and which Boiardo had for a long time undertaken to anatomize. It just so happened that at this point, after the completion of Book 2, Pico burst into prominence and formulated his own very different kind of response to the same cultural problem, a response that I strongly suspect Boiardo found unacceptable—which would not be surprising, even apart from any possible reading of Orrilo, given what we know of the poet's experience, vision, and character.

There are abundant high spirits in the satirical invention of this episode; but high spirits are the order of the day when the aristocrat dons the *servus's* robes and tricks and freedoms and gestures. Just as the "slave's" twisty inventions are put forth in the service of ultimately serious goals—namely, his own freedom, and the freedom of mistreated or misguided youth to be fruitful and multiply, and so continue the familial line—so, too, are the artist's: satire is always a serious business. So that the incident of Orrilo makes one of an interesting set of codas to the central concerns of the poem: a pointed moment of warmth and wit that does something to leaven, though it can hardly redeem, the apocalyptic notes of the *Innamorato*'s broken finale.

THE ARTS IN FERRARA

Figure 1: Francesco del Cossa, *March* (lower register).
Ferrara, Palazzo Schifanoia, Hall of the Months.

Figure 2: Cosmè Tura, *Madonna Enthroned.*
London, National Gallery.

Figure 3: Cosmè Tura, *Madonna and Child in a Garden*.
Washington, D.C., The National Gallery of Art.

Figure 4: Anonymous, *The Meeting of Solomon and the Queen of Sheba.*
Houston, The Museum of Fine Arts.

Figure 5: Francesco del Cossa, *April*.
Ferrara, Palazzo Schifanoia, Hall of the Months.

Figure 6: Francesco del Cossa, detail of *April* (upper register). Ferrara, Palazzo Schifanoia, Hall of the Months.

Figure 7: Anonymous, *Scene from the Story of the Argonauts*.
Madrid, The Thyssen-Bornemisza Museum.

Figure 8: Antonio Pisanello, Lionello d'Este. Portrait medal (obverse).
Florence, Museo Nazionale del Bargello.

Figure 9: Antonio Pisanello, *Portrait of Lionello d'Este*.
Bergamo, Accademia Carrara.

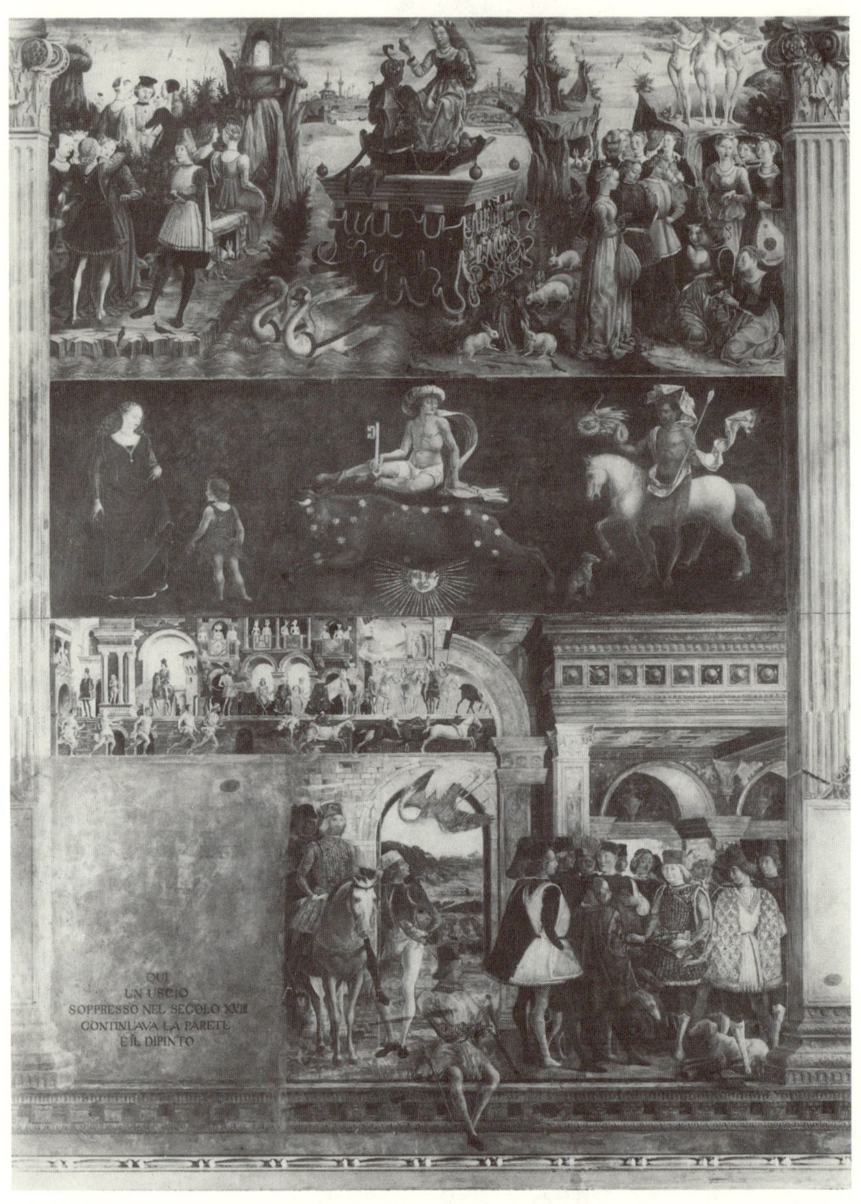

Figure 10: Francesco del Cossa (and Cosimo Tura),
Triumph of Venus and Taurus. Ferrara, Palazzo Schifanoia.

Figure 11: Andrea Mantegna, View toward the walls with scenes of
Return of Cardinal Francesco Gonzaga from Rome and Ludovico Gonzaga and his family.
Mantua, Camera degli Sposi, Palazzo Ducale.

Figure 12: Diagram of a wall.
Scandiano, Camerino dell'Eneide.

Figure 13: Scandiano, Rocca Nuova.

Figure 14: Nicolò dell'Abate, ceiling.
Scandiano, Camerino dell'Eneide.

Figure 15: Drawing of a soldier.
Scandiano, Cortile d'Onore.

Figure 16: Nicolò dell'Abate, *Book V of Aeneid*.
Scandiano, Camerino dell'Eneide.

JOSEPH MANCA

Boiardo and the Visual Arts in Ferrara: Comparisons and Convergences

IT IS NOT MY INTENTION HERE to explore any of the particular questions about Boiardo's literary efforts, but instead to look at the relationship between the visual arts in Ferrara and Boiardo's writings. This essay will cover two main topics: first, the formal or stylistic similarities that exist between Boiardo's poetry and the work of his countrymen who were artists. Secondly, aspects of Ferrarese art that, like Boiardo's works, reveal traditional, medievalizing, or otherwise conservative features in both style and subject matter. Of course, despite the Renaissance ideal of *ut pictura poesis*, it is problematic to compare Boiardo's poetry to contemporary painting. Boiardo was an aristocrat and poet who used words, mostly describing acts of love and war. The Ferrarese painters were largely of working-class origins. Their physical craft was very different from that of a poet, and their subject matter generally consisted of traditional Christian imagery. Yet, there was an overlap between Boiardo's audiences and the spectatorship in Ferrara for the visual arts, and the parallels between the work of the poet and that of local artists indicate shared expectations among the public in Estense Ferrara of the later fifteenth century.

In turning to the visual arts, one cannot help but be struck by the single-mindedness of the criticism of Quattrocento Ferrarese painting. According to the conventional wisdom, art from Ferrara was related to the central Italian Renaissance style but, in contrast, contained some inherent atavism that made it expressionistic, agitated, and downright neurotic and disturbing. Critics see Cosmè Tura as being some demonic parallel to Andrea Mantegna, and Ercole de' Roberti as a kind of nervous Ghirlandaio.[1] There has been a reluctance to see in Ferrarese art the beauty that comes simply from its otherworldliness, from its departure from mundane and vulgar reality that brings the viewer into a realm of brittle surfaces, spiralling mountains, hard enamel colors, strange physiognomies, and garments that are bent and shaped like metal. Indeed, here is the first of the convergences that we might note between the Ferrarese painters and Boiardo: a thirst for novelty, romantic escapism, and transportation to an impossible realm in which wonderfully improbable things can happen. Like Boiardo, Ferrarese painters depicted an idealized and unreal world. This is not to imply that artists or the writer were engaged in a frightened flight from reality. On the contrary, their productions can better be understood as magisterial reformations of the world, imaginative evocations of ideal realms. Both Boiardo and Ferrarese painters worked for noble clients who had the confidence to be able to let go of this world temporarily and experience unreal and beautiful fantasies.

Despite the differences in form—poetry versus the visual arts—there are similarities between the writings of Boiardo and Ferrarese painting even in narrower aspects of style and narrative approach. For example, there is a parallel in Ferrarese painting to Boiardo's sudden jumps from place to place, his discontinuities of narrative, and his quick changes of mood, emotion, and description (figure 1). The complications found in Boiardo's *Orlando Innamorato* recall those in Ferrarese art, especially narrative painting, in which the settings are fragmented and complex, and the storyline and the action do not always seem to correspond. Boiardo's interlacing is reminiscent of the discontinuity of space and pictorial presentation characteristic of numerous Ferrarese painted works of the same period. It is this lack of consistency and continuity that some viewers habituated to a Florentine or central Italian mode apparently find repugnant about Ferrarese art, but we might imagine that when turning to enjoy a local painting, Boiardo's listeners found this kind of fragmentation and disjuncture exciting.

Boiardo stated that his *Orlando Innamorato* is full of variety, that one can pluck and choose different, multicolored flowers at will from his garden (3.5.1–2). Certainly, variety is a fundamental characteristic of Ferra-

---

[1] Seminal expressionistic interpretations of Ferrarese painting appear in Roberto Longhi, *Officina ferrarese (1934), Ampliamenti (1940), Nuovi ampliamenti (1940–1955)* (Florence: Sansoni, 1956); Sergio Ortolani, *Cosmè Tura, Francesco del Cossa, Ercole de' Roberti* (Milan, 1941); Benedict Nicolson, *The Painters of Ferrara: Cosmè Tura, Francesco del Cossa, Ercole de' Roberti, and Others* (London: Elek, 1950); and Eberhard Ruhmer's *Tura: Paintings and Drawings* (London: Phaidon, 1958) and *Francesco del Cossa* (Munich: F. Bruckmann, 1959).

rese visual art. While a peculiar unity does in some sense come through, essentially Ferrarese painting of the later Quattrocento is one of diverse detail, of a wonderful and unabashed variety of colors, textures, and individual objects, sometimes rendered with minute and searching detail. This variety appears in paintings as well as in sculptural projects, such as Domenico di Paris's highly dense and decorative Sala degli Stucchi in the Palazzo Schifanoia and the ornate marble portal of the same palace. An incredible variety is found in the pages of the famous Bible of Borso d'Este and other local manuscripts of the later fifteenth century.[2] For their part, Ferrarese easel and mural painters tended to seek, not the more unified painterly vision favored in nearby Venice, but a manner based on parts. One can be forgiven, therefore, for standing in front of a Ferrarese painting and simply delighting in its particulars.

Another convergence between the writer and artists from his city is that Ferrarese painting, again not unlike Boiardo's poetry, especially his *Orlando Innamorato*, is vivid and peculiar: it is calculated to have an immediate effect on the viewer. Ferrarese art is often informed with a certain vernacular simplicity and a bluntness that sometimes borders on coarseness. Frequently, as in Boiardo's epic, there is a hyper-real quality to the details, even though the entirety is marvelously unlikely. Sometimes this attention-getting takes the form of primitive energy and violence (one of Boiardo's own fortés), as in Tura's *Saint George and the Dragon* (Ferrara, Museo del Cattedrale), while in other works the viewer is struck by subtler features, such as strange physiognomies and unusual landscape elements such as sharp, rocky outcroppings.[3] In short, despite the complication, the intricacies, and the sophistication of it all, there is in Ferrarese art something that is immediately grabbing. Even casual visitors to the National Gallery in London will stop and do a double or a triple-take before the *Madonna Enthroned* from Tura's Roverella altarpiece (figure 2), with its bizarre Madonna, peculiar green and pink architecture, and finely wrought sculptural details. Ferrarese art of the later Quattrocento is in large part direct and instantly eye-catching, all of this analogous to Boiardo's descriptive technique as found in his great romance.

Another similarity between Boiardo and the visual arts is in the ironic

---

[2] The Bible, which is located in the Biblioteca Estense in Modena (MS. V.G. 12), is illustrated in Adolfo Venturi, *La Bibbia di Borso d'Este riprodotta integralmente* (Milan, 1937).

[3] Tura's *Saint George and the Dragon* is illustrated in Ruhmer, *Tura*, figures 17 and 18.

and even humorous tone that breaks forth repeatedly in his *Orlando Inna-morato*. Some art historians might not agree that this is true also of Fer-rarese painting from the period. Indeed, a review of the criticism of Quat-trocento Ferrarese painting indicates that very few find the art ever to be intentionally funny. To be sure, it has other serious aspects to it as well, but the art of Ferrara is not in essence characterized by *Angst*, nervousness, and disturbance. On the contrary, it frequently has an ironic, tongue-in-cheek air to it, being infused with subtle wit, double-entendre, and quiet, knowing humor. Whether in an absurd fold of drapery, a humorously impossible rock formation, or a sophisticated nonchalance of action in dramatic narrative, Ferrarese painting is marked by a clever wittiness.[4] Clearly, the patrons and public for painting and poetry wanted to be enter-tained, and they apparently preferred not to have only a deadly serious tone in their art and literature.

I want to turn to the second theme of this paper, namely, the survival of medievalizing traits in Ferrarese art. Certainly, the medieval quality of the *Orlando Innamorato* is, because of differences of form and subject mat-ter, not exactly equivalent to that found in Ferrarese visual art at the time. Still, the evidence suggests that in Ferrara there was a desire to see reviv-als of past themes and styles, a strong traditionalism in all of the arts.

I stated earlier that a fundamental aspect of Ferrarese art is its unreali-ty, its encompassing of a different, better world than that of quotidian life. If this is true, there is no reason why Ferrarese art would not also retain Gothic characteristics. Indeed, if what the public wanted was to see a cre-ative, idealized vision set before their eyes, then we would fully expect that Gothic features might endure in Ferrarese art, for the International Gothic style was a lovely, affected, and gracious departure from reality, an elegant escape from this world. And we do see in Ferrarese art a lingering Gothicism, just as we find an enduring taste for traditional subject matter in Boiardo.

A good example of Gothic survival can be found in a painting by Cosmè Tura, his *Madonna and Child in a Garden* in the National Gallery of Art in Washington (figure 3). Some earlier writers believed that this must be a very early work by him, the obvious Gothic character suppos-edly a last gasp of the International style, still present before Tura saw cen-tral Italian Renaissance examples and changed his manner. But, without

---

[4] See also my *Art of Ercole de' Roberti* (New York: Cambridge Univ. Press, 1992), 2–3 and "Friedrich Vogelfrei's Ferrarese Notebook," *Artibus et Historiae* no. 24 (XII) (1991): 65–73.

conducting a Morellian analysis of the details of the painting, it can be said that nothing about the execution, technique, drapery style, physiognomic forms, lighting, coloring, etc. indicates that this is necessarily an early work. On the contrary, it seems to be a mature work, made in 1465–70 or so, a general dating accepted by most recent writers.[5] Tura's picture is, therefore, a striking phenomenon: it is a conscious reversion, a purposeful recapitulation of Gothic art. The flat placing of the leaves behind the figures, the painting of little gold highlights on these leaves, the gentle attitudes and facial expressions of Mother and Child, the cursive shapes of the raised gesso frame, and the inclusion of tiny, miniature-like figures of the Annunciation above are all clear aspects of the Gothic style. Whoever the patron, Tura had reason to think that a conservative work of this type was appropriate. This painting makes it fully understandable that in 1469 Borso d'Este sent Tura on a mission to nearby Brescia to study some now-lost works of the late Gothic painter Gentile da Fabriano.[6] There was no prejudice against the International style even at so late a date; indeed, Borso apparently regarded Gentile as a positive model for study and imitation, as reflected in Tura's *Madonna and Child*.

Numerous Ferrarese paintings of the late Quattrocento show this persistence of earlier stylistic traditions. One of the notable ones is the *Meeting of Solomon and the Queen of Sheba* in the Museum of Fine Arts in Houston, a fascinating *tondo* by an anonymous Ferrarese master (figure 4). This work is difficult to date; some writers put it at 1470 or so, although I think that it may predate that by a decade or more.[7] In any case, it is strongly Gothic, with its punched gold, elegant, elongated female figures, Gothic architectural elements, and charming anecdotal incidents of hawkers, monkeys, and fighting dogs. Another *Solomon and the Queen of Sheba* by this artist is certainly later, perhaps dating to the 1470s. This work, now in Boston

---

[5] For catalogue entries see Ruhmer, *Tura*, 173, and Fern Rusk Shapley, *Catalogue of the Italian Paintings*, 2 vols. (Washington: The National Gallery of Art, 1979), 1: 509–10.

[6] Tura was sent on a mission to Brescia to study the paintings by Gentile that were in chapel of the Broletto, painted for Pandolfo Malatesta in 1414–19. The cycle included a representation of *Saint George and the Dragon*; see Keith Christiansen, *Gentile da Fabriano* (Ithaca: Cornell Univ. Press, 1982), 16–17 and 134–35. For documentation of Tura's visit, see Adolfo Venturi, "Cosma Tura genannt Cosmè, 1432 bis 1495," *Jahrbuch der Königlich preussischen Kunstsammlungen* 9 (1888): 14–15.

[7] For recent discussions of the *tondi* in Houston and Boston see my "A Ferrarese Painter of the Quattrocento," *Gazette des Beaux-Arts* sixth series, vol. 116, year 132 (Nov. 1990), 157–72, and Daniele Benati, cat. no. 77 in *Le Muse e il principe: arte di corte nel Rinascimento padano*, 2 vols. [exh. cat., Milan, Museo Poldi-Pezzoli] (Milan: Franco Cosimo Panini, 1991), 2: 300–7.

in the Museum of Fine Arts, has many of these same Gothicizing, decorative features, although they are somewhat less emphatic than in the earlier Houston version. These works show that traditionalizing stylistic tendencies were surviving quite nicely still by the 1470s or so.

This kind of artistic conservativism is revealed in some fresco fragments that have recently been discovered in the church of San Paolo in Ferrara, again by an anonymous artist.[8] Various scenes were uncovered, but I want to draw attention to a section of one with elegant, blond women, who in their elongation, fair hair, long fingers, and tiny lips are still in the International tradition. These figures appear in a scene from the life of Saints Cosmas and Damian. This fresco is datable to 1476, indicating that in the last quarter of the Quattrocento a suave medieval current was still present in Ferrarese art. These women are reminiscent of Gothic representations of gatherings of beautiful ladies, a tradition also present in the *tondi* in Houston and Boston.

It should be stressed at this point that there were essentially two formal trends in Ferrarese art of the later Quattrocento. The first was a kind of crumpled, angular mannerism that is an abstracted, stylized, and bizarre variant on the Early Renaissance style in Italy. This was undoubtedly the dominant of the two trends. The second strain consisted of conservative, elegant Gothic forms, which were also sometimes prominent. Both of these modes, though, can be related to Boiardo, the first in its variety, disjuncture, and fantastic unreality, and the Gothic style in its otherworldly quality, and its traditional and retrospective air. Ferrarese viewers apparently sought splendid illusions and art beyond the mundane, so of course these seemingly contradictory styles could exist simultaneously, even in a single work.

We find these two stylistic modes in the best known of Ferrarese painting projects, the frescoes in the Hall of the Months in the Palazzo Schifanoia.[9] In the lower register of Cossa's month of March, which I believe is one of the greatest paintings of the Quattrocento, the angular mannerism that many associate with the Ferrarese school is brought to full fruition (figure 1). The fragmented landscape itself, the jolting jump from place to

---

[8] See Giorgio Branchini and Anna Maria Visser Travagli, "Relazione preliminare delle ricerche condotte nel primo chiostro di San Paolo a Ferrara," *Critica d'Arte* 56, nos. 5–6 (January–June 1991): 29–43, especially figs. 24–26.

[9] See illustrations in Ranieri Varese's *Atlante di Schifanoia* (Modena: Edizioni Panini, 1989), *passim*.

place, and the crowded, active movements of figures place this work squarely in the Ferrarese manneristic tradition of the later fifteenth century. Even the architecture forms a fantastic variant on the Renaissance current that was unfolding in a more strait-laced fashion elsewhere in Italy.

Another mode is found, though, in Cossa's famous Love Garden in the upper register of the month of April (figures 5 and 6). The mood is gentle, the movements of the figures are slow, and this is undoubtedly a recreation of the Gothic Love Gardens found in earlier pictures of the Quattrocento. Even the emphasis on flirtation and aristocratic leisure is rooted in medieval tradition, despite the presence of the classical deities Venus and Mars.

The rest of the cycle of the Hall of the Months contains this contrast, and further confirms that Ferrarese painting of the later fifteenth century is a mixture of Gothic and mannered Renaissance. For example, the Master of September has a witty, energetic, and angular style in his Forge of Vulcan and Triumph of Vulcan, while the adjacent Master of August takes a very different approach, with bright colors, doll-like figures, and comparatively simple, static garments. Here were two artists, one avant-garde and the other conservative, one revolutionary and the other Gothicizing and traditional, working together perhaps on the same scaffolding.

What became of these Gothic survivals, so obvious from the 1450s to the 1470s? It is clear that even later a traditionalism endured, although to be sure such features did finally wane. There was a growing taste for classicism in the Ferrara of Ercole I, demonstrated most obviously in the style of the Erculean Addition. Yet, the Gothic past retained a place in the local scene. It is enough to recall that from 1476 until about 1529 *oltremontane*, medieval hangings of the *Roman de la Rose* remained throughout this time in the *sala grande* of the Castello.[10] Surely made in the usual northern style (that is, in a late Gothic mode), they could easily have been removed if there had been some dogmatic shift in taste away from Gothic style or subject matter.

Some paintings of the 1490s made in Ferrara still have this kind of chivalrous spirit. The series of the Argonauts, carried out by an anonymous Ferrarese master and his collaborator, are painted in a fairy-tale style (figure 7).[11] The landscapes are formed of lightly painted, insubstantial

---

[10] These "cortine ricamate" are discussed by Nello Forti Grazzini, *Arazzi a Ferrara* (Milan: Electa, 1982), 39.

[11] This series of six paintings, which seems to be carried out by two different artists

little hills. The foliage in this series consists of small rounded trees adorned with golden drops of lighting, all very much in the Gothic tradition. The figures stand in easy, elegant poses, and they seem—in good late medieval, aristocratic tradition—not to be doing very much. Even the miniature ships are in the late Gothic manner, strongly resembling ornamental ships that one sees in late medieval reliquaries and other works of art. The author of these Argonaut ships was most likely imitating a northern late-Gothic source, adding to the late medieval character of the series as a whole.

A similar kind of retrospective air appears in the work of the 1490s by Ercole de' Roberti, even though he was in general not a Gothic revivalist. A small diptych that he made in the early 1490s (probably for the Duchess Eleonora d'Aragona because a work of this description was in her inventory) includes a quite consciously retrogressive use of perspective in the landscape. Ferrarese painters, even the more progressive ones, had little hesitation in turning to conservative stylistic practices when it seemed to them suitable for the commission and the patron.[12]

Some documented but now-lost works from the 1490s further indicate a continuation of traditional styles and subject matter in Ferrara. In 1494 the Ferrarese painter Fino Marsigli painted various rooms at Belfiore with animals such as tigers and wild boars, continuing a tradition of late Gothic mural decorations showing exotic animals and hunting scenes.[13] Another room at Belfiore by Marsigli represented figures set against green foliage backdrops.[14] This latter work must have been quite traditionalizing, perhaps not so different in appearance from the Hall of the Sibyls in the Casa Romei, a cycle dating forty years earlier, which has female figures placed about the room against a backdrop of green, flattening bushes, and a low trellis.[15]

Other rooms from Belfiore dating to the last quarter of the Quattrocento are noted by Giovanni Sabadino degli Arienti in his description of

---

(not Roberti or Costa, as is often argued), is discussed in Manca, *Roberti*, 184–85.

[12] The pair, representing the *Adoration of the Shepherds* and the *Dead Christ* (London, National Gallery), is discussed in Manca, *Roberti*, 62–64 and 143–45.

[13] For documentation see Adolfo Venturi, "L'arte ferrarese nel periodo d'Ercole I d'Este," *Atti e memorie dell R. deputazione di storia patria per le provincie di Romagna* 7 (1889): 388–89.

[14] Venturi, "L'arte ferrarese," 389.

[15] Illustrated in Cetty Muscolino, *La Casa Romei: Una dimora rinascimentale a Ferrara* (Bologna: Univ. Press, 1989), 19–22.

Ferrara from *circa* 1497 published by Werner Gundersheimer. These rooms included scenes of dancing, hunting, and other representations of exotic or wild animals, some of these (perhaps those documented) as being by Fino Marsigli.[16] Gothic traditions were only slowly waning in Ferrara, and it is striking that as recently as the decade before Raphael painted his *School of Athens*, and several generations after the commencement of the artistic Renaissance in Florence, the Ferrarese were happily surrounding themselves with merry murals of boar hunts, jousting, and the dancing of fancily clad men and women.

I would like to conclude, as a coda but also as an aspect of the survival of traditional taste in Ferrara, with at least a mention of Boiardo's own eye for art. Motivated by his own pleasure in looking, and also by the need to help his listeners and readers visualize details of his tale, the poet takes the opportunity to describe works of art that he mentions in his *Orlando Inna-morato*. An extended example of this comes in the recounting of how Fior-delisa and Brandimarte gazed at length at a prophetic fresco cycle repre-senting heroes in battle in Febosilla's loggia (2.25.25–58). Boiardo's observations here have largely to do with the content and not the style, and there is nothing surprising about the poet's fascination with scenes of victorious cavaliers, or with his interest in foretelling future Este glory. In any case, a few of his observations do seem to indicate some stylistic aspects that Boiardo liked. He starts by saying that the works were made of "gold leaf and the finest colors," so the materials themselves were appealing to him, apart from any questions of handling of paints, shadowing, color harmonies, and so forth. Although Leon Battista Alberti, in his *De pictura* of 1435, had frowned on the use of real gold in paintings, Boiardo has no problem with this, and the physical splendor of the cycle was thus impressive for him.

In a similar vein, Boiardo more than once in his description of this imaginary cycle mentions the sharp juxtaposition of colors. He notes the placing of gold lettering against an azure field. Elsewhere he remarks on an imperial eagle painted white on a blue background. In another place he seems to like the contrast between black and white eagles. Admittedly this is not much to go on, but it does suggest that Boiardo was pleased by the application in painting of simple, contrasting, decorative colors or tones. This passage is useful as a reminder that the *Orlando Innamorato* itself com-

---

[16] See Gundersheimer's *Art and Life at the Court of Ercole I d'Este: The "De Triumphis Religionis" of Giovanni Sabadino degli Arienti* (Geneva: Librairie Droz, 1972), 70–72.

prises such clarity and sharply outlined detail, not unlike that found in contemporary Ferrarese painting. At any rate, his praise of such simple contrasts could have been written fifty years earlier, or one hundred years earlier. Boiardo's eye for coloring, if we are to judge from his description of this imaginary cycle, was late medieval, not yet complicated by the kind of pictorial subtlety and fine distinctions that were to develop in painting in the later fifteenth and, especially, the early sixteenth century.

Further insight into Boiardo's sensibility toward the visual arts can be gained from a review of his description of the stone portal representing the story of the Labyrinth and the Minotaur seen by Orlando in Morgana's underworld (2.8.13–18). Boiardo is clearly most fascinated by the material used rather than the style per se, noting that the stone door is inset with gold, pearls, enamel, and various gems. A few lines later Orlando comes across a marvelous statue of a king by a riverbank, a work that Boiardo indicates was made of gold, rubies, pearls, and diamonds. Michael Baxandall has demonstrated that the documentary evidence from the later Quattrocento indicates that the emphasis was shifting away from materials themselves toward matters of technique and style.[17] In this light, Boiardo certainly is allied with the older, medieval-based tradition, and his "period eye" for color and materials was decidedly late Gothic.

In conclusion, Boiardo's sense of fantasy, his love of disjunctions and interlacings, his avowed love of variety, and his taste for forcible, vernacular description and sharp exciting incidents were analogous to the work being done by Ferrarese artists of his time. In addition, the survival of the Gothic spirit in Boiardo's writings and in Ferrarese art throughout the fifteenth century indicates a continuing taste for a retrospective, medievalizing style; the aristocratic gatherings, Love Gardens, and boar hunts in Ferrarese art and literature demonstrate the perseverance of late Gothic subject matter. Boiardo's poetry was in consonance with the work of Ferrarese artists from the time, despite their different art forms. It would happen soon that a new kind of painting would come to the fore in Ferrara. Even then the work of poets and painters would converge. Although the potential subject of separate paper, one could argue that Ariosto's elegant, refined verses and sophisticated literary style have much in common with the harmonious, Giorgionesque manner of Dosso Dossi, the idyllic landscapes of Ortolano, and the classicism of Garofalo.

---

[17] Michael Baxandall, *Painting and Experience in Fifteenth Century Italy* (Oxford: Clarendon Press, 1972), 14–17.

JODI CRANSTON

Commemoration, Self-Representation, and the Fiction of Constancy in Este Court Portrayal

"PRINCES," WRITES PIETRO ARETINO IN 1548, "who consider themselves to be like God, when shown every thing in which they are present, take more notice of a portrait taken from life, in which they can look at themselves, but which can never demonstrate to them the immortality of written memory."[1] Commenting from his own experience as a writer, as a close friend of Titian (who portrayed sacred and secular rulers), and as an observer of biographies and portraits for more than a century, Aretino theorizes how each mode of portrayal, of representing and commemorating an individual, evokes a particular temporal condition, either the instantaneousness of painting or the longevity of words. Princes, in Aretino's estimation, prefer to be portrayed in paint rather than in words, for the painted portrait allows them to see themselves in life and how others will see them after death, whereas a memoir or biography exists completely only after their death. Asserting the priority of written over painted portraits, Aretino here responds to and articulates aesthetic concerns that had begun almost a century before in the Este court in Ferrara and other courts in

---

[1] "I principi, che per istimarsi da quanto Iddio, al quale ogni cosa se gli mostra in presenzia, fanno piu conto d'un ritratto tolto da sembianza, in cui se stessi vagheggiano, che in quante imagini mai potesse rassemplargli la immortalità de la memoria." Pietro Aretino addressed the letter, dated April 1548, to Sebastiano Fausto da Longiano. For the complete letter, see Paola Barocchi, ed., *Scritti d'arte del cinquecento* (Milan and Naples: R. Ricciardi, 1971), vol. 1, 257.

Italy, a concern, that is, of how to represent and perpetuate the fame of a ruler.

As an avid collector of ancient medals, Leonello d'Este, duke of Ferrara from 1441 to 1450, was aware of the powerful legacy sustained through the currency of the profile. Inspired by his numismatic interests, Leonello called for a competition for his painted portrait between Jacopo Bellini and Pisanello, who was already known in Ferrara for his portrait medals of Leonello (figures 8 and 9). The differences of the two completed pictures surprised the duke, and he attempted to persuade the two artists to reconcile their dissimilar renderings of his features.[2] His response to the pictures, his desire for true likenesses of "ritratti al naturale," and apparent confidence in the power of art to replicate nature, affirm one of the central discourses of Renaissance aesthetics, one that would later occupy, among others, Pietro Aretino, as we have seen.

Figuring immmortality in paint and in words is a continuing objective among Leonello's successors, Borso (who ruled 1450–71) and Ercole (who ruled 1471–1505). Correlated to Leonello's desire for verisimilitude is his succesors' recognition of painted and verbal portrayal as a transmitter of political rhetoric, on the one hand, and the rhetorical nature of painting and poetry in general, their ability to "make that which is not seem to be," as Castiglione writes of painting, on the other.[3] The situation of the literary and pictorial portrayal of the Este court within the dialectic of seeming and being illustrates how the portraits of both Borso and Ercole attempted to attain the elusive combination of immortality and resemblance described by Aretino.

The power of portraiture in general had been suggested already in 1435 by Leon Battista Alberti in his commentaries, *De pictura*. "Through painting," Alberti writes, "the faces of the dead go on living for a very long time."[4] With rhetorical finesse Alberti enunciates the powerful intimacy between portraiture and the memory of the dead as a reminder to, as well

---

[2] Jacopo Bellini's winning portrait is now lost. For Leonello d'Este's remarks on the portraits ("uixque precibus meis reconciliastos . . .") see Michael Baxandall, "A Dialogue on Art from the Court of Leonello d' Este: Angelo Decembrio's 'De Politia Litteraria' Pars LXVIII," *Journal of the Warburg and Courtauld Institutes* 26 (1963): 314. See also Joanna Woods-Marsden, " 'Ritratto al Naturale': Questions of Realism and Idealism in Early Renaissance Portraits," *Art Journal* 46 (fall 1987): 209–16.

[3] Baldassar Castiglione, *Il libro del Cortegiano*, eds. Amedeo Quondam and Nicola Longo, (Milan: Garzanti, 1992), 6.

[4] Leon Battista Alberti, *On Painting*, trans. Cecil Grayson, (London: Penquin Books, 1991), 60.

as one perpetuated by, the living. Significantly, Alberti uses the example
of a ruler's portrait, that of the deceased Alexander, to demonstrate the
ability of painting to make the absent present and of representing the dead
to the living many centuries later.[5] Not merely a rhetorical topos, this
complex association between portrayal, memory, and temporality implicit
in portraiture assumes an explicit ideological role in the commissions of
Borso d'Este and then Ercole d'Este. Independently continuing the family
tradition of self-commemoration and the fiction of constancy, they nevertheless extended the modes of such ducal representation beyond that of
the static, everlasting profile portrait favored by Leonello. Instead, the two
major projects sponsored, the Salone dei Mesi frescoes in the Palazzo Schifanoia and Matteo Maria Boiardo's poem *Orlando Innamorato*, respectively
portray each ruler in real or described *logge istoriate*, which overtly manipulate time and its destructive power.

The tradition of courtly mural cycles, in large part deriving from ekphrastic descriptions of picture galleries, is, as recent scholarship has demonstrated, profoundly aligned with courtly self-portrayal and the ruler's
body as a site for the grafting and production of social and political ideologies.[6] Important and frequently cited examples for Renaissance studies are
the Salone dei Mesi (figure 10) and the Camera Picta in Mantua (figure
11).[7] However, the frescoes at the Palazzo Schifanoia, with the smiling
Borso d'Este representing good and just government, here from the month
of April, and at the Camera Picta, representing relationships of authority,
are significant, yet distinct, examples in such discourses on power. Whereas the Camera Picta suggests the possibility of successors with the fictive
curtains covering two of the four walls, the Salone dei Mesi does not represent the unknown and the uncertain future and secrets of the state.[8]

---

[5] Alberti, *On Painting*, 60.

[6] Loren Partridge and Randolph Starn, "Room for a Prince: The Camera Picta in
Mantua, 1465–1474" in *Arts of Power* (Berkeley and Los Angeles: Univ. of California
Press, 1992), 81–148.

[7] Giovanni Sabadino degli Arienti (Sabadino) in his *De triumphis religionis* describes
fresco cycles with portraits in the two country residences of the Estense: at Belriguardo,
there is a scene of Ercole d'Este in the company of his courtiers; at Belfiore, a *loggia* enclosed a series of frescoes that represented Alberto d'Este and his attendants hunting. For
Sabadino's text and a description of his account, see Werner Gundersheimer, *Art and Life
at the Court of Ercole I d'Este: The "De triumphis religionis" of Giovanni Sabadino degli Arienti*. Travaux d'Humanisme et Renaissance 127 (Geneva: Librairie Droz, 1972), 21–23. I
am grateful to Jo Ann Cavallo for bringing these additional fresco cycles to my attention.

[8] For a discussion on the significance of the fictive curtains in the Camera Picta, see

Borso's effective and good government, in contrast, is as rhythmic and pre-dictable as the twelve months that structure the calendar year and his self-representation. The mode of calendar landscape, in which human activi-ties such as the women harvesting in the foreground are emblematic of the different seasons, is altered here so that even in the face of inevitable change Borso is always present and constancy is assured.

Aside from an ideology that results from apparent constancy—Borso's repeated representation within a calendar—there is the related assertion of power through Borso's manipulation of the calendar as a means for struc-turing his self-representation, his manipulation of time. Time is never innocently or naturally expressed: never known by and for itself, and hav-ing no essence except for its constant deferral, time always signifies some-thing else. Recognizing the variety of mechanisms and ways for recording time, Leonardo da Vinci, for example, wrote in his notebooks: "We do not lack for ways to divide and measure these, our miserable days."[9] A ca-lendar is one such example of a no-less motivated means of signifying time than a clock, repeating the syllables of words, or musical notes.[10] Borso's activities, as literal parallels to the signs of the zodiac and to the gods and goddesses, are installed as the earthly personifications of each month. Rep-resenting the months with a ruler's activities, and portraying a ruler and his activities in any calendar format, but especially in one that unites mor-tal time in the lowest register, cosmic time in the middle register, and mytho-historical time in the upper register, cosmologizes the lived time of Borso and humanizes cosmic time.[11] The result is a connection between the fictional time of memory—what Borso accomplished—of a general con-cept of before and after implicit in the succession of the months, the abso-lute time of past, and a perpetual repetition of the now mediated through the astrological signs and the presence of the image before us.

Daniel Arasse, "Il programma politico della Camera degli Sposi, ovvero il segreto dell' immortalità," *Quaderni di Palazzo Te* 6 (1987): 45–64. Arasse discusses the curtains not in terms of unknown successors, however, but as revealers and concealers of the secrets of the state.

[9] "Non ci manca modi ne vie di compartire e misurare questi nostri miseri giorni." Codice Atlantico 12b, Biblioteca Ambrosiana, Milan. Published in *The Literary Works of Leonardo da Vinci*, ed. Jean Paul Richter (New York: Phaidon, 1977), vol. 2, 243.

[10] For the varied means of expressing time, see Paul Ricoeur, *Time and Narrative*, trans. Kathleen Blamey and David Pellauer (Chicago: Univ. of Chicago Press, 1988), vol. 3, 12–22.

[11] Ranieri Varese, "Tempo e tempi a Schifanoia," Abstract for *Ferrara, La corte degli Estensi e il loro mecenatismo* (Copenhagen, 1987).

Sensitive to the narrative possibilities of time, the temporal suspension and manipulation offered by poetry, Boiardo in Book 2, Canto 25 describes a *loggia istoriata* in the palace inhabited by the fairy Fesobilla which proleptically portrays and commemorates Ercole d'Este and the family's successful defense of the Church.[12] Setting out the lines that follow as the rhetorical exercise of ekphrasis, the narrator claims ignorance of the frescoes' maker and the means of their making:

> I can't say who the artist was
> Who had depicted on those walls
> The great events that were to come:
> I don't know how he learned of them...[13]

Pretending to be doubly uninformed, the narrator distinguishes his description as original *invenzione* by not referring to his authority, Turpino, and implicitly suggests that written ekphrasis has prophetic powers not possessed by painting. As mentioned earlier, painting, synecdochically theorized by portraiture, has the power to record the past, the faces of the already dead.

Boiardo's poetry, by claiming to make the not yet living forever present through the fictional, visual medium of that which commemorates the dead, engages the topos later called the *paragone* between painting and poetry, but which often included music and sculpture. Comparisons of the effectiveness and affectiveness of various media, suggested by Alberti and fully developed by Leonardo and successors, arose from ancient writers comparing painters and sculptors to poets and orators, and from the Renaissance interest in the panegyric.[14] Engaging artists and non-artists alike, the *paragone* literature, although often repetitive, documents the Renaissance concern over the nature and legitimacy of any signification. Foremost among the terms of the comparison is the temporal nature of each mode, the longevity of each medium to capture and preserve the beauty and transience of all mortal things, and the instantaneous nature

---

[12] For similar *logge istoriate*, particularly in the poetry of Tasso, see G. Baldassari, "Ut poesis pictura. Cicli figurativi nei poemi epici e cavallereschi" in *La corte e lo spazio: Ferrara Estense*, eds. Giuseppe Papagno and Amedeo Quondam (Rome, 1982), 605–35.

[13] Matteo Maria Boiardo, *Orlando Innamorato*, trans., Charles Ross (Berkeley and Los Angeles: Univ. of California Press, 1989), 2.25.43. All subsequent citations are taken from this edition.

[14] For the most complete discussion of the *paragone*, its origins and development, consult Claire Farago. *Leonardo da Vinci's Paragone* (New York: E. J. Brill, 1992).

of painting, the multiple views of sculpture, and the gradual unfolding of poetry and music. "Now," Leonardo da Vinci writes, championing painting, "see what difference there is between hearing an extended account of something that pleases the eye and seeing it instantaneously.... Yet the works of poets must be read over a long span of time."[15] Offering his challenge to advocates of painting's superiority, Boiardo suggests ironically that such paintings in Fesobilla's courtyard, although narrated, thwart the temporal progression of the poem itself. When Doristella asks Brandi-mart "What are you doing here?... / Wasting time staring at that thing? Don't you know what you have to do?" (2.25.57), she implies that he wastes the literal time of the poem and postpones the future by viewing, since it is a future that depends on the heroic actions of the fictional, narrated present.

But for the dedicatory subject of the *Orlando Innamorato*, Ercole d'Este, the notion of viewing his personal history as a loss of time, if not mildly insulting, defines the nature of portraiture in general: the portrait, as a trace of the mortal, always signifies a loss wrought by the passage of time even as the portrait serves as an actual or potential permanent record. As a signifier of time through being or lack of being, the pictorial or literary portrait was thought by some to represent the character of the portrayed, although Renaissance writers continually questioned the ability of paint to represent the interior qualities. Consequently, Boiardo's proleptic portrait excludes any final judgement on Ercole's character, an omission that the narrator ascribes to the painter of the fictive frescoes. Completing his ekphrasis, the narrator states:

> Above his head there were some words,
> Written in gold, and this they told:
> "If in this painting I could show
> The virtue of the human soul,
> No figure in the world would be
> More royal, fine, or fit for fame.
> But I can't make my hand design
> What is beyond the human mind." (2.25.56)

The inability of painting to portray or signify the imminent, the presumed failure of the hand to portray the mind, is a recurring Renaissance theme taken over from Martial's description of a portrait of the young Marcus

---

[15] *Leonardo on Painting*, ed. Martin Kemp (New Haven: Yale Univ. Press, 1989), 23.

Antonius Primus: "Would that Art could represent character and mind! / There would be no more beautiful painting on earth."[16] Boiardo alters this topos so as to suggest that Ercole's soul is beyond comprehension in either words or paint, and thereby pretends that such unrepresentability is the result of great eternal character and not because of an undetermined future that prevents the final or, as Ariosto would later suggest in the *Orlando Furioso*, any judgement of a person after death.

Significant here is not Boiardo's ekphrastic portrayal of Ercole in a fictive picture gallery but his explicit engagement of the terms of the *paragone*, especially those relating to temporality, to portray Ercole. Responding to and developing themes that occupied successive artists and writers on aesthetics, Boiardo very consciously manipulated that which is only known through representation: time, interior thoughts, and virtues. In a related way, the frescoes in the Salone dei Mesi manipulate time through the structure of the calendar in order to portray Borso as a personification of time and personified by time. Often the notion of power is claimed by scholars through art's courtly origins; however, in Este Ferrara, this power was achieved specifically by harnessing time and thereby sustaining the fiction of constancy, which had been initiated at mid-century by Leonello.

---

[16] For the Renaissance interest in depicting the spirit, see Martial, *Epigrams*, trans. D. R. Shackleton Bailey (Cambridge, MA, and London: Loeb Classical Library, 1993), X. xxxii. 5–6; John Shearman, *Only Connect... Art and the Spectator in the Italian Renaissance* (Princeton: Princeton Univ. Press, 1992), 110–11. Many of the issued raised in this essay are developed more fully in my dissertation, "Dialogues with the Beholder: The Poetics of Portraiture in the Italian Renaissance" (Ph.D. diss., Columbia University, 1998).

KATHERINE A. McIVER

The Room and the View:
A New Look at Giulio Boiardo's
Private Apartments at Scandiano[1]

We are seen, therefore we are...the good courtier performs his part remembering where he is, and in the presence of whom, with proper devices, apt poses and witty inventions that may draw on him the eyes of the onlooker.[2]

AWARE OF THE DUBIOUS MANEUVERINGS of his relatives to obtain dominion over Scandiano and of his own prolonged wait of nearly three years to become invested as count of Scandiano by Ercole d'Este, Giulio Boiardo, like Castigione's "good courtier," refashioned his projection of self.[3] Clear-

[1] This article is a revision of a paper presented at the College Art Association Conference held in San Antonio, Texas, in January 1995. Preliminary research for this project was supported by an NEH Summer Seminar (summer 1994): "Constructing the Image of the State, the Family and the Individual in Renaissance Florence and Venice," led by John T. Paoletti and Wendy Stedman-Sheard. I wish to thank Gary Radke and John Paoletti for their insightful critiques of earlier versions of this paper. My thanks, also, to Charles Ross and Jo Ann Cavallo for their editorial comments.

[2] Baldassare Castiglione, *The Book of the Courtier*, trans. Charles Singleton (Garden City, NY: Anchor, 1957), 72.

[3] The apparent rift between the two branches of the family (see lineage chart on page 294) dates back to Feltrino Boiardo's death in 1457: Feltrino had left provisions for his son Giulio Ascanio to become count as well as stating that both Matteo Maria Boiardo and Giulio Ascanio's widow, Taddea Pia, would maintain control of Scandiano and surrounding territories (Odoardo Rombaldi, Roberto Gandini, and Giovanni Prampolini, *La*

ly preoccupied with his own self-image, in the 1540s Boiardo commissioned Nicolò dell'Abate to paint an innovative decorative program for his Camerino dell'Eneide (figure 12) that would show him to be "a man of letters, an intellectual and a generous person."[4] Located in the heart of the apartment complex, the Camerino was situated, as Leonbattista Alberti recommended, at the flank of the Rocca Nuova (figure 13), overlooking the public piazza and the garden on one side and the Cortile d'Onore on the other.[5] Giulio Boiardo's self-fashioning begins in the Cortile d'Onore

------

Rocca Nuova di Scandiano e gli affreschi di Nicolo dell'Abate [Reggio Emilia: Casa di Risparmio, 1982], 20). What is unclear at this point is why Giulio Ascanio's son, Giovanni, did not become count at his father's death. According to rumor, in late 1474 Taddea Pia maneuvered to take over Scandiano: along with her brother Marco Pio, Lord of Carpi, Pia plotted to poison Matteo Maria. However, their accomplice who was to do the deed, Simone Bioni, had a change of heart, confessed, and the plot failed; Aderito Belli, *Storia di Scandiano* (Reggio Emilia: Stabilimento Tipografico G. Notari & Figli, 1925), 32. Neither Rombaldi et al., *La Rocca Nuova*, 20–25 nor Giambattista Venturi, *Storia di Scandiano* (Modena: G. Vincenzi e Compagno, 1822), 96–98 mention this plot. The Este reacted by splitting up the Boiardi holdings between Matteo Maria, who received Scandiano, Gesso, and Torricella, and Giovanni, who received Arceto, Salvaterra, Casalgrande, Dinazzano, and Montebabbio. This incident may be related to the 1469 plot against Borso d'Este that that involved two Pio brothers.

Taddea Pia's plotting did not end here: after Matteo Maria death on December 12, 1494, she challenged Camillo's right to rule (Rombaldi et al., *La Rocca Nuova*, 25); Camillo died mysteriously in 1499. In 1500, Giovanni Boiardo became the count of Scandiano and the territory of the Boiardi was once again reunited. Giovanni supposedly then drove Matteo Maria's widow, Taddea Gonzaga, and daughters out of the Rocca. Gonzaga appealed to Isabella d'Este, who in turn wrote to her father Ercole on their behalf. The Este remained unresponsive. It has been suggested that the Este preferred to pacify the Pio rather than appease the Gonzaga. See Giulio Reichenbach, *Matteo Maria Boiardo* (Bologna: Nicola Zanichelli editore, 1929) and Werner Gundersheimer, *Ferrara: The Style of a Renaissance Despotism* (Princeton: Princeton Univ. Press, 1973). Even after Giovanni Boiardo became count, Taddea Pia wanted Scandiano, perhaps for the Pio family, Rombaldi et al., *La Rocca Nuova*, 26. It is of interest here to note that in the same year (1500) the Pio of Carpi received Sassuolo from Ercole d'Este (Thomas Tuohy, *Herculean Ferrara* [Cambridge: Cambridge Univ. Press, 1996], 144). One cannot help but wonder if the two events are not connected.

[4] Leandro Alberti in his *Descrittione di tutti Italia* (1550; reprint, Cologne: Baum, 1567, fol. 328*v*) describes Giulio Boiardo as "hora illustra questo luogo Giulio, figliolo di Giovanni parente di Matteo Maria sopra detto suo degno ingegno, lettere e liberalita." Also of interest, in about 1544, Ercole Gonzaga commissioned a motet in Giulio's honor from Jacquet of Mantua; it is titled *Cantemus Domino*.

[5] For the most comprehensive study of Nicolò dell'Abate's frescoes see: Rombaldi, *La Rocca Nuova* and Giambattista Venturi, *L'Eneide di Virgilio dipinto in Scandiano* (Modena: G. Vincenzi e Compagno, 1821). For his views on architecture see Leonbattista Alberti, *On the Art of Building in Ten Books*, trans. Joseph Rykwert, Neil Leach and Robert Tavernor (Cambridge, MA: MIT Press, 1992), 292–93, 299.

where scenes from Matteo Maria Boiardo's *Orlando Innamorato* were interspersed with the "stemmi" of various families connected to the Boiardi and where Nicolo dell'Abate painted a series of frescoes that included a group of figures making music (late 1530s). It continues above, on the second floor of the Rocca Nuova in Giulio's Camerino, which was decorated with twelve scenes from Virgil's *Aeneid* disposed above monochrome battle scenes and surmounted by lunettes depicting city and landscape scenes. Female *all'antica* figures adorned the eight pendentives and directed the viewer's attention to the center of the ceiling where Nicolò's octagon (figure 14) depicted a group of people with musical instruments looking down on the room below.

Drawing on a number of popular literary sources like Leonbattista Alberti's treatises on architecture and the family, and Baldassare Castiglione's *Book of the Courtier* (1528), Boiardo also called on the authority of the ancient past for a historical model for his court through his use of Virgil's *Aeneid* as the major decorative element. At the same time, he paid tribute to Matteo Maria Boiardo, whose *Orlando Innamorato* contains numerous references to Virgil. It is quite possible that Giulio was appealing to the good name of his cousin to cleanse his own, bringing to mind the old adage "the sins of the father. . . ." What emerges, then, is a picture of a man who was clearly aware of the past and its implication and who manipulated not only Virgil's text, but also Alberti's in an effort to fashion his identity and, perhaps, to vindicate himself of the alleged murder of Matteo Maria's son by emphasizing his honor and virtue and, thereby, justifying his right to rule Scandiano.

While previous scholarship on the Camerino has noted the faithfulness with which Nicolò dell'Abate followed Virgil's text for his paintings, the

---

Along with the Camerino dell'Eneide, Giulio Boiardo's complex of rooms included the Salone delle Feste, a library, and his bedroom. The Camerino was a rectangular room with a fireplace, one door opening to Giulio's bedroom, and a second door opening onto the landing of a spiral staircase. Unfortunately, the rooms are no longer in their original state; the frescoes have been removed from the walls and are in the Galleria Estense in Modena. We can reconstruct the general layout of the rooms and their decoration from archival documents and architectural plans. Stefano Maccarini (*La Committenza dei Boiardo di Scandiano nel XVI secolo*, tesi di Laurea, Istituto universitario di architettura di Venezia, 1986) proposes various reconstructions for the Camerino, as well as discussing the activities of Terzo Terzi who was at the Rocca during its reconstruction. Reference to the scenes from Matteo Maria Boiardo's *Orlando* and the "stemmi" in the Cortile are found in numerous descriptions of the Rocca from the period. Following the extensive renovations of the Rocca by Giovanni Boiardo and his son, Giulio, the building was referred to as the Rocca Nuova.

historical context of the frescoes has never been explored in detail nor has anyone examined just how the Camerino and its decoration was used to validate Giulio's role as count of Scandiano.[6] On the most obvious level, as Langmuir suggests, the vertical progression of frescoes from the battle scenes through the *Aeneid* cycle to the octagon illustrates the general idea of the foundation of the cities of this region five hundred years before the foundation of Rome. As such, they are analogous to the legendary founding of Rome as told in the *Aeneid,* which established a heritage for the ancient Romans, allowing Augustus to claim his ancestry as divine since Aeneas was the son of the goddess Venus and the mortal Anchises.[7] It might be worthwhile to restate the legend: the Modenese region was first populated by Umbrians who founded many cities there and lived in peace and harmony until the Tuscans came. They struggled for decades until the Tuscans gained control of the land (represented by the monochrome battle scenes in the Camerino). The fact that when he landed in Italy Aeneas was able to raise an army from among the Tuscan-Umbrians, in his fight against the Rutoli, proves that the Modenese region antedates Rome by about five hundred years (represented by the Aeneid cycle).[8] The legend culminates in post-antique history, which reaches its height in the contem-

---

[6] Basic bibliography on the Aeneid cycle that has not already been cited includes: Alfredo Fabrizi, "L'Eneide nei dodici quadri di Nicolò dell'Abate," *Capitolium* (1930): 506–16; Walter Bombe, "Gli Affreschi dell'Eneide di Nicolò dell'Abate nel Palazzo di Scandiano," *Bollentino d'Arte* X (1931): 529–53; Sylvie Beguin, *Mostra di Nicolo dell' Abate: Catalogo critico* (Bologna: Edizioni Alfa, 1969); Erika Langmuir, *The Early Narrative Cycles of Nicolo dell'Abate* (Ph.D. diss., Stanford University, 1972) and her article: "Arma Virumque . . . Nicolo dell'Abate's Aeneid Gabinetto for Scandiano," *Journal of the Warburg and Courtauld Institutes* 39 (1976): 151–70. Giovanni Battista Venturi (1821) was the first to write about the frescoes and to acknowledge their faithfulness to Virgil's epic. In the 1930s, Alfredo Fabrizi and Walter Bombe Virgil summarize the frescoes at Scandiano and note their remarkable faithfulness to Virgil's text. Sylvie Beguin published the only existing monograph on Nicolò dell'Abate that summarizes the previous literature; she sees the Camerino frescoes as paying homage to Matteo Maria Boiardo. Langmuir provides the most comprehensive research on the *Aeneid* paintings to date. In her article, she focuses on the methods of narration employed by Nicolò as examples of episodeic illustration, but does not relate them to the history of the Virgilian iconography; rather she ties the frescoes to foundation myths current in the period without any attempt to contextualize them.

[7] Langmuir, "Arma Virumque," 157, sees the vertical ordering of the frescoes as a temporal metaphor: ancient to modern.

[8] Lodovico Vedriani, *Historia dell'antichissima citta di Modena* (Modena, 1666), 14–16; see also Annio da Viterbo, *Archiloco de tempi—Ditte candiano della guerra troiana* (1498, reprinted 1543), 131.

porary Boiardi who were represented in the octagon, therefore, establishing Giulio Boiardo's lineage.[9]

It is of interest to note, here too, that both Vedriani and Tiraboschi suggested that this foundation myth was well known in the late fifteenth and early sixteenth centuries.[10] In other words, anyone who was allowed into the Camerino would have understood the reference to the myth of origins of the Modenese region and to Giulio's lineage. It is my contention that we must go beyond this simple reading of the frescoes to explore the reasons behind the commission and to examine just why Giulio Boiardo felt the need to validate his position as count of Scandiano and to enhance his self-image.

As will become evident, it is through the decorative programs of both the Cortile d'Onore and the Camerino dell'Eneide that Giulio Boiardo maneuvers to position himself and his court solidly among the provincial aristocrats of the Ferrarese who included the Sanvitale of Fontanellato and Castelguelfo, the Pallavicini of Busseto and Cortemaggiore, and the Pio of Carpi and Sassuolo. Both the "stemmi" and the *Orlando* imagery in the Cortile speak to issues of power and family, while the vertical progression of frescoes in the Camerino, from the *Aeneid* cycle to the lunettes that depicted the active courtier at leisure, which culminate in the ceiling octagon, show a kind of apotheosis of Giulio himself.[11] Indeed, the overall imagery of Giulio's Camerino gives us a portrait of a man who is more erudite and sophisticated than his predecessors, and who claims to have, like his eminent ancestors Feltrino and Matteo Maria Boiardo, a "thorough grounding in Virgil, a taste for history and an awareness of the pleasures of the marvelous."[12]

The Rocca Nuova and the Cortile d'Onore

Giulio's apartments in the Rocca Nuova were part of an ambitious renovation and expansion campaign initiated in about 1500 by his father, Giovanni Boiardo when he became count of Scandiano. Built in the mid-

---

[9] Langmuir, "Arma Virumque," 157.

[10] Vedriani, *Historia dell'antichissima città*, 14; Girolamo Tiraboschi, *Memorie storiche Modenesi* (Modena, 1793), 1.

[11] I wish to thank Charles Ross for suggesting the "apotheosis" idea to me.

[12] Charles Ross, "Poetics at the Court of Leonello d'Este: Virgil, the Marvelous, and Feltrino Boiardo in the Competing Discourses of Angelo Decembrio's *De politia literaria*," in *The Court of Ferrara and Its Patrons* ed. by Marianne Pade, Lene Waage Petersen and Daniela Quarta (Modena: Edizioni Panini, 1990), 55–69.

thirteenth century, the Rocca came into the possession of the Boiardi when Feltrino Boiardo was invested as the first count of Scandiano by Niccolo III d'Este in 1423.[13] The renovations of the Rocca undertaken by Giovanni, grandson of Feltrino, included the extension to the east of the original structure, that is the Rocca Nuova, and the construction of a symmetrical façade with two towers following the model of the Castello in Ferrara and the Rocca at Fontanellato. Giulio Boiardo, Giovanni's second son, continued the campaign after his father's death, transforming the structure into an urban villa.[14]

The main entrance of the Rocca Nuova, marked by a small tower, leads to the central courtyard, the Cortile d'Onore, which united the old with the new structure; it was arcaded and had a loggia facing the entrance. In about 1520, Giovanni Boiardo commissioned paintings for the interior walls of this Cortile; scenes from the *Orlando Innamorato* were interspersed with various "stemmi" of families connected to the Boiardi including the Estensi, Gonzaga, Pio, Gambara, and Pallavicini.[15] Just how and where the painted imagery was displayed is unclear. Moreover, we do not know for certain which scenes from the *Orlando* were depicted in the Cortile.[16] Considering the apparent rift between the two branches of the family, it is significant that any reference to Matteo Maria is made at all.[17] Moreover, it is of greater importance to note that in 1544 Giulio Boiardo sponsored a performance of Matteo Maria's play *Il Timone* in the

---

[13] After Niccolo III d'Este's death, he became Leonello d'Este's courtier and close friend. Rombaldi et al., *La Rocca Nuova*, 9–19.

[14] The building was modified again in the 1580s, the 1640s, and during the eighteenth century. Rombaldi et al., *La Rocca Nuova*, 72–74. Together Giulio and Silvia transformed the medieval structure into a Renaissance palace rich with paintings, sculpture, precious objects, and a notable library that contained copies of Annibale Caro's *Aeneid*, Matteo Maria Boiardo's *Orlando Innamorato* and other works. Silvia Sanvitale was highly educated and had a particular fondness for Virgil's *Aeneid*; she played a major role in the decorative campaign of the Camerino. See my forthcoming article "Two Emilian Noblewomen and Patronage Networks in the Cinquecento," in *Beyond Isabella: Secular Women Patrons in Renaisance Italy*, eds. Sheryl Reiss and David Wilkins (St. Louis: Sixteenth Century Press).

[15] Rombaldi et al., *La Rocca Nuova*, 122. Other "stemmi" in the courtyard included those of the Contrari, Sacrati, Correggesi, Martinenghi, Malaspini, Collalto, Sfiondati, and Tassini families.

[16] Given the nearly contemporary Loggia Leone in the Castel Buonconsiglio at Trento painted by Romanino, we might assume that the scenes were limited to the enclosed space of the loggia rather than dispersed around the walls of the courtyard.

[17] The use of Matteo Maria's *Orlando* for the decoration of the Cortile suggests that the poet's fame lasted longer locally than previously throught.

Cortile in honor of Giberto Pio, signore of Sassuolo;[18] coincidently, Nicolò dell'Abate's frescoes in the Camerino would have been completed by this time.

Boiardo's *Orlando Innamorato* creates, as Ross notes in his introduction to his translation, "a world of valor and beauty" by portraying Charlemagne's knights on a variety of martial and amatory adventures. In the poem fierce individualism battles aristocratic loyalty, a conflict also characteristic of Ferrara and the poet's sovereign, Ercole d'Este, to whom the work was dedicated. Love and enchantment lure the *Innamorato's* heroes, Orlando and Ranaldo, away from the defense of Paris, their chief military obligation to Charlemagne. Often within the work, fields and streams, the settings for love, "are contiguous to the poem's battlefields, for the *Orlando* is not just a love story, but an imaginative chronicle of Christiandom's conflict with North Africa and Asia."[19] One can imagine the Cortile d'Onore painted with such imagery and with soldiers (figure 15) displaying familial "stemmi" interspersed among them. In fact, in the *Orlando* itself, as various courtiers of Charlemagne's court make their entrances into tournaments, battles and so on, they are described in full armor and by their "stemmi."[20] Giovanni Boiardo would certainly have been aware of Matteo Maria's soldier imagery and may have consciously appropriated it for his display of familial connections in the Cortile d'Onore. More to the

---

[18] Considering the function of the space and its painted decoration, it is of interest to note that a loggia was a customary outdoor site for celebrations and performances. Two theatrical productions were recorded at Scandiano in 1544 in honor of Giberto Pio, signore of Sassuolo: the "Tragidia d'Egisto" written by Tommaso Mattacoda, physician and poet of Scandiano, and Matteo Maria Boiardo's "Il Timone" (Rombaldi et al., *La Rocca Nuova*, 79).

[19] Charles S. Ross, *Matteo Maria Boiardo: Orlando Innamorato* (Berkeley and Los Angeles: Univ. of California Press, 1989), 2–4, 9. See Giambattista Venturi's *Storia di Scandiano* for reconstruction drawings. The scenes from Matteo Maria's epic poem no longer survive and the soldier in the plate exists in a drawing after the fresco. Venturi identifies this figure as Giovanni Boiardo by the coat of arms on the shield, an eagle and crown, and by the dragon crest on his helmet that was appropriated from the Fogliani coat of arms. Located over the primary entrance of the courtyard, Venturi suggests, Nicolò dell'Abate's concert scene represents Giovanni Boiardo's three sons Giambattista, Giulio, and Ippolito with their mother Giulia Gambara.

[20] A description of a loggia in Book 1, Canto 6 of the *Orlando* gives us some insight as to why and how the walls of the courtyard may have been painted: "The count admired the loggia, which was painted on its three façades. The painter had his craft so mastered, Nature had been eclipsed by art. Orlando stood before them, staring, reading a noble story there of ladies and barons bold; each figure's name was carved in gold"; Stanza 49. Stanzas 50–53 give more detail of what was depicted.

point, the Boiardo family's use of Matteo Maria's *Orlando* does not reflect, so much, an interest in the humor and complex plot of the epic poem as it does their concern for self-aggrandisement—especially if one considers the great themes of the *Orlando*—"nobility, worth and courtesy."[21]

The intimate relationship that both Feltrino and Matteo Maria Boiardo enjoyed with the Este was never realized by either Giovanni Boiardo or his son Giulio. While both of them maintained an active role in Ferrara and participated frequently in various Este functions, neither Giovanni nor Giulio lived at court for extended periods nor did they have close personal associations with particular members of the Este family.[22] Perhaps this desire for a similar intimacy with the Este was the catalyst for the decoration of the Cortile d'Onore and, more importantly, for the decorative program of Giulio's Camerino dell'Eneide. Though Giulio Boiardo created a court not unlike that of the Este with a court humanist, a court musician, and so on, he seems to have been driven to demonstrate his equality with his more illustrious ancestors, Feltrino and Matteo Maria Boiardo. Indeed, Giulio's marriage to Silvia Sanvitale in 1523 brought the family eminent connections. Her father, Francesco Sanvitale was the brother of Giangaleazzo Sanvitale, the lord of Fontanellato, who commissioned Parmigianino to paint his portrait and stufetta in the 1520s. Her mother, Laura Pallavicina, was friendly with the Sforza of Milan and with the Farnese of Parma, particularly Pope Paul III who came to visit her at Scandiano in 1543 and who surely saw Giulio's Camerino dell'Eneide.[23]

---

[21] Ross, *Matteo Mario Boiardo*, 9, 14–15; see also note 19 above. In the *Orlando*, as Ross notes, Matteo Maria blends medieval chivalry with Virgil's *Aeneid*, thus transforming Virgil into French romance, perhaps his greatest invention. Boiardo's *Orlando* not only reflects his knowledge of Virgil, but also of Angelo Decembrio's *De politia litteria*, which was written in the 1440s and set in the court of Leonello d'Este. Feltrino Boiardo had an ongoing argument with Leonello because he prefers Livy to Virgil; Decembrio's speakers move from one episode to another in much the same way as Matteo Maria narrates his epic poem. Growing up at the court of Ferrara, while Feltrino was courtier to the Este, provided Matteo Maria with an intimate look at court life and with acess to the Este library, which contained most of the classical writers, contemporary literature, and romances of chivalry; Ross, *Matteo Maria Boiardo*, 11–12.

[22] Rombaldi et al., *La Rocca Nuova*, 77–78. Giulio did develop a friendship with Ippolito II d'Este in the 1540s, though it was never as intimate as the relationships of Feltrino and Matteo Maria Boiardo with the Este. See Vincenzo Pacifici, *Ippolito II d'Este, cardinale di Ferrara* (Tivoli, 1920), 22–23.

[23] Rombaldi et al., *La Rocca Nuova*, 77–79. The anonymous "Historia dell'origine et huomini illustri della famiglia Sanvitale," busta 883B, Archivio Sanvitale, Archivio di Stato, Parma, gives an extensive description of the family.

The Camerino dell'Eneide and Giulio Boiardo's Self-Image

The Camerino itself falls within the studiolo tradition; the most significant models are Isabella d'Este's in Mantua, her brother Alfonso's Camerino d'Alabastro in Ferrara, and Federico da Montefeltro's in Urbino.[24] The Scandianese Camerino functioned as a small private study for the family and privileged guests; it housed sculptures, coins, gems, and collections of archaeological marvels and was characterized in contemporary documents as a "jewel."[25] The room was a place for the study and handling of precious objects and an escape from the cares and duties of the outside world. The close association of private rooms and open landscapes, which stems from classical antiquity, is founded on the refreshment of the soul. This association underlies the typical position of private rooms over a garden landscape at Scandiano and elsewhere.[26] The collections contained within this room along with its decorative program suggests that Giulio Boiardo, following the example laid out by both Alberti and Castiglione, was modeling himself after the ideal humanist.

Looking more closely at the decoration of the Camerino, we begin with the lowest level, the basamento where Nicolò painted monochrome battle scenes, only fragments of which survive and are in the Galleria Estense in Modena. These scenes, unlike those from the *Orlando* in the Cortile, are not connected to any literary text; rather they give the general idea of battle and are based on engravings after the battle scenes in the Sala di Costantino in the Vatican.[27] The battle imagery is surmounted by

---

[24] For Isabella d'Este and her studiolo see: Clifford Brown, "The Grotta of Isabella d'Este," *Gazette des Beaux-Arts* 89 (May–June 1977): 151–71, and 91 (January 1978): 72–82, and Sylvia Ferino Pagden, ed., *La Prima Donna del Mondo: Isabella d'Este Furstin und Mazenatin* (Vienna: Kunsthistorisches Museum, 1994). For Alfonso d'Este and his studiolo see: Charles Hope, "The Camerino d'Alabstro: A Reconstruction of the Evidence," in *Bacchanals by Titian and Rubens*, ed. Gorel Cavalli-Bjorkman (Stockholm: Nationalmuseum, 1987), 25–42 and "The Camerini d'Alabastro of Alfonso d'Este," *Burlington Magazine* 113 (1971): 641–50, 712–21. Federico da Montefeltro's studiolo at Urbino dates from the 1470s but was well-known in courtly circles and much admired.

[25] Rombaldi et al., *La Rocca Nuova*, 104. See also Geminiano Prampolini, "Cronaca di Scandiano dal 1543," MSS. Turri A113, Biblioteca Municipale Panizzi, Reggio Emilia, and Francesco Morsiani, "Supplemento all cronaca di Prampolini," MS. Turri C38, Biblioteca Municipale Panizzi, Reggio Emilia.

[26] Paul Holberton, "The Choice of Texts for the Camerino Pictures," in *Bacchanals by Titian and Rubens*, ed. Gorel Cavalli-Bjorkman (Stockholm: Nationalmuseum, 1987), 58.

[27] In 1821 Giambattista Venturi commissioned engravings of the battle scenes as well as of the female all'antica figures.

Nicolò's *Aeneid* cycle. As the largest paintings in the room, full of color and activity, these scenes were positioned at approximately eye level and were separated from each other by pilasters. Restricting the illustrations of the *Aeneid* to clearly demarcated uniform pictorial fields gave them a textual logic and clarity. The frescoes were arranged around the walls of the room in a way that compelled the viewer to read the cycle as if reading a text, beginning from the left as one entered the room. Representing each of the twelve books of the *Aeneid* with a multitude of episodes allowed the viewer to identify with the characters of the story as the drama unfolded around the walls of the room.

Within each panel, the arrangement of episodes begins at the upper left and circulates through the middleground to the last episode at the lower, far right, thus generating a pattern of movement that leads to the next fresco (figure 16).[28] Each scene is a narrative within a landscape; Nicolò's approach to landscape was not only decorative, subordinating it in favor of the subject, but he used it as a strategy for organizing the epic poem. In each scene, the landscape controls the viewpoint and dictates the narrative path by separating and locating episodes of the story; action is set within landscape as words are set to music.

Nicolò's frescoes are the earliest, most complete extant illustrations of the *Aeneid* in mural form.[29] Rather than monumental paintings, engravings from printed books like Sebastian Brandt's edition of the *Aeneid*, printed in Strasbourg in 1502, were the obvious source that Nicolò consulted for the program—following the advice of Giulio Boiardo's court humanist, Sebastiano Corrado.[30] The literariness of the depictions of the

---

[28] Langmuir, "Arma Virumque," 161, 166–67.

[29] In the Quattrocento, Virgil's *Aeneid* was a popular subject for the decoration of cassoni panels, miniatures, and other so-called minor arts. The only three monumental paintings of the subject prior to Nicolò's include Perino del Vaga's of a single scene of *The Shipwreck of Aeneas* in the Palazzo Doria in Genoa; it was commissioned by Andrea Doria in 1527. In the mid-1530s, Giulio Romano painted a cycle of the Trojan War based on both Homer and Virgil for Federico Gonzaga; the cycle decorated the Sala di Troia in the Palazzo Ducale in Mantua.

[30] Virgil's poem was very popular in the first decades of the sixteenth century; a number of translations were available all over Italy. Sebastian Brandt's edition contained 138 engravings by Johannes Grunninger, a copy of which was in Ferrara in this period. Nicolò's textual source may have been Annibale Caro's translation of the *Aeneid*. A printed edition is documented in a mid-sixteenth century inventory of the Boiardo library (Rombaldi et al., *La Rocca Nuova*, 108–9). Sebastiano Corrado, a native of Arceto, was at Scandiano in the 1530s, returning again in the 1540s. He wrote a commentary on the first book of the *Aeneid* and dedicated his first public work, the *Ciceronian Quaestura* pub-

Aeneid distinguishes them from Dosso Dossi's *Aeneid* scenes painted in the 1520s for Alfonso d'Este's Camerino d'Alabastro, which are usually cited as the model for Nicolò. Dosso's cycle was disposed as a frieze around the Camerino under the cornice. Unlike Nicolò's frescoes, Dosso's illustrated only one episode of each book. In fact, Nicolò's resolution of how to illustrate the complex iconography of the epic poem was to situate the story in a place, like the poet's own method. Both Nicolò and Virgil include landscape; like the poet, the painter uses the land and sea as a structure for him to accommodate the multitude of *Aeneid* episodes.[31] By the manner in which he depicts the scenes, Nicolò transforms the classical themes of the *Aeneid* into chivalric legend. As Matteo Maria Boiardo does in his *Orlando*, Nicolò revives the medieval ideal of the courtier. The ancient funerary games in honor of Anchises from Book 5, located in the middleground of the fresco are, for instance, interpreted by Nicolò as medieval chivalric tournament rather than as a historic recording of the events.

Though comprehensive in nature, Nicolò dell'Abate's *Aeneid* cycle is not all inclusive; certain episodes are omitted and others emphasized. Nicolò excluded almost all episodes that involved extreme emotion such as anger; when violence is shown, as in Book 12 with the death of Turnus, it is interpreted in a detached manner. He also avoided erotic scenes and those that contain omens, magic, prophecy, and metamorphosis, while stressing those favoring virtuous qualities.

The episodes included from each book suggest that either Nicolò dell'Abate, Giulio Boiardo, or Corrado was familiar with Cristoforo Landino's commentary on the *Aeneid* (published in 1480) and Leonbattista Alberti's *Della Famiglia* (published about 1450). According to Landino's Christian, Neoplatonic assessment, the *Aeneid* could be understood as a paradigm for the praise of virtue and condemnation of vice; it was seen as a handbook of moral philosophy—the emphasis of Nicolò's cycle, which consistently includes those episodes that exemplify virtuous acts while surpressing those that carried themes of vice.[32] Further, Alberti's treatise

---

lished in Venice in 1537, to Giulio Boiardo. He also tutored Boiardo's children and was characterized as "un grammatico e profondo conoscitore di Virgilio, Cicerone e Valerio Massimo."

[31] The classical model for the division of poetry into twelve parts established by Virgil in literature was employed by Nicolò perhaps at the suggestion of Corrado. Rombaldi et al., *La Rocca Nuova*, 104; Langmuir, "Arma Virumque," 157.

[32] Craig Kallendorff, "Cristoforo Landino's *Aeneid* and the Humanist Critical Tradition," *Renaissance Quarterly* 36 (1983): 519–46. Since this is a common reading of the

outlines for his "good prince" such virtues as "honorable ways, courteous and praiseworthy relationships among citizens, steadfast deeds, faith and diligence." Thus, like the scenes from the *Aeneid* in the Camerino, Alberti's text stresses honor and virtue, while condemning vice.[33] Boiardo manipulates both text and image as a strategy to recoup his image.

Above the *Aeneid* cycle are the lunettes that are generally seen as illustrations of court life showing a falcon hunt, duck hunting, a fair, a naval scene, and so on. In general, the lunettes reflect an idyllic arcadian setting suggesting, perhaps, Virgil's *Eclogues* or Matteo Maria Boiardo's imitation, the *Pastoralia*.[34] Landscape, as far back as classical antiquity, was associated with ideas of refreshment of the soul and escape from the world, an idea closely related to the function of the studiolo. Thus, the room offered a relief from serious business, intellectual delight, and distraction from the world through music, literature and art—all three present in Giulio's Camerino.[35] Moreover, the range of subjects included in the lunettes resembles the list drawn up by Alberti for villa decoration: "We are particularly delighted when we see paintings of pleasant landscapes, of harbors, scenes of fishing, hunting, bathing, of country games and flowers and leafy views."[36] Alberti stresses the pleasing and restorative effects of landscape, and the importance of variety, while also emphasizing that different types of landscape are appropriate to the differ-

---

Aeneid, Corrado may have referred to an early commentator such as Fulgentius or Silvestris. See Kallendorff's *In Praise of Aeneas: Virgil and Epideictic Rhetoric in Early Renaissance Italy*, (Hanover: Univ. Press of New England, 1989) and Bettie Forte, "Vergil's Aeneid in Literature and Art in the Italian Renaissance," *Vergilius* 28 (1982).

[33] Leonbattista Alberti, *Opere volgare: i libri della famiglia*, ed. Cecil Grayson (Bari: Giuseppe Laterza e Figli, 1960), 1: 198–201.

[34] Early scholarship on the lunettes, such as Walter Bombe's article, suggested that the lunettes depicted scenes from the life of Matteo Maria Boiardo, "Gli Affreschi," 529–53. This has been refuted by Erika Langmuir, "Arma Virumque," 152, 155–56. The lunettes, whose range of subjects lacks an easily identifiable theme, depict modern, contemporary life. Charles Ross has suggested in private correspondence that since the lunettes relate to Virgil's *Eclogues*, the "*Aeneid* represents epic achievement" of Matteo Maria. According to Ross, "All editions of Virgil included the lines about trading the oaten reed for trumpet stern, a model of the poet's career: pastoral to epic." The lunettes, then, "might suggest the necessity of pastoral, that Boiardo could write the great epic romance because he lived the pastoral life, an interesting and novel reading of one's cultured ancestor." Equally provocative to me, if we recall the scenes from the *Orlando* in the courtyard below, is Giulio's apparent need to associate himself with his more illustrious cousin.

[35] Holberton, "The Choice of Texts," 57–60.

[36] Rykwert et al., *On the Art of Building*, 299.

ent temperaments of the viewer. Recall, here too, the location of the Camerino on the second floor of the Rocca Nuova overlooking a garden; once again Giulio followed Alberti's ideal.[37] The lunettes, then, blend the arcadia of the past with contemporary perscriptives for an idyllic villa setting.

One lunette shows a figure standing in a landscape, often identified as Matteo Maria Boiardo writing his *Orlando*. Another hypothesis suggests he is Nicolò dell'Abate sketching the various castelli of the Boiardi. Indeed, in a number of the lunettes, the cityscapes and background castelli may reflect Boiardi property.[38] In one lunette, for example, where a woman points to a castello on a hill, the structure may represent Casalgrande, which overlooked Scandiano. The representation of various castelli could illustrate the uniting of the once-divided holdings of the Boiardi under Giulio's rule—a sort of golden age. The lunettes, then, are depictions of modern life as distinct from the antiquity portrayed in the monochromes and the *Aeneid* cycle. The lunettes, often seen as paying homage to Matteo Maria Boiardo, more likely emphasize the activities of the ideal courtier, the possessions of the Boiardi, and the idyllic restorative nature of landscape settings—a panorama of modern court life and culture.

Above the landscape lunettes, the female all'antica figures in the pendentives, known only through engravings, directed the viewer to the octagon in the ceiling; the top edge of each pendentive corresponded to each side of the octagon where twelve figures are shown outlined against the sky and clouds, leaning on a balustrade singing, playing musical instruments, or listening. A freize of stylized leaves and large pods decorated the border of the octagon. The couple formed by the man with the white-plumed hat and the woman in the large-sleeved dress may be Giulio Boiardo and Silvia Sanvitale. The remaining figures are traditionally identified as other members of the family, a mix of generations that may include the poet Matteo Maria Boiardo, Giulio's brother Giambattista, and Silvia's mother Laura Pallavicina, who was living at Scandiano at this time. The court musician and composer Jugdulus Menon and the artist Nicolò dell'Abate may also be depicted.[39]

---

[37] Rykwert et al., *On the Art of Building*, 299.

[38] It is unlikely that this is a portrait of anyone in particular; see note 28 above. For illustrations of the lunettes, see Rombaldi et al., *La Rocca Nuova*.

[39] Venturi, *Storia di Scandiano*, 100–3; Langmuir, "Arma Virumque," 156–58; Beguin, *Mostra di Nicolò dell'Abate*, 55–56; and Rombaldi et al., *La Rocca Nuova*, 114–17, all discuss the various identifications of those depicted in the octagon. Girolamo Tira-

Looking more closely at the octagon, it is of interest to note that Silvia and Giulio smile down on those who enter the room, inviting the viewer to come forward and become an active participant in the activities that will soon take place there. This interaction between viewer and painted image is not unlike Garofalo's figures in his ceiling fresco (1520s) in the Palazzo Costabili in Ferrara, who seem to wait for a cue from below before taking up their instruments to begin their performance.[40] Moreover, like Garofalo's ceiling or like Mantegna's frescoes in Camera Picta (1460s) in the Palazzo Ducale in Mantua, the overall fresco program of the Camerino should be read as a part of court ritual and rhetoric.[41] The visual display of frescoes in the Camerino, then, with their blending of medieval chivalry and ancient epic, are again manipulated to express Giulio's sense of his self-worth.

On another level, the imagery of the Camerino is more complex than a simple reading of it as an illustration of the mythic origins of the Modenese region allows. The *Aeneid* cycle, the lunettes, and the ceiling octagon are particularly significant for the creation of Giulio Boiardo's self-image, while the monochromes and pendentive figures serve a purely decorative function. Recalling the manner in which the *Aeneid* scenes are depicted, it becomes apparent that the cycle is meant to suggest, by analogy, Giulio's own moral virtue and to support his right to rule Scandiano—both controversial issues. The spectre of Matteo Maria seems to loom over Giulio Boiardo. Indeed, Giulio, who appears in the ceiling octagon with Silvia Sanvitale and their court, is shown through the imagery of the Camerino to be a man of nobility and honor who is gracious, gallant, and courteous like his more illustrious ancestors Feltrino and Matteo Maria Boiardo. What Matteo Maria creates in words in his epic poem, and is visible in the Cortilie d'Onore below, Giulio has his painter Nicolò dell' Abate create in pictures—a world that combines medieval chivalry and

---

boschi in his *Biblioteca Modenese* (Modena, 1781, vol. 1), 300, identifies the figures in the octagon as Matteo Maria Boiardo's family. Only the figures of Giulio Boairdo and Silvia Sanvitale are universally identified as such.

[40] For an illustration of the Costabili ceiling, see my article, "Vedere la Musica: Depictions of Music Making in the Sixteenth-Century Italian Villa," *RIdIM Newsletter* 17 (fall 1992): 4, #1.

[41] Mantegna's oculus has been connected to courtly games evoking a sense of jest and humor in an otherwise serious environment; see Randolph Starn and Loren Partridge, *Arts of Power: Three Halls of State in Italy, 1300–1600* (Berkeley and Los Angeles: Univ. of California Press, 1992), 118. Perhaps, Nicolò's octagon should be seen more in this light.

classical epic with contemporary life. Giulio is not simply paying homage
to his ancestors and tracing his ancient and noble lineage, he is making a
statement about his own individualism and, at the same time, validating,
through ancestral connections, his right to rule Scandiano. As Leonbattista Alberti suggests, through the appropriate decoration a man can bring
honor to himself, his family, and his city.[42]

As we move from the public space of the Cortile d'Onore with its clear
declaration of lineage and power (the "stemmi" and Matteo Maria's *Orlando*) to the private and more intimate space of the Camerino, the message
becomes personal. While the Cortile introduces the Boiardo family and
links Giulio to his famous cousin, the *Aeneid* cycle in the Camerino connects Giulio first to his ancient ancestors and, by analogy, to his more
contemporary relative Feltrino Boiardo, first count of Scandiano. Secondly, Giulio links himself to Matteo Maria whose *Orlando*, with its references to the *Aeneid* and to the Este court, parallels in conception the epic
nature and comprehensiveness of the Camerino decoration. Through his
sophisticated literary program Giulio validates both his courtly status and
his individuality. Moreover, through the Camerino frescoes, Giulio presented himself as an intellectual equal of Feltrino and Matteo Maria
Boiardo. Indeed, Giulio Boiardo totally manipulated his environment to
create a programmatic statement about his own image and his place in the
world.

---

[42] Rykwert et al., *On the Art of Building,* 292–93.

Boiardo Family Lineage Chart

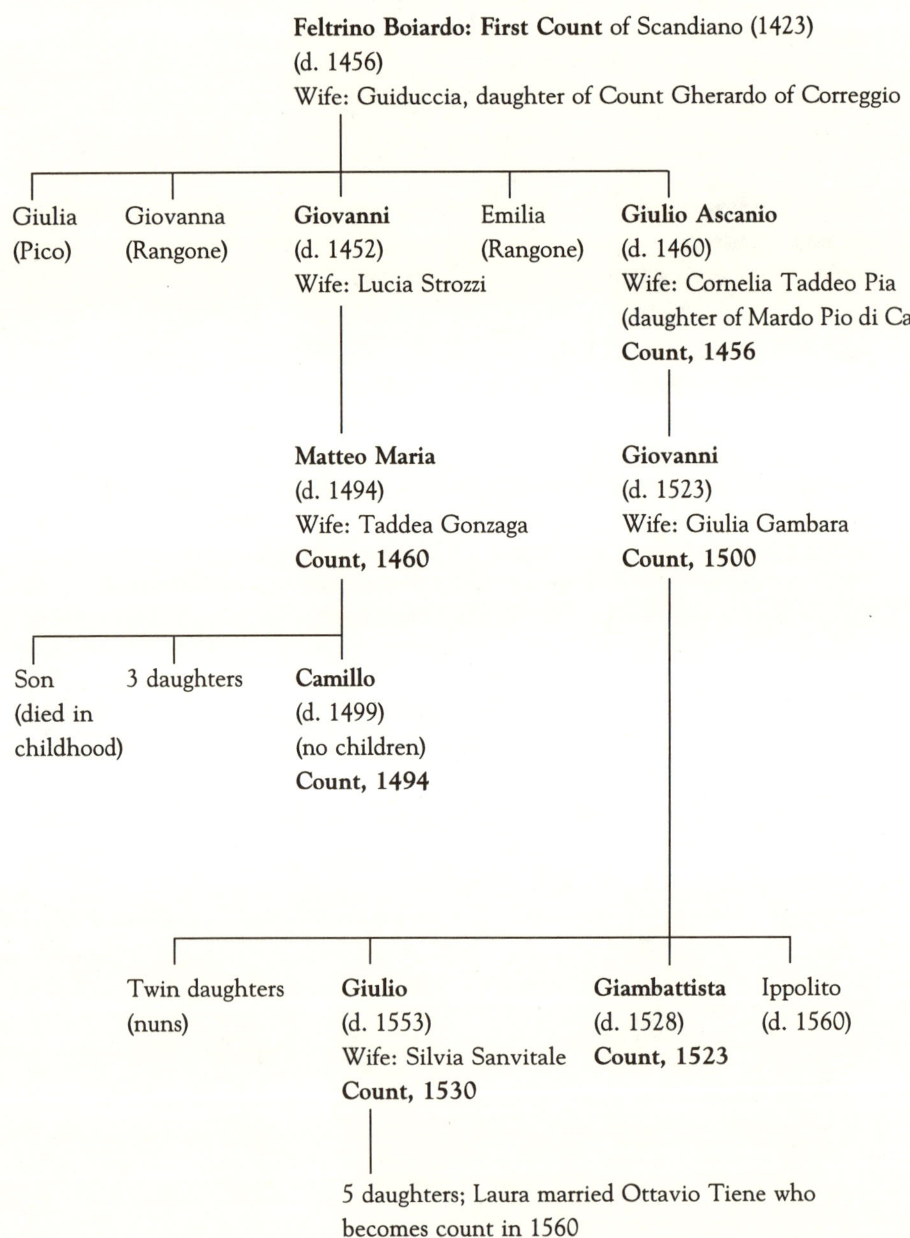

LEEMAN L. PERKINS

Musical Culture in Late Quattrocento Ferrara: Local Traditions and Foreign Influences

For Lewis Lockwood, Colleague and Friend

DURING THE RELATIVELY LONG AND PROSPEROUS reign of Duke Ercole I, the Ferrarese court became a musical center of international renown. Paradoxically, although Boiardo was at the time a significant figure among the duke's familiars, the historical significance of this rather extraordinary state of affairs would not necessarily be evident to one who viewed fifteenth-century Ferrarese culture primarily through the lens of the Scandianese's poetry. Unlike some other poets of the period, his verse was rarely set by composers of either the fifteenth or the sixteenth centuries.[1] What is more, Boiardo's references to music-making in *Orlando Innamorato* are relatively few in number, given the length of the poem, and are all quite conventional in nature. They invariably reflect the customary uses for music in courtly society during the Middle Ages, often much as they are described by earlier French romances[2]: trumpets, drums, and bells for ostentatious ceremony but also for jousts, wars, and alarms; instrumental music and songs for dancing; and songs for entertainment and leisure.[3] As

---

[1] Alfred Einstein, *The Italian Madrigal* (Princeton: Princeton Univ. Press, 1949), I: 426–28.

[2] For a detailed study of the uses of music portrayed in the fifteenth-century French romance *Cleriadus et Meliadice*, see Christopher Page, "The Performance of Songs in Late Medieval France, A New Source," *Early Music* 10 (1982): 9–21.

[3] See Appendix I: References to Music in Boiardo's *Orlando Innamorato*.

we shall see, these traditions continued to be very much in evidence still at the Ferrarese court of Ercole I.

With respect to music, however, despite the evident excellence of the ducal chapel—or perhaps because of it—there is a good deal more to say about foreign influences than local traditions. Although it is apparently possible to draw parallels between Boiardo's poem and its French antecedents, the literary tradition of fifteenth-century Italy at that point was surely much more autonomous than the musical one. In fact, if one were to assess Ferrarese culture solely on the basis of its music, the result would surely give greater comfort to those who would claim with Nordström that "in all that concerned higher culture as a whole, ["renaissance" Italy] long remained a French province,"[4] than to those who believe, with Burckhardt, in the uniqueness and originality of the contributions of the men and women of the rinascimento in laying the cultural foundations for the modern world.

As is widely recognized, at the turn of the fifteenth century music was in a uniquely anomalous situation on the Italian peninsula. Its cultivation there stood in sharp contrast to the stunning display of native talent and skill in literature, architecture, and the visual arts. Moreover, music as a sounding art could offer no parallels to the achievements of Greek and Roman antiquity in other areas capable of drawing it into the growing enthusiasm for classical culture. Unlike buildings, paintings, sculpture, poetry, or even prose, surviving examples of which could be studied first hand and eventually taken as models, no music survived in a retrievable written form from any earlier than the eleventh or twelfth centuries—the very period so often referred to by the writers of that and later times as the *intervallum* or *lacuna* between the glory that had been and the *fons et origo* of the recently perceived rebirth of culture.[5]

All that was then known about the music of ancient civilization came from one of two sources. There were, on the one hand, the scattered remnants of a highly developed theoretical system, the cosmologically inspired

---

[4] The assertion, as cited by Wallace K. Ferguson, *The Renaissance in Historical Thought* (Cambridge, MA: The Riverside Press, 1948), 379, is from the study by J. Nordström, *Moyen Age et Renaissance, essai historique* (Paris, 1933).

[5] Concerning the use of these terms and their eventual application to music by authors of the fifteenth and sixteenth centuries, see Leo Schrade, "Renaissance: The Historical Conception of an Epoch," *Kongressbericht der Internationale Gesellschaft für Musikwissenschaft Utrecht, 1952*; reprinted in *Twentieth-Century Views of Music History*, ed. by William Hays (New York: Charles Scribner's Sons, 1972), 114–25.

writings of the Greek "harmonists," which were very difficult to relate to the musical practice of the fifteenth century; and on the other, mythical tales of the miraculous effects that had once been achieved by skilled performers such as Apollo, Orpheus, Amphion, and even the shadowy Pythagoras. In neither case did the surviving lore have much to do with the uses of music in the households of the upper nobility, such as the Este family in Ferrara. Those customs reflected much more clearly the traditions of medieval courtly society, especially as they were exemplified by the customs and style of long-established royal houses.

The performing musicians most indispensable to the reputation of these noble patrons were the trumpeters. Their function was to advertise the presence of their lord visually by their livery and the devices sometimes displayed on banners hung from their instruments, and sonorously with fanfares used to announce his arrival at the gate of a town or castle, his presence on the field of battle, or his entry into the lists of a joust.[6] Given their role (and by analogy the bugler of a "modern" army), it is unlikely that many of them were musically literate; their instrumental skills, however, consummate, were apparently learned without benefit of notation, and, so far as we know, their repertory was solely monophonic.[7]

During moments of leisure in hall or chambers, both singers and players could be called upon to provide entertainment. For small groups in relatively intimate surroundings, recreation or amusement often involved the use of soft-sounding instruments,[8] including harps, lutes, flutes, bowed strings, and the human voice. These were usually heard one at a time, but by the fourteenth century one can at times assume polyphonic combinations as well.[9] In such circumstances voice and soft instruments were also used occasionally to accompany dancing.[10] Loud winds such as shawms (loud double-reeds, distant ancestors to the oboe) and slide trum-

---

[6] See, for example, Edward H. Tarr, "Trumpet," *The New Grove Dictionary of Musical Instruments* (London: Macmillan, 1984), 3: 641–53.

[7] For the contexts in which trumpets are sounded in Boiardo's poem, see below, Appendix I: References to Music in Boiardo's *Orlando Innamorato*, A. Conventional Uses for Trumpets, Drums, and Bells.

[8] During the Middle Ages, the primary distinction made in the classification of musical instruments was between those of loud and soft sonorities, termed *haut* and *bas* by the French.

[9] For passages in Boiardo's poem in which singing and playing have a recreational role, see Appendix I: B. Singing and Playing as Social Recreation.

[10] For passages in Boiardo's poem in which singing or playing of soft instruments accompanies dancing, see Appendix I: C.1. Dancing to Songs and Soft Instruments.

pets (ancestors to the trombone) made music for dancing in larger spaces for more numerous assemblies.[11] The wind players were often heard in a characteristic ensemble that is sometimes pictured on a balcony above a great hall filled with feasting or dancing nobles. Such a band usually consisted of three shawms, but a slide trumpet sometimes replaced a shawm on the lowest bass part. Unlike the trumpeters, all of these musicians were probably expected to be conversant with the notation of the period and capable of holding their own in the performance of complex polyphonic music.

At the wealthiest and most opulent of courts, most notably those of a powerful duke or king, a group of clerics and singers served the chapel where the ruler and his familiars usually observed privately—if ostentatiously—the rites of the Christian liturgy.[12] Traditionally, the musical portions of these services were sung to the plainchant that had been codified over the centuries by the medieval church. Increasingly in the fifteenth and sixteenth centuries, however, special religious feasts and noteworthy occasions in the life of the court were given added luster by presenting in brilliant polyphonic settings central elements of the liturgy: the Ordinary chants of the mass (in particular), the Vesper hymns, the Magnificat, processional antiphons, and devotional and celebratory verse. In such instances, the cleric-musicians of the chapel had to be able to perform such works, and those who were most appreciated (and most generously rewarded) were also capable of composing them.

Music at the Este court had long been organized according to this pattern when Ercole I came to power in 1471. As early as 1445 Leonello had in his employ at least one trumpet, two *piffari*, the famed lutenist Pietrobono, and nine cleric-singers for his chapel. What is more, the number of musicians in each of these categories increased steadily until the end of his rule in 1450.[13] Significantly, in the light of subsequent developments in the musical institutions of the court, it was said of Ercole that, "in order that the fame of his deeds should shine forth clearly . . . he built a chapel . . . in a royal manner," which he "embellished . . . most honorably and sumptuously with furnishings, books, and gold reliefs," and that

---

[11] For passages in Boiardo's poem in which loud instruments accompany dancing, see Appendix I: C.2. Dancing to Loud Instruments.

[12] There is no direct mention in Boiardo's poem of music in a liturgical context.

[13] See the chronological list of musicians named in the archives of the Este court as given by Lewis Lockwood, *Music in Renaissance Ferrara 1400–1505: The Creation of a Musical Center in the Fifteenth Century* (Cambridge: Harvard Univ. Press, 1984), 316–17.

"he ordered singers to be brought from France, who celebrated the divine service marvelously with very sweet harmony."[14] I shall return presently to the surprising matter of importing chapel singers from the north.

Borso d'Este, upon his accession as Marquis of Ferrara, chose to dissolve the chapel choir, apparently preferring to leave the liturgical needs of the court to the clergy and musicians of the local cathedral. By contrast, he maintained an even larger group of secular musicians. In 1462, for example, his payment rolls show a total of fifteen: five trumpets, three *piffari*, a trombone, a singer, the lutenist Pietrobono, a keyboard player, and three others whose function is not specified.[15]

Under Ercole I, therefore, it is not so much the constitution of the musical establishment of the court that strikes the observer as it is the scope it assumed and the rapidity with which it was organized (see Table 1). As the first full year of his reign as duke of Ferrara came to a close, Ercole already had in his service eight trumpeters, five players of soft instruments (some of whom were singers as well), five shawm players or *piffari*, and seventeen cleric-singers. Significantly, moreover, in the years that follow (at least for which the payment records appear to be reasonably complete) the musical forces of the court were seldom fewer in number.

In 1474, and again in 1481 and 1482 when Ferrara was on the eve of war with Venice, only four trumpets were listed, but in other years there were as many as twelve or thirteen. Similarly, except for 1482 and 1483, when the two states were actually engaged in the conflict, there were as few as five other instrumental and chamber musicians only in 1473 and in 1490. Most of the time there were at least seven, often there were as many as fifteen or sixteen; of these at least three or four, and at times six and seven, are designated *piffero* or *trombone*.[16] When hostilities broke out with the Serene Republic, the duke's trumpeters were probably assimilated into his armies (and thus, perhaps, paid as soldiers rather than as musicians). As for the chamber musicians, it seems unlikely that all of them would have been dismissed, even though their names do not appear in the

---

[14] J. Ferrariensis, *Excerpta ex Annalium Libris* (before 1556), 32, as quoted and translated by Lockwood, *Music in Renaissance Ferrara*, 44–45.

[15] See the chronological list of musicians named in the archives of the Este court in Lockwood, *Music in Renaissance Ferrara*, 317–18.

[16] These figures have been extracted from the yearly lists summarized by Lockwood, *Music in Renaissance Ferrara*, Appendix V, 318–28.

Table 1. Musicians in the Employ of the Este Court, 1472[17]

Trumpeters:
Andrea trombeta
Bazo d'Arezzo trombeta
Daniele trombeta
Guasparo [de alemagna] trombeta
Luzido [de Norsa] trombeta
Marco d'Arezzo trombeta
Raganello trombeta
Zilio trombeta

Chamber Musicians ("musici," "piffari," and "tromboni"):
Pietrobono dal Chitarino
Francesco Malacise [suo] tenorista
Jacomo dell'arpa sonadore
Andrea della Viola
Zampaulo della Viola

Stefano da Savoia piffaro
Corrado d'Alemagne piffaro
Zanino de Polo da Venezia piffaro
Zoanna d'Alemagna piffaro
Piedro de Augustino trombone

Chapel Musicians:
Andrea da Mantova cantore tenorista
Carles
Costantino Tantino [maestro de fare organi in Modena]
Domenico contrabasso
Girolamo [da Ferrara] soprano
Jaches cantore
Jacheto chievre [de Cambrai?]
Jacheto contratenore
Jacheto de Nemport cantore
Marino cappellano
Nicolo d'Olanda
Piedre [de Nantes de Bretagna, soprano?]
Udorigo tenorista
Zoanne Brebis
Zoanne Gon maestro de' putti
Zoanne Polster
Zorzo Prando

---

payment records of the court during this period.

In the surviving roles of Ercole's chapel musicians, the specifications of a part or voice range for a number of them indicates clearly that, like the singers in Leonello's chapel, they were trained in the performance of mensural polyphony. During the decade preceding the war they numbered between nineteen (in 1479) and thirty-four (in 1474).[18] However, the evidence suggests that the chapel choir had to be temporarily disbanded soon after the war was declared. There is no trace of them in court accounts in either 1482 or 1483, and when, in the following year, cleric-singers figure once again on the ducal payroll, they number only nine. Thereafter, by contrast, there are never fewer than thirteen, and most of the time they are between nineteen and twenty-two strong—an unusually large choir for the period. Surprisingly, as many as thirty-five or thirty-six are occasionally listed in the accounts (e.g., 1499 and 1504, the year before Ercole's death). During the final two decades of Ercole's rule, his chapel was served by twenty-four or more musicians in at least eight years.[19]

Who were the musicians drawn to Ercole's service? What were their regions of origin, and where were they trained? To begin, it is striking to see the number of wind players qualified in court documents as *d'Alemagna*. Naturally, some caution is called for in interpreting the meaning of that term; in the pay records of the court it could apparently point to any of the northern regions then considered part of the Holy Roman Empire, including the Low Countries and Switzerland. Still, both the players and the makers of wind instruments in German-speaking cities were reputed to be among the best in the world, and trumpeters and shawm and trombone players continued to be identified in payment records by their transalpine origins until the end of Ercole's reign.

The chamber musicians, by contrast, seem to have been for the most part natives of the Italian peninsula, and a number of them were in fact from local families. The della Violas were part of a dynasty of Ferrarese musicians who served various members of the Este household from the 1460s (at the latest) until well into the sixteenth century. And the famous lutenist and singer, Pietrobono dal Chitarino (ca. 1417–97), who served

---

[18] In 1473–74, Ercole apparently experimented with a double choir in which boy choristers were an important component. Fourteen singers are labeled *garzoni todeschi* in the accounts for the first of these two years, and ten in those for the second, after which they disappear from the surviving records. See Lockwood, *Music in Renaissance Ferrara*, 157–58, 319.

[19] Lockwood, *Music in Renaissance Ferrara*, 318–28.

Borso d'Este not only as a musician but also as *barbiere* and is first mentioned in court payment records as early as 1441, was almost certainly a native son of Ferrara.[20] I shall return presently to his contribution to music-making at the Este court and to the more general implications of that activity for the development of an indigenous repertory of solo song in the Italian vernacular.

The chapel singers were recruited from the outset from musical centers north of the Alps, in particular France, Flanders, and the Low Countries, and in most years these northern imports constituted as a body the majority of the choir. This was probably in large measure because the cathedrals and collegiate churches in the areas mentioned were remarkably successful in producing musicians skilled in the performance and composition of polyphony, whereas in Italy training of that kind seems to have been the exception rather than the rule. Nonetheless, Ercole was always able to include among his chapel singers a respectable number of cis-alpine musicians: four in 1472, when the choir was organized, and usually between eight and eleven through the remainder of the century—excepting, of course, the early 1480s when Ferrara was at war with Venice.[21]

More significant than the regional origins of the singers, however, both for the repertory available to the choir and for its reputation abroad, were the composers included among its members. Without exception, these were from northern centers. The first cited in court accounts is Johannes Brebis, whom they identify as *Franza cantadore*. He was in Ercole's employ already in 1471, when the chapel choir was first being formed, and he served, at times as *maestro di cappella*, until his death in 1479. By fifteenth-century standards his known works are relatively few in number and limited as to genre. There is on the one hand a motet in praise of Ercole, a very competent piece of polyphony written perhaps to celebrate Ercole's accession as duke (or one of the first anniversaries of that event), and on the other an indeterminate number of much simpler hymn, psalm, and Magnificat settings for Vespers of Lent and Matins of Holy Week. Many of the latter were copied into a pair of manuscripts intended for use in the ducal chapel that constitute the first sizeable collection of polyphony for double chorus now known (see Table 2: MSS. Alpha M.1.11 and 12).[22]

More prolific, perhaps, and certainly better represented in the sources

---

[20] Lockwood, *Music in Renaissance Ferrara*, 98–108.

[21] Lockwood, *Music in Renaissance Ferrara*, 98–108.

[22] Concerning Brebis, see Lockwood, *Music in Renaissance Ferrara*, 161f, 250–57.

of the period was Johannes Martini, originally from Brabant, who is consistently referred to in court documents as *cantadore compositore*. He may have come to Ferrara from Constance and joined the ducal chapel as early as January 1473.[23] Except for a hiatus of ten months spent in the chapel of Duke Galeazzo Maria Sforza of Milan in 1474, Martini served at the Ferrarese court until his death in 1497. During that time he played a leading role in the ducal chapel, directing its activities as *maestro di cappella*, recruiting singers, and compiling and composing repertory for the choirbooks that were copied for its use. He may even have taught music to Ercole's children, most notably Isabella d'Este, whose skills as a performer and seminal role as a patron of music are widely known.

Martini's share of the music performed at court—a good deal of which was inscribed in collections compiled for the use of the its musicians—includes both sacred and secular pieces. He collaborated with Brebis in composing the large repertory for double chorus mentioned earlier (see Table 2: MSS. Alpha M.1.11 and 12). In addition, at least seven of the eighteen cyclical Ordinaries constituting the most extensive collection of polyphonic music for the liturgy of the mass known to have been copied for use in the ducal chapel have likewise been attributed to Martini, and others among the five anonymous works may also be his (see Table 2: MS. Alpha M.1.13). This would suggest that the majority of the ten or eleven masses ascribable to Martini in the surviving sources were either written expressly for Ercole's choir or were at some point included in its repertory.

The composer's name is also found with a modest number—seven—of motets. None of them was included in the choirbooks copied for the court during the fifteenth century, but one, *Perfunde coeli rore*, celebrates the wedding of Ercole to Eleanora of Aragon in 1473. Another, a setting of the *Salve regina,* is constructed over chant melodies that make of it a fervent prayer for peace; it may have been prompted by the cruel war with Venice in 1482–84. A third, *O beate Sebastiane,* is a plea for protection against the plague and may have been occasioned by any of several serious outbreaks of the disease in the 1480s.[24]

Turning to secular repertory, Martini is the best represented among the composers whose works were included in the handsome collection of pieces

---

[23] A Giovanni d'Alemagna, whose appointment to the chapel choir is dated January 27, 1473, is thought to be Martini; concerning the composer's contributions to the musical life of the Ferrarese court, see Lockwood, *Music in Renaissance Ferrara*, 167–72.

[24] Lockwood, *Music in Renaissance Ferrara*, 258.

Table 2. Musical Sources Compiled for the Este Court, 1479–1505[25]

Modena, Biblioteca Estense

MS. Alpha M.1.11 (Lat. 454), 1479–81. Contents: polyphonic psalm, hymn, and Magnificat settings by Johannes Martini and Johannes Brebis (odd-numbered verses); music for Vespers during Lent and Matins of Holy Week.

MS. Alpha M.1.12 (Lat. 455), 1479–81. Contents: complement to M.1.11 (with even-numbered verses) for use with double chorus; also portions of two settings of the Passion.

MS. Alpha M.1.13, 1481. Contents: eighteen polyphonic Mass Ordinaries, all but one without attribution in the source; composers identified by concordances include Johannes Martini (seven), Guillaume Faugues (two), Johannes Vincenet (one), Petrus de Domarto (one), Caron (one), Guillaume Dufay (one), and Gaspar van Weerbecke (one); five remain anonymous.

MS. M.1.2, 1504–5. Contents: ten polyphonic masses with attributions to Jacob Obrecht (five), Josquin (two), Okeghem (one); two others may also be by Obrecht.

Modena, Archivio di Stato

Frammenti musicali, 1481. Contents: incomplete segments of the Agnus Dei from masses by Antoine Busnois (*Missa L'homme armé*) and Alexander Agricola (*Missa Je ne demande*); these fragments were once part of a large collection of masses like MS. Alpha M.1.13.

Rome, Biblioteca Casanatense

MS. 2856, 1479–81. Contents: repertory of 123 secular pieces for three and four parts; most of them are chansons without text; composers include Martini (twenty-three), Agricola (nineteen), Busnoys (eleven), Hayne van Ghizeghem (nine), Loyset Compère (six), Johannes Okeghem (five), Josquin Desprez (four), and eighteen other, mostly northern, composers.

---

[25] Lockwood, *Music in Renaissance Ferrara*, 217.

identified in a 1495 inventory of the ducal library as *cantiones a la pifarescha*. This singular expression is apparently a reference to the fact that all the songs in this repertory (ninety-eight on French, nine on Italian, five on Dutch, and one on macaronic verses) have been copied without their text and were in fact intended for the use of instrumentalists (see Table 2: MS. 2856 of the Biblioteca Casanatense in Rome).[26] Of the 123 compositions copied into the manuscript, twenty-three are ascribed unequivocally to Ercole's chief musician. (He is also named for two others with conflicting attributions.)

Other composers of greater or lesser stature were associated with Ercole's chapel for much shorter periods of time, but his crowning achievement in recruiting composers undoubtedly came shortly after the turn of the century when he was able to attract to the Ferrarese court two masters of international reputation, both of them born and trained in the North. The first of these was Josquin Desprez, clearly the most admired composer of his day. Then came Jacob Obrecht, whose reputation very nearly equaled that of the older man.

Josquin was apparently a native of Picardy who may have received his initial musical instruction as a choirboy at the collegiate church of St. Quentin. He arrived in Ferrara in April 1503 to assume the duties of *maestro di cappella* but left about a year later for Condé-sur-l'Escaut where he was installed as the provost of the chapter of the collegiate church of Notre Dame. He may have been seeking the latter position for some time, for he lived out the remainder of his life in Condé. He was replaced in Ferrara by Obrecht, who had been chapelmaster in a series of northern cities, including Bergen-op-Zoom (his family home), Bruges, and Antwerp. He reached Ferrara in the late summer of 1504, but unfortunately fell victim to the plague in February 1505, shortly after Ercole's own demise.[27]

As Lockwood has observed, the chapel singers were generally paid considerably less well than either the trumpeters or, in particular, the wind players—the only notable exceptions being composers of the extraordinary stature of a Josquin or an Obrecht. Even a musician as central to the musical life of the court as Johannes Martini was paid less than a squire to a

---

[26] Concerning Martini's compositions, see Lockwood, *Music in Renaissance Ferrara*, 167–72, 233–40; cf. Lockwood, *The New Grove Dictionary of Music*, 11: 726–27.

[27] Lockwood, *Music in Renaissance Ferrara*, 210. Concerning Obrecht, see the comprehensive new study by Rob C. Wegman, *Born for the Muses: The Life and Masses of Jacob Obrecht* (Oxford: Clarendon Press, 1994).

man of arms and only slightly more than half of what was paid a crossbow-man.[28] Nevertheless, the recruitment of twenty to thirty cleric-musicians skilled in the performance (and composition) of polyphony was a very con-siderable enterprise; the duke's correspondence is filled with references to searches and negotiations for musicians capable of enhancing the quality—and the reputation—of his musical establishment.

Moreover, in practical terms the maintenance of a small army of trum-peters, instrumentalists, and singers was a considerable drain on Ercole's fi-nancial resources. In 1476, for example, he spent approximately 2,680 lire on his *trombeti, musici, piffari,* and *tromboni,* and about another 4,070 for his chapel musicians, for a total of nearly 6,750 lire. That sum represents 5.8 percent of his total expenditures if one includes the sums paid out to members of his family. And if these domestic subventions are set aside, he spent nearly ten percent of his income on the music of the court in that particular year.[29]

Why did Ercole take such trouble and go to such great expense for the music of his court? A clue as to his intentions may be gleaned from a com-ment included in a letter written on August 14, 1502, by Girolamo da Se-stola, more familiarly known as Coglia, musician and man about the court who, among other things, often acted as the duke's agent in procuring music and musicians for the chapel. Coglia had been recruiting singers, and he urged the duke to engage Josquin to head up the chapel choir. His argument is a compelling one:

> My Lord, I believe that there is neither lord nor king who will now have a better chapel than yours if Your Lordship sends for Josquin. Don Alfonso [d'Este] wishes to write this to your Lordship and so does the entire chapel; and by having Josquin in our chapel I want to place a crown upon this chapel of ours.

Such a comment implies a conscious decision on Ercole's part to pur-sue in this, as in other areas, what might be termed the politics of ostenta-tious display, a strategy by which the most powerful and firmly seated courts of western Europe attempted to establish in the minds of all—sub-jects, allies, and enemies alike—the legitimacy of hereditary claims to the

---

²⁸ Lockwood, *Music in Renaissance Ferrara,* 179–84.

²⁹ The calculations were made by William F. Prizer, "North Italians Courts, 1460–1540," *The Renaissance from the 1470s to the End of the 16th Century,* ed. Iain Fenlon (Englewood Cliffs, NJ: Prentice Hall, 1989), 136.

right to rule. In such a context the maintenance of an impressive roster of musicians in all three of the conventional categories—trumpeters, singers and instrumentalists for secular entertainments, and cleric-singers for the chapel choir—can be seen as yet another manifestation of a culture deeply rooted in medieval tradition. In this sense, the music of the court functions in a manner analogous to other forms of public spectacle and artistic patronage deployed by ruling nobles to demonstrate their magnificence.

As Roy Strong has suggested, magnificence came to be viewed as a virtue by Renaissance rulers generally. They seem to have taken to heart Aristotle's assertion, that,

> great expenditure is becoming to those who have suitable means
> . . . acquired by their own efforts or from ancestors or connections,
> and to people of high birth and reputation . . . for all these things
> bring with them greatness and prestige.[30]

For Ercole, "all these things" appear to have included, in addition to the patronage of art and music, appropriate demonstrations of religious piety, the building and decoration of churches and sumptuous palaces, the organization of splendid processions and "royal" entries, the sponsorship of tournaments and jousts, and the presentation of theatrical spectacles. Significant examples of each can be documented during his reign.[31]

That Ercole was familiar with the Aristotelian concept is suggested by the careful definition given magnificence by Giovanni Sabadino degli Arienti in his *De triumphis religionis*, a paean to the Estense glories that was written for and dedicated to the duke.[32] Assuming that this work was prepared in direct response to a ducal commission, or at least with Ercole's knowledge and approval, it can be read as a catalogue of the achievements

---

[30] The passage is from the *Nicomachean Ethics*, as quoted by Roy Strong, *Art and Power, Renaissance Festivals 1450–1650* (Woodbridge and Suffolk: The Boydell Press, 1984), 22.

[31] See Lockwood's discussion of "Music for Court Festivals and Theater," *Music in Renaissance Ferrara*, 278–87; court spectacles of various types are examined with instructive examples by Strong, *Art and Power, passim*.

[32] Sabadino introduces the fifth book of the essay with the following: "Sequitaremo ala narrata tua liberalitate ducale, religiosissimo Principe, Signor mio charo, l'alta virtù dela magnificentia, la quale in ogni cosa con singulare gloria ostendi, perchè pensi non più ala religione che al preclaro sangue convenirsi. La magnificentia dunque considerare si debbe che in cose sumptuose, grande et sublime consiste"; see the edition by Werner L. Gundersheimer, *Art and Life at the Court of Ercole I d'Este* (Geneva: Librairie Droz, 1972), 50.

and activities seen by its author as contributing to his patron's reputation. The importance of elegant buildings beautifully decorated is apparent from Sabadino's detailed description of the Este palaces in and around Ferrara and the wall paintings that graced them. In addition, Sabadino gives careful attention to Ercole's involvement in brilliant public festivals, his assiduous attendance at a regular round of liturgical and devotional exercises, his generous patronage of local religious institutions, and even the establishment of a *cappella di cantori*. The implication, clearly, is that Ercole saw all such matters as essential to the persona of the magnificent prince that he aspired to be.[33]

That the music of the court was viewed in this light is confirmed, in my opinion, by the circumstances in which the ducal chapel was reestablished and the care with which its growing reputation was nurtured. When Ercole came to power in 1471, Borso, who earlier by his generosity had persuaded Emperor Frederick III to bestow on him the title of duke of Modena and Reggio, had just barely succeeded in having Pope Paul II elevate the marquisate of Ferrara to a dukedom.[34] This made it possible, perhaps in a sense even necessary, for Ercole to compete with the duke of Milan, Galeazzo Maria Sforza, his most obvious Italian rival, in displays of the kind capable of enhancing his status with his own subjects and with neighboring polities. Interestingly, nowhere is that cultural emulation more evident than in the recruitment of singers for the respective ducal chapels. Like Ercole, Galeazzo Maria announced his intention to found a *cappella di cantori*—a choir capable of embellishing the liturgical observances of his court with polyphony—in 1471. From that moment on the correspondence of the two magnates shows them vying constantly with one another for the best musicians, and their rivalry ended only with Sforza's assassination in 1476.[35]

The models for both men in their pursuit of magnificence were evidently those courts in which the medieval traditions of kingship had been maintained most continuously. A certain nostalgia for what was perceived as former glories is surely evident in Boiardo's recreation of the medieval romance. For Ercole, the most obvious paradigm was the royal court of

---

[33] The passage in question, found in Gundersheimer's edition, *Art and Life at the Court of Ercole I d'Este*, 89, is quoted and translated by Lockwood, *Music in Renaissance Ferrara*, 158.

[34] Lockwood, *Music in Renaissance Ferrara*, 88.

[35] Prizer, "North Italian Courts, 1460–1540," 138–39.

Naples under the rule of Alfonso V of Aragon, with which he was intimately familiar. He had been sent there to live at the age of fourteen (in 1445) and stayed for eighteen years (until 1463). Ercole's royal host maintained a sizeable musical establishment in the best medieval tradition, including trumpeters, singers and instrumentalists for secular entertainments, and a large chapel choir.[36]

A less immediate but perhaps more powerful example was the royal court of France, with which the Este rulers of Ferrara were traditionally allied. There was, in addition, Duke Philip the Good of Burgundy, self-styled "plus que roi," whose heady dynastic ambitions were reflected in the founding of the Order of the Golden Fleece (ostensibly to organize another crusade to free Jerusalem from the Infidels), the organization of lavish festivals such as the celebrated *banquet du voeu*, and the maintenance of a chapel choir that was the envy of all Europe. It is surely not without significance that the leading composers at both courts—Busnoys for the duke of Burgundy and Okeghem for the king of France—came to be represented in the repertory of the Ferrarese chapel (see Table 2: Modena, Archivio di Stato, Frammenti musicali and MS. M.1.2 of the Biblioteca Estense).

One is inclined to ask, finally, whether or not the musical strategies of Ercole's putative politics of magnificence were a success; was the substantial investment of time and means needed to constitute and maintain such a large and varied musical establishment warranted by the results obtained? In short, to put the question in crass modern terms, did Ercole get value for his money?

If one turns first to the secular musicians, that question is not easily answered. Aside from polyphonic songs, such as those included in the Casanatense MS. 2856, the repertory heard at court was apparently for the most part unwritten. Only exceptionally did some of the dance tunes find their way into surviving written sources, and their song repertory is equally difficult to trace. For even the most celebrated among them, Pietrobono Chitarino, there is not a single notated composition with a secure attribution. Nonetheless, the lutenist's fame was widespread, and praises such as those sung by the poet Antonio Cornazano in his *Sforziade* must also have redounded to the credit of his Ferrarese patron.[37]

---

[36] See Allan W. Atlas, *Music at the Aragonese Court of Naples* (Cambridge: Cambridge Univ. Press, 1985), especially chapter 2, "The Royal Chapel," and chapter 5, "Music for Secular Entertainment."

[37] For the pertinent passage in Italian with a commentary in English, see Nino Pir-

From our present vantage point, moreover, it seems likely that melodic formulae such as Pietrobono must have adopted in singing both lyrical and narrative poems contributed substantially to the development of the *frottola*, a genre of accompanied solo song based on poetry in the Italian vernacular. Such pieces began to circulate in considerable numbers around the turn of the century, especially in the printed collections of the Venetian printer Ottaviano Petrucci. The verse forms used in either case were strophic in nature, including such patterns as *terza* and *ottava rima*. These predictable structures lent themselves readily to musical declamation with a limited number of musical phrases that could be combined in various ways, modified, transformed, and, as remembered, be repeated from stanza to stanza and reused from song to song.[38]

And what of the chapel singers, especially the highly paid composers that Ercole attracted to his court late in his life? Did they contribute anything more to the duke's reputation for magnificence than a repertory of polyphonic masses, such as that contained in the choirbook copied for the choir in 1504-5,[39] a skillful performance of which would likely dazzle visitors to the Este court? Among the works of Josquin at least two were and still are linked with Ercole's name. One of these, a magisterial setting of Psalm 50, *Miserere mei, Deus*, is cited by Teofilo Folengo as having been written at the duke's request.[40] The motet in question is so extraordinary in its conception, so imposing in its length, and so moving in its effect that it has been compared, not without some justification, to Michelangelo's *Last Judgment*.[41] Given the work's reputation at the time, it is indeed striking that its genesis was linked to Ercole's patronage; I know of no other motet of the period for which a similar connection has been so specifically made.

---

rotta, "Music and Cultural Tendencies in Fifteenth-Century Italy," *Music and Culture in Italy from the Middle Ages to the Baroque* (Cambridge: Harvard Univ. Press, 1984), 93–96.

[38] An interesting example of such procedures was offered by the musicians of Ex Umbris during the concert given at Corpus Christi Church on the last day of the Columbia conference (9 Oct. 1994). The melodic-harmonic pattern known as "Ruggiero" was adapted most effectively for the recitation of "The Meeting of Rugiero and Bradamante" from Book 3, Canto 5 of Boiardo's *Orlando Innamorato*; cf. their compact disk, "O Triumphale Diamante": *Music from the Court of Ercole I of Ferrara* (Comune di Scandiano: Berni, GL/100, 1996). Concerning the formula in question, see Richard Hudson, *The New Grove Dictionary of Music*, 16: 323–24.

[39] See Table 2: Modena, Biblioteca Estense, MS.M.1.2.

[40] The pertinent passage, taken from Folengo's *Opus Merlini Cocai Poete Mantuani Macaronicorum*, is cited in Lockwood, *Music in Renaissance Ferrara*, 261.

[41] See the comments of Edward E. Lowinsky in his edition of *The Medici Codex of 1518*, Monuments of Renaissance Music (Chicago: Univ. of Chicago Press, 1968), 3: 199f.

Even more arresting as a tribute to the duke's magnificence, however, is Josquin's *Missa Hercules Dux Ferrarie*, composed, perhaps, as early as 1480–81, when Josquin was presumably in the service of Ascanio Sforza with whom he may have spent the year in Ferrara. It is based on a *soggetto cavato*, a secular *cantus firmus* derived directly from the duke's Latinized name and title. By extracting the vowels from the three words in which these are expressed and matching them with solmization syllables from the Guidonian hand, Josquin generated a short musical phrase, thus:

H<u>e</u>rc<u>u</u>l<u>e</u>s D<u>u</u>x F<u>e</u>rr<u>a</u>r<u>ie</u> = re, ut, re, ut, re, fa, mi, re.

This becomes the structural foundation for the mass and is heard in three-fold statements in each major section of the work, first from D-sol-re, then from a-la-re, a fifth higher, and finally from d-la-sol-re, at the upper octave (see Plate xx). In the Credo Josquin has made of his Herculean *cantus firmus*, a palindrome in which the three-fold ascending pattern of the Et incarnatus is answered in retrograde by a descending one in the Et in spiritum sanctum. Conversely, in the Agnus Dei the composer begins with a descending trifold statement in retrograde that is countered by the as-cending series for the concluding section of the mass.

In light of the referential and symbolic meanings that the *cantus firmus* of the polyphonic Mass Ordinary was generally expected to carry, it is tempting to speculate as to the nuances of meaning that might have been conveyed to the knowledgeable listener of the period by Josquin's *soggetto cavato*. The Trinitarian imagery of the three-fold statements would surely have escaped no one. And it is likely that the progressive elevation of pitch in its presentation was perceived as symbolic of the duke's increasing stature as patron, prince, and warrior. The palindrome of the Credo might even have been intended as a reference to Ercole's well-known piety, sug-gesting that although exalted in the flesh, he was humble in spirit, espe-cially before the Lamb of God.

Whatever the composer's intentions in this respect—or the listeners' constructions of them at the time—it is clear that Ercole's patronage of music, in particular his interest in the remarkable creative imagination of one of the most gifted composers of the age, gave rise to a remarkable monument to his magnificence. Even today, each time the mass is per-formed, his name and ducal title are woven into the sacred texts of the li-turgy, linking him symbolically to the central act of Christian worship. What could he have done, either as ruler or as patron of the arts, that would have more effectively assured that "the fame of his deeds should shine forth clearly . . . and the glory of his name be known everywhere"?

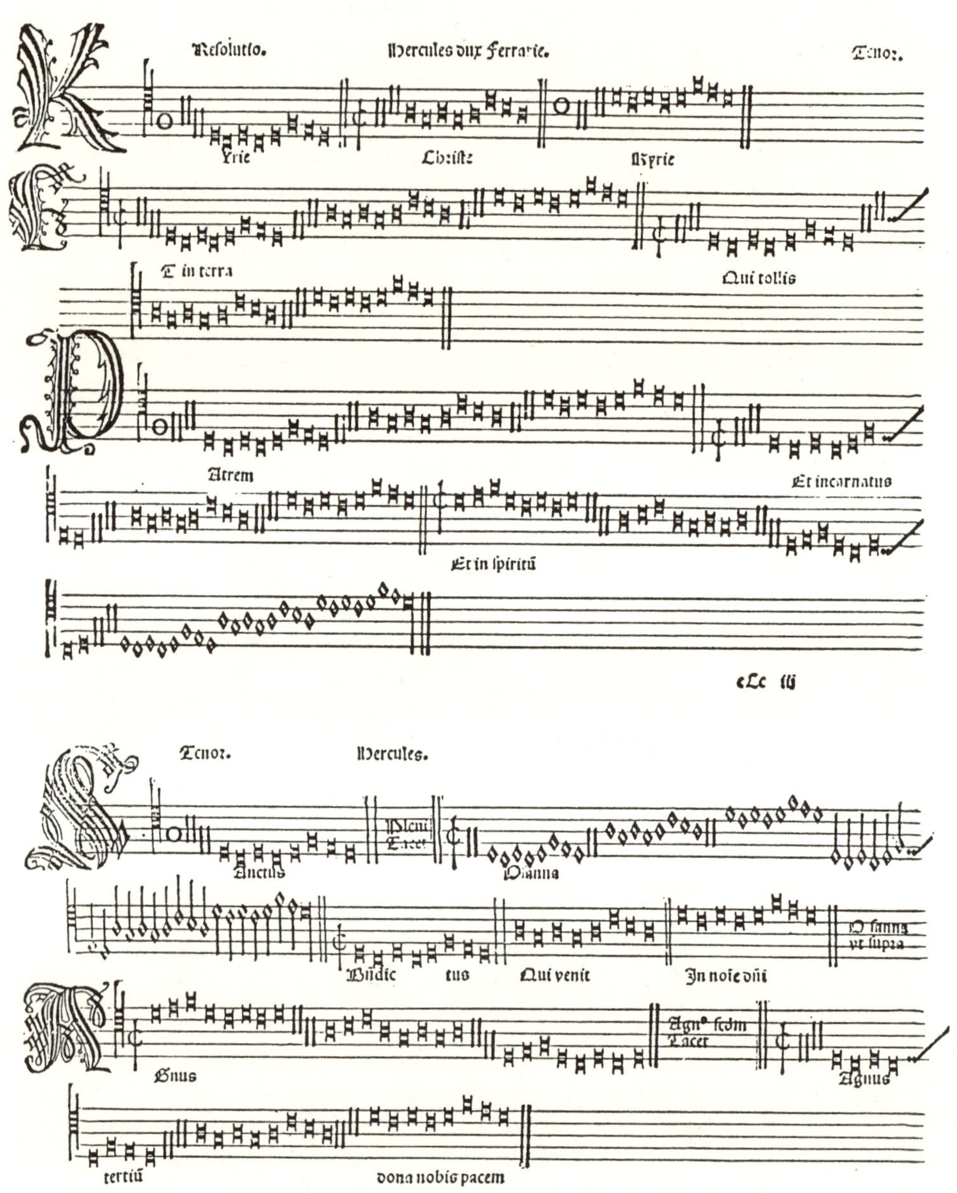

Missa Hercules Dux Ferrarie.
Missarum Josquin Liber secundus (Venice: Octaviano Petrucci, 1505).

Appendix 1. References to Music in Boiardo's Orlando Innamorato[42]

A. Conventional Uses for Trumpets, Drums, and Bells

1.1.11:   the sounding of bells, trumpets, and drum during the celebration of Pentecost in Paris.

1.7.5:   trumpets, drums, and bells resound during battle as Paris attempts to fend off Gradasso.

2.23.21:   trumpets play as the battle of Montalbano is engaged.

2.24.1:   trumpets described as rousing the warrior to battle.

2.24.22:   trumpets, horns, and drums accompany King Marsilio's entrance into the fray.

2.27.31:   pealing bells and sounding trumpets mark the celebration of Fiordelisa's reunion with her parents at Liza.

2.28.4:   King Agramante dancing with ladies of his court on a portico overlooking the sea (no music is mentioned) is distracted by the horn call of Brandimarte, come to challenge him.

2.29.50:   trumpets, drums, and horns sound as Agramante joins battle at Montalbano.

B. Singing and Playing as Social Recreation

1.8.7:   as pre-prandial entertainment at Angelica's Pleasure Palace, three maidens sing, another plays (apparently as a polyphonic ensemble) while others do a round dance, encircling Ranaldo.

1.8.10:   as post-prandial entertainment the music of harps and lutes, during which a seductive message is whispered in Ranaldo's ear.

1.12.11:   writing verses and singing songs among the social pleasures in which Prasildo engages when he falls in love ("Versi compone e canta in melodia").

1.14.42:   at Dragontina's Aquilante takes the soprana, Chiarone the tenor, and Brandimarte the contra tenor as they sing together, obviously in polyphony.

2.31.2:   Boiardo's "singing" (referring to the poem) described as a means of helping his listeners to set aside their cares and worries.

3.1.57:   Mandricardo is entertained by a lady who sings to a lyre of famous deeds and tales of love: "con la lira a sé facea tenore" implies polyphonic performance.

---

[42] Compiled by Charles Ross, whom I should like to thank for sharing with me the results of his search for references to music in Boiardo's poem.

<h2 align="center">C.1. Dancing to Songs and Soft Instruments</h2>

2.8.57:   Fay Morgana, as the figure of Fortune, dances as she sings a song, the text of which Boiardo "quotes."

2.13.41:   to celebrate the return of King Manodante's son (Brandimart), his subjects throng to the piazza and dance to the sound of instruments; tambourines, harps, and lutes are specified.

2.15.43-45:   the god of love and three maidens dance naked in the clearing near Merlin's fountain before pelting Ranaldo with flowers.

2.31.45:   Brigliadoro stops to drink at a fountain and sees in the water women singing and dancing.

2.31.48:   Orlando enters a palace and sees maidens doing a round dance; there is no mention of music as accompaniment, but Boiardo then refers again to his "singing."

3.1.63:   Mandricardo slays the giant come to challenge him, and directly the ladies of the court begin a round dance as they play string and wind instruments (presumably soft winds) and sing joyous songs.

3.7.8:   Naiades revel and dance in the Laughing Stream; no music is specified but is of course implied.

<h2 align="center">C.2. Dancing to Loud Instruments</h2>

2.1.31:   in Africa, at Agramante's court, maidens dance on a platform to the music of trumpets, drums, and shawms (*piffari*).

2.28.43-44:   during the feast at Agramante's court, a drummer comes down from the platform where, presumably, instrumentalists were placed to provide music for the dance (only the drummer is identified), and reminds Agramante of his duty to return to battle.

3.7.29:   Gradasso frolics with the Naiades, who dance to the sound of trumpets.

<h2 align="center">D. Literary Traditions and Miscellaneous References</h2>

1.22.49:   as Ordauro steals away with Leodilla, the wife of Folderico, he sings as they ride.

2.1.3:   Boiardo, in the tradition of lyric poets such as Homer and Virgil, proposes to sing of the events he is about to recall.

2.4.1-2:   at the beginning of the canto, the poet invokes again tradition; he refers to singing of love in the *Canzoniere* and seeks inspiration for the story at hand.

2.13.5:   Fay Morgana sings incantations as she gathers herbs by moonlight.

2.27.1:   at the beginning of the canto Boiardo invokes the legend of Arion, whose music charmed the creatures of the sea, and claims to have surpassed him.

BOIARDO'S

MINOR WORKS

ROBERT J. RODINI

Aphasia and the Divided Self:
Boiardo's *Amorum Libri Tres*

IN THE TRADITION OF ITS Petrarchan paradigm, "Voi ch'ascoltate in rime sparse," ("You who listen to my scattered verse") the opening sonnet of Boiardo's *Amorum Libri* establishes an important temporal dynamic between past and present as it situates the one hundred and eighty poems of the collection thematically.[1]

> Amor, che me scaldava al suo bel sole
> nel dolce tempo de mia età fiorita,
> a ripensar ancor oggi me invita
> quel che alora mi piacque, or mi dole.
>
> Così racolto ho ciò che il pensier fole
> meco parlava a l'amorosa vita,
> quando con voce or leta or sbigotita
> formava sospirando le parole.
>
> Ora de amara fede e dolce inganni

---

[1] For this paper I have used the recent edition of Boiardo's *canzoniere* with the facing-page English translation by Andrea di Tommaso, *Amorum Libri. The Lyric Poems of Matteo Maria Boiardo* (Binghamton, NY: Medieval & Renaissance Texts & Studies, 1993). Di Tommaso bases his Italian text on the edition of Pier Vincenzo Mengaldo (1962). All references will be to the *initial* poem number in the Di Tommaso edition; English translations are those of Di Tommaso, used with the kind permission of the publisher.

l'alma mia consumata, non che lassa,
fuge sdegnosa il püerile errore.

Ma certo chi nel fior de' soi primi anni
sanza caldo de amore il tempo passa,
se in vita è vivo, vivo è sanza core.

Amor, who warmed me in his gentle sun
back in my easy days of youthful bloom,
invites me to reflect once more today
on that which pleased me then and now gives pain.

So now I've gathered all those musings here
that maddened thought addressed to me in love
when, with a voice now cheerful, now forlorn,
I formed my words accompanied by sighs.

And now my soul, so wearied and consumed
by disappointed trust and sweet deceits
flees from my youthful error in disdain.

But yet I know that he whose flowering youth
is passed away without the warmth of love
may seem to live, but lives without a heart.

The Petrarchan echo in Boiardo's "quel che alora mi piacque, or mi dole," ("that which pleased me then and now gives pain") is also present in the association of love with folly, of desire with the disintegration of the self, and of the poetic voice with the inability to find expression. Andrea di Tommaso has observed that "[w]hereas Petrarch begins [his *canzoniere*] with discreet fragments and creates the illusion of continuity, Boiardo begins with the illusion of felicitous unity and deconstructs it into a world of unredeemable fragments."[2] In other words, there is a trajectory from seeming order to disorder, from apparent wholeness to dispersal and disintegration. One might argue that the incipit sonnet sets the stage for this progression in that it already problematizes the joys of youthful love, framing the text with the opening declaration that love once fired the poet's spirit and the closing proclamation that youth without love is a living death, and, at the same time associating youthful love with error and deception: "püerile errore" and "dolce inganni." One might say that the

---

[2] Di Tommaso, introduction to *Amorum Libri*, 25.

opening sonnet strikes the major structural chord of the collection as it plays the joys of youthful passion against the bittersweet awareness of its follies and ephemeral nature.

Marking the starting point of this trajectory from what Di Tommaso has called the "illusion of felicitous unity" toward a fragmentation are, I would argue, two important strategies. First, the poet actually names the object of his desire, going so far as to inscribe ANTONIA into the weave of the opening lyrics. And Antonia is explicitly associated with the restoration of order to the universe, with the coming of a Golden Age:

> Con lei ritorna quella antica vita
> che con lo effetto il nome de oro avia,
> e con lei inseme al ciel tornar ce invita.

> With her returns that ancient life which bore
> the name of gold as well as its effect,
> and she invites us back to heaven with her. (4)

Sonnet 14, "Arte de Amore e forze di Natura," ("All Love's old skills and all of Nature's powers"), both names the beloved and associates name with miracle.

The first point, noted above, distinguishes the poet from his predecessor, Petrarch, or his near contemporary, Maurice Scève (1501?–60?), in that Boiardo is actually able to articulate the name of his beloved, to inscribe her into his verse. The aphasic condition of poets such as Petrarch and Scève, which precludes the possibility of generating the beloved's name, seems not to hold as the *Amorum Libri* opens. The second point associates in a stilnovistic/humanistic way Antonia's beauty with natural order and fruition.

> Dovunque e' passi move on gira il viso
> fiamegia un spirto sì vivo d'amore
> che avanti a la stagione el caldo mena.

> Al suo dolce guardare, al dolce riso
> l'erba vien verde e colorito il fiore
> e il mar se acqueta e il ciel se raserena.

> Wherever she walks by or turns her eyes,
> a spirit full of love bursts forth like fire
> which well before its time brings summer's warmth.

> Before her peaceful gaze, her gentle smile,

> the grass grows green, the flower takes on its hue,
> the sea turns calm, the sky serene above. (6)

One might say, then, that the "whole" Antonia, named and defined, given an essentiality, initiates Boiardo's exploration into the world of Eros: for example, each of the first seven sonnets begins with the letters of her Christian name; they are followed by a madrigal (*mandrialis*) and six sonnets, each beginning with the letters of her surname; the final one in the sequence is also an acrostic sonnet, each verse beginning with a letter of her Christian and surname: ANTONIA CAPRARA.[3] If, then, both Petrarch and Scève struggle toward a poetic creation of the beloved, a struggle marked by an inability to verbalize her name and therefore gain "physical and semantic possession," to quote one critic, Boiardo's *canzoniere* begins with a seeming victory and complete possession.[4]

However, the body of the text of the *Amorum Libri* develops the problematics that the incipit sonnet posits. That is, there is a progressive unraveling of the ordered universe, a growing loss of possession of Antonia, that is expressed through patterns of what I will call "aphasic discourse,"

---

[3] In an earlier version of this paper, I was reminded by an anonymous reader—to whom I am grateful—that an important antecedent for Boiardo's acrostic lyrics is more than likely Boccaccio. The *Amorosa Visione* was arguably an important text in Boiardo's conception of his lyric cycle: like Boccaccio's work, Boiardo's is strongly marked by stilnovistic tradition and Ovid; its opening sonnets acrostically herald the vision about to be revealed. As Charles Ross has aptly noted, Boiardo's "visual effects are aerial, depending on gradations of light," suggesting, I would add, its proximity to the dream world of Boccaccio's poem. And it might be profitable to keep in mind the words of Vittore Branca regarding Boccaccio's work: "... the marvellous dream somehow invests the poem with a broadly autobiographical sense, as though it were a vision of his own life stripped of its contingencies and considered for the import of its moral experiences." See, respectively, Charles Ross's review of Di Tommaso's translation of Boiardo's *Amorum Libri* in *Renaissance Quarterly* 48/4 (1995): 861, and Vittore Branca's introduction to Giovanni Boccaccio, *Amorosa Visione*, trans. by Robert Hollander, Timothy Hampton, and Margherita Frankel (Hanover: Univ. Press of New England, 1986), xix.

[4] Kenneth E. Cool, "Scève's Agony of Expression and Petrarchan Discourse," *Stanford French Review* 3 (1979): 193–210. "It was Petrarch who inaugurated this onomastic tendency in the love poetry of the Renaissance. His paranomastic re-arrangements of Laura's name semantically motivated the thematics of his poetry. The lesson was not lost on Scève. In fact, he even gives a certain priority to the name of the Tuscan poet's beloved in his own poetry (i.e., the repeated usage of 'l'aure'). As for his own lady's name, he uses it sparingly, almost not at all.... This absence of nomination is totally congruent with the thematics of silence or suppressed expression. Conferring a name on the beloved is an act of both physical and semantic possession, a state to which [Scève] never accedes. On the contrary, his poetry exists in a kind of verbal limbo of designation, never quite managing to affix the object of desire with a durable identity." (205)

and a loss of identity and wholeness on the part of the poet, all directed—
to paraphrase Di Tommaso—toward fragmentation.[5] Book 3 of the *canzoniere* is, not insignificantly, riddled with indicators of disintegration and
contingency. The poet's voice, which had initially signalled his possession
of Antonia by declaring her name and by making onomastics one with the
poetry, becomes a "moriente voce" ("dying voice"; 125); the poet, experiencing his own undoing—"vo mancando a poco a poco" ("I continue dying bit by bit"; 128)—declares that he has lost self-identity: "a gran fatica
me cognoscerai" ("it will be hard for you to know it's me"; 170). And the
verse becomes replete with verbs such as "rodere," "limare," "mutare,"
"disfare" ("wear way," "file down," "change," "undo"), all of which
were anticipated in the incipit sonnet where he laments "l'alma mia consumata" ("my soul, so wearied and consumed"), and which begins to per-
meate even Book 1 with images of undoing, consuming, impotence, and
madness: "Ormai del mio furor per tutto sciassi" ("my madness is by now
exposed to all"; 16). Like Petrarch before him and the mad Orlando after
him, he becomes the sign—the "segnale," as Ariosto would have it—of desire's undoing.[6] He is the "exemplo," he states in Book 2, of what desire
has wrought (109).

One might argue, with Di Tommaso in mind, that the poet structures
the *canzoniere* as follows: wholeness and a sense of self, which are based on
the illusory nature of desire and unbridled passion ("... ed io non ho po-
tere / di ratenere il fren come io solia"; "... and I have not / the power to
rein it in as once I would"; 33) and therefore represented in the figuration
and naming of the woman, or the object of desire, are undermined by the
scrutiny of the rational faculties and the passage of time, and are ultimately found to be insubstantial. At the same time, he draws the collection toward a conclusion with a plea that his freewill be crushed, unable as he is
to accept fully what reason dictates:

> Lèvame tu, mio Dio, da tanto male,
> rompe lo arbitrio che donato m'hai
> poiché a mio danno per sciocheza lo uso.[7]

---

[5] See note 2 above.

[6] Ludovico Ariosto, *Orlando Furioso*, 24.1.6.

[7] As I note elsewhere, Boiardo's language in his *canzoniere* anticipates that of Michelangelo. This tercet is echoed—in its images and its language—in the first tercet of Michelangelo's "Vorrei voler, Signor, quel ch'io non voglio" ("I wish to have, my Lord,
that which I do not want"): "Squarcia 'l vel tu, Signor, rompi quel muro / che con la

> Deliver me, my God, from so much grief,
> and crush the will that you have given me,
> since I am using it to harm myself. (177)

The focus of this essay is on five thematic and rhetorical fields that seemingly dominate the discourse of the *Amorum Libri* and that subvert the sense of control and possession, which the opening lyrics might be said to declare. They are all fields that have to do with fragmentation and that therefore and inevitably refer back to the Petrarchan Ur-Text.

In the collection, *time* works as a type of corrosive, the poet constantly pitting the present against the past and, essentially, the integral being of a former time against his present state. Prefiguring Ronsard, Boiardo bemoans time's undoing and its destructive effects on beauty.[8] But the bottom line is that it is always personalized; that is, time passes and he, the poet, is no longer what he once was. The examples multiply, with elegiac moments such as the following:

> Sperai con tal desir, e fui sì presso
> al fin del mio sperar, che io vuò morire,
> pensando ora che fui, che sono adesso.

> I hoped with such desire, and was so near
> to having hopes fulfilled, that I want to die
> now thinking what I was and have become. (143)

It is against this backdrop of temporal contingency and instability, with a semantic play between past and present tenses ("sperai," "fui," "io vuò morire," "che sono adesso"; "I hoped," "I was," "I want to die," "what I have now become")—harking back to Petrarch and anticipating the self-analysis of Orlando in *Orlando Furioso* 23—that the other fields of discourse I wish to consider are situated.

If the poet gives a wholeness to the woman at the beginning of the collection by naming her and thereby implicitly declaring his own integral being and control, he plays these notions against the persona of the poet as it evolves beyond the frame of the initial lyrics; that is, within the body

---

suo durezza ne ritarda / il sol della tua luce, al mondo spenta!" ("Rend that veil, you, O Lord, break down that wall / which with its hardness keeps delayed from us / the sun of your light, extinguished in this world").

[8] See sonnet 46.

of the text of the *canzoniere*, the poetic persona is marked by division and subsequent disintegration.

The concept of the self divided becomes a major trope in the one hundred and eighty poems. One example of many will suffice, one which pointedly associates division with the lady: "che per star sieco son da me diviso" ("that longing to join it, I am disjoined"; 93).[9] The fundamental importance of this trope is underscored by the fact that the poet situates the place and anniversary of its beginnings with spatial and temporal deictics: "questo loco" and "oggi."

> (a) In *questo loco*, in amoroso riso
> se incominciò il mio ardor, che resce in pianto;
> tempo fallace e ria fortuna, *quanto*
> *è quel ch'io son da quel che era diviso!*
>
> In *this very* place, with love-filled laughter,
> my ardor, which is now a plaint, was born;
> deceitful time and wicked fortune, *how*
> *distant I am from what I was!* (112)
>
> (b) *Oggi* ritorna lo infelice giorno
> che fu principio de la mia sagura.
> [....]
> ed *io son da quel che era sì mutato*,
> de isdegno, de ira e sì de angoscia pieno
> che il giorno riconosco, e non me stesso.
>
> *Today* returns that most unhappy day
> that was the very source of my misfortune.
> [....]
> And *I'm so different from the way I was*,
> so full of anger, anguish, and disdain,
> that I can recognize the day, but not myself.
>   (116; emphasis mine)

The divided self—"son da me diviso" (93)—results in an erosion of the poet's being. The key verb is "consumare," but, as I mentioned earlier, companion verbs such as "rodere," anticipating the tactile imagery of Mi-

---

[9] In addition to references to the divided self cited in the text, see also numbers 9, 11, 12, 13, 17, 33, 65, 66, 112, 128, 132, amongst others.

chelangelo, express both a spiritual and corporeal wearing away: "Pur me destino de lasciare amore / prima che 'l corpo mio sia sfatto in tuto" ("Indeed my plan is to abandon love / before my flesh is totally corrupted"; 97). Not surprisingly, this type of spiritual, moral, and corporeal disintegration is associated with a loss of control and potential madness, foreshadowing both the language and the process of Orlando's loss of self in the central episodes of Ariosto's romance.

At the semantic level, the tropes of temporal contingency and the ephemeral, the loss of wholeness and mutability, have two important corollaries in the *Amorum Libri*. The first is a pervasive verbal paralysis that contradicts, one might say, the verbal control marking the poet's acrostic sonnets. That is, the collection begins with semantic possession and control, expressed in the articulation of Antonia's name; and it proceeds with the poet experiencing difficulty or incapability of articulation. The second corollary is found in the poet's insistence that he cannot mimetically represent; he can only state similarities.

In an article on poetic aphasia, Michael J. Giordano has discussed Petrarch and Maurice Scève's association of what I have called disintegration, and what Giordano calls dispersal or fragmentation, with verbal paralysis.[10] The discussion holds true for Boiardo in that his sense of the dissolution of the world around him ("etade rea"; "intemperate age"; 4), its moral tenor, his lady's loss of compassion, and his own disequilibrium all result in an inability to verbalize. Though at times he celebrates the correlation Antonia:speech ("quella per cui formo le parole"; "her for whom I fashion all my words"; 74), or chides the facility with which he poeticizes ("Deh, come leve n'escon le parole!"; "Alas, how light the words are as they issue"; 67),[11] the text is fraught with a sense of fundamental impotence when it comes to significant representation of his love and of his lady's beauty:

> ché tanta è tua belleza e nobilitate,
> e di tal maraviglia,
> che esser da noi cantata se disdegna,
> e chiede magior trumba.

---

[10] Michael J. Giordano, "Aphasia, Surrogate Discourse, and Scève's *Délie*," *Language and Style* 16 (1983): 262–83.

[11] See the important observations on Boiardo and the word in Claudia Micocci, *"Zanze" e parole: studi su Matteo Maria Boiardo* (Rome: Bulzoni, 1987), chapter 1.

> since so much beauty and such nobleness,
> so marvelous to see,
> disdain the humble song I offer them,
> and seek a brighter trumpet. (50)

Ironically, perhaps, one of the fullest declarations of the poet's verbal inadequacy and paralysis introduces a *canzone* that follows immediately upon the sonnet in which he acrostically names his beloved:

> Chi troverà parole e voce equale
> che giugnan nel parlare al pensier mio?
> Chi darà piume al mio intelletto ed ale
> si che volando segua el gran desio?
>
> Se lui per sé non sale,
> né giunge mia favella
> al loco ove io la invio,
> chi canterà giamai de la mia stella?
>
> Who will discover words and voice so matched
> that in their utterance they reach my thought?
> Who'll grace my intellect with feathered wings
> and let it soar to meet my great desire?
>
> If it fails to rise alone
> and my discourse cannot reach
> that place to which I send it,
> who'll ever sing the praises of my star? (15)

The *canzone* both personalizes and universalizes verbal paralysis before the spectacle of Antonia's beauty.

Critics such as Michael J. Giordano and Kenneth Cool have closely studied types of aphasic discourse and strategies of compensation, especially as they relate to Maurice Scève, and in the context of Roman Jakobson's several writings on linguistic aphasia. The fifth and final rhetorical field I wish to consider in Boiardo's collection reflects the linguist's discussion of similarity disorders in linguistic aphasia. Giordano states Jakobson's position: "One suffering from a similarity disturbance has difficulty in producing meaningful substitutions deriving from the metaphoric axis: [these are characterized by] metalingual constructions, synonyms, antonyms, failure to shift from an index or icon to a corresponding verbal symbol.''[12] Boiardo makes it clear that there is no correspondence between the beauty that he perceives and his intellect's ability to represent it: "La sua materia è . . . / tal ch'io non la scio dir come io la veggio" ("That body is of choicest alabaster, . . . [so] that I cannot describe it as it appears"; 31). The following sonnet elaborates this trope of non-correspondence:

> Perché non corresponde alcuno accento
> de la mia voce a l'aria del bel viso?
> [. . . .]
> Ben ho più volte nel pensier stampite
> parole elette e nòtte sì süave
> che assai presso giungneano a sua belleza;
>
> ma poi che l'ho legiadramente ordite,
> par che a ritrarle el mio parlar se inchiave
> e la voce mi manche per dolceza.

> Why is it that the sounds made by my voice
> can't match the look in her angelic face?
> [. . . .]
> How many times my thoughts have been imprinted
> with words well-chosen and with pleasant sounds,
> that come so close to equaling her beauty!
>
> But, once I have them gracefully in order,
> it seems as though my speech cannot repeat them,
> as ecstasy deprives me of my voice. (32)

Finally, then, in the Jakobsonian context, one could say that a compensatory lyric strategy is to fall back on devices such as synonyms or, in Boiardo's case, on the frequent use of verbs that introduce an attempted comparison, or a failure in making a comparison: "rasumigliare," "comperare" ("resemble," "compare") as well as "non sumiglia," "non è equale" ("does not resemble," "is not equal"). In lyric 49, after noting that nothing in the universe approximates his lady's beauty—". . . ad altro che a se stessa non sumiglia"—he concludes, paradoxically, that his creativity derives from her beauty:

------

[12] Giordano, "Aphasia," 266–67, is referring to Roman Jakobson, "Towards a Linguistic Classification of Aphasia Impairments," *Roman Jakobson: Selected Writings II: Word and Language* (The Hague: Mouton, 1971), 289–306.

> Questo è il monstro ch'io canto sì giolivo,
> dal qual lo inzegno e la alta voce piglio,
> di cui sempre ragiono e penso e scrivo. [13]

> This is the wonder that I praise so joyfully
> from which I take my voice and inspiration,
> of which I always think and write and speak.

There is a vacillation between the woman as source of poetic expression and the woman as "monstro" or "wonder," who blocks creativity, who can seemingly be re-figured only through a discourse of resemblance or "figures de la ressemblance," to use Michel Foucault's term.[14] To a lesser degree, certainly, than with Petrarch and Maurice Scève, but significant nonetheless, is the fact that the collection is marked by its reference to the poetic enterprise, to the act of writing.[15] The poetic enterprise is arguably the major trope of both Petrarch and Scève's lyric collections. This paper attempted to suggest that a kind of structural reversal in Boiardo's *Amorum Libri* problematizes poetic expression by deconstructing or dispersing the voice that opens the lyric sequence and that is only illusory in its wholeness and control. It had seemingly given semantic expression and, therefore, essentiality to Antonia, but the ensuing verses, in exploring the emotional world of the poet, give lie to the possibility of a truly mimetic poetry.

---

[13] See Petrarch, *Canzoniere*, 129, 52: "in guisa d'uom che pensi e pianga e scriva" ("like a man who thinks and weeps and writes").

[14] See Cool, "Scève's Agony of Expression," 195 n. 5.

[15] See the discussion of Petrarch in Cool, "Scève's Agony of Expression," 194–95.

NANCY DERSOFI

Staging Timon the Misanthrope

IN ADAPTING *TIMON FOR THE STAGE*, Boiardo transformed the comic hater of gods and men found in Lucian's *Timon the Misanthrope* into a protagonist whose misanthropy makes him a figure of suffering; and like Shakespeare's *Timon of Athens*, Boiardo's *Timone* confounds criticism. Although Boiardo's play is not generally counted among Shakespeare's sources, there is a kinship calling for comparison between the two portrayals of a character whose disillusionment with wealth and moral indignation against flatterers and parasites make all mankind his enemy. Timon, a character whose story is neither typical nor exemplary, acquired theatrical form and dimension in the cultural surroundings of Ferrara at the end of the fifteenth century. Among the actors on that social stage was Girolamo Savonarola, whose sermons against worldly vanity rebuked elaborate theatrical display at Ferrara and elsewhere. I propose here to survey the interests and values of Boiardo's Ferrara, and to suggest that Savonarola's influence touches both Boiardo's and Shakespeare's visions of a Renaissance misanthrope.

Boiardo composed *Timone* when Ferrara was entering a period rich in theatrical activity and invention. On January 25, 1486, a production of Plautus's *Menaechmi* was played in vernacular translation on "a new stage shaped like a city made out of planks and painted with houses"[1] built for the occasion in the New Courtyard (*Cortile Nuovo*) of the ducal palace. The following year saw the first performance of Niccolò da Correggio's *Ce-*

---

[1] Cited in Nino Pirrotta and Elena Povoledo, *Music and Theatre from Poliziano to Monteverdi*, trans. by Karen Eales (New York: Cambridge Univ. Press, 1982), 302.

falo and a performance in the vernacular of Plautus's *Amphytrion*, both presented in the outdoor courtyard of the ducal palace on a "tribunale of wood and planks painted with houses, in the image of a castle and a city."[2] For *Amphytrion*, there was a Paradise where Jove could appear in a sky illuminated by lamps "burning...behind thin black curtains, and shining like stars; and there were children dressed in white representing the planets."[3] Opposite sat Duke Ercole I d'Este with his guests, the Marquess of Mantua, ambassadors of the duke of Milan, and other foreign dignitaries, citizens, and scholars. The duchess Eleanora, accompanied by her ladies with their sons and daughters, looked down from her balcony. For the wedding festivities of Isabella d'Este and Francesco Gonzaga in 1489, performances were moved into the great hall of the ducal palace, which was used again in 1491 for *Menaechmi*, Terence's *Andria*, and another *Amphytrion*. The traditional speculative date for *Timone* is 1490-91, before performances at Ferrara were interrupted, from 1492 until 1498, while Ferrara was in mourning and under the threat of French invasion. After 1498, performances resumed and were held every year during Carnival. Five Plautine comedies performed in 1502 for festivities celebrating the marriage of Alfonso d'Este to Lucrezia Borgia closed the first chapter in a theatrical history that by its end had laid the foundation for modern European theater.

After Ercole's death in 1505, Ferrara's dukes sponsored Ariosto's comedies, beginning with *La Cassaria* in 1508. Theatrical and musical entertainments included performances by Ruzante and his troupe of actors and singers in 1529 and in 1532. In stage design, the idealized urban perspective view that would characterize Renaissance scenography, emerged in Ferrara as an image of the "città ferrarese."[4] A permanent court theater, probably envisaged in the first years of the sixteenth century, was planned and constructed in the years 1529 to 1532. *Timone*, composed in the early years of experimentation and renewal, is one of the works marking the transition from narrative and lyrical forms to the rebirth of stage comedy.

The play is based on a dialogue by Lucian of Samosata (a village in Syria). Born about A.D. 120, Lucian studied rhetoric and Greek, and became a traveling lecturer before migrating to Athens, where he developed a variety of dialogue that combines philosophical dialogue with satirical

---

² Pirrotta and Povoledo, *Music and Theatre*, 303.
³ Pirrotta and Povoledo, *Music and Theatre*, 303.
⁴ Pirrotta and Povoledo, *Music and Theatre*, 315–17.

comedy. In his *Timon the Misanthrope*, Timon, having squandered his inherited fortune on false friends and learned from poverty the value of hard work, complains to Zeus that the gods no longer punish the wicked. When Zeus offers to restore Timon's wealth, Timon renews the vow he made in poverty, to live alone and scorn all men: "Friendship, hospitality, society, compassion—vain words all. To be moved by another's tears, to assist another's need—be such things illegal and immoral. Let me live apart like a wolf; be Timon's one friend—Timon."[5] No sooner does Timon acquire new gold than the parasites who consumed his wealth return, only to be driven off by Timon's stones.

Quattrocento humanists produced numerous imitations and translations in Latin and in the vernacular of Lucian's work,[6] among them a Latin translation of *Timon* that was the basis for Galeotto dal Carretto's *Timon greco*, dedicated to Isabella d'Este and performed in 1498. Boiardo's source was a vernacular translation by Niccolò Leoniceno.[7] Boiardo also remembers the Greek original by having Lucian appear as Prologue to say he has changed his language from Greek to Italian under the benevolent authority of Duke Ercole d'Este whose practical interest in theater probably influenced the play's division into five acts, each subdivided into scenes.[8] The play's animated dialogue gives further testimony to the work's claim on comedy. Focusing on the mordant, even "tragic" wit of Boiardo's dialogue, Antonio Franceschetti demonstrates the play's fundamental "comicità," claiming that Boiardo wrote a comedy conceived in the spirit of the Latin theater of Plautus.[9] Thus, an ancient source, five-act structure, and a theatrically expressive voice regulate Boiardo's contribution to the emerging genre of stage comedy. Stage directions in the author's hand

---

[5] H. W. Fowler, trans., *The Works of Lucian of Samosata* (London: Oxford, 1905), 46.

[6] Marcello Aurigemma notes that fifteenth-century writers were extremely interested in Lucian, and that Boiardo translated other of Lucian's compositions. In *Timone*, the novelty of bringing a Greek rather than a Latin author to the stage was paramount. See M. Aurigemma, "Il 'Timone' di M. M. Boiardo," in *Il Boiardo e la critica contemporanea*, ed. Giuseppe Anceschi (Florence: Leo S. Olschki, 1970), 30.

[7] See Antonia Tissoni Benvenuti and Maria Pia Mussini Sacchi, eds., *Le Corti padane: Teatro del Quattrocento* (Turin: UTET, 1983), 473 n. 2. Tissoni Benvenuti is the editor of *Timone* and the author of the introduction and notes to that text.

[8] Ercole d'Este's correspondence with Battista Guarino indicates the duke believed a play should have a coherent plot, a balanced number of characters, and a five-act dramatic structure; see Tissoni Benvenuti and Mussini Sacchi, *Le Corti padane*, 18–19.

[9] Antonio Franceschetti, "Ispirazione comica e dimensione umana nel 'Timone' del Boiardo," *Yearbook of Italian Studies* 6 (1987): 82.

affirm his expectation that the play would be staged, although no reference has been found to any performance of *Timone* at the court of Ferrara.

Visually, the action takes place in Jove's heaven and on Timon's earth. Boiardo's stage directions call for a set designed to accommodate an action played on upper and lower levels and equipped to lift Mercury to Heaven mechanically (*per machina*) after his visit to Timon in Act 3. Although the two-level set is typical of sacred drama, a similar stage is required for mortals on earth and the divinities in heaven in *Amphytrion*, the staging of *Timone* may have been imagined in a similar classicizing context.

Boiardo's first scene, as in Lucian, finds Timon,[10] hoe in hand, ranting to Jove about the injustice of men and the weakness of the gods. As the ground where Timon ekes out his scant living is neither a pastoral landscape nor an urban space, the author seems indifferent to the scenic norms prescribed for comedy by Vitruvius. If Timon's Athens resembles Ferrara, however, its stage image differs from that of other Renaissance cities. Ferrara, observes Ludovico Zorzi, is a "città di campagna," where the close relationship between town and country mirrors the economic dependence of the urban center on the surrounding countryside. Ferrarese stage design reflects the nature of a territory that is neither urban nor bucolic, neither *rinascimentale* nor medieval, but a combination of the two.[11] Scenic design in other cities in the Po Valley shows a similar approach to the city as part of a greater territorial space. At Padua, for example, Ruzante is mindful of the distinction between *Pava / pavan*: the city of Padua (*Pava*) and its surrounding countryside (*pavan* or *pavano*).[12]

Although Vitruvius's descriptions of the scenery appropriate to tragedy, comedy, and pastoral drama have no apparent bearing on Boiardo's play, the influence of the Vitruvian tradition on the idea of theater at Ferrara does appear in a treatise in Italian by Pellegrino Prisciano, librarian to Duke Ercole, who worked from 1486 to 1501 on *Spectacula* (in the sense of "spectacles"); the document was based on Vitruvius's Greek architectural treatise and its Latin translation by Leon Battista Alberti, both published in 1485–86. Supervisor of stage design at Ferrara, Prisciano writes in his dedication to the duke:

---

[10] I use the English spelling of the protagonist's name throughout.

[11] Ludovico Zorzi, *Il Teatro e la Città* (Turin: Einaudi, 1977), 6.

[12] Zorzi, *Il Teatro e la Città*, 6–7.

> We should praise your Highness for assembling your most faithful
> and loving populace at so many spectacles, so well planned; you
> delight your people and instruct them in social living, and you
> invite them to study and become men of learning, to the honor
> and great good of the entire Republic.[13]

The goal of teaching men how to live well in society guided theatrical life
at the court of Ferrara.

In *Timone*, the lesson in social living is ambivalent. As in Lucian's satire, the play excoriates the flatterers and parasites who feed at Timon's
table until he has exhausted his wealth, and then deny him help or comfort. More difficult to interpret and reconcile with the case for living well
in society is Boiardo's characterization of Timon, whose fall from wealth
to poverty leaves him adverse to all human company. His role, anticipated
in an *Argumento* and developed especially in a fifth act composed of
material new to the parent text,[14] reveals a protagonist whose heart is
divided between ideal sociability and its absolute renunciation. Like
Shakespeare's Timon, he eludes definition as a character who may be tragic, heroic, noble, or simply unfinished.

In an illuminating discussion of the two "Timone," Lienhard Bergel
says that Boiardo's play is not a character study; rather, its subject is
"richeza."[15] The theme of wealth is developed in the contrast between
Timon and a character named Filocoro, the former unable to use his
wealth rationally, the latter taught to distinguish between foolish spending
and the prudent use of money. Poverty makes Timon a hater of men, but
not a Christian stoic who has truly and gladly renounced the world. His
very hatred for the world, his misanthropy, reveals an ongoing emotional
engagement with humanity; for Shakespeare's Timon, wealth is symbolic

---

[13] The text is published in Ferruccio Marotti, *Lo spettacolo dall'Umanesimo al Mani-
erismo* (Milan: Feltrinelli, 1974), 54. This and all subsequent translations from Italian are
my own.

[14] The main additions are the *Prologo*, *Argumento*, and the entire fifth act, although
smaller additions occur throughout the play. M. Aurigemma regards these interpolations
as part of a complete "rereading" and "remediation" of the original; see Aurigemma, "Il
'Timone' di M. M. Boiardo," 31.

[15] See Lienhard Bergel, "I due 'Timone': Boiardo e Shakespeare," in *Il Boiardo e la
Critica Contemporanea*, edited by Giuseppe Anceschi (Florence: Leo S. Olschki, 1970),
73–80.

of innate human corruption, and his realization of its worldly importance destroys him.[16]

Revisiting the question of Boiardo's characterization of Timon, I would say that Boiardo, responding to Filocoro's story and its happy ending, has deepened and complicated the character of Timon. Boiardo gives his Timon a psychological history narrated in the exposition, and a wounded inner-self discovered through the action. Bergel argues convincingly that Timon is not a true stoic, content to retreat from society into monastic isolation; but neither is he a true misanthrope, following Lucian's example of a man motivated and satisfied by hatred of men. Boiardo's Timon desires a courteous society, generous and moved by love. Society's failure to requite his expectations leaves him rejected in the manner of a lover spurned. It is from this perspective that I wish to compare Boiardo's and Shakespeare's characterization.

Lucian's Timon had spent his wealth humanely, according to Hermes, who reports that "it was kindness and generosity and universal compassion that ruined him."[17] Boiardo, in his *Argumento*, offers insight into his protagonist's reckless misuse of his inheritance by inventing a father whose obsessive pursuit of wealth ruined his health so that he died prematurely, leaving his fortune to an unseasoned son. Timon came to value wealth inappropriately, confusing wealth with love and wasting his inheritance as he tried to buy the love he had been denied in his early youth. Inexperienced and good natured, he fell victim to a "taste for honor" and the false world of flatterers. Poverty taught him something about himself as well as others, so that aware, now, of his earlier recklessness, he acknowledges: "With abundance and refinement / I destroyed my life and my self / becoming proud, wicked, and inflated" (3.144–46).[18] The lesson extends to relationships between men and women; in love, says Fame at the beginning of the fourth act, men complain of being betrayed when they are, in fact, the betrayers.

Shakespeare puts Timon's extravagant life and promiscuous use of money on stage. In the first act of *Timon of Athens*, Timon offers his friends a banquet accompanied by a masque performed by ladies as Ama-

---

[16] Bergel, "I due 'Timone': Boiardo e Shakespeare," 78.

[17] Fowler, *The Works of Lucian of Samosata*, 33–34.

[18] "Cum abondancia e cum delicatece / mi destrusse la vita e la persona / superbo iniquo e tumido me face," in Tissoni Benvenuti, 'Timone,' in *Le Corti padane*, 516. All further citations are from this text.

zons. With them is Cupid, who speaks to the barren sensuality of Timon's hospitality:

> The five best senses
> Acknowledge thee their patron and come freely
> To gratulate thy plenteous bosom. There,
> Taste, touch, all, pleas'd from thy table rise;
> They only now come but to feast thine eyes.
>   (1.2.123-27)[19]

Yet, even while they partake of the feast, Timon's coffer is empty. Not only does the host misjudge his guests, he fails to see that his generosity is hollow and his pending destruction self-inflicted.

Boiardo and Shakespeare both follow Lucian in their assessment of Wealth: Poverty teaches the true nature of wealth; Plutus, wealth's personification, wears a charming mask to hide his blind, pale self; Arrogance, Folly, Vainglory, Effeminacy, Insolence, and Deceit escort him. Wealth produced by hard work may appear to be useful socially, but is, in fact, antisocial, dividing men from one another and driving them into isolation. Thus when Zeus (Jove) restores Timon's wealth, Timon affirms its solitary, isolating character, calling himself "Misanthropos" and retreating to a lonely place—a castle, a tower, a cave—big enough to live in alone and, when dead, in which to lie.

As in Lucian's text, word of Timon's renewed wealth quickly spreads, and his flatterers return hastily. The rocks that Lucian's Timon uses to drive off the second round of flatterers become, in Shakespeare's play, stones served with warm water in covered dishes. Reversing the function and spirit of the play's earlier banquet, this third act anti-banquet is a kind of inverse last supper: "Uncover, dogs, and lap" (3.6.85), Timon commands. The meal not only portrays the false humanity of Timon's friends, but symbolizes the host's lost humanity. Boiardo, on the other hand, develops the story of the second treasure, adding new characters and a new episode to a plot that is narrated, for the most part, by a figure called Auxilio.[20]

---

[19] William Shakespeare, "Timon of Athens," in *The Riverside Shakespeare* (Boston: Houghton Mifflin Company, 1974), 1450. All further citations are from this text.

[20] The figure of Auxilium derives from Plautus's *Cistellaria*. Mauda Bregoli Russo examines the parallel roles of Lucian (Prologue) and Auxilium in "Tecnica di Contrasto e Fini Moraleggianti nel 'Timone' di M. M. Boiardo," in *Studi di critica boiardesca* (Naples: Federico & Ardia), 25–27.

In this subplot, Timon, hiding his restored gold in the grave of a countryman named Timoncrate, finds more buried gold. The story of this second treasure is that Timoncrate, judging (correctly) that his son Filocoro would squander his inheritance, left only part of his wealth at the time of his death, but obtained his son's promise, sworn in mutual love, to open a sealed letter after ten years had passed. The letter directs the son to reopen the grave where the rest of Timoncrate's gold awaits him. The father anticipated Filocoro would use the second lot of gold rationally and be: "no longer prodigal, but liberal, spending and dispensing with reason" (5.382–83).[21] This theme is an important alternative to Timon's story, demonstrating the prudent use of wealth and adding a further dimension to the play's theme of parental relationships. Boiardo emphasizes the topic in the closing speech of the first act: "What bear or tiger or even wilder beast / takes no care for its offspring? / Only the asp behaves insanely towards her young" (1.235–37).[22] Yet, Timon almost thwarts Timoncrate's plan when he finds the gold and decides to make himself Timoncrate's heir, knowing that the true heir is in prison for debt.

Before choosing his final course of action, however, Timon confronts two characters invented to establish a political and moral context for his misanthropy. When two servants whom the imprisoned Filocoro had sent to Timoncrate's grave approach the site, Timon threatens to strike them dead. "Have you been made the king of Athens?" (5.232)[23] asks Parmeno, deploring the tyrant who threatens decent men. Timon asserts further dominion over Siro, whom he recognizes as the slave of Cremate, a free Athenian citizen, although Siro denies that he is beholden to a free man. Cremate, he says, is a slave to avarice, adding for good measure that a free man fears neither poverty nor wealth, nor does he bend to fame. Filocoro's servants reflect the free spirit their master inherited, and teach Timon that he cannot be Timoncrate's heir any more than he can be his son. A chastened Timon, remembering that wealth is meretricious, decides to return to his solitary life, retreating into a natural world of absolute frugality. His image of solitude is beguiling, evoking pastoral tranquility rather than cruel poverty:

---

[21] "El giovene fia tratto de pregione; / più prodigo non fia, ma liberale, / servendo e dispensando cum ragione"; 'Timone,' 555.

[22] "Quale orso o tigre o qual fiera più strana / non ha de la sua schiata conoscenza? / La aspide sola e contra a' figlii insana"; 'Timone,' 494.

[23] "Or sei tu forsi fato re de Atene"; 'Timone,' 549.

> On some high hill or in a lonely wood
> I'll feed on native fruits,
> and slake my thirst at some spring.
> And when the winter boughs shed their leaves,
> in the hollowed trunk of a great oak
> falling branches will make my bed,
> or I'll take shelter in some cave. (5.307–13)[24]

His image evokes a Petrarchan solitude, and his words give voice to the pain of a lover whose impossible, unrequited love for humanity grieves him beyond endurance. In this pastoral moment, Timon imagines repose and solace, not hatred. Here, Boiardo gives a new frame to his tale and an original interpretation of his protagonist. Timon repudiates a world that reduces love, friendship, and honor to material terms, and he rejects the enslaving power of materialism in favor of a pastoral place that invites dreams of a golden age to replace a society that has traded love for wealth.

This vision recalls the role of another man of Ferrara, Fra Girolamo Savonarola, who in the 1480s and early 1490s was preaching poverty, simplicity, and the renunciation of worldly vanities. "Pride, lust, and avarice . . . are the roots of all evils,"[25] he told the Florentines. In Ferrara, Ercole d'Este had already taken heed. By 1490 Ferrara was a city in which vanities were burned and sumptuary laws enforced. "Small wonder," writes Werner Gundersheimer, "that Girolamo Savonarola, after having left Ferrara in disilluion with its worldliness as a young friar, admired and praised the zealous Duke who consulted him in anxious and soulful letters."[26] Preaching divine punishment for social injustice, and condemning the rich for their greedy exploitation of the poor, Savonarola saw himself the instrument of a new social order and of the moral reconstruction of Italy. Boiardo's Timon is a character whose disillusionment is likewise absolute. What he had mistaken for love is revealed to him as hypocrisy and greed. With Savonarola he shares the ideal of renouncing all worldly vanities for poor simplicity. Thus reduced, Timon becomes the world's most unrequited lover.

---

[24] "In qualche monte o in qualche selva strana / mi pascerò de' fructi che vi nascano, / e cacerò la sete a la fontana"; 'Timone,' 552.

[25] Girolamo Savonarola, "Trattato sul Reggimento e Governo della Città di Firenze," in *Savonarola*, ed. G. Dore (Turin: Società Editrice Internazionale, 1928), 182.

[26] Werner L. Gundersheimer, *Ferrara: The Style of a Renaissance Despotism* (Princeton: Princeton Univ. Press, 1973), 197–98.

After his momentary glimpse into pastoral simplicity, Timon reverts to his misanthropic temper, driving off Siro and Parmeno and, in a closing soliloquy, offering the cord around his waist to any countryman wanting to hang himself. Shakespeare echoes the tragic tones of this gesture in *Timon of Athens* in a passage probably derived from Plutarch's lives of Antony and Alcibiades. Shakespeare recasts his protagonist in a plot issuing from the Athenians' ingratitude toward Alcibiades, a captain and patriot banished by the Athenian Senate as he seeks mercy for a friend, one whose crimes were outweighed by "comely virtues." A true friend, Alcibiades is a patriot able to overthrow Athens' corrupt Senate by force of arms. Timon contributes his gold. However, when the senators of Athens approach him for gold, he answers with a mixture of irony and heartbroken truth: "But yet I love my country" (5.1.189). Irony triumphs when he speaks of his tree ready for whoever wishes to hang himself. Alcibiades strikes against only those senators who were Timon's enemy and his own; but Timon dies before Alcibiades extends to Athens the olive branch of peace together with his sword, promising to speak later to the memory of "noble Timon." Boiardo ends his play with a narrative by Auxilio, who closes the story with assurances that Siro and Parmeno will share in their new-found wealth with Filocoro and live among the citizens of Athens.

Both Boiardo and Shakespeare set their protagonists within plot structures designed to fulfill a social promise, whether of wealth constructively used or of a corrupt society restored to decency. Their visions of Timon coalesce in that both authors present a hero who suffers for loving too much. The tragic tones of their vision recall the dark meditations Savonarola brought to the Renaissance. Eugenio Garin has said that "without Savonarola, certain of Michelangelo's most tragic tones would be unthinkable."[27] Among the darkest tones in Renaissance theater are those of Timon, who places Savonarola's severe message in view of the public he challenged. Audiences, however, turned away. Shakespeare's play was not performed during his lifetime; Boiardo's play may have suffered the same dismissal of non-performance. Indeed, Savonarola's preaching may, ironically, have been influential in surpressing performances at Ferrara[28] from 1492 to 1498, the year when Savonarola was executed in Florence.

---

[27] Eugenio Garin, *La Cultura del Rinascimento* (Bari: Edizioni Laterza, 1971), 126.
[28] This speculation was suggested by Charles Ross.

INDEX

also Metamorphoses); portrayal of Medea, 36, 85–86; stories of the Argonauts and of Theseus, 78n. 5, 79n. 11, 83, 85–86

paintings. *See* arts, visual

palazzo incantato, in the *Furioso*, the Laughing Stream in the *Innamorato* as model for, 98

Palazzo Schifanoia: Hall of the Months, 266–67, 273–74, 277; Sala degli Stucchi of Domenico di Paris in, 263

palindrome, use in Josquin's *Missa Hercules Dux Ferrarie*, 311

Panizzi, Antonio, 205n. 1, 237n. 2

Paradise Lost (Milton), 90n. 64

Paradiso (Dante), 154n. 8

paragone literature, 275–77

parents, fooled by children, 143, 143n. 16

Paris: Orlando's return to, 109; Orlando's surreptitious departure from, 111–12; Rinaldo sent back to, 109n. 25

Paris, Battle of, in the *Innamorato*, 98–99, 98n. 2, 102–4, 125–27; erased and rewritten in the *Furioso*, 98–99, 105, 119, 127–34; Laughing Stream episode between the Battle of Montealbano and, 101, 109

Parker, Patricia, 137n. 2

parody: of Osiris, Orrilo as in Book 3, 252; of passage of the soul through this world, in the *Innamorato*, 13

Parzifal (Wolfram von Eschenbach), 148

passion. *See* desire; lust

Pastoralia (Boiardo), 290

Patch, Howard R., 43

Paul II (pope), 308

Paul III (pope), 286

Paul the Apostle, as an authority for Pico in the *Oration*, 243

peace, choosing discord over, Boccaccio on in the *Filocolo*, 201

peacock: Origille's conceit compared to, 179; reference to in Ovid's *Metamorphoses*, 179n. 9

peacock-lady, in garden at Orgagna in Book 2, 159

Pegasus, 118n. 37

pendentives, in the Camerino dell' Eneide, adorned with female *all'antica* figures, 281, 287n. 27, 291, 292

Penitence: advisement to Orlando, 60, 69–70, 74, 91; personification of in Morgana's underworld, 35

Perceval, or the Story of the Grail (Chretien de Troyes), 55–56, 89, 89n. 61

perfidy, Origille's, 177, 186

Perfunde coeli rore (Martini), 303

Perino del Vaga, *The Shipwreck of Aeneas*, 288n. 29

Perkins, Leeman L., 295–314

perspective, retrogressive use of, in Ferrarese visual art, 268

Petrarch, 138, 213, 337 (*see also Remedies for Fortune Fair and Foul*); influence on Pico, 239, 242n; poetic aphasia, 324; poetry as paradigm for Boiardo's *Amorum Libri*, 317–18, 319, 320n. 4, 322, 327

Petrucci, Ottaviano, 310

Pettinelli, Rosanna Alhaïque, 83n. 33

Phaedo (Plato), 196n

Philip the Good of Burgundy, 309

Philochorus, 80–81

Philoxenus, 51n

Pico della Mirandola, 1, 241n. 8, 245 life and works contrasted with Boiardo's, 238–40 new philosophy, 237–38, 239–45, 248; Boiardo's response to, 248–57 seen as Boiardo's target in satire of Orrilo, 252–54

Pietrobono dal Chitarino, 298–302, 309–10

piffari (pipers), 298–300, 306

Pigna, Giovan Battista, 110n. 27

Pimander (Ficino's translation of the *Cor-*

NOTES ON CONTRIBUTORS

ALLEN MANDELBAUM is W. R. Kenan, Jr., Professor of Humanities at Wake Forest University and Professor of the History of Literary Criticism at the University of Turin. Author of five verse volumes, of which the principal are *Chelmaxioms* and the *Savantasse of Montparnasse,* he is also the verse translator of the *Aeneid,* for which he won a National Book Award, the *Divine Comedy,* the *Odyssey,* and the *Metamorphoses,* as well as the *Selected Poems* of Ungaretti and the *Selected Poems* of Quasimodo. He is co-editor of the *California Lectura Dantis,* with the *Inferno* volume forthcoming this year.

JO ANN CAVALLO is Associate Professor of Italian at Columbia University and director of its Summer Program in Scandiano. Her publications include *Boiardo's* Orlando Innamorato: *An Ethics of Desire* (1993) and articles on early Christianity, Dante, Boiardo, Ariosto, Tasso, Giordano Bruno, and Elsa Morante. She is also a contributor to the forthcoming *Dante Encyclopedia* and *The Encyclopedia of the Renaissance.*

CHARLES ROSS is Professor of English and Comparative Literature and Assistant head of the Department of English at Purdue University. He has translated Boiardo's "Orlando Innamorato," published by the University of California Press in 1989 and currently available as an abridged paperback in the Oxford World's Classics series. He is the author of "The Custom of the Castle from Malory to Macbeth" (1997) as well as articles on Virgil, Dante, Boiardo, Shakespeare, Milton, and Nabokov. He is currently translating the "Thebaid" of Statius.

DAVID QUINT is Professor of English and Comparative Literature at Yale University. His recent books are *Epic and Empire* (1993), a translation of Ariosto's *Cinque Canti* (1996), and *Montaigne and the Quality of Mercy* (1998).

JAMES NOHRNBERG has been Professor of English since 1975 at the

University of Virginia, where he has taught Shakespeare, Spenser, Milton, allegory, and the Bible. He taught previously at University College in the University of Toronto, Harvard, and Yale; in 1987 he gave the Gauss Seminars in Criticism at Princeton. His books are *The Analogy of "The Faerie Queene"* (1976, 1980) and *Like unto Moses: The Constituting of an Interruption* (1995). Besides other work on Spenser and Scripture, he has also published essays on allegory, Homer, Dante, Milton, and Thomas Pynchon.

MICHAEL MURRIN is Professor of Comparative Literature, Divinity, and English at the University of Chicago. He is the author of *The Veil of Alleghory* (1969), *The Allegorical Epic* (1981), and *History and Warfare in Renaissance Epic* (1992). He is currently working on a study of trade and romance.

WERNER GUNDERSHEIMER is Director of the Folger Shakespeare Library and Adjunct Professor of History at Amherst College. He has written extensively on the court and culture of Ferrara in the fifteenth and sixteenth centuries as well as on various topics in the history of sixteenth-century France, Machiavelli, and other Renaissance subjects. He is currently working on the history of the emotions in late sixteenth-century Italian thought.

MANUELE GRAGNOLATI studied classics at the University of Pavia (Italy). He received his Masters in Italian Literature from the University of Paris IV Sorbonne. He is currently a doctoral candidate in the Department of Italian at Columbia University, where he is teaching "Literature Humanities" and writing his dissertation entitled "The Triumph of Body: Identity, Pain, and Resurrection in Dante's 'Commedia'." He is the author of articles on the poetry of Giovanni Pascoli, Filippo Tommaso Marinetti, and Bonvesin da la Riva.

JOHN McMICHAELS began his study of Boiardo at Scandiano in 1996. He read a draft of the essay presented in this volume at the 1997 conference of the American Association of Italian Studies. His essay, "The Lady Rises: Stoicism and Spenser in Milton's *Comus*," will appear in the 1998 *Renaissance Papers*. A doctoral candidate in English Renaissance and comparative literature at the University of South Carolina, he is currently working on a study of rhetoric as allegory in Shakespeare's plays.

RICHARD F. SORRENTINO earned his Ph.D. in Italian at Columbia University in 1994, with a specialization in the *Orlando Innamorato*. His thesis, titled " 'Vera istoria' and 'Bella istoria': Boiardo and the Carolingian Legend in Italy," was an exploration of the relations between the poem, its reception, and development of the chivalric romance in and around Florence and Venice. He is currently at work on a volume on the cultural history of the chivalric romance in Italy.

MICHAEL SHERBERG is Associate Professor of Italian at Washington University in St. Louis. He is the author of *Rinaldo: Character and Intertext in Ariosto and Tasso* (1993) as well as editor of Torquato Tasso's *Rinaldo* (1990). In addition to Boiardo, Ariosto, and Tasso, he has written on Boccaccio and Machiavelli.

KATHLEEN CROZIER EGAN is a part-time lecturer in Italian at Yale University, where she received her Ph.D. in 1996. She is currently working on a translation of the anonymous romance *Spagna*.

JOSEPH MANCA is Associate Professor of Art History at Rice University. He has written numerous studies of Italian art of the fifteenth and sixteenth centuries, including *The Art of Ercole de' Roberti* (1992) and *Cosmè Tura: The Life and Art of a Painter in Estense Ferrara* (forthcoming).

JODI CRANSTON is a graduate student in art history at Columbia University and has completed her dissertation, "Dialogues with the Beholder: The Poetics of Portraiture in the Italian Renaissance."

KATHERINE A. McIVER is Assistant Professor of Art History at the University of Alabama at Birmingham. She has written several articles on the artistic patronage of Giulio Boiardo, his wife Silvia Sanvitale, and other women patrons in northern Italy in the sixteenth century. She is currently working on a book titled *In the Shadow of Ferrara: Giulio Boiardo and Self-Imaging under the Este*.

LEEMAN L. PERKINS is Professor of Music at Columbia University. He has edited the complete works of the sixteenth-century composer Johannes Lheritier (1969) and the collection of fifteenth-century chansons known as the Mellon Chansonnier (1979). He is currently general editor of the series Masters and Monuments of the Renaissance, published by the Broude

Trust, in which five volumes have appeared to date. In addition to numerous articles and reviews, he is the author of a comprehensive study, *Music in the Age of the Renaissance,* which will be published later this year.

ROBERT J. RODINI is Professor Emeritus of Italian Studies at the University of Wisconsin, Madison. His research interests include Renaissance lyric poetry, romance, and theater. He has written widely on Renaissance lyric poetry, comic theater, and on translation.

NANCY DERSOFI is Professor of Italian and Comparative Literature at Bryn Mawr College. She has published a monograph and numerous articles on the sixteenth-century playwright/actor Angelo Beolco, called Ruzante, and a English translation of his comedy *L'Anconitana/The Woman from Ancona* (1994). She has contributed studies on Reniassance authors to *Italian Women Writers* (1994) and to the *Feminist Encyclopedia of Italian Literature* (1997).